Catholics in England
1950–2000

Catholics in England 1950–2000

Historical and Sociological Perspectives

Edited by

Michael P. Hornsby-Smith

Institute of Social Research
University of Surrey

CASSELL

Cassell
Wellington House, 125 Strand, London WC2R 0BB
370 Lexington Avenue, New York, NY 10017-6550

© Michael P. Hornsby-Smith and contributors 1999

First published 1999

British Library Cataloguing-in-Publication Data
A catalogue record for this book is available from the British Library.

ISBN 0-304-70527-6 (paperback)

Typeset by BookEns Ltd, Royston, Herts.
Printed and bound in Great Britain by
TJ International Ltd, Padstow, Cornwall

Contents

Part III: Sociological Perspectives

Tables

The Contributors

Frank Boyce is a former Dean of the Faculty of Education at De La Salle College of Higher Education, Manchester. He now combines teaching at Liverpool University's Department of Continuing Education with researching community history in the dockland areas of the city. He has published several essays on the dockland's communities and is currently writing a book on the subject.

Timothy J. Buckley CSSR is a Redemptorist priest who produced a report for the Catholic Bishops of England and Wales on the pastoral situation about marital breakdown and the various support groups which have emerged for separated and divorced Catholics. He was awarded a PhD for his research by London University in 1996.

Philip L. Daniel KCSG, KCHS was educated in the 1930s at the London School of Economics. During the war he served as a staff officer on Lord Mountbatten's HQ in Burma. As a civil servant he retired as a Director of New Towns and for many years was a Planning Inspector. He has been President of the Newman Association, was a member of the National Council for the Lay Apostolate and the Laity Commission, and for many years Chairman of the Parliamentary Committee of the Catholic Union. He is currently Chairman of the Catholic Council for Polish Welfare.

Mary Eaton is Vice-Principal at St Mary's University College, Strawberry Hill, where she was formerly head of the Department of Sociology. Her published works include *Justice for Women* (Open University Press, 1986) and *Women After Prison* (Open University Press, 1993). She is co-editor of and contributor to *Commitment to Diversity: Catholics and Education in a Changing World* (Cassell, forthcoming).

Michael P. Fogarty graduated from Oxford in PPE and is the author of *Christian Democracy in Western Europe 1820–1953* (Routledge & Kegan Paul, 1957). He has been involved in a wide range of political and Catholic activity in Britain and Europe and has an honorary doctorate in political and social science from the University of Leuven/Louvain. He was Professor of Industrial Relations in the University of Wales and has held senior posts at the Economic and Social Research Institute, Dublin, and the Policy Studies Institute, London. He is President of the Movement for Christian Democracy.

John Fulton is Professor of Sociology at St Mary's University College, Strawberry Hill. He is the author of *The Tragedy of Belief* (Clarendon, 1991) and co-author of *The Politics of Spirituality* (Clarendon, 1995). With Peter Gee he has edited *Religion and Power: Decline and Growth* (BSA Sociology of Religion Study Group, 1991) and *Religion in Contemporary Europe* (Edwin Mellen, 1994). He is co-author of *Young Adult Catholics and the Millennium* to be published by University College Dublin Press in 2000.

Sheridan Gilley is Reader in Theology in the University of Durham. He is author of *Newman and His Age* (Darton, Longman & Todd, 1990), co-editor (with Roger Swift) of *The Irish in the Victorian City* (Croom Helm, 1985), *The Irish in Britain 1815–1939* (Pinter, 1989) and the forthcoming *The Irish in Britain: The Local Dimension* (Four Courts Press). He has written some two hundred articles on aspects of modern European, British and Irish Christian history.

Mary J. Hickman is Reader in European Studies and Director of the Irish Studies Centre at the University of North London. She is the author of *Religion, Class and Identity: The State, the Catholic Church and the Education of the Irish in Britain* (Avebury, 1995), which grew out of her PhD in Sociology at the Institute of Education, London University. She is co-author of *Discrimination and the Irish Community in Britain* for the Commission for Racial Equality (1997).

Michael P. Hornsby-Smith is Emeritus Professor of Sociology at the University of Surrey. His publications include *Catholic Education* (Sheed & Ward, 1978), *Roman Catholics in England* (Cambridge University Press, 1987), *The Changing Parish* (Routledge, 1989), *Roman Catholic Beliefs in*

England (Cambridge University Press, 1991) and, with John Fulton and Margaret Norris, *The Politics of Spirituality* (Clarendon, 1995). He co-authored *Roman Catholic Opinion* (Department of Sociology, University of Surrey, 1979) with Ray M. Lee.

Ian Linden worked as a university teacher in Africa in the late 1960s and 1970s and is the author of *The Catholic Church and the Struggle for Zimbabwe* and *Revolution in Rwanda* and articles on African studies and aspects of Christianity in Africa. He joined the Catholic Institute for International Relations' southern Africa desk in 1980 and became General Secretary in 1986. He has written on issues of international economic justice, human rights and contemporary Christian thought. He has doctorates in Neurosciences and in African Studies from the University of London and an honorary doctorate from Southampton University.

John Marshall CBE qualified in medicine at the University of Manchester. His first academic appointment was Senior Lecturer in Neurology in the University of Edinburgh, from where he moved to London University, first as Reader and then Professor of Clinical Neurology. For forty years he worked with the Catholic Marriage Advisory Council (now Marriage Care) as a counsellor and medical adviser undertaking many research projects into the psychological aspects of Natural Family Planning. He was a member of the Papal Commission on Birth Control.

Mildred Nevile MBE worked for seven years for the Young Christian Students before joining the Sword of the Spirit/CIIR where she was General Secretary for 28 years. She was Secretary for several years of the Lay Apostolate Committee which prepared delegations of English Catholic organizations for the three World Congresses of the Laity in Rome. She recently retired as Chair of the Churches' National Housing Coalition and as a Trustee for CAFOD. In 1987 she took an MA in Theology and Religious Studies at Leeds University.

Bernadette O'Keeffe is Assistant Director of the Von Hugel Institute and a Fellow of St Edmund's College, Cambridge. She is a sociologist and has undertaken research in Church of England, Roman Catholic and independent Christian schools. Her publications include *Faith Culture and the Dual System*, and she is editor of *Schools for Tomorrow*, and co-editor of *The Contemporary Catholic School: Context, Identity and Diversity*. She sat for several years on a working party set up by the Catholic Bishops' Conference on the Catholic School and Other Faiths.

James Sweeney CP is a Scottish Passionist, author of *The New Religious Order: The Passionists and the Option for the Poor* (Bellew, 1994). For many years he has worked with religious orders, facilitating chapters and renewal processes. He is currently engaged in research and writing as senior research associate of the Von Hugel Institute at St Edmund's College, Cambridge. He was awarded a PhD in Sociology from London University.

Preface and Acknowledgements

I know all about you: how you are neither cold nor hot ... but only lukewarm
(Revelation 3.15–16)

This volume originated in one of a series of conferences which have been held in the Sociology Department at the University of Surrey since 1981. In June 1998, under the auspices of the Institute of Social Research in the Sociology Department, a conference was held on the theme *The Catholic Church in England and the New Millennium*. The conference brought together a number of social scientists, chiefly sociologists and historians, who had researched some aspect of contemporary English Catholicism, together with a number of people with long experience in a wide range of Catholic organizations who were known to have a social science background from which to interpret their own experiences.

The conference took as its point of departure the book edited by Bishop Beck to celebrate the centenary of the restoration of the hierarchy of England and Wales, *English Catholics 1850–1950* (Burns Oates, 1950). The aim of the conference was to review the major social and religious transformations of the fifty years since the centenary. However, the term 'English Catholics' tends to discount the massive contribution of immigrant Catholics. At the time of the 1971 Census, nearly half the Catholics in England and Wales were either first- or second-generation immigrants and half of these were from Ireland. The title of this book, therefore, reflects more accurately the focus on Catholics currently living in England. It also leaves open the question of the religio-ethnic identity of those, particularly from Ireland, who have an immigrant ancestry.

Second, since only around 3–4 per cent of the Catholics in England and Wales live in Wales and most of the data used in this book refer to the situation in England, it is a reasonable simplification to focus on Catholicism in England. Third, while a few members of other Churches define themselves as Catholics, its usage in this book is confined to members of the Roman Catholic Church.

This book, which is the fruit of the conference, is, then, avowedly social-scientific in its attempt to bring a reasonably detached perspective to bear on the changes which England's largest minority has experienced, particularly over the past half-century. While most of the contributors shared a strong sense that the vision of the Second Vatican Council had not been fully realized, they have all tested their analyses against empirical and historical evidence. This volume offers the most comprehensive collection of research-based evidence about English Catholicism in the second half of the twentieth century so far available.

The year 2000 not only represents the beginning of the third millennium of Christianity, but for English Catholics marks the 150th anniversary of the restoration of the hierarchy of England and Wales after the post-Reformation penal times. In 1950 the centenary was celebrated defiantly and triumphalistically. Just over a decade later English Catholicism appeared to reach a high-point after massive post-war migrations from Ireland and to a lesser extent mainland Europe. What has happened since? The various contributions in this book together throw much light on the transformations which English Catholicism has faced over the past fifty years. They show how there was a grateful appropriation of the post-war social, and especially economic changes, but a much more ambivalent take-up of the vision behind the Vatican Council's reforms.

One might judge the Church's performance in the past half-century to be lukewarm, certainly not prophetic, but showing a greater awareness of the obligation not only to ameliorate suffering and need but also to seek for their causes and to address them through individual and collective action. Furthermore, such action was no longer interpreted solely in confessional terms but increasingly pursued alongside other Christians and people of good will. An end-of-century report might say 'could do better'; it remains to be seen how English Catholics will face the challenges of the twenty-first century.

We wish to record our gratitude to an anonymous trust for a generous grant towards the cost of the conference from which came the various contributions in this book. I am grateful, too, to Gianne Allen for her secretarial assistance in connection with the conference and subsequently. The sharpening up of the analyses of the changing nature of English Catholicism benefited greatly from the contributions at the conference of Margaret Archer, David Barker, Sylvie Collins, Gerard Grace, Dominic McDonnell, Terry McLaughlin, David Martin, Robert Leaper, James O'Connell and Judy Scully. We wish to express our grateful thanks to various informants and interviewees who assisted us in the collection of the data reported in the various chapters of this book. I am particularly indebted to Dominic McDonnell for his helpful suggestions which led to the restructuring of the conference themes in a way suitable for publication. Ruth McCurry at Cassell gave a wonderfully prompt acceptance to our proposal for publication in time for the millennium.

I also wish to record my heartfelt thanks to my wife, Lennie, for her love and forbearance and her continuing support and understanding during the first three months of my 'retirement' when *the book* seemed to consume every minute and thought of every day.

Part I

Introduction

A Transformed Church

Michael P. Hornsby-Smith

A Time of Jubilees

We are living through a period of jubilees and other anniversaries which draw attention to our past and to distances travelled and directions of current movement. In 1997 we celebrated 1400 years since St Augustine came to Britain. It is nearly 150 years since the restoration of the Catholic hierarchy. The *Catholic Herald* celebrated its centenary in 1988 and *The Tablet*, next, 150 years since its foundation in 1840 (Walsh, 1990). It is 75 years since the founding of the Irish Free State, over 50 years since the end of the Second World War, and 25 years since the United Kingdom joined the Common Market. The Catholic Institute for International Relations (CIIR) was born as the Sword of the Spirit in 1940 (Walsh, 1980) and the Newman Association was founded in 1942 (Cheverton *et al.*, 1992). The first Catholic People's Week was held in 1945 (Baily, 1995). Marriage Care, formerly known as the Catholic Marriage Advisory Council (CMAC), celebrated its golden jubilee in 1996 (Marshall, 1996). The Catholic Housing Aid Society (CHAS) was founded in 1956 (Howes, 1996). The Student Cross pilgrimage to Walsingham in Holy Week started some fifty years ago in 1948 (Bryden, 1998). It is now forty years since Pope Pius XII died in 1958 and, according to Frank McHugh (1987), with the accession of Pope John XXIII was heralded in the present era of change in the Church.

A whole generation of Catholics has now grown up in the years since the Second Vatican Council (1962–5). It is thirty years since Pope Paul VI published his encyclical *Humanae Vitae* (1968), and nearly two decades since the National Pastoral Congress (NPC) in Liverpool (Anon., 1980; 1981) and the first visit of a reigning pope to Britain, neither of which appear to have had any lasting consequence (Hornsby-Smith, 1982a; 1982b; 1982c; 1991; Scurfield, 1982; Hornsby-Smith *et al.*, 1983). It is also twenty years since the first (and only) national survey of *Roman Catholic Opinion* (Hornsby-Smith and Lee, 1979). Shortly afterwards Cumming and Burns (1980) edited an inquiry into the state of the Catholic Church in Britain and Ireland. Archer (1986) argued that there were two Churches and that one consequence of changes since Vatican II was the 'oppression' of traditional working-class Catholics by new middle-class 'progressives', a thesis which led to considerable debate (Hamnett and Mills, 1987; Hornsby-Smith, 1987a; 1987b).

Apart from its symbolic significance in cosmic terms at the end of the second millennium since the time of Christ, the year 2000 is also the 150th anniversary of the restoration of the hierarchy in England and Wales. Fifty years ago the centenary was commemorated by a volume edited by the then Bishop Beck. This provides an interesting and instructive point of reference for this present collection. Beck noted that 'While accounts of the notable personalities [by which he meant Archbishops of Westminster, in particular] are not wanting, very little exact information is available concerning the details of Catholic history, diocesan and parochial, and of the growth and movement of the Catholic community' (1950: vii). The concerns were for maintenance and consolidation. Thirteen of the nineteen chapters were written by clergy. Fifty years later only two of the fifteen chapters in this present volume have been written by clergy, both with doctorates in sociology, an indication, perhaps, of a significant transformation in the nature of the Church in England.

In the Beck volume there are chapters on the Westminster Archdiocese, bishops, Cardinal Newman, 'old Catholics and converts', the religious orders, the Catholic press and Catholic literature. Four chapters reflect Catholic concerns with education and there are chapters on Irish immigration, the (consequential) growth of the Catholic community, and 'the care of the poor'. The content of this present volume reflects both the consolidation of English Catholicism over the past half-century and also the way in which the greater acceptability of Catholics in English society has resulted in a greater self-confidence and a changed agenda. It is still necessary to reflect the strong immigrant background of many Catholics and acknowledge the post-war waves of immigration not only from Ireland but also from Catholic countries such as Poland and Italy.

The focus of attention now, however, is the second generation. Social change since the Second World War and the religious changes since the Second Vatican Council have led to major generational changes among Catholics.

The papal encyclical *Humanae Vitae* (Paul VI, 1968) probably turned out to be a watershed and accelerated the trend for increasing numbers of English Catholics to make up their own minds on contraception and reduce the areas where previously clerical control had been accepted. Over the past half-century there have been significant changes in many aspects of Catholic institutional life. Chief among these must be the educational institutions and the strength and nature of the dual system. But parishes and religious orders have also been transformed and there has been a massive reduction in the salience of extra-parochial Catholic organizations. The dissolution of the defensive walls around the previously distinctive Catholic subculture (Hornsby-Smith, 1987b) raises questions about the distinctiveness of English Catholics as they enter the new millennium. The extent to which Catholics make a significant contribution to public life might also be taken as an indicator of their emergence from the defensiveness of the 'fortress Church'. While there are clear continuities, especially in respect of immigration and Catholic schools, this is a notably different agenda from that of fifty years ago.

There is no doubt that there have been enormous social and religious changes over the past half-century. Britain lost an empire and slowly and reluctantly adapted to the end of the imperial era. The threat of nuclear annihilation dominated politics for four decades, and economic reconstruction on a global scale and the emergence of new technologies transformed lives and introduced insecurities not anticipated fifty years ago. The aim of this book is to consider the position of English Catholics in this changed social, cultural, economic and political context and, at the beginning of the third millennium in the Christian era, to address four main sets of questions:

1　Who are the English Catholics now and how distinctive are they?
2　What has happened to them and how have they been affected by the past half-century?
3　What special contribution, if any, do they make to English society?
4　What are their main concerns and in what direction are they heading as they enter the new millennium?

Whereas the Beck volume was primarily historical and institutional in its concerns and orientation, in this book we report on the current state of social research-based knowledge about English Catholicism in the second half of the twentieth century. Our aims are primarily analytical and interpretative. Although not all the contributors are sociologists by training, all have addressed their particular task in a social-scientific manner so that, as far as is possible, the collection will provide as authoritative and empirically-grounded an analysis of a substantial segment of English society at the turn of the millennium as it is possible to give at this time.

Part II includes two chapters by historians reflecting on some aspects of the enormous transformations which have occurred during the second half of the twentieth century and five analytical testimonies from key players in various areas of the institutional life of English Catholicism.

It must be admitted at the outset that the empirical sources available are somewhat limited and there have been no major studies of English Catholics since *Roman Catholic Opinion* (Hornsby-Smith and Lee, 1979). Just as Bishop Beck noted gaps in the available data fifty years ago, so we might note a relative paucity of research-based analysis even in such central areas as the patterns of assimilation or adaptation of the various Catholic immigrant groups; generational differences in patterns of belief and practice; the changing role of women in the Church and the impact, if any, of the feminist movements both within the Church and in the wider society; changing patterns of Catholic family life and sexuality; the historical significance for the Catholic community of the transformations in the former teacher training colleges or in the ways in which priests are trained in the seminaries; the claims that easier ecumenical relationships are essentially secularizing; the major transformations in the Catholic priesthood; the significance of the decline of Catholic organizations; or the influence of Catholics in public life, especially politics and the trade unions, and so on.

The six chapters in Part III, all of which are founded on empirically based research, go some way to fill the gaps in our knowledge. They also point to a steadily increasing body of doctoral and ongoing research. Even so, it is clear that much work remains to be undertaken by new generations of social scientists. It is our hope that this present volume will be an encouragement to them. We believe that the somewhat eclectic coverage in the thirteen substantive chapters and testimonies in this book, in sum, provide a very good overview of the state of English Catholicism at the end of the twentieth century.

In terms of weekly attendances, Roman Catholicism is the largest mainstream Church in England (Brierley, 1991). We wish to affirm our belief that the study of social and religious transformations which it is experiencing is likely to be both analytically valuable, in terms of its contribution to studies of the impact of modernity on mainstream religion, and a rewarding research enterprise.

Overview and Major Themes

It is sobering to note the pessimism in Cardinal Heenan's address to the Church Leaders' Conference in Birmingham just seven years after the end of the Second Vatican Council (*The Tablet*, 16 September 1972). Given the conciliar emphases on participation and dialogue it must have been disappointing, to say the least, to hear him start by saying: 'I must confess that I am never over-confident of hearing God's voice at conferences'! He was particularly scathing about the development of 'discussion – words before and often instead of deeds', and what he called 'the cult of talk'. He was alarmed at the rising numbers of sociology students since 'this is almost certain to bring requests for fresh surveys'! Quoting a recent German survey he opined that the results did not surprise him and he was 'doubtful of their value in planning future pastoral strategy'. In sum, 'we simply do not know the state of the Church. The state of any Church is known only to God.' Given these views it is perhaps not surprising that Heenan had not been inclined to save the Newman Demographic Survey or that he felt that 'the chief heresy is ... modernism', which he predicted 'will re-appear as the chief threat to the Church of tomorrow'.

One consequence of the proliferation of meetings for consultation was that 'clergy are less free' for home visiting in spite of the truth of the old saying that 'a house-going priest makes a church-going people'. While Heenan was right to point to some unintended consequences of the growing bureaucratization in the Church, my impression is that the pastoral strategy of regular parish visiting has always been something of a generalized myth, fuelled by stories of the 'petty' or 'benevolent tyrants', powerful Irish priests in the crowded cities of Victorian England (McLeod, 1974; Samuel, 1985), or the routines in the atypical Liverpool parish of St Catherine as reported by Conor Ward (1965) in the late 1950s. (But see Frank Boyce's chapter in this volume and his references to Anthony Kenny's (1986) experiences as a Liverpool curate.) Four years after *Humanae Vitae* Heenan was also saddened by the 'revolt against papal authority'. The expectation was that the laity, or the 'simple faithful' as Heenan was fond of calling them, should know their place and have a proper sense of the 'authority of God and the magisterium of His Church'.

The liturgical and disciplinary reforms which emanated from the Second Vatican Council also raised howls of heartfelt protest from fearful traditionalists. The social anthropologist Mary Douglas devoted a whole chapter of her book *Natural Symbols* (1973) to the symbolic consequences of the loss of the rule about Friday abstinence for 'the Bog Irish'. It had significance as a symbol 'of allegiance simply by [its] lack of meaning for other cultures' (1973: 62). While perhaps it 'became a wall behind which the Catholics in England retired too smugly' (ibid.: 64), nevertheless, 'Friday no longer rings the great cosmic symbols of expiation and atonement: it is not symbolic at all, but a practical day for the organization of charity. Now the English Catholics are like everyone else' (ibid.: 67). Adrian Hastings saw the issue as 'a matter of not cutting off the vast subterranean religious roots of the shepherdless multitude of the untheological' (1986: 665).

It is one of the aims of this book to explore the extent to which these fears of the early post-conciliar years have been realized, to trace the nature of the transformations which have undoubtedly taken place, and to offer an evaluation of them and of the strengths and weaknesses of the Roman Catholic Church in England as it faces the third millennium. We set out to investigate these tasks under five broad headings.

Ethnic and Generational Variations

There is a need to offer an interpretation of the patterns of assimilation and cultural retention on the part of the main Catholic immigrant groups. Analysis of the 1971 Census 'Country of Birth' tables suggested that around one-quarter (1.4 million) of those who identified as Roman Catholics were first-generation immigrants. Half of these were born in Ireland (North and South) and the bulk of the rest were born in Europe, for example Poland and Italy. The 1971 Census was unusual in providing data on second-generation immigrants, that is those one or both of whose parents had been born outside Great Britain. Further analyses showed that an additional one-fifth of Catholics (1.1 million) were second-generation immigrants (Hornsby-Smith, 1987b: 24–6).

Data from the 1981 and 1991 censuses show that the number of people in England who were born in Ireland remained just over three-quarters of a million (1.6%) while the number of Polish-born people declined to 68,000 by 1991. The number of people born in the countries of the European Union have increased in recent years. Those born in Italy more that doubled between 1981 and 1991 to 84,000. The number of people born in New Commonwealth countries increased by one-third of a million between 1981 and 1991 to 1.6 million (3.4%). These figures suggest that there are in England around 580,000 Catholics who were born in Ireland, 50,000 born in Old Commonwealth countries, 200,000 born in New Commonwealth countries and around 430,000 born in mainland Europe. These figures can be compared with the estimates for 1971 which indicated that around one quarter of Catholics in England and Wales had been born outside Great Britain, half of them in Ireland (Hornsby-Smith, 1987b: 25).

What has happened to these immigrants and their children in the past two or three decades? Have they been substantially assimilated or have they adapted in different ways? On the whole there have been few empirically grounded research studies which have investigated these matters. Mary Hickman (1990; 1995), for example, has argued that in spite of the attempts of Catholic schools to make Irish Catholics more culturally acceptable to the indigenous population, some Irish retain a strong Irish identity through to the second and third generations. She reports on the identities of teenagers of Irish descent in Chapter 10. She argues strongly against the view which I have expressed elsewhere (1987b: 116–32) that Irish Catholics have very largely been assimilated into the Catholicism of this country.

While there has been virtually no research on the experiences of black Catholics in England, there seems little reason to doubt that on the whole the response of indigenous Catholics to black incomers was frequently hostile and exclusionary (Lubin *et al.*, 1991). Indeed, Spencer argued that the Catholic community in Britain was incapable of playing an integrative role in relation to black Catholics in any way comparable to that played in the nineteenth century in relation to the Irish (1973: 130).

It is also important to note the extent to which immigrant Catholics have approached the levels of social mobility of non-immigrant Catholics and have dispersed widely throughout the different regions. There do not appear to be more recent data than those from the 1978 national survey which suggested that 'Irish Catholics appeared to converge towards the English norm by the second generation but immigrants from outside the

British Isles experienced considerable downward mobility in both the first and second generations' (Hornsby-Smith, 1987b: 88).

Among the first post-war generation of English Catholics it is commonly noted that there have been substantial levels of alienation on the part of their children (Bull, 1993; Miller, 1995a; 1995b). In what ways do these 'new generations' differ from older generations of Catholics? What are the new ways of 'being a Catholic'? How best can these be interpreted? Can one speak of the failure of socialization in home, school and parish or has there been a major transformation in the understanding of what it means to be a Catholic (Hornsby-Smith, 1997)? Given the importance of these questions for the future of the Church in this country it is surprising how little research has been undertaken. The prejudice and antagonism towards sociology illustrated by Cardinal Heenan, and the assumption that a clerical workforce knew all the answers anyway, goes some way to explaining the omission. John Fulton in Chapter 9 reports some important new research in this area. (See also Mary Eaton in Chapter 12.)

Family Life and Sexuality

Support for family life and a traditional sexual ethic have always been strongly emphasized by Catholics. But there have been strong indications of major changes in recent decades and a substantial convergence towards the norms of the general population on matters such as contraception and divorce, though to a lesser degree, abortion (Hornsby-Smith, 1987b: 89-115). It is now thirty years since the Abortion Act made abortion legal in Britain, and it is estimated that in that time some 5 million abortions have been carried out (*Briefing* 27/10 (16 October 1997), p. 5). While the research basis for inferring that the publication of Pope Paul VI's encyclical *Humanae Vitae* in 1968 was the major factor in the transformation of Catholic attitudes is not as strong in England as perhaps it is in the United States, there is, nevertheless, strong evidence from the 1970s for heterodox views on issues of marital and sexual morality among English Catholics, especially on contraception and divorce. Clerical authority became increasingly contested in the areas of personal morality and increasingly confined to more specifically 'religious' issues (Hornsby-Smith, 1991: 164–89).

In the early post-war years the sanctions against marriage outside the Church were extreme and uncompromising and were supported in the main by ordinary members of the distinctive Catholic subculture in a 'fortress' Church. By contrast, pre-marital sexual intercourse was simply a human failing. It is unlikely that there are any longer significant community sanctions against 'marrying outside the Church' and, seemingly, cohabitation is a 'normal' practice. Whereas in half the marriages celebrated in Catholic churches in 1960 both partners were Catholics, by the late 1990s the proportion was around one third. There seems little doubt that Catholic marriages are just as likely to break down as anyone else's. Timothy Buckley in Chapter 11 addresses some of the issues arising and reports on research with a number of groups which have emerged to provide support for those whose marriages have broken down.

Jack Dominian has reflected on some of the major changes in the area of the Church and human sexuality. At the celebration in 1991 at York University of the fortieth anniversary of the Union of Catholic Students (UCS), he observed that the world of the first post-war generation of Catholics, with a 'strong fear of sin, guilt and sex' has changed radically. 'The young of the last twenty years are much less afraid to be themselves and don't want a Church to save them from their guilt and fear.' They have assumed the right to 'make up their own minds about right and wrong', liberated themselves from paternal forms of authority, and show an awareness of Christ's liberation from fear. 'The young are infinitely more aware of love ... Where genuine love is present, [they believe] there God exists.' The 'loss of the sense of hell' (Lodge, 1980) and the replacement of the 'rule of law' as clerically defined by 'the rule of love' as subjectively interpreted, has had a major, and almost certainly irreversible impact on Catholic practice, notably in the matter of contraception, but also in such matters as the pastoral care of those remarried after divorce, where again, the primacy of love is increasingly asserted.

It should be acknowledged that the English bishops, in their interventions at the 1980 Synod on the Family and their *ad limina* visit to Rome in 1997 (*The Tablet*, 1 November 1997), appear to be discreetly aware of these pastoral concerns. At the Synod Cardinal Hume admitted that 'pastors need to learn from married couples, *who have a special authority in matters relating to marriage*' (*Briefing* 10/32 (10 October 1980), p. 2; emphasis added) and Archbishop Worlock referred to the divorced and remarried who 'often long for the restoration of full eucharistic communion with the Church and its Lord' (ibid., p. 3).

During the past half-century the role of women in society has changed considerably. Married women with children are increasingly employed in the labour force and the feminist movement has contributed to changing attitudes towards women and their place in society. The Church can reasonably be said to lag far behind the rest of society in coming to terms with changing norms and expectations. The National Board of Catholic Women (NBCW) published the report *Do Not Be Afraid* (1991) on the responses of Catholic women to a discussion paper *Women: Status and Role, Life and Mission*. Mary Brogan (1992), President of the NBCW has reviewed the involvement of members of the Newman Association, encouraged by such giants as Barbara Ward (Lady Jackson). Mary Eaton in Chapter 12 reflects on some intergenerational changes among Catholic women. It can, however, safely be admitted that this is one area where further research remains to be done.

Institutional Life

There is little doubt that there have been major changes in Catholic institutions over the past half-century and it is a matter of some importance to map these changes and interpret them in the context of global processes of modernization and the working out of the implications of the Second Vatican Council which ended over three decades ago. Transformations in Catholic institutions and their significance may be considered in four areas in particular: schools and colleges; parishes; religious orders; and recognized Catholic organizations.

First, though, it is necessary to place an analysis of Catholic institutional life in England into an appropriate context. Fifty years ago, in the days of the 'fortress' Church, the complex network of Catholic institutions provided the main elements of a segregated Catholic 'pillar' (Spencer, 1973: 128). The associational life of Catholics could be almost entirely segregated. Catholics were inducted soon after birth into Catholic parish life; they attended Catholic schools where they were taught by Catholic teachers who had been trained in Catholic training colleges; their religious life was often enriched by retreats and other such activities given by members of the religious orders; they were members of a wide range of Catholic organizations which catered not only for their spiritual needs but also for their social needs, providing appropriate opportunities for the selection of a marriage partner. While employment was usually found in the wider secular society, normal associational life within the network of Catholic institutions served to reinforce a 'collective-expressive' involvement in the Church. Hammond (1988) has suggested that this leads to an 'involuntary, immutable' form of communal religious identity.

However, with the massive social changes which have taken place in recent decades and the growth of a plurality of leisure pursuits, together with the softening of previous religious antagonisms encouraged by the reforms of Vatican II, the defensive walls of the fortress Church have been largely dissolved away. In these changed social circumstances, Hammond has suggested that there tends to be a low local involvement with an 'individual-expressive' involvement in the Church and a more voluntaristic, 'transient, changeable' religious identity. Tensions resulting from the early stages of this transition were reported by Joan Brothers (1964) in her study of the impact on parish life of extra-parochial Catholic grammar schools in Liverpool in the early 1960s.

It is important to bear these contextual issues in mind when considering the evidence of apparent institutional decline since the mid-1960s. For England and Wales, the number of parishes in 1996 was 2,856 compared to 2,320 in 1965. On the other hand, Mass attendances have declined from 1.9 million to 1.1 million and the number of priests from 7,808 to 5,732. Child baptisms have fallen from 134,055 to 74,848 and receptions from 14,803 (in 1960) to 6,133. Total marriages fell during this period from 46,480 (in 1960) to 17,294. Catholic organizations are notoriously shy about membership figures but there seems little doubt that there has been a very substantial collapse of recruitment to many of those organizations which were so salient up to the 1960s: the Union of Catholic Mothers (UCM), the Catholic Women's League (CWL), Children of Mary, Legion of Mary, Knights of St Columba, the Newman Association, the Young Christian Workers (YCW), and so on. (See in this volume Chapter 6 by Mildred Nevile and Chapter 12 by Mary Eaton.) What is suggested here is the importance of investigating not simply the decline of institutional life but its transformation at a time of considerable social and religious change.

That Catholic institutions are not dead was apparent in the appendix to the bishops' document *The Common Good* (1996: 34–5), which identified a wealth of Catholic resources. There are, for example, eighteen diocesan welfare agencies with more than 1,500 staff and a turnover of at least £30 million a year spent on children, the elderly, handicapped and homeless. There are 2,000 primary schools and 450 secondary schools, with around three-quarters of a million pupils, 35,000 teachers, seventeen sixth-form colleges and six colleges of higher education. The Catholic community contributes nearly £20 million every year towards the maintenance and improvement of school buildings. The Catholic Fund for Overseas Development (CAFOD), raised £39.4 million in voluntary income in 1995. There are around 70 marriage counselling centres. The St Vincent de Paul Society (SVP) reports 1.5 million visits each year by 18,000 volunteers to people in need in their homes, prisons and other institutions. There are more than 10,000 male and female members of religious orders in nearly 300 religious communities. Around 200 Justice and Peace groups are to be found around the country. The Bishops' Conference has set up an office for refugee work and there are other organizations such as the Catholic Housing Aid Society (CHAS) and the Catholic Association for Racial Justice (CARJ). There is also a very healthy collection of Catholic newspapers and periodicals (Walsh, 1992).

In 1995 as its first contribution to the Millennium celebrations, the Bishops' Conference of England and Wales established the Catholic Agency for Social Concern (CASC) to 'provide a focus for work on social issues' in this country and 'with the aim of ensuring that an "option for the poor" is incarnate in the life of the Church at national and local level' (CASC, 1998: 2). In its first two years CASC has undertaken an extensive programme of information-gathering, networking, advocacy and empowerment around the issues of poverty and social exclusion, contributing to the national debate on *The Future of Welfare* and the welfare implications of the enlargement of the European Union. In its forthcoming publication *Contributing to the Common Good: Yesterday, Today and Tomorrow* it will review the way in which the Catholic Church in this country has adapted its responses to perceived social needs over recent decades and identified new directions which it can make in the light of current needs.

In general it can be argued that Catholic institutional life has not declined so much as been transformed over the past four or five decades.

Education

The post-war expansion of the Catholic education system in the years following the bitter battles which led up to the 1944 Butler Education Act was a triumph of administrative competence and quiet but persistent diplomacy. By the early 1970s just under one million children were being educated in nearly 3,100 Catholic schools (Hornsby-Smith, 1978: 169–70). With the decline in the birth rate from the mid-60s, however, a constant contraction subsequently was inevitable so that by 1996 809,000 pupils were being educated in 2,438 schools. In 1975 there were around 10,000 students (perhaps 85 per cent of them Catholic) in the thirteen Catholic colleges of education (ibid.: 196). With the closure of La Sainte Union College in 1997 (about which see the correspondence in *The Tablet*, May–September 1997) after two decades of contraction and transformation, the Catholic colleges of higher education have been reduced to five: Newman College, Birmingham; Trinity and All Saints University College, Leeds; Liverpool Hope University; Digby Stuart College, a Constituent College of Roehampton Institute, London; and St Mary's University College, Twickenham. Heythrop College became part of London University in 1971 and the Maryvale Institute, Birmingham, is an Affiliated Institute of Maynooth University, an Associated Institute of the Open University and is an Associated College of Hull University.

It is important to reappraise the educational strategy of the English Catholic community (and distinguish it from that negotiated by Scottish Catholics). The construction, defence and consolidation of the separate Catholic schools system and the extended arm of institutions of higher education, originally to train Catholic teachers for these schools, consumed an enormous proportion of the human and financial resources of the Catholic community for decades. But in recent years it has had to adjust to major shifts of government educational policy in the context of considerable demographic change. It is important to evaluate the traditional strategy as well as the reasons for and the consequences of the shifts of policy over the past decade or so. Following Berger (1973) and Whyte (1981), I have suggested (1996; see also 1999, forthcoming) that the educational strategy of the Church in England shifted from the 'intransigence' of the 'closed' Catholicism of the early post-war years to the 'accommodation' strategy of a more 'open' Catholicism in recent years. A significant indicator of the shift of emphasis from educational provision to educational content, processes and outcomes was the report *Signposts and Homecomings* (Konstant, 1981) and the shift of name from the Catholic Education Council to Catholic Education Services. Bernadette O'Keeffe discusses the reordering of Catholic perspectives in the new multicultural context in Chapter 13.

Parishes

It is necessary also to consider various aspects of continuity and change in Catholic parishes (Hornsby-Smith, 1989), the consequences of the declining numbers of priests, the rhetoric and the reality behind the notion of collaborative ministries, and the implications of the major liturgical reforms legitimated by the Second Vatican Council. The *Catholic Directory* for 1998 reports that there were 4,030 diocesan priests for England and Wales in 1996 but that 628 of these were retired. In addition there were 1,682 religious priests (1998: 908). In 1996/97 there were 109 clergy obituaries and 117 ordinations of priests and 35 deacons (1998: 899-902). The loss of over 2,000 priests in the past thirty years has not been made up by the recent gain of over 400 former Anglican clergy, more than 100 of whom are married (*The Tablet*, 1 November 1997) or by 395 permanent deacons in 1996. The *Catholic Directory* also reports that there were 2,673 parish churches in 1996 and an additional 1,049 chapels open to the public. Weekly Mass attendance was estimated to be 1.1 million in 1996 (1998: 910). However, the priesthood in England is 'greying' (Louden, 1998) and it is apparent that the number of priestless parishes will steadily increase. Yet there are few signs that the implications of these changes have been taken seriously or that a massive co-optation of trained lay catechists and paid parish assistants has been promoted. The Rite of Christian Initiation for Adults (RCIA) is far from general though sacramental preparation is now more frequently carried out in parishes rather than schools.

Arguably, the talk about collaborative ministries, for example in *The Sign We Give* (Bishops' Conference, 1995), is so much rhetoric which is simply not widely practised or experienced in many parishes. It could be claimed that priests are experiencing increasing demands on their time as a result of increasing expectations for consultation and lay participation, and processes of democratization and bureaucratization. Given the increasing demands being made of them, it is probably only to be expected that home visiting has largely disappeared. There is clearly a case for a rethinking of the pastoral priorities of a declining number of priests and the greater involvement of lay people in a wide range of pastoral ministries. In this connection, the warning given by the Pope to the bishops in response to their latest *ad limina* visit that 'Pastors have a duty to foster the charisms, ministries, and different forms of participation by the people of God, without adopting notions borrowed from democracy and sociology [*sic!*] which do not reflect the Catholic vision of the Church and the authentic spirit of Vatican II' (*The Tablet*, 1 November 1997) seems unnecessarily negative and defensive.

It is in the parishes that most Catholics have experienced the reforms emanating from the Second Vatican Council. We have already noted the reservations of Mary Douglas and others at the loss of the traditionally distinctive Catholic practices of fasting and abstinence and the easing of regulations regarding holy days of obligation. Such changes can be interpreted as an accommodation to modernity, making it easier to live in a pluralist society, and recognizing the realities of the everyday lives of ordinary people and, in particular, work demands such as shift work and unsociable hours.

The most obvious changes in recent decades have been liturgical and have included the use of the vernacular, lay readers and eucharistic ministers, the 'kiss of peace' and girl altar servers, and, with the 'loss of the sense of hell', declining Mass attendance (but possibly less frequent but regular attendance), much more frequent reception of Holy Communion but a huge decline in private confession together with a strong latent desire for more opportunities for general absolution. The younger generations, in particular, do not regard missing Mass on Sundays as a mortal sin in the way their parents did and in consequence will happily receive communion whenever they do attend. Public triumphalistic demonstrations of Catholic identity, for example in Whit or Corpus Christi processions, have not been replaced and there has been a decline of para-liturgies such as Benediction, exposition of the Blessed Sacrament, and the Stations of the Cross. It is likely that there have also been corresponding reductions in family prayers and the saying together of the rosary.

Given that the parish is probably the most important Catholic institution in the everyday lives of most lay people, it is surprising that there has been so little research undertaken to explore variations between parishes, relationships between priests and lay people, structures of power and authority, processes of decision-making, adaptation to the reforms deriving from the Second Vatican Council, and so on. Brian O'Sullivan (1979) described his experiences as parish priest in a relatively 'open' parish in Surrey. There have also been a handful of notable and interesting doctoral researches. Theo Koopmanschap (1978) studied changes in Liverpool Catholicism in the 1970s. John Leslie (1986) studied resistance to change in a North Midlands parish in the 1980s. Desmond Ryan (1996) offered a rich portrait of parish life as it was experienced mainly by priests in around one-third of the parishes in the Birmingham Archdiocese in 1990/91. Stephen Louden (1998) carried out a survey of parochial clergy in England and Wales in 1996 and received 1,482 completed returns (a 42 per cent response rate). He focused in particular on clergy stress and 'burnout'. (See also *The Tablet*, 19 September 1998.) In this book, while we have no particular study of parish life, Sheridan Gilley in Chapter 2 addresses the issue of liturgical change from a traditionalist perspective, Mary Eaton reports some reflections by Catholic women on their parish experiences in Chapter 12, and Frank Boyce addresses the responses at the local parish level to the problems arising out of urban regeneration in Liverpool in Chapter 3.

Religious Orders

Third, it is necessary to assess the nature of the contribution of the religious orders to the Catholic Church in England and the ways in which they have adapted to the major social and religious changes of the past half-century. They represent important nodes of autonomy in the Church and it is not surprising that they have been responsible for so much innovative change in spite of the dangers of the 'routinization' of the founder's 'charisma' (Weber, 1968: I, 246–54; III, 1121–3). They have made an immense contribution in education and also in health and social welfare. But inevitably, following the call for renewal at the Second Vatican Council, they have been called upon to undertake a radical reappraisal of their particular vocation. This has resulted in some significant shifts in orientation on the part of some religious orders. While there have been studies of religious change in individual religious orders, such as the Passionists (Sweeney, 1994; see also his Chapter 14 in this volume), a serious study of the changes among religious orders generally remains to be undertaken. It seems likely that with the increasing professionalization of education, health and welfare work, there has been a significant shift of concern. This appears to have been out of education and into a range of pastoral work, for example as parish sisters or in the hospice movement or attempting to plug some of the gaps left by the welfare state, such as addressing the needs of the homeless and other deprived groups, such as refugees, victims of torture, and psychiatric patients.

The *Catholic Directory* reports that there were 1,286 convents for women in 1996 (1998: 910). In 1997 there were 1,842 priests in religious orders, 286 brothers and 8,101 sisters, a total of 10,229 in religious orders. This total, which does not include contemplatives, is one quarter down since the mid-1980s and reflects both the ageing of many in the religious orders but also longer-term shifts in patterns of work which have greatly expanded opportunities for women in, for example, education, health and social work. Comparisons between the mid-1980s and mid-1990s suggests that many of those who retired from full-time work in education and health may have moved into part-time work in the social and pastoral ministries. It is also of note that the number of religious from England who are working overseas included 445 priests, 440 brothers and 908 sisters in 1994. Finally, it is worth recording the observation of one informant that the structures of decision-making in the female religious orders 'are a million years ahead of the Church generally'. In other words, they, in particular, have taken the conciliar call for renewal in the light of contemporary needs very seriously indeed.

Organizations

The fourth area of institutional change concerns the steady decline in many of the Catholic organizations which had played such an important part in the lives of Catholic laity a generation ago. The *Catholic Directory* lists 145 distinct Catholic societies in England and Wales (1998: 710–22). One hypothesis which might be considered is that there has been a radical shift from confessional lay-led but hierarchically-controlled organizations, mobilizing the defiant collectivism of a defensive subculture in a fortress Church, to autonomous and lay-led and usually ecumenical organizations for the mobilization of individual expressions of a Christian social commitment and activism. Among the former type one might consider the Catholic Parents' and Electors' Association (CPEA) and such parish-based organizations as the Union of Catholic Mothers (UCM), the Catholic Women's League (CWL) and the Catholic Young Men's Society (CYMS). Examples of the latter type would include the Catholic Institute for International Relations (CIIR), the Catholic Housing Aid Society (CHAS), the Catholic Association for Racial Justice (CARJ), Church Action on Poverty (CAP) and the Churches' National Housing Coalition (CNHC).

An alternative hypothesis, suggested by Mildred Nevile (see Chapter 6), is that up to the early post-war years there was a 'self-induced deference' towards ecclesiastical authority. But over time, autonomous lay organizations gradually became emancipated from this assumption. One notable example of this was her robust response following a challenge from Cardinal Heenan over the matter of the Wiriyamu massacre, that CIIR did 'not speak for the Catholic Church and have never claimed to do so. The CIIR is an independent lay organization' (Walsh, 1980: 32). The Catholic Union, too, especially in the past two decades through the work of its Issues Committee, firmly asserted their freedom from 'direct constraints ... from ... ecclesiastical authority' (Daniel, 1997a; 1997b).

Under this heading we might also consider the changing structures of consultation and advice within the Church in England. This has developed considerably in the post-conciliar years. A number of provisional commissions were set up in 1967 to advise the Bishops' Conference on various aspects of its task. The work and scope of these commissions was subsequently evaluated and recommendations made for more permanent commissions to advise the bishops on such matters as ecumenism, education, international justice and peace, and social welfare, and 'to encourage the laity ... to play their full part in the mission of the Church in the modern world' (Bishops' Conference 1971: 14). There were ambiguities in the structure and working of these commissions, however, between advice and executive action, and with a mixture of technical experts and representative members (Hornsby-Smith and Mansfield, 1975; Mansfield and Hornsby-Smith, 1975) and following a review of the working of the commissions and of their perceived needs (1982), the Bishops' Conference restructured itself with five departments, each with a number of committees under episcopal chairmen. There were also a number of recognized consultative bodies (such as the National Board of Catholic Women and the Catholic Union) and Conference Agencies, such as CAFOD and the recently established Catholic Agency for Social Concern (CASC). The restructuring was intended to emphasize the primary role of the bishop in his diocese.

Critics of the current arrangements have argued that the changes were regressive in constraining lay advice and action and unrealistic in neglecting the national dimension of the Church's involvement in such matters as justice and peace (see, for example, correspondence in *The Tablet*, December 1982–February 1983). Philip Daniel (see Chapter 5) has also argued strongly that there has been a decline in the amount of dialogue between the bishops and lay people since the introduction of the present structure of the Bishops' Conference.

Catholic Culture

Consideration also needs to be given to the changing nature of the Catholic subculture in English society. Was Mary Douglas right to assert that 'now the English Catholics are like everyone else'? Twenty years ago Peter Coman wrote that:

> The gradual assimilation through education and mixed marriage, the dissent over traditional teaching in birth regulation, the questioning of the limits of papal authority, the gradual substitution of English for Latin in the liturgy, the tentative movements towards ecumenism, the softening of traditional disapproval of mixed marriages and the abolition of Friday abstinence all pointed to the weakening and erosion of the traditional Roman Catholic sub-culture. (1977: 105)

Is there any longer an identifiable Catholic culture, in terms of norms, values, beliefs and practices, which is distinct from that of other religious groups and ethnic communities? There is little doubt that with the dissolution of the defensive walls surrounding the Catholic community in the solvent of post-war social change and post-Vatican II religious change, there has been a very substantial degree of convergence between Catholics and the rest of the population in England. That this was the case was indicated by the 1978 national survey of *Roman Catholic Opinion* (Hornsby-Smith and Lee, 1979; Hornsby-Smith, 1987b; 1991). They have a significantly higher religious commitment than people generally (Gerard, 1985: 74–5) and over one third of those attending church services each weekend are Catholics. In spite of much general convergence on values they continue to be much more restrictive in their attitudes towards abortion than the population generally. Largely because of the great number with Irish ancestry a higher proportion of them vote Labour.

Yet Catholics have changed over the past half-century. Not everyone is happy with the changes and there have been losses as well as gains. Sheridan Gilley in Chapter 2 identifies a number of the more significant losses. At the end of the twentieth century Catholics are not so certain or arrogant and exclusive about their faith as they claimed to be fifty years ago. They are more questioning of authority and moral teaching, though probably not of creedal doctrines. There has been a decline in the salience which sin and damnation once had. It is likely that there have been significant changes in their forms of piety and spirituality. They are, for example, much more likely to study Scripture, while there has been a reduction in devotions deriving from a high ultramontanism. While there continue to be generally good relations between Catholic laity and their priests, it can in no way be claimed that Catholics are priest-ridden. Increasingly, Catholics are likely to make up their own minds over an ever-widening range of issues (Hornsby-Smith, 1991).

What is the contribution of Catholicism to the cultural life of the nation? In the 1950s Catholic graduates used to be reminded that Pope Pius XII had given them the twofold task of permeating contemporary thought and contributing to the service of the Church. How have the increasing numbers of Catholic graduates influenced the intellectual climate of the nation? How influential have Catholics been in post-war literature, the arts or the media generally? Is there an 'intellectual emptiness' (Hastings, 1986: 477; quoting Hugh Trevor-Roper writing in 1953)? One suspects that, apart from the distinctive contributions of novelists such as Graham Greene, Evelyn Waugh and David Lodge, the cultural contributions of Catholics have not been insignificant but have been hidden in general processes of post-war embourgeoisement and advancement into academia, the civil service, the professions and the media. As Adrian Hastings observes of Waugh's great Second World War trilogy *Sword of Honour*, 'the Catholic is just the best sort of unassuming Englishman' (1986: 478). It seems very likely that the Catholic tradition of defensiveness persists and has, if anything, become more entrenched.

Public Life

The final theme, perhaps the most important, which it is necessary to consider is the contribution of Catholics to the life of the nation and to public life, not only in the traditional areas of social welfare but also in politics, the trade unions, industry and commerce. Do they bring a distinctive social morality to bear in politics or the market-place? Have they outgrown the historical legacy of defensiveness or 'keeping their heads down'? Frank McHugh (1982; 1987) has argued that an old-style 'objectivist' Catholicism on social and political issues, associated with hierarchically led forms of Catholic Action gradually gave way to a more socially rooted concern with social needs and problems. The key turning point for him was 1958 when Pius XII died and Professor Fogarty resigned from the Executive of the Catholic Social Guild (CSG) in protest at clerical domination. By 1967 Family and Social Action (FSA) was making a strong claim for the lay voice to be heard in the Church (McHugh, 1982: 99).

The low representation of Catholics among MPs is well known. Is it that Catholics, as well as reflecting a historical defensiveness, are also indolent or 'burnt out'? A former President of the Newman Association has suggested that 'prophesy is the chief business of the educated Layman' (Wright, 1992: 54). But are Catholics in England a 'domesticated denomination' or a 'prophetic Church' (Hornsby-Smith, 1987b: 157–81)? Over the tragedy of the conflict in Northern Ireland, for example, Catholics in England kept a notoriously low profile. Are Catholics renowned for their work in non-governmental organizations and campaigning groups? Certainly, there has always been a strong Catholic presence among the leadership of Church Action on Poverty (CAP), whose first Director was John Battle, now a Labour government minister, and the first chair of the Churches' National Housing Coalition (CNHC) was Mildred Nevile. The lay-led Catholic Institute for International Relations (CIIR) has achieved international and governmental recognition for the quality of its research and its contacts with 'partners' in Third World countries (Walsh, 1980; Linden, Chapter 8 in this volume).

Another question which it is important to consider is the general orientation of Catholics towards the European project of greater economic, social and political integration. Because of their strong international links, one might suppose that they were generally favourably disposed, in spite of the opposition of maverick Catholics such as Bill Cash, MP. This was, indeed, the case in the early days of European Christian Democracy (Papini, 1997; Keating, 1996) and Catholics have been strongly represented in the recently established Movement for Christian Democracy (see Fogarty, Chapter 7 in this volume).

Given the Irish background of many Catholics in the major urban centres, it is not surprising that they have been active in the labour movement, both in the Labour Party and in the trade union movement (Hornsby-Smith and Foley, 1993). There remains a major story to be told here of the struggles of the Catholic Left in a Church climate of anti-communist hostility and, not infrequently, hysteria. There is a lovely story of two communist miners' leaders, Mick McGahey and Joe Daly, robustly singing 'Faith of Our Fathers' in a railway hotel after a union meeting and claiming it was a great revolutionary song! Another significant investigation which needs to be undertaken is the subtle, and possibly insidious, influence of the Catholic 'Right'. (For a sloppily written conspiracy theory see Clifton, 1993.)

There is a general perception that Cardinal Hume, who has been the leader of the Church in England and Wales since 1976, has contributed greatly to the respectability of the Church, though whether this is a good thing or not is disputed (Bunting, 1998). The bishops' statement on *The Common Good* (1996) in the run-up to the 1997 General Election was well-regarded though lay groups protested that they had not been consulted in its preparation (see, e.g., the *Catholic Herald*, 15 November 1996). Increasingly, it seems that socially aware Catholic activists are participating in ecumenical campaigns such as the Real World Coalition (Jacobs, 1996).

Outline of the Book

This book, then, offers a response from Catholic social scientists and 'insiders' to some of the research themes which have been identified. The chapters in Part II offer a number of historical perspectives on the changes over the past half-century. In Chapter 2 Sheridan Gilley outlines a traditionalist concern that with the reforms of the Second Vatican Council, something of value in the traditional Catholic culture might have been lost. How the social and religious changes have been experienced at the grass-roots level has been described by Frank Boyce in Chapter 3. He also raises important questions about the extent to which traditional parish structures have failed to adapt to shifts in the nature of local social needs.

The remaining five chapters in Part II all provide important testimonies from key players in the Catholic life of the past half-century. John Marshall, who was a member of Pope John XXIII's Pontifical Commission for the Study of Population, Family and Births, reports on his own researches as a key participant over several decades with the Catholic Marriage Advisory Council (CMAC) in Chapter 4. Philip Daniel has been a life-long member of numerous Catholic organizations, including the Laity Commission, and the National Council for the Lay Apostolate (NCLA). For many years he was the Chairman of the Issues Committee of the Catholic Union, which addresses itself mainly to articulating Catholic social and moral concerns through Parliament and by direct consultation with the government of the day. In Chapter 5 he expresses the concern that since the restructuring of the Bishops' Conference in 1983 there has been a significant decline in the amount of dialogue between the bishops and representatives of lay people. The changing nature and salience of Catholic organizations is reviewed in

Chapter 6 by Mildred Nevile, who was for many years General Secretary of the Catholic Institute for International Relations (CIIR) and more recently has chaired the Churches' National Housing Coalition (CNHC). Some aspects of the role of Catholics in public life have been reviewed by Michael Fogarty, President of the Movement for Christian Democracy (MCD), in Chapter 7. In Chapter 8, Ian Linden, the present Executive Director of CIIR, has identified some of the ways in which Catholic approaches to aid and development have shifted in recent years.

The six chapters in Part III offer some sociological perspectives on change in English Catholicism over the past half-century. All are based on empirical researches, using a rich variety of research methods including surveys, interviews, life-histories, and participant-observation, in a number of key areas of concern. John Fulton in Chapter 9 outlines some early findings from important recent research into the religious beliefs and moral attitudes of young Catholic adults. In Chapter 10, Mary Hickman reports on her research into teenagers of Irish descent in London and Liverpool. In Chapter 11, Timothy Buckley reports on his important research undertaken in the first half of the 1990s and originally commissioned by the Marriage and Family Life Committee of the Bishops' Conference, into the ways in which Catholics have tried to cope with the realities of marriage breakdown and the various support groups for divorced and separated Catholics. Mary Eaton in Chapter 12 addresses the still largely neglected matter of the changing place of women in the Church and reflects on women's changing perspectives on their experiences at the parish level. In Chapter 13, Bernadette O'Keeffe provides a major overview of changing perspectives of Catholic schooling which takes seriously the multicultural and multi-faith character of their student bodies. In Chapter 14, James Sweeney reports on some of the difficulties which religious orders have faced in responding to the conciliar call to renewal.

Taken together, we believe that the empirically grounded researches and informed testimonies and experiences collected in this book provide a significant base from which to interpret the major transformations which have undoubtedly occurred in English Catholicism over the past half-century. Chapter 15 in Part IV of this book attempts to identify some of the key strands and also to assess where the Church is at, and in what direction it is moving as it enters the third millennium.

Part II

Historical Perspectives

2

A Tradition and Culture Lost, To Be Regained?

Sheridan Gilley

Culture and Community

Cultural counter-revolutions often occur in unseen ways, from a range of disciplines which suddenly come together, to alter a world view or to recover an old one. Such cultural revolutions create revolutions in religion, for religion is always communicated through culture, and Catholicism in England has been in decline and in crisis for a generation, in part because of its sudden abandonment of a culture which once communicated it effectively. This culture embraced prayer and worship, art, architecture and music, literature, custom and convention, sign and symbol, a cycle of feasting and fasting, and the life of a whole range of institutions from schools and charities to sodalities, confraternities and guilds, and every other kind of voluntary association.

'Culture' is a rather vague and spongy term, but it may serve to cover Nicholas Lash's definition of the efforts at understanding and applying Scripture as 'the concrete, the life, activity and organisation of the Christian community ... in its "active reinterpretation"' (Lash, 1986: 23), recognizing that 'community' is a term almost equally spongy. Yet even if there are difficulties of definition here, the time is ripe for a proper evaluation of the partly Irish and partly English Catholic culture and community which came to grief in the swinging 1960s, and left a whole generation of Roman Catholics caught between ecclesiastical nostalgia and a half-digested modernism. There has been a fashion in certain quarters to denigrate the older Catholicism as belonging to an outdated ghetto, English and Irish, from which the changes that followed in the aftermath of the Vatican Council can only be seen as a liberation. The sheer decline of a once flourishing institutional Catholicism in England since the 1960s suggests the inadequacy of this view, which too often failed to distinguish between baby and bathwater. The elements for a reaction against this attitude to pre-Vatican II Catholicism in this country come from a number of scholars, by no means all of them Catholic.

The Irish Experience

One such area of scholarship has been the sympathetic study of Irish Catholic experience, a subject first urged by a great old authority on the Victorian era of an earlier generation, George Kitson Clark, who wanted a far deeper enquiry into the general religious legacy of the nineteenth century (Kitson Clark, 1965: esp. 147, 165-6 on the Irish). His influence coincided with the movement in the 1960s, in part suggested by the *Annales* school in France, to write history from below as well as from above; to rescue ordinary people, in the socialist E. P. Thompson's famous phrase, from 'the enormous condescension of posterity'.

The Roman Catholic Church was especially attractive to such study, being the only major religious body in Britain which could claim a large practising predominantly working-class membership. The results of this study have been uneven; but there has been, over the past quarter of a century, an accumulation of local essays and monographs partly or wholly on Irish Catholic communities, in London, by Lynn Lees (1979), Raphael Samuel (1985) and Hugh McLeod (1974; 1984; 1996), in Southwark, by Alan Bartlett (1988), and in Manchester, by Steven Fielding (1993). Of these writers, Samuel was a saintly secularized Jew, and the doyen of the grass-roots historians of the British working class; none of the others is Roman Catholic, and all have worked or work in secular universities. All show something of that affection for the Irish Catholic community which socialist historians tend to show for the old British working class, and are less interested in the Church as such than in the Irish Catholic experience of it. One by-product of this scholarship has been the three volumes of essays on the Irish in England which I have co-edited with Roger Swift (Swift and Gilley, 1985; 1989; and forthcoming). The religious element has been only one theme in these volumes, but the essays on religion within them are fairly representative of the discipline as a whole.

McLeod is especially interesting in his study of Catholicism in its European context (McLeod, 1981), while his latest book makes comparisons between London, Berlin and New York (1996). One of his many insights in an essay on New York is that part of the strength of Irish Catholicism lay in extra-ecclesiastical ritual and in private devotions, like those to the Sacred Heart, the Virgin and saints, which were least under the authority of priests (McLeod, 1989). It is one of the many paradoxes of the so-called lay-oriented 1960s that the Church should have suddenly seemed to abandon these lay devotions, in favour of a solitary concentration on the Mass, which always requires a priest; just as, in an age of vernacular liturgy, it also precipitated the abandonment of a large body of vernacular hymnody which was connected with them.

A good deal of this sort of study has been devoted to Irish religious practice, and though large numbers of immigrants lapsed from the formal profession of their faith, it is the Church's successes, as Fielding puts it, which are the more striking. Even in secular terms, the Church before Vatican II is acknowledged to have conferred individual identity and communal discipline, as well as being a central provider of education and charity. Irish Catholics everywhere had a local, a national and an international consciousness supplied by a combination of Irish national-ism and Catholicism (Gilley, 1984). Even where the dominant theme is one of sectarian conflict, the Irish Catholic tends to get the sympathy for the underdog, as in Frank Neal's study of Liverpool (1988) and Tom Gallagher's of Glasgow (1987). The recent historians of anti-Catholicism, John Wolffe (1991) and Denis Paz (1992), write with even-handed sympathy. Mary Hickman (1995) has argued that the English Catholic Church, especially in its schools, had Anglicizing and denationalizing attitudes to Irish nationalism, which is largely if not wholly forgotten by all except the most recent generation of immigrants. Otherwise, the dismissiveness about the Catholic tradition and culture of the immediate past that one finds in much post-Vatican II writing has had very little encouragement from its historians.

This study has been confined to historians, and has had little impact on theologians, even though for decades Catholics of Irish birth or descent have probably been the largest body of worshipping Christians in these islands. It is remarkable that in spite of the emergence of liberation theology, there has been so little reflection by the Catholic Church in England on its own history as one which was persecuted and predominantly poor. Equally, there is little reflection, in an age of feminism, on a British religious tradition more often practised by women than by men, though what can be done has been shown in miniature by Susan O'Brien (1992), and there is now a large body of more general literature on the feminization of nineteenth-century Catholicism (Ford, 1996).

Even the modern rhetoric of community has made little of the creation, up to the 1960s, of one of the most impressive religious communities in Britain in the modern era. It is almost as if the Church began talking about community in the 1960s at exactly the moment when this community began to dissolve, in part through the dissolution or decay of the societies, sodalities, guilds and confraternities through which Catholic community was expressed, institutions which from the sixteenth century have been the very life-blood of lay Catholicism (Châtellier, 1989). Any reflection upon the Catholic future must look to this legacy from the past. Such a study must be selective; the sheer destitution of so many of the Irish immigrants in this country was of the stuff of tragedy. Yet even when most embattled, and for all of the distressing incidence of violence, drunkenness and a culture of poverty among some which so greatly disheartened the young John Carmel Heenan (Heenan, 1971: 71–3), Catholic communities also had collective values, especially to do with family loyalties, religious and moral behaviour, self-sacrifice and self-discipline, solidarity and charity. These have to be recovered, with the authority of the Church which ordered them, if Catholics are to keep alive the idea that there are values that are Catholic, and which are not simply those of the increasingly secular society around them.

Popular Devotion

A further drawback in the works so far described is that most of them go only until the end of the Victorian era or the Second World War, notable exceptions being Hickman's work and Ziesler's study of Birmingham (1989). Moreover they do not always penetrate far into the religious experience of the community as such – McLeod is an exception, Gerard Connolly (1985) another – to recapture the particular characteristics of popular devotional life. Even here, however, there are excellent things, as in Leon Litvack's essay on Irish Catholic vernacular hymns (1996) and, alone and supreme in its field, Mary Heimann's great recent work, *Catholic Devotion in Victorian England* (1995). Here are two recent scholars, neither of them Catholic, recovering a whole Catholic culture which has been quite recently lost. In many ways that culture was embellished in the twentieth century, and certain of the most popular hymns, like the Marian 'Bring flowers of the rarest', were not Victorian; their sense, however, of continuity with their Victorian past was complete. There is a need for a first-class scholar to do for twentieth-century Catholic devotion what Heimann has done for the nineteenth, a study which places that devotion in the solid context of Catholic community history.

One very striking work which tries to do justice to the values of the working-class Catholicism of the twentieth century is Anthony Archer's splendidly rebarbative *The Two Catholic Churches: A Study in Oppression* (1986), based on the parish of St Dominic's in Newcastle; an attack on the destruction from within of the separate rituals and disciplines which for a working-class Catholic defined Catholicism, and their replacement by a religion only accessible to a yuppified and educated middle class. The old liturgy was imposed without class discrimination or difference on all social classes; it was class blind. The new liturgy, with its 'lay participation', fell quickly into the hands of the best-educated and literate. Of course, there was verbal participation before Vatican II in the dialogue Mass, as well as in the silent following of the text by anyone educated enough to read the service in a bilingual Missal, quite apart from joining the choir in singing the plainchant proper of a Sung or High Mass, or the Ordinary of the *Missa de Angelis*, especially the Credo III known to everyone. There was also material 'participation' by rich and poor in the provision of fabrics and furnishings: altars, statues and windows.

The oddity, as Archer puts it, was that the Church abandoned the whole rich language of non-verbal symbolism at the very moment that anthropologists were discovering it. As a consequence 'participation' was grossly redefined in terms of actual verbal participation, and in the process of discarding non-verbal participation in non-verbal ritual, and participation in the holy time and silence, visually through the elevation of the Host, aurally through the ringing of bells to punctuate the rite, and by gesture, in kneelings and crossings and bowings of the head, the special claim of Catholicism in these islands, to be the Church of the poor, was gradually lost. There seems to have been little understanding of the faith of the non-Mass-going poor, Catholic and non-Catholic, who would rather slip into church to say a prayer and light a candle. The modern liturgists forgot that the Mass is essentially an action, 'not a mere form of words – it is a great action, the greatest action that can be on earth. It is, not the invocation merely, but ... the evocation of the Eternal. He becomes present on the altar in flesh and blood, before whom angels bow and devils tremble' (Newman, 1848: 328). The old liturgy conveyed this sense of the eternal to all, whereas charismatic Catholicism by contrast, 'did not attract working class people' (Archer, 1986: 226).

Catholics in Politics

The marginalization of working-class Catholicism had other, social, causes, in the break-up of working-class neighbourhoods and the destruction of the wider working-class culture with the socialism which it espoused. One dimension of that culture which needs recovery is a tradition of political radicalism. It is a Jewish scholar, Geoffrey Alderman (1989), in his history of London Jews, who has provided a tantalizing glimpse of the Catholic Labour tradition of the East End, the Jews being a group somewhat similar to the Irish in their poverty, alien culture, exotic religion and ambiguous relationship to a better-off constituency of co-religionists. The inter-war political co-operation of Jews and Catholics in the East End, under the aegis of a devout Jew and crook, 'Morry' Davis, reflects the wider fact that as Colin Pooley (1989) has shown, the Irish were not 'ghettoized' in areas of segregated housing, but were generally scattered through the community; and that as Steven Fielding (1993: 55) has put it, their Catholicism was 'an organic, accepted feature of working class life'.

The work of the devoutly Catholic John Wheatley, the founder of the Catholic Socialist Society and the first Labour minister for housing, has been usually a subject of scholarship by non-Catholics (Gilley, 1989; Wood, 1990). This is the consequence of the fact that, as J. H. Whyte (1981) has argued, unlike Catholicism on the continent on both the right and left, British Catholicism was 'open' insofar as British Catholics never set out to found their own political parties, and have largely voted Liberal and, later, Labour. Dermot Quinn (1993a) has made a splendid contribution to the study of Victorian political Catholicism, but the history of political Catholicism in Britain in the twentieth century is only in its beginnings (Buchanan, 1996). The leftward tendency of the Irish Catholic diaspora dates from the nineteenth century, when it received the official blessing of Cardinal Manning in England, Cardinal Gibbons in Baltimore and Cardinal Moran in Australia (Gilley, 1987). What is perhaps still more striking is that the papal teachings on social justice from Pope Leo XIII's *Rerum Novarum*, itself the subject of several excellent commemorative scholarly volumes (Furlong and Curtis, 1994; *Rerum Novarum*, 1997), chartered a precise middle course, a third way, between the extremes of liberal *laissez-faire* capitalism and collectivist secular socialism, which is just about the place to which our politics has come today. The local embodiment of the papal vision was the Distributist movement associated with Chesterton and Belloc, both anti-socialist and anti-capitalist, and it still awaits an historian to write its history (Quinn, 1993b; Thorn, 1997).

Critical Distance

Yet there is a sense in which Catholicism, for all its aspirations to be a part of mainstream culture, from the Duke of Norfolk down to the East End stevedore, was also separate from it and a judgement upon it. This is in spite of the fact that there was a much smaller distance before 1960 between Catholic and non-Catholic sexual ethics, given that the Church's teaching on abortion and homosexuality had the support of the law, and that even artificial contraception was certainly not universally practised, indeed was largely a moral taboo, at least before 1940 (Taylor, 1965: 165-6). Indeed Anglicans regarded the Catholic Church as scandalously lax in absolving sin in the confessional and granting annulments.

It is precisely this sense of a critical distance from the life around them which Catholics have lost in winning respectability and acceptance, even while the Catholic sexual ethic has become increasingly distinctive. It was the exoticism of Catholicity, its strong cultural sense of the otherworldly reality and glory of God, which provided the critical distance, in part in liturgy, in part in the aspiration to chastity and poverty in the religious orders, however far they fell short of their ideal. Either Catholicism is distinctive, or it is nothing: as it is both in the world but not of it; as it transforms and judges it. The symbol of separation was the religious habit, and it is striking that it is only religious orders which still wear the habit – Benedictines, Dominicans, Carmelites – which still have novices. Of course, the habit does not make the monk, but the monastic habit was itself a statement about critical distance and, here again, Catholicism too often lost the baby with the bathwater.

The Catholic Cultural Achievement

The fast diminishing religious orders of women have only recently found their historian in Susan O'Brien (1988), and we need a study that would do for Catholicism in our century what Eamon Duffy has done for the later Middle Ages in England, in his magnificent *The Stripping of the Altars* (1992). Patrick O'Sullivan, the editor of the excellent series *The Irish World Wide*, on Irish immigration throughout the modern era (O'Sullivan, 1992-7), has remarked that reading Duffy's book was like a return to his childhood. The Cambridge historian John Morrill in his introduction to the recent monograph on Christopher Dawson, another intellectual of the old Catholicism who has been rediscovered, remarks that Duffy's book 'reads uncomfortably like a lament for a liturgical vandalism visited in modern times upon the English-speaking world by ICEL'. Duffy's text is in places an undisguised apologetic for a range of devotions which a large part of the Church too drastically abandoned. As Morrill says, Duffy 'examines a system of belief and practice which functioned as well as man-made structures ever function and demonstrates how that system could be wilfully ripped away from a people unprepared for something so much less universal in appeal' (Caldecott and Morrill, 1997: 8). Duffy's book is one of a number – by Jack Scarisbrick (1984), Richard Rex (1993) and Christopher Haigh (1987) – which have reclaimed the early sixteenth century for Catholicism by arguing with much greater sophistication, and in a manner which all historians of the era have been compelled to recognize, for what looks like an older vision of a Merrie England which was Catholic.

If this is one reminder of English medieval Catholicism, there is another in the courses on the history of art which are burgeoning at so many of our universities. This history, in its religious aspect, is very largely the history of the Western Catholic art which was the setting of the old Latin liturgy, in building styles which run from Romanesque and Gothic to the Renaissance and Baroque. Again, the historic Anglican cathedrals and churches of this country are crowded with visitors, and there is a deeper interest in the chapels of Nonconformity. Within this wide spectrum there is a much greater awareness of the artistic achievement of the Catholic nineteenth century. The world of architectural history is also now pioneering a new understanding of the great British shrines of pre-Vatican II Catholicism. Here the pre-eminent figure is the prolific Rory O'Donnell (1983), an Inspector of Historic Buildings at English Heritage, and also now a member of the Art and Architecture Committee of Westminster Cathedral and of the Historic Churches Committees of the dioceses of Westminster and Middlesbrough. O'Donnell is noted for his brilliantly erudite expositions of Catholic church interiors and furnishings, especially the great wedding cake high altars, the dramatic foci of the buildings, so often their greatest art works and so often sadly vandalized in the wake of Vatican II (O'Donnell, 1994a; 1994b; 1997).

Recent conferences on architectural history at Dundee and Leuven have shown a real liturgical and architectural understanding of the proper use of these buildings and of their architects (Sanders, 1997). The main interest, of course, lies in Augustus Welby Pugin, one of the few genuine English cultural revolutionaries, and the greatest English Catholic designer-artist and architect of the modern era, the subject of a number of recent books and of a recent magnificent exhibition at the Victoria and Albert Museum (Atterbury and Wainwright, 1994), as well as the designer of the Lord Chancellor's wallpaper. There is also a deeper appreciation of other great Catholic architects like John Francis Bentley, who designed Westminster Cathedral, and Sir Giles Gilbert Scott, whose Anglican Liverpool Cathedral is one of the finest churches in the world, and of the richest and most creative British Catholic patron of the arts in modern times, the third Marquess of Bute (Mordaunt Crook, 1981). Here Roman Catholic scholarship can benefit from its proximity to the study of the great Anglo-Catholic architects, William Butterfield, George Edmund Street and John Loughborough Pearson, whose churches, when reordered, have not also been vandalized. Nevertheless, it is notable that no one has yet dared touch the very finest of Catholic church interiors, that of Westminster Cathedral, with its great baldacchino, the huge and glorious symbol of the sacramental heart of Catholicism.

Liturgical Loss

The modern liturgical loss has been aural as well as visual. Andrew Beards, who lectures at Ushaw, has pointed out the special virtues of an ancient liturgical language. Our Lord prayed and read in the synagogue in the *lingua sacra* in Hebrew, and indeed may have done so at the Last Supper, rather than in his vernacular Aramaic, while in Russia, the Ukraine, Armenia and Ethiopia, Christian communities, under Communist pressure or other persecution, have been held together by liturgies in otherwise defunct and now solely ecclesiastical languages. Beards suggests that such *linguae sacrae* manifest 'the pilgrim movement beyond time into eternity', by adding to the normal transparency of language a sense of what lies veiled or concealed in the great mystery of God (Beards, 1992: 37).

This, of course, addresses what was said as well as sung. There is now the extraordinary situation where the Church's music in plainsong and Palestrina, in the Masses of Haydn and Mozart, sell by the tens of thousands as tapes and CDs and are popular in the concert halls, and are bought by sophisticated and secular young people for use in 'chilling out'; indeed are heard everywhere except in church. A particular tragedy was the disappearance of the glories of the old liturgy, the sequences, hymns and canticles of transcendent beauty – *Puer natus* at Christmas, *Attende Domine* in Lent, *Pange lingua* on Maundy Thursday, *Vexilla regis* and *Crux fidelis* on Good Friday, *Victimae paschali laudes* and *O filii et filiae* at Easter, *Veni Sancte Spiritus* at Pentecost, *Lauda Sion* at Corpus Christi, the four seasonal antiphons to the Virgin, with the *Ave maris stella* and *Salve mater*, as well as the *O salutaris* and *Tantum ergo* of Benediction. Many of these chants were well known to parish choirs and in secondary schools run by religious orders. There is no reason why they cannot be made part of a modern liturgy as markers to the seasons, as indeed they are in translation among High Anglicans. The most intellectually sophisticated defender of the old liturgy is not simply a liturgist but the sociologist Kieran Flanagan (1991), who has pointed out the sociological naivety of the modern liturgical conceptions of simplicity, intelligibility, community and participation (Flanagan, 1991: also Nichols, 1996 for a summary). In the same way it took the anthropologist Mary Douglas (1973: 59–76) to see the point of Friday and Lenten fasting: an aspect of religion controlled from the kitchen and more recently the refrigerator and, according to John Bossy (1975) (of course before refrigeration!) a central element in the early modern formation of English Catholicism.

This may partly suggest that liturgy is too important to be left to liturgists, but there has also been a deeper philosophical movement towards an understanding of the relationship between theology and liturgy. This is the idea, described by Gavin D'Costa, of 'a *living tradition* characterised by various *dogmas* and *practices* that facilitate a structured co-habitation with the object of study, appropriate to that object', as enunciated by Michael Polanyi and Thomas Kuhn in science, Hans-Georg Gadamer in the humanities and Alasdair MacIntyre in moral philosophy (D'Costa, 1998: 120). This legitimation of tradition is significant in itself, associated as it is with the idea that in any enterprise there is a vast body of assumptions and presumptions, which we must assume to argue anything, indeed which in a sense define our own consciousness about ourselves, as argued vigorously by Newman in the nineteenth century, so much as to bring him under the suspicion of scepticism. This means that in, say, terms of reader-response theory, every text requires an interpreter, so that one cannot have a Bible without a Church: a position which disposes at a blow of the classical Protestant appeal to the Bible alone. As the great Orthodox theologian George Florovsky puts it of the Church of the Fathers, 'Scripture belonged to the Church, and it was only in the Church, within the community of right faith, that Scripture could be adequately understood and correctly interpreted' (1972: 75). So in D'Costa's words, the theologian is accountable 'to a living tradition (which means music, art, pilgrimage, local customs, festivals, the bible and magisterium ...)' as these reflect or embody a knowledge of God (1998: 126). Thus knowledge is not simply an external historico-critical study of texts, but an intuitive and imaginative knowledge learned in prayer and worship, upon one's knees. This whole idea, as D'Costa recognizes, is a challenge to the notion of a secular university without preconceptions; as if secularity was not itself a tradition with its own assumptions and presumptions.

The larger context of this movement of ideas has been the attempt by philosophers and theologians to recognize and to try to repair what T. S. Eliot called the 'dissociation of sensibility' wrought by the Enlightenment, 'between thought and feeling, between the mind and the heart', in which the scientific paradigm of knowledge produced a Romantic reaction which was itself an evidence of the dissociation, so that religion with much else was assigned to a subjective realm of feeling and the imagination (Louth, 1983: 1). Thus the study of the Bible in English and German Protestant Departments of Theology embraced an historico-critical method which treated the biblical texts in an allegedly 'disinterested' scientific spirit which, when taken to its logical conclusion, was by its own first principles inimical to the faith of its professors. Much Roman Catholic neo-scholasticism adopted something of the same sort of positivist rationalism, but was preserved from rationalist self-destruction by a combination of the apophatic sense of the mystery of God and the sheer force of the magisterium until the 1960s, when the removal of that pressure left Catholic universities and seminaries in countries of predominantly Protestant tradition singularly vulnerable to a similar corruption. 'A Christian culture without a doctrinal foundation is all bosom and no backbone' (Nichols, 1997: 401), and the softening of the backbone after 1965 deflated the bosom.

The oddity is that this began at the very point when the academy began to have reservations about its own wisdom in the matter; departments of theology in this country, which have raised up a whole generation of RE teachers in the older method, are beginning to experience a reaction which, while not rejecting the sounder aspects of historico-critical scholarship, are recognizing that this requires a profounder understanding of its relationship to Christian tradition and worship. Indeed as Louth has said, traditional Christianity cannot survive in such an environment, for such traditional Christianity claims that 'through certain specific events in the past God has revealed himself to men' (1983: 16).

The whole idea of a 'critical distance' between Christianity and modern secular culture is of desperate importance to liturgy. The non-Roman Catholic philosopher Catherine Pickstock, one of the new Cambridge school of radical orthodoxy, whose best-known member is probably John Milbank, has recently written a brilliant work arguing that Aquinas's doctrine of transubstantiation is the sole preservative against the nihilism preached by the high priests of postmodernity like Derrida. Pickstock also argues that the 'stammering repetitions' of the old Latin rite, its complex sentences with conjunctions and subordinate clauses, so unlike the functionalist and streamlined aridity of modern language, are the apt expression of a complexity of thought and action in which the believer approaches the great mystery of God and withdraws from Him renewed, only to return to Him again. Like a number of her tribe, Pickstock writes with a passionate unintelligibility that bars her work to non-philosophers. Moreover, she overestimates the uniformity of the medieval rite, which included our own English Sarum use, and there is a Protestant edge to her underestimation of what Duffy says about the participation of the laity in the medieval Mass. What is also notable about these Cambridge philosophers, however, is their critical attitude to modern liberal consumer society as a culture of death, which refuses to make the traditional incorporation of the rituals of death into life (Pickstock, 1998: 101–19). Of Pickstock herself, her reviewer Gerard Loughlin (1998) has written recently in *The Times Literary Supplement* that in her 'turning of philosophy to liturgy, she offers that now most rare thing, a powerful and original contribution to theology'.

Pickstock's argument ruthlessly contrasts the richness of traditional liturgy with its banal and barren modern translation. This transformation has other critics. Of the arguments for the liturgical changes of the 1960s, the archaeological one, that the Church must reproduce the liturgical arrangements of the fourth century, has suffered shipwreck altogether on one major point, that priests and people faced one another in the Mass; all the evidence is that for the Church's central rite, clergy and congregation faced towards the east and Jerusalem and the rising sun (Gamber, 1993: 77–90). The Church has never, of course, lost an essential part of the meaning of the rite, that it is not only a meal but a sacrifice, in which Christ eternally offers himself; but there is a desperate need for a re-emphasis of this theme in what the ancient Church called 'the awesome and terrible rites' in which the sacrifice is taught and conveyed through the splendour of liturgy.

This kind of thought seems to have had little effect so far on our philosophers and theologians, though John Saward (1997) has begun the interpretation in an English idiom of *the* theologian of the contemporary Church, Hans Urs von Balthasar, whose works are being translated from German and whose ideas underlie many of the Vatican's pronouncements, including those on the ordination of women. Indeed this is a matter on which Rome now has some highly sophisticated women defenders in the very home of feminism, the United States (Butler, 1996). There seem to be no such equivalents in England. Nor do we have in England a philosopher and theologian like the contemporary French thinker Jean-Luc Marion, who combines, in the words of Graham Ward, a 'fraught marriage of postmodernism and Catholic ecclesial orthodoxy' (Ward, 1996: 198). There are, however, now tremendous opportunities for a new era in Catholic thought, drawing upon Catholic scholarship abroad, in a way not seen since the period between the wars, with figures like Maritain and Gilson. Encouraged by encyclicals like *Aeterni Patris* (1879), twentieth-century neo-scholasticism itself deserves reconsideration. It had its text-book side, but was a very varied phenomenon as an effort to be creative in response to modernity. It has also helped form a range of modern Catholic theologians like John Finnis, Professor of Law and Legal Philosophy at Oxford, the scourge of ethical relativism in the Church (Finnis, 1983; 1991; 1993a; 1993b; Grisez, 1983; and Grisez *et al.*, 1994).

Catholic Literature

Some part of the recovery of the best of Catholic thought and tradition must also have reference to the neglected realm of Catholic literature. This was once vast: Fr Stephen Brown lists some three and a quarter thousand novels and tales by Catholic writers in the Central Catholic Library in Dublin in 1940 (Brown, 1940). One convert writer who is still a living force is Cardinal Newman, the subject of studies innumerable, as appears in the annual bibliographies published by the kind and learned Sisters of The Work at Littlemore. It is striking that before Vatican II, Newman and the Oratories that he founded and which kept his memory were regarded as liberal, and that since the Council they have come to seem conservative, in spite of the fact that Newman's life and thought remain one place where Catholics and Anglicans can talk easily to each other. The realization in 1990 of Newman's dream of an Oxford Oratory has added another centre to the small number of places in which the new rite of the Mass is splendidly celebrated in something like the old way. Quite apart from a large body of theological thought and scholarship which is part of the inheritance of all English Christians, Newman's work itself constitutes the most powerful apologetic and polemic in English for Roman Catholicism, so that the most liberal thinker learns some orthodoxy from him. As the only English-speaking theologian of the first rank in the modern era, he remains, as the convert Catholic novelist Muriel Spark has declared, the great convert-maker of the Catholic Church , and the converts he makes are inescapably drawn into a robustly Catholic Roman Catholicism (Gilley, 1997).

The other convert writer and convert-maker who might one day be raised to the altars of the Church is Gilbert Keith Chesterton, whose whole life, like Newman's, was directed against liberalism in religion. It is possibly significant that Chesterton is more honoured in the United States and in Canada, where Fr Ian Boyd edits *The Chesterton Review*, though he now again has his own centre for study, in association with the Centre for Faith and Culture run by Stratford Caldecott in Oxford, whose connection with T. & T. Clark has resulted in a large number of fine works of Catholic scholarship. The latest book about Chesterton, by a former Lutheran pastor David Fagerberg (1998), has the endearing title *The Size of Chesterton's Catholicism*. Chesterton's greatest virtue is that he is always in a good humour as he slays his dragons to the left and right of him. Yet Chesterton is also to be seen in the literary setting of the inter-war years in which the Church received converts of the very highest literary quality, of whom the best-known are Evelyn Waugh and Graham Greene, on both of whom there is now an enormous literature. An oddity of the polemic of some Catholics against pre-Vatican II Catholicism is their failure to address the issue of why it was so attractive to converts of the highest culture; and why after the 1960s it ceased to be so. If the working-class community of largely Irish origins gave Catholicism one kind of strength, then the literary and cultural Catholicism of the converts gave it another.

There has, of course, been from the time of Bernard and Wilfrid Ward a knowledge in English Catholicism of its own history which is scholarly, critical and sympathetic: a tradition represented in the Catholic Record Society and the periodical *Recusant History*, and in recent years by such excellent monographs as Vincent Alan McClelland's on Catholic higher education (1973) and by Richard Schiefen's life of Cardinal Wiseman (1984), and from outside the Church, by Edward Norman's work on the nineteenth-century Church (1984). It is alarming, however, that there seems to be no recognition of this subject in Catholic schools, and that most Catholics remain profoundly ignorant of their own history. Again, most Victorian Catholics still await biographers. One underestimated figure is Newman's rival, Cardinal Manning, the subject of an excellent monograph by Alan McClelland 37 years ago, which demonstrated his greatness as a social activist and politician (McClelland, 1962). David Newsome has also recently written eloquently about him (Newsome, 1993), while an elucidation of Manning's development from Anglican to Catholic by Professor McClelland's pupil Fr James Pereiro, the head of the Opus Dei house in Oxford, has just been published. He shows that Manning's high ultramontanism was rooted in the growth of his conception of the universal office of the Holy Spirit, which underlies whatever is true in the traditions outside the Church (Pereiro; 1998). Fr Pereiro's work demonstrates the breadth of vision of an ecclesiastic too often dismissed as a narrow sectarian.

The Catholic culture of the inter-war years had a richness which is described with a breathless and tantalizing brevity by that one-man publishing industry, Fr Aidan Nichols, in his magnificent new work on seven major twentieth-century English Dominican theologians (Nichols, 1997). The publishing houses of Sheed & Ward, run by Frank Sheed and Maisie Ward, themselves the authors and translators of a multitude of books in the realms of history, literature and theology; Hilary Pepler's St

Dominic's Press at Ditchling, and the worlds of René Haig and Eric Gill; the philosopher and historian E. I. Watkin; the translations from the French by Barbara and Bernard Wall; the poet and artist David Jones, and the Oxford circles of the scholar Gervase Mathew, the polymath and wit Ronald Knox and the great Jesuit Martin D'Arcy, the subject of a recent excellent biography (Sire, 1997), and J. R. R. Tolkien, whose predominantly Anglo-Catholic reading-group, the Inklings, was an exercise in proto-ecumenism; these could constitute the basis of a major collective study of the English Catholic mind at the very height of its powers.

Post-War Gain and Loss

Nichols writes that

> After the Second World War, ... English Catholicism was by no means as sclerotic and dull as is sometimes alleged. Institutionally, indeed, it went from strength to strength, and was strongly, even effortlessly, convinced of its future. It continued to attract, in the war years and beyond, converts of the greatest intellectual distinction, whether prospective or already achieved: the philosopher Elizabeth Anscombe, the anthropologist E. E. Evans-Pritchard, the poet Edith Sitwell. To some degree, however, it suffered a closing in of cultural horizons. (Nichols, 1997: 45)

How this happened is a major subject in itself, given the more fundamental dissolution, as Nicholas Lash (1977) has described it, of the elitist culture of which the high Catholic literary, philosophical and liturgical culture was a part, in what could now be described as 'dumbing down', just as the Church's working-class base was also eroded away.

Of course, there was gain as well as loss, in the repudiation of past bigotries and in a new co-operation with other Churches and religious traditions. The past cannot be restored as it was, nor should it be, and it might seem pointless to recommend the virtue of the world now lost in a populist avalanche of vulgar consumerism and hedonistic secularity. This chapter has not been about how such a recovery could be made, but about the recent modern scholarship which has taken a kinder and more perceptive view of the Roman Catholic Church in England as it was. Any intelligent discussion of the future must have a proper understanding of the past, and it is now an open question whether Catholicism, which simply means the universal, can offer a coherent vision to a world lost, on some accounts, in the fragmented condition of postmodernity, and so, as in Christopher Dawson's view, complete and fulfil all other traditions; or whether it simply adds to the existing fundamentalisms. But if Catholicism in England is to be renewed, then it must first rediscover its own tradition and culture; and for that it requires a proper knowledge of philosophy and theology, as well as of its own history.

3

Catholicism in Liverpool's Docklands: 1950s–1990s

Frank Boyce

Where there is no vision, the people perish
(Proverbs 29.18, Authorized Version)

Kirkby and Urban Reconstruction

At the beginning of the 1950s the Catholic Church in Liverpool entered a period of post-war reconstruction and expansion. During the Second World War, Merseyside was the focus of sustained aerial attacks which caused extensive damage throughout the region, but especially to the central and dockland areas of the city. During the blitz in May 1941 the parish churches of St Brigid's, St Mary's, and Holy Cross, situated in the Vauxhall area, were destroyed. By 1954 all three had been rebuilt and damage caused to Catholic churches in other parts of the city had been repaired.

The northern dockland's municipal wards of Scotland, Vauxhall, Everton and Kirkdale, constituted the traditional heartland of Liverpool's Catholic community and was one of the most densely populated sectors of any city in Britain. In 1938 the estimated Catholic population alone was 100,000. Its sixteen parishes, all within close proximity to each other, were staffed by more than eighty priests. The Sisters of Notre Dame were invariably appointed to headships of the parochial infant and junior schools, and to headships of senior girls' elementary schools (*Quarant Ore Guide*, Archdiocese of Liverpool, 1938).

Urban redevelopment schemes introduced by the Liverpool City Council in the late 1920s had led to the movement of hundreds of families to new council estates on the outskirts of the city. In the immediate post-war years, the City Council returned to its policy of urban redevelopment and renewal. This had a number of consequences for the Catholics of Liverpool. The first related to the development of Kirkby as an overspill housing estate and a light industrial zone. These were developed during the 1950s and 1960s mainly for young families, the majority of whom came from the docklands and inner-city areas.

Between 1952 and 1965 seven new Catholic churches were built there together with parochial primary schools. Two purpose-built comprehensive schools provided inter-parochial secondary education for children between the ages of eleven and eighteen. This massive rate of building brought heavy financial burdens upon parishioners and priests (Scott, 1967: 151).

From the early stages of its development, Kirkby began to take on a distinctive character. Its population increased from 52,080 in 1961 to 59,700 in 1971, nearly three-fifths of whom were under 25 (Hart, 1971). Some of its first residents jokingly referred to their new town as 'frontier land'. Without adequate shopping centres or transport facilities, many of them struggled to come to terms with the traumas and doubts of leaving their close-knit communities. Some returned frequently to their old neighbourhoods and friends in the city, to shop and to keep in touch. Many people who continued to live in central city areas travelled to Kirkby's new industrial estate every day to work in the factories (Mays, 1962: 94).

The experience of spending their formative years in the docklands provided many of Kirkby's first generation with the resilience and determination needed to overcome the emerging social problems of their new town. In the early 1960s, Kirkby was frequently in the pages of the national tabloid press, partly because the town had been chosen by BBC television as the setting of its popular police drama, *Z Cars*. It also became noted for the anti-social behaviour among elements of its juvenile population.

Multinational companies were encouraged to invest in Kirkby because of enhanced grants and tax concessions from Harold Wilson's Labour government. Companies, in return, promised long-term employment. But by the mid-1970s, the promises began to fade. Factories closed in rapid succession and fell into decay. More than half the town's available workforce joined the ranks of Merseyside's long-term unemployed, and Kirkby's image as an area of social deprivation was sealed.

A more positive aspect of Kirkby's developing community was the increasing general awareness among many of its people, that sectarianism, which had blighted Liverpool's religious and political past, was giving way to more tolerant attitudes between people of different Christian traditions. Wartime experiences in the armed forces and the shared troubles of enduring bombing raids, are sometimes suggested among reasons for this break with the past. But in allocating houses on the new estates, city council officials did not discriminate between people's religious beliefs. There was, therefore, a greater religious mix of people living as neighbours in the new estates than had been the case in the old city-centre neighbourhoods.

In the absence of alternative leisure activities, the Catholic parish clubs soon became a popular feature of social life in the early years of Kirkby, not only for Catholics but also for non-Catholics. In time, young families became more concerned with forging a sense of community with their new neighbours and coming to terms with Kirkby's emerging social problems than maintaining the old religious barriers. Even among those who remained in the central and dockland's neighbourhoods, attitudes were changing, although there were occasional reminders that old sectarian animosities still existed in the minds of a minority (Heenan, 1974: 235–8).

This significant break with Liverpool's religious and political sectarian past culminated in 1992 with the signing of *The Kirkby Covenant*. The spirit of Christian partnership which had been forged by the Church leaders on Merseyside, Archbishop Derek Worlock, Bishop David Sheppard and Dr John Newton, led to a covenant between a Methodist church, three Anglican churches and seven Catholic churches in the township. For Worlock, Sheppard and Newton this event 'was an astonishing achievement ... representing many years of careful preparation, exchange and mutual support in face of industrial and social hardships' (Sheppard and Worlock, 1994: 14).

The declaration of intent, with its echoes of Old Testament imagery and language, was read to a packed congregation by representatives of the local community. It was a moving summary of past struggles, and endorsed a commitment to God, and to the future of the people of the town:

We have reflected on the stories of our people ... of their common suffering, poverty and joy in the inner city of Liverpool for nearly one hundred years. We have thought again of the exodus which led us together to the new land of Kirkby, and of the fading of the old divisive memories and the deepening discovery of our common Christian Faith. Particularly in the past twenty years we have been conscious of the presence of the Spirit, leading us to a sharing in the understanding of our various traditions. We have prayed together, worshipped together, given public testimony to our common Faith, and joined steadfastly together to repel attacks on the dignity and helplessness of our people ... (ibid.: 15)

Inner-City Parishes

While the Church was managing successfully to meet the spiritual and educational needs of Catholics in the expanding suburbs, it became obvious that urban redevelopment would have long-term consequences for the Catholic communities remaining in the inner-city areas. Between 1961 and 1971, the population in the Catholic wards, Central, Everton, Melrose, Sandhills, and Vauxhall, declined by 48 per cent from 74,746 to 38,541 (Hart, 1971: 7).

As slum houses were demolished, so they were replaced with three- and five-storey tenements and blocks of multi-storey flats, mainly for families who had opted to continue to live within their old neighbourhoods. When, in the late 1970s, the Liverpool City Council attempted to rehouse people from this type of accommodation to new housing developments outside the dockland's neighbourhoods, they met with considerable resistance. A new spirit of community and solidarity emerged which enabled the people of the Vauxhall area to mount and sustain a long campaign to assert their right to be rehoused in their own neighbourhood.

During the 1950s and 1960s, the Department of Social Science at the University of Liverpool encouraged several research projects to establish the extent to which communities were being affected by urban development, improved access to secondary education and prospects for employment. (See, for example, *Neighbourhood and Community*, 1955; *The Dock Worker*, 1956; Mays, 1962; Vereker and Mays, 1961.) Particularly relevant for the purposes of this study is Conor Ward's (1965) study, *Priests and People* while Joan Brothers's (1964) *Church and School* and Kokosalakis's (1971) essay on authority structures also consider important aspects of institutionalized Catholicism in Liverpool. Conor Ward provides a detailed profile of the structures of a typical Liverpool Catholic parish at this time.

Ward demonstrates that in 'St. Catherine's' (a parish which straddles the southend docklands and a late Victorian residential area) parishioners considered that personal contact between priests and people was 'extremely important' (ibid.: 57). The key elements in this contact were the system of house visitations which enabled priests to visit families every six weeks, and membership of parochial societies and clubs, which provided further contact between priests and people: 'The priests spent some time at all gatherings of parishioners from confraternity meetings to dances and domino drives. They were also to be seen regularly in the men's club and in the youth club' (ibid.: 61).

Forty-eight per cent of householders interviewed were involved actively in parish societies and 25 per cent of these were acknowledged 'leaders' in all forms of parish life. The personal relationships which existed between priests and parishioners were, according to Ward, the most important single factor in the social structure of the parish. People expressed 'a sense of belongingness and a consciousness of an ideal parish'. Ward comments that 'the parishioners in general appeared to be proud of its achievements and anxious about its progress' (ibid.: 44).

In a period when the number of parish clubs was increasing, not only in the new parishes of Kirkby, but also in the older parishes of Liverpool, St Catherine's appeared to be in a time warp. Parishioners wanted a club where husband and wife could together socialize with other parishioners. Eventually, the parish priest of St Catherine's reluctantly agreed to a change in the rules of the men's club which would allow members to bring their wives or fiancées to the club socials on Saturday nights.

Among the features provided by Catholic clubs were inter-parochial social evenings, when the entertainment usually included professional performers, singing groups and bingo sessions, the latter providing a major source of income towards the cost of building new Catholic schools. In time, inter-parish celebrations contributed to the reduction of parochial rivalry which had been a traditional feature of Catholicism in Liverpool, especially between parishes in the docklands. Parish clubs were controlled by committees of lay people keenly supervised by parish clergy. Deals were struck between committees and local or national breweries towards the cost of building or converting suitable premises.

St Catherine's, with fewer than 2,000 parishioners, represented a small parochial unit compared with parishes in the north end. While their fellow Catholics were experiencing the upheavals of urban redevelopment, the parishioners of St Catherine's were benefiting from living in a stable area in which 'the living conditions were in general ... fairly good' (ibid.: 42).

Eighty-two per cent of Ward's sample of householders preferred parochial rather than inter-parochial schools. They believed that 'every parish should have its own school ... The children grow up with pride in their own [parish] and ... get to know their own priests ... parents, teachers and priests of the parish can know one another' (ibid.: 45). But this was a period when all-age parochial schools were slowly being phased out to comply with the requirements of the 1944 Education Act. While infant and junior provision remained part of the traditional parochial structures, secondary provision developed through a system of inter-parochial secondary schools.

One of Archbishop Heenan's problems on taking up his appointment in Liverpool in July 1957 was the inadequacy of Catholic secondary school provision. One of the causes of this was rooted in the education debates of the 1930s, a turbulent period in Liverpool's political and sectarian history (Waller, 1981: 340–3). In 1933, the majority of Catholic elementary schools in the city were classified as overcrowded and lacking in basic amenities, a situation, the Board of Education warned, that 'could not be excused or tolerated'. The controversy arising from the 1936 Education Bill prevented any real improvement being effected in Catholic elementary schools, or the reorganization of secondary schooling, until after the Second World War. Even as late as 1958, 15 per cent of Liverpool children aged thirteen-plus were still receiving their education in unreorganized, all-age primary schools, The majority of these were Catholic, but permission to rebuild had been refused due to economic stringency (Mays, 1962: 25–6).

By the end of the 1950s, five new Catholic secondary modern schools had been opened in the Kirkdale and Vauxhall areas. By the mid-1960s, this number had more than doubled with the opening of new secondary modern schools in Garston, Huyton, Anfield and other areas of the city. But there remained a further educational problem which concerned the archbishop. Although there were many convent schools there were 'few grammar schools for boys. A boy at a county primary school had a one in five chance of qualifying for a place in a grammar school. A boy at a Catholic primary school had only a one in twelve chance of a place in a Catholic grammar school' (Heenan, 1974: 246). With the co-operation of the city council, Heenan quickly obtained permission to convert a former orphanage into the Cardinal Allen grammar school for boys (ibid.: 247). Two additional grammar schools were built in the Croxteth area during the 1950s. But, as Joan Brothers (1964) was to discover, the influence of inter-parochial grammar school education on the attitudes and values of young Catholics became a matter of concern for many parish priests.

While St Catherine's parish appears to be a somewhat self-satisfied, rather cosy, traditional community, with its priests enjoying the confidence and high esteem of its people, and with little more than petty irritations reported between them, Ward does raise the question of whether the traditional parish structures were 'suitable to meet the needs and multiple problems of a modern urban civilization'. He concludes: 'It could be said perhaps that the system of ecclesiastical organization ... arose in the somewhat different circumstances ... of the nineteenth century and that in some respects it had not as yet adapted itself sufficiently to the new conditions and to a changed situation in the mid-twentieth century' (Ward, 1965: 117). Regrettably, Ward does not give examples of what he means by 'the needs currently arising', or 'the new conditions ... in the mid-twentieth century'.

A different slant on parish life in Liverpool during the 1960s is provided by Anthony Kenny in his autobiography *A Path From Rome* (1986). Kenny served as a curate in two Liverpool parishes between 1959 and 1963. He later resigned from the priesthood and left the Catholic Church. His subsequent distinguished academic career as a philosopher included a tenure as Master of Balliol College, Oxford. His first parish was a 'busy city mission' in a run-down area of the city which was experiencing problems of unemployment and inadequate housing. As families were moved out to Kirkby it was felt that the parish was losing its base, and by 1959 the population had reduced to 3,500. The contrasting life-styles of the parish clergy and their parishioners became a source of concern:

> Shortly before I arrived, the ample but antiquated presbytery had been completely renovated, at a cost of £25,000. As hardly any of our parishioners can have lived in a house worth more than £2,000, this fact was a source of embarrassment, and, to me at least, uneasy conscience. We ate good, and often expensive, food ... the parish priest was generous with cocktails, and there was wine on the table several times a week. Considered absolutely, our lives were not very

luxurious ... But they contrasted uncomfortably with the lives of our parishioners. (Kenny, 1986: 153)

Unlike the parishioners and clergy of St Catherine's, Kenny was sceptical about the system of house visiting because it was mainly concerned with collecting money: 'Each Friday from four until ten we would visit fifty or so houses in our area, to greet the parishioners and to collect their offerings, spending between five and ten minutes with each household ... It was quite exhausting' (ibid.: 153–4). Kenny considered his years in the inner-city were 'the most depressing of his life' (ibid.: 159). Curates were not encouraged to make any close social contacts with the people, but:

We were expected to drop in at the Young Men's Club and drink the sweet dark beer provided for the aged clientele. Teenagers attended the Youth Club, which the junior curates supervised: one came to dread the nights of overloud music and the occasional fights to be sorted out ... it would not have been easy to make friends in the parish, even if that had been encouraged. (ibid.: 158)

Anthony Kenny could not be regarded as a typical Liverpool priest. Unlike most of his colleagues, he was willing to take a public stand on political issues. In April 1962, for example, he became involved in a controversy with a local priest who had defended the use of nuclear arms against communist aggression. By December 1962, he had written several articles and pamphlets and addressed public meetings on the politics and morality of nuclear warfare. Inevitably, this level of public involvement became a source of concern to Archbishop Heenan. Following an article written by Kenny on Pope John XXIII's encyclical *Pacem in Terris* (in Walsh and Davies, 1984: 45-76), published in *The Catholic Pictorial,* the archdiocesan newspaper, Kenny received a letter from Heenan which included the following:

Two bishops in whose diocese the *Pictorial* circulates have complained to me about your comments on the Pope's encyclical. I think you probably do not realise how different it is writing for the kind of semi-literate public which reads the *Pictorial* and, for example, the *Tablet* or *Clergy Review*. Educated readers will dismiss the view of a priest if they do not agree with him. The simple

Catholic is likely to accept whatever a priest writes in a Catholic paper as part of the teaching of the Church. (ibid.: 185)

Kenny's autobiography provides numerous insights into parish structures. His years as a curate in Liverpool coincided with a period of transition: the approaching break-up of traditional parish structures; the changing relationships between priests and people which frequently led to a mutual loss of confidence between them; then the questioning of authority within the Church, the topic researched by Kokosalakis (1971).

While Ward (1961), Kokosalakis (1971) and Kenny (1986) provide insights into Catholic parish structures during the 1960s, it is, perhaps ironically, Heenan's account of his arrival in Liverpool as the city's new archbishop in 1957 which conveys a sense of the enthusiasm and loyalty of the 'semi-literate' and 'simple' Catholics towards their church leaders. The Catholic community's fidelity to its religion was often expressed through community celebrations. Special events, such as sacerdotal jubilees or parochial visits from the archbishop, were observed with elaborate processions in the parish church, through brightly decorated streets with improvised altars and congratulatory slogans painted on walls. The papal flag, together with those of the Irish Republic and the local football teams, added to the variety of colours on display.

This custom was an indication of the people's regard for their priests and archbishop. It reached its peak during the episcopate of Archbishop Richard Downey (1928–53); Downey's gift of oratory, his wit, and his willingness to engage in political as well as religious controversy, contributed to his popularity throughout the archdiocese. He thrived on what he called 'mammoth demonstrations of faith' such as the centenary celebrations of Catholic Emancipation in 1929 at Thingwall Park. He addressed regular functions and open-air meetings in defence of Catholic schools. He travelled widely to raise money to fulfil his ambition to provide his fellow Liverpool Catholics with 'a cathedral in our time'.

By contrast, Downey's successor, Archbishop William Godfrey (1953–7), although Liverpool-born and widely respected, never enjoyed the popular acclaim from his people that they had given to Downey. When John Carmel Heenan arrived in Liverpool in 1957 for his enthronement as the successor to Godfrey, the people's enthusiasm for their archbishop was rejuvenated: 'Liverpool was alive with ebullient friendliness and religious fervour ... it is renowned for demonstrative faith and the love of the laity for their clergy . . . the Catholics of Liverpool, practising and lapsed, educated and unlettered, share their esteem for their archbishop' (Heenan, 1974: 218, 221).

On the Sunday after his enthronement, and in spite of a city-wide bus strike, more than 40,000 people attended an open-air service on the site of the future Metropolitan Cathedral, to welcome their new archbishop. Heenan wrote that 'thousands unable to gain admission to the grounds gathered in the surrounding streets. It was a magnificent demonstration of faith which filled me with courage at the beginning of my new task. This was a period of intense zeal in the Catholic Church' (ibid.: 222). The majority of people who filled the cathedral site and crowded the streets were from the working-class parishes of the city. Heenan, like Downey before him, found on visiting these parishes that his arrival 'was made into a gala for the whole neighbourhood. Houses were decorated and streets were closed while I made my way to the sick (ibid.: 223).

When Heenan left Liverpool in September 1963 to become Archbishop of Westminster, the *Liverpool Daily Post* estimated that 10,000 people crowded into Lime Street station and its surrounding streets to watch his departure. He was succeeded as Archbishop of Liverpool by George Andrew Beck (1964–76) and Derek Worlock (1976–96), neither of whom, in spite of their outstanding pastoral achievements, attained the level of popularity within the Liverpool Catholic community that Heenan had enjoyed. His departure from Lime Street, with the station's platforms thronged with people singing 'Faith of our fathers', brought to an end the long tradition of public religious demonstrations in support of Catholic leaders in the city. There was to be nothing like it again until the visit of Pope John Paul II in 1982.

Community Development

The social transformation of the northern docklands which began in the 1950s gathered momentum during the 1960s and 1970s. Between 1968 and 1978, there were several grass-roots initiatives which challenged the authority of local institutions. The first of these, the Scotland Road Residents' Association, was an attempt to challenge the decision of the Liverpool City Council to construct the Kingsway Tunnel (a second road link between the city and the Wirral), in their neighbourhood, with the inevitable loss to the community of a popular shopping centre and a further shift of population to new housing estates. The Residents'

Association provided the impetus for the establishment of the Vauxhall Neighbourhood Council.

The second initiative was the opening of the Scotland Road Free School, which provided an alternative to traditional schooling. Its founders argued that institutionalized forms of education, which emphasized classroom discipline and stressed social conformity, were failing local children. Influenced by the educational theories of Thomas Dewey, Paulo Freire, and A. S. Neill Summerhill, two teachers resigned from their teaching posts in nearby Catholic secondary schools, gathered support from three sympathetic newly qualified graduates, and launched their experiment in a vacant school building in the summer of 1971.

The third and most successful initiative was the formation in 1978 of the community group, The Eldonians. Like their neighbours in the Residents' Association, the Eldonians began as a protest group. In their case the protest was against a City Council proposal to build a new by-pass road through the north end of the city, which would inevitably lead to a further depopulation of the Vauxhall area. The Eldonians gained the support of Archbishop Derek Worlock, Bishop David Sheppard and Margaret Thatcher's government, in negotiations with the city's Liberal Council, and later, during a period of confrontation with the city's Militant-led Labour Council. The success of the Eldonians has been described by one of its members as 'an inner-city fairy story'.

The thread that linked these community initiatives was the belief that with community solidarity, determination and positive action, 'anything was possible'. The proposal to designate Scotland Road as a dual carriageway and link road for the Kingsway tunnel included proposals to demolish dozens of well-established neighbourhood shops, small business premises, banks, post offices, a public library and two parish churches: St Brigid's (one of the churches rebuilt after war-time destruction) and All Souls.

In response to these proposals, an association was formed under the chairmanship of the headmaster of a local Catholic primary school. In an interview the secretary described the origins of the association:

> We formed the association ... because we had read all about the new tunnel in the *Liverpool Echo* and nobody on the Council had thought of consulting us beforehand. Here we were, knowing nothing about their plans, and wondering where we would be living in twelve months' time. Then some of the shops that were to be

demolished had been in business since the beginning of the 1900s. So we organized meetings and decided to find out what local people really felt about the plans. The YCW at Our Lady's, Eldon Street, and the Legion of Mary in St Sylvester's, visited homes throughout the area. Most people objected to the tunnel; they wanted to stay in Scotland Road, but they also wanted improvements: better street lighting, play areas for children, an improvement in the environment. We organized meetings; some councillors came; the chief constable, we wanted more policing; we wanted improvements to housing – so the City Housing Officer came. They were all patronizing – 'amazed' to find us so articulate! But we lost the battle! (Interview with Mrs B. J., January 1989)

However, it was this failed attempt to reverse a Council decision that became the seed-bed for the establishment later of the Vauxhall Neighbourhood Council. The City Council offered to fund a research project proposed by the university's sociology department for the purpose of identifying the specific social and educational needs of the people of the Scotland and Vauxhall areas. The project workers obtained premises in a vacant parochial elementary school which later became the administrative centre of the Vauxhall Neighbourhood Council.

The results of the research led to the appointment of several trained community workers, funded by the City Council. A welfare rights office and a law centre were opened to assist the unemployed and victims of petty crime in the area. There followed the formation of a tenants' association, a youth service and the provision of various sports initiatives. In 1972, the monthly community newspaper, *The Scotty Press*, was founded and continues with a healthy circulation today. Its editor and staff claim that 'it is the longest serving community newspaper in the country'. Classes were added to Vauxhall's education programme in response to people's interests.

In the early 1980s, a dispute between Centre workers, over the issue of adult education provision, led to a split. There was a feeling that the Centre was failing to give a sufficiently high profile to its adult education programme. The breakaway group was established at the Rotunda College in the Kirkdale area of the city. This continues to function successfully with financial support from the University of Liverpool and the City's Community College.

In 1989, the Vauxhall Neighbourhood Council co-operated with

Merseyside housing agencies to launch the Athol Village, a project to build good quality rented accommodation on an extensive stretch of derelict land to the west side of the Leeds and Liverpool canal. Currently under construction, on the site of the former Anglican parish church of St Martin's-in-the-Fields, is a new complex which will house all the community activities of the Neighbourhood Council at a cost of £3.4 million; all but £369,000 will be funded through Objective One Status sources. The Centre will include community business and technology training, a library and a bowling green. Most of the Centre's staff live in the Vauxhall and Scotland areas and remain under contract to Liverpool City Council.

The Scotland Road Free School lasted four years. The first intake of 30 pupils included children whose parents had chosen to 'opt-out' of formal education. All came from neighbourhood Catholic secondary and primary schools. Consequently, local priests closed ranks in their opposition to the school, some issuing warnings to parents who were considering transferring their children to the Free School. Nevertheless, there was considerable support for the experiment from the community. Regular fund-raising events were held throughout the area and parents gave assistance with school projects and outings. The teachers, all without salaries, eked out an existence with the help of unemployment benefits and the generosity of local people, some of whom provided the staff with food and accommodation.

Taking as their motto 'Education in the community by the community', teachers found philosophical and practical support for their experiment in a child-centred approach to learning. Therefore, there was an emphasis on the use of pupils' everyday experiences of living within the Scotland Road community. There was no formal curriculum or timetable. Free School teachers argued that young people should be 'guided' towards an understanding of the meaning of freedom. They criticized traditional schooling because it suppressed individuality and led children to confuse freedom with licence 'to do as you please irrespective of the consequences'.

Although the experiment appeared to succeed in its first phase, lack of money and resources began to affect administration and to sap the idealism of the staff. Reluctantly, Liverpool City Council agreed to offer limited funds on condition that the school opened its doors to children who had been excluded from other primary and secondary schools in the city. The acceptance of this deal eventually led to the demise of the Free

School in 1975. The mixture of local children with children from other areas led to a deterioration in behaviour. Roots with the local community began to weaken. People who had enthusiastically supported the school began to lose heart.

With its closure, Free School pupils had difficulty in returning to formal education. Catholic schools complied with the wishes of local priests and resolutely refused to re-admit pupils on the grounds that they were ill-disciplined and 'backward' in the basic subjects. Consequently the City Council allocated them to rehabilitation units established for pupils with histories of truancy and misbehaviour. Ironically, two of the original pupils of the Free School interviewed recently, and now owning successful businesses in the Liverpool area, disclosed that they send their own children to public schools!

The Eldonians took their name from Eldon Street, the street in which their parish church of Our Lady had been opened in 1854. Designed by E. W. Pugin, the church was described in the 1870s as 'a jewel in a dust-heap', thus signifying the contrast between its distinctive architectural features and the squalor of its surroundings. By the 1970s, most of the nineteenth-century housing had disappeared. Our Lady's was a parish consisting of blocks of three- and five-storey council tenements which straddled Vauxhall Road. At that time Vauxhall was the centre of the north end industrial area, dominated by the massive sugar refinery of Tate and Lyle, the British American Tobacco Company, and a complex of smaller businesses.

In 1978, the Liberal City Council proposed the demolition of the walk-up tenements in Eldon Street, Burlington Street and Portland Gardens. Although few denied that the demolition of these properties was long overdue, the proposed dispersal of the residents to estates on the city's outskirts provoked strong reaction. Consequently, the Eldon Community Association was formed to investigate alternative schemes for housing developments within the Vauxhall area and to resist a further phase of depopulation. In 1980, the community joined a campaign, supported by trade unions, against the closure of the Tate and Lyle factory. Inevitably, the factory closed and redundancy notices were served on 1,700 people, mostly local residents.

The Eldonians did, however, achieve an early success in that the Liberal Council agreed to explore with them the possibility of building new houses within Vauxhall. Subsequently, a partnership was formed between the Eldonians and Merseyside Improved Housing Association.

With the assistance of the Association's architects and builders, a section of Portland Gardens was proposed for upgrading, with a further section proposed for conversion to modern bungalows for elderly residents. Plans were also discussed for building modern houses on neighbouring sites when these became available after the demolition of former industrial properties. The Tate and Lyle factory was one such site. With the encouragement of the then Secretary of State for the Environment, Patrick Jenkin, and English Heritage, a comprehensive investigation of the site was made, funded by the Merseyside Task Force. The outcome was favourable and in May 1985 the Eldonians were encouraged to apply to the City Council for permission to convert the site from industrial to residential use.

The Liberal Council was ousted by Labour in the 1983 municipal elections. The new Council, dominated by its Militant wing, refused to approve the Eldonians' application on the grounds that the Eldonians' plans did not comply with the Council's Urban Regeneration Strategy. They had already decided on a plan of their own to regenerate the Vauxhall area. They also argued that the Tate and Lyle site was a potential health hazard and was, therefore, unsuitable for housing.

The Urban Regeneration Strategy, launched in 1984, was the major piece of legislation introduced by the Labour Council. Fourteen inner-city areas, and three on the outer estates, were designated as priority areas for the massive house-building programme to which the Council had committed itself in its election manifesto. Between 1983 and 1987, more than 5,000 council houses were built (Taaffe and Mulhearn, 1988: 159).

Nevertheless, the Urban Renewal Strategy was opposed locally and nationally, mostly for ideological reasons. The housing charity Shelter, for example, considered the housing programme a recipe for disaster. *The Morning Star* (30 January 1985) objected because tenants would have no control over their rented properties. The programme did not allow for housing co-operatives, and the Council refused to co-operate with the voluntary sector in financing housing associations. (For a fuller discussion of the complexities of local politics in Liverpool during this period see Parkinson, 1985; Charles, 1986.)

The refusal to approve the Eldonians' application to build on the Tate and Lyle site is often explained on the grounds that the Militant Tendency was opposed to any housing developments which were not under the full control of the elected Council. This was the view of Archbishop Derek Worlock and Bishop David Sheppard in discussing the role of Councillor

Tony Byrne, considered by the two prelates to be the architect of the Urban Regeneration Scheme. They recognized that he 'was a man who lived simply and was utterly dedicated' to improvements in housing. But they were critical of his 'authoritarianism [which] was most evident in his opposition to housing co-operatives, which he saw as possessing an unacceptable degree of freedom and flexibility' (Sheppard and Worlock, 1989: 227).

Byrne, Jesuit-educated, was not a member of the Militant Tendency, but he shared his colleagues' belief that 'with very little resources, the first task was the designated priority areas and to house people in the greatest need. To have given housing co-ops the £6.5 million being demanded would have meant severely cutting the council's housebuilding programme' (Taaffe and Mulhearn, 1988: 161). The Eldonians appealed against the decision of the Council and sought advice and support from Sheppard and Worlock. The archbishop consented to give evidence at the public hearing:

It happened that the public hearing of the Appeal was held in Liverpool at a time when we had to declare ourselves openly against the confrontational tactics of the Militants. This coincided with Neil Kinnock's public challenge to Derek Hatton at the Labour Party Conference in October 1985, so it was at a critical time that I was called to the hearing as a witness. In the temporary courtroom in the City Library, which was filled for the occasion by applauding Eldonians, I assumed the mantle of a prophet as I testified on their behalf: 'I share the view of many that the next decade will see the development of the riverside area bordering the Mersey. The work of reclamation, begun at the Garden Festival and the Albert Dock, will continue along the waterfront below Vauxhall. It would be an injustice if the present families in the Vauxhall community were to be denied the opportunity to share in the benefits of this facility.' (Sheppard and Worlock, 1989: 210–11)

The public opposition of the bishops to Militant politics in Liverpool, together with their view that the Eldonian Housing Co-operative could be linked with the Government's own programme for the regeneration of Merseyside, strongly influenced the Secretary of State for the Environment. Consequently Patrick Jenkin upheld the public inquiry's recommendation that approval be granted to the Eldonian project. The response of the Council, through the chairman of the Building

Subcommittee, suggested a conspiracy between government, bishops and the Eldonians (Taaffe and Mulhearn, 1988: 161).

Sheppard and Worlock continued their public and active support of the Eldonians, making 'several visits to the Department of the Environment and the Merseyside Task Force to try to press the matter forward' (Sheppard and Worlock, 1989: 211). In the autumn of 1986 a financial package and permission to proceed with the building programme were confirmed, and in November of that year, Worlock and Sheppard were the principal guests at

> A great celebration [which] took place in the packed church in Eldon Street ... in pouring rain a procession formed to go, as it were in pilgrimage, to the site which was to be the cherished Eldonian Village ... Across the street, in the windows, on the back of the service booklet, the message was plain: 'Our thanks to Archbishop Derek, to Bishop David and to all our friends. WE DID IT BETTER TOGETHER.' (ibid.: 211–12)

The wording of the slogan provided them with the title for their book.

The success of the Eldonians started with that victory. In 1986, tenants moved into the converted tenement blocks; the Government awarded a £2.1 million grant towards bringing the Tate and Lyle site up to greenfield standard; the Task Force funded £4.5 million to the Co-operative for the building of new houses on the site. In May 1989 Phase 1 of the Eldonian Village was officially opened by Prince Charles. Since then, Phase 2 has been completed on land adjacent to the first development.

The Eldonians have now become a successful model of urban regeneration, a success which has been recognized both nationally and internationally. In recognition of their support, the names of Derek Worlock and David Sheppard are now enshrined in Village street names. On the occasion of the official opening of the Village, Archbishop Worlock wrote: 'For my part I would want to single out their remarkable community solidarity. This has combined well with their faith and in their recognition that in many matters they may turn in friendship to those able to offer them the professional advice needed in the complex tasks they have tackled' (*The Eldonian*, 3 May 1989).

In an attempt to place the Eldonian experience in a theological context, a priest serving in the parish, during and after the first successes of the Housing Association, wrote that for the Eldonians:

what really matters is growing together as a concerned and loving community. They will go to any lengths to resist injustice being done to themselves and their neighbours. They believe in the dignity of ordinary people like themselves and they will do all they can to help others realize their own dignity and to make sure it is respected, especially by those in public positions of responsibility. This is the vision of life they believe in and want to share with others. It is this attitude to life that they are trying to pass on to their young people by the living witness of their own committed lives. (From correspondence with Revd Kevin Kelly)

The Eldonians' success continues. They are now a community-based housing association, building houses in partnership with Wimpey Homes for sale as well as for rent to non-Vauxhall residents. They have moved away from their own 'parish' area into other districts of Vauxhall. On the site of the demolished Catholic church of St Gerard stands 'St Gerard Majella Close', a scheme completed in 1989 for tenants of pensionable age. There is now a Community Trust, a registered charity, which arranges social and religious activities for local people, ranging from day trips to Knowsley Safari Park to trips to Lourdes.

In a colourful and attractively produced brochure, the Trust is described as fulfilling 'a vital role in the Eldonian culture that encourages people to socialise and help one another. No one is forgotten or left on their own.' Some examples of the range of facilities are listed: regular visits from a chiropodist, an optician and a dentist, while a hairdresser pays a weekly call. The Village has its own hall, day nursery, community centre, outdoor sports facilities and a multi-use indoor sports centre. These have all been completed with funding from private sources, and from the Merseyside Development Corporation. Like the Vauxhall Neighbourhood Council, all the staff of the Eldonians are recruited locally, although there are specialist workers; for example, some of the medical and care staff are 'outsiders'.

Since the recent demise of Liverpool's Irish Centre, Irish cultural activities, such as dancing and music tuition, take place at weekends in the Village Hall. There is a possibility that, in due course, an Irish-Liverpool Heritage Centre will be set up there. The Leeds and Liverpool canal has been cleaned and two brightly painted canal barges – one called *The Eldonian* – are ready for service during the tourist season. The Eldonian Village Hall and Administrative Centre are the centrepieces of the first phases of development. Vauxhall Road itself is currently being improved with extra pedestrian crossings, safety islands and speed restrictions. To these have been added a new link road which crosses the canal giving access to 'Eldonian Quay', the site currently under development for executive houses.

The Eldonian Community Trust has partnerships with Merseyside business employers such as Littlewoods, Carlsberg, the City Council and various housing trusts. Through these contacts, training and educational facilities are made available, and there is a recent proposal to establish a purpose-built information technology centre for community use, on the basis of a 'drop-in' facility. The overall management of the Eldonians is structured around six committees. Some members are elected by residents, others because of particular areas of expertise. The parish priest of St Anthony's parish, Scotland Road, is a member of the Trust and Management Committees.

Community developments pioneered by the Vauxhall Neighbourhood Council and the Eldonians will continue well beyond the Millennium. From their inception both organizations had different priorities. The Vauxhall Council's first task was to provide welfare, education and related services. For the Eldonians the priority was to provide houses, with the aim of maintaining the remnant of what had once been a densely populated neighbourhood. The extent of the Eldonians' achievement can be seen in the impressive housing and community developments which dominate Vauxhall Road and adjacent areas. The achievements of the Vauxhall community are not so evident in terms of bricks and mortar (apart from the Athol Village estate and the forthcoming Centre), but in the range of services available daily throughout the neighbourhood and the commitment of the community workers.

Although there is no evidence of hostility between the management of the two organizations, neither is there much evidence of co-operation. The reason may be rooted in different political ideologies. The Vauxhall Neighbourhood Council retained strong financial and political links with Liverpool's former Labour Council and the Labour Party, and has used those links effectively to obtain financial support from European sources. The Eldonians, on the other hand, took control of their own destiny and are not allied to any local political groups. Eldonian leadership consisted mainly of former dockers and factory workers from Tate and Lyle with trade union experience who were quick to adapt to the entrepreneurial climate generated by Margaret Thatcher's government.

The achievements of the Eldonians and the Vauxhall Neighbourhood Council have been remarkable considering the baselines from which they started. However, high levels of unemployment together with their associated problems continue. Whereas unemployment in Liverpool doubled between 1971 and 1991 from 11 per cent to 22 per cent, that in Vauxhall increased from 16 per cent to 45 per cent (*Liverpool Community Atlas*, John Moores University, 1991). Twenty-two per cent of the residents suffer from long-term illness and 81 per cent of households have no car. The population is steadily ageing and the proportion aged 60 and over has increased from 14 per cent in 1971 to over 20 per cent in 1991. Over 10 per cent of pupils of the Vauxhall area, currently in secondary education, live in lone-parent households (Liverpool Education Directorate, April 1998).

A Failure of Vision?

At the beginning of the twentieth century the Catholic Church in Liverpool faced the future with confidence. Sixty years of extraordinary growth during the nineteenth century were followed by thirty years of consolidation. The arrival of the twenty-first century, however, at least in the docklands areas, is likely to continue the period of contraction which commenced in the 1960s.

The demographic changes which have taken place over the last thirty years have led to an extended process of rationalization. Between 1968 and 1996, five docklands parishes have been closed and the vacant sites sold for redevelopment. The church of St. Alban, closed in 1991, is in the process of renovation and conversion to an outdoor pursuits centre. Three parishes have merged. St Mary's Church, currently a centre of ecumenical ministry in the city, is up for sale. Further closures and mergers are likely in the near future. The age profile of the eleven priests still serving in the area shows a significant weighting towards the over-sixties age group. Given the current shortage of priests in the archdiocese, it is unlikely that they will be easily replaced.

Some organizational changes introduced by the archdiocese in recent years seem to have by-passed the docklands parishes. Of the 81 permanent deacons throughout the archdiocese, none serve in the docklands. The archdiocesan Youth Service has active centres in Norris Green, Toxteth and Speke, but none exist in Vauxhall. The Vauxhall deanery, along with Kirkby and Old Swan, is one of only three deaneries without a marriage-contact group. Local priests claim that about 10 per cent of Catholics living in Vauxhall attend Sunday Mass regularly, although Baptism and First Communion are joyfully celebrated by extended families and at considerable expense. Contact between some of the priests and their parishioners seems minimal. Sodalities and parish organizations which were part of the old parish structures no longer exist. Gone also are the social aspects of parochial life. Churches are open only at Mass times.

On a more positive side, the Jesuits at St Francis Xavier parish, now merged with the former Franciscan parish of St Mary of the Angels, have participated in effective community work across Everton's traditional religious divide since the mid-1980s. A group from the parish, working in co-operation with the neighbouring Anglican parish of St Peter's, are in contact with a Catholic–Presbyterian group in Portadown, Northern Ireland, and hopeful that a regular series of community exchanges may be effected. An order of nuns have a convent in a high-rise block of flats in the Holy Cross parish, from which they combine parish visiting with full-time nursing and welfare work.

Catholics in the Vauxhall area have, in the past, identified closely with their parishes, and have looked with respect upon their priests and sought guidance from them. With very few exceptions, this tradition has died. People now identify more closely with the Eldonians and the Vauxhall Neighbourhood Community Centre. Out of the process of regeneration have emerged individuals of vision, determination and strong leadership, with a deep commitment towards improving the quality of life for residents of the area. This level of involvement and commitment has not, so far, been matched by the Catholic Church. The influence of local clergy in this process has been marginal. While the 'secular' organizations are facing the Millennium with confidence, with well researched and well resourced programmes, Catholicism seems to be drifting.

For more than a century the people of Vauxhall provided the numerical strength of the Catholic Church in Liverpool. Through their parishes, they helped to establish a vibrant devotional and social tradition which now exists only in the memories of an older generation. That Catholicism will survive in the regenerated urban villages of Vauxhall is highly probable. But questions on the structure and forms of ministry which may be appropriate for the people living there have yet to be faced.

4

Catholic Family Life

John Marshall

The Augustinian Inheritance

Catholic family life is a subject to which it is difficult to apply the methodology of scientific observation. Information about age at marriage, interval between marriage and having children, family size, and so on can be obtained from published demographic data, but the inner dynamics of family relationships and behaviour in private are not easily revealed. Some information does emerge from psychological studies but these are usually concerned with people for whom stress has reached a level which makes them seek outside help (see e.g. Dominian, 1975; 1981; Dalrymple, 1995; Marshall, 1995; 1996). The inner workings of 'normal' families remain shrouded in mystery, though some important sociological studies have been undertaken by researchers at the Marital Research Centre, now One-Plus-One, which was founded by Dr Jack Dominian (see, for example, Thornes and Collard, 1979; Brannen and Collard, 1982; Mansfield and Collard, 1988).

These difficulties beset the study of all families. They are no greater for Catholic families, but are of particular significance because Catholic families attract special interest. This is because the Roman Catholic Church has prescribed the sexual behaviour of its members in a way that no other religious group has ever attempted. In traditional textbooks of moral theology, for every page dealing with sins against social justice as many as one hundred were devoted to sexual sins. The latter were subjected to such detailed scrutiny as the morality of different positions for sexual intercourse and embraced such abstruse concepts as the degree of pleasure which might be enjoyed without sin during sexual intercourse between husband and wife.

These concerns reflect an ambivalence about sexual pleasure and sexual intercourse present in the official Church from the time of St Augustine. (The term 'Church' requires definition. It is often applied to the Pope and Roman Curia in such phrases as 'the Church teaches', whereas the Church is the entire body of the baptized, known since the Second Vatican Council as the 'People of God'. To avoid ambiguity, the term 'official Church' will be used in relation to the Pope and Curia.) The official Church adopted the Augustinian view that the enjoyment of sexual pleasure in intercourse between husband and wife was only justified by the intention to have a child. Excluding conception from intercourse was a mortal sin. Even when conception was not deliberately excluded, sexual intercourse for any other reason than to have a child was venially sinful. Pope Gregory the Great went even further and said that even when conception was intended, sexual intercourse was venially sinful because the pleasure it aroused was likely to be immoderate.

What effect did this teaching of the official Church have on the lives of Catholic families? This is difficult to assess. In the United States Michael Novak persuaded thirteen married couples to report on their experiences of marriage and what sexuality in marriage actually meant to them as persons and as Catholics (1965: xiii) but until recently there has not been a similar study in this country (but see Marshall, 1995).

Despite the preoccupation of the official Church with the minutiae of sexual behaviour, public pronouncements were couched in general terms. Divorce, birth control, abortion and sexual intercourse before and outside marriage were condemned but more detailed teaching was not conveyed in the public forum. It was through the confessional that more detailed teaching was undertaken. The requirement that every member of the Church must confess in private to a priest at least once a year and the constant urging to more frequent confession, monthly or even weekly, underpinned this. Indeed, many of the official answers to moral questions originated from this source; they were responses to questions raised by confessors through their bishops or in other ways. The secrecy of the confessional prevents us obtaining a picture of the intimate side of family life from this source but, fortunately, there are other indications, albeit indirect, which give us some insight into how Catholic families conducted their lives.

Prior to the twentieth century, birth control was not an important issue. It is true that couples have sought to limit family size by various means from the beginning of history, but overall it was not a pressing need. Indeed, high infant mortality and the value of child labour gave the large family an advantage. However, progressive industrialization and urbanization increased the risk of childbearing for women and provided the stimulus for the birth control movement in Great Britain and the United States around the turn of the twentieth century. The success of the movement, despite strong opposition, not only from religious groups but from a broader swathe of society, led to a gradual decline in family size. At first, Catholic families did not share in this decline, so much so that the large family became synonymous in popular parlance with the Catholic family and was the butt of many jokes. But gradually, from the 1920s onwards, Catholic families began to follow the national trend so that today there is no significant difference in family size between Catholics and non-Catholics.

Family Planning

How was this reduction in family size achieved by Catholics? It was certainly not by Natural Family Planning (NFP); the work of Ogino and Knaus on the timing of ovulation was only published in 1929 and it was not until the 1950s that the knowledge was applied in a practical manner in the development of the Basal Body Temperature Method of Natural Family Planning (Marshall, 1963). Meantime, the official Church did not leave its members in any doubt about the grave evil of birth control. In 1930, Pope Pius XI in his encyclical *Casti Connubii* described contraception as a 'criminal abuse' (§53) and said that those who practise it 'do something which is shameful and intrinsically immoral' (Pius XI, 1930: 25; §54). However, he declared that 'virtuous continence' (§53) was permissible with the consent of both parties.

Some Catholics endeavoured to follow this course by 'living as brother and sister', which was the phrase commonly used at that time. This came to light when couples sought help from marriage counsellors or teachers of NFP in organizations such as the Catholic Marriage Advisory Council (CMAC; now Marriage Care), which was founded by a group of Catholic laypeople in 1946 (Marshall, 1996). Couples spoke of the stress they endured; as one husband said: 'For about two and a half years we had abstained and as a result my wife was on the verge of a nervous breakdown and our marriage was very hollow.' Or, a woman speaking:

'we abstained for six months which was rather a sad time. Although ... outwardly there was nothing amiss, but inwardly something was missing' (Marshall, 1995: 44–5, 51). What percentage of Catholics followed this course is not known but it was probably a minority.

For the majority of Catholics, the solution lay in *coitus interruptus*. Evidence of this comes from the use of the term 'Catholic method' by workers in Family Planning clinics to which Catholics were beginning to turn. The spread of the term indicates that the attendance at a clinic of a Catholic who had been practising *coitus interruptus* was a common occurrence. How did Catholics reconcile the use of *coitus interruptus* with the teaching of the official Church? It was through genuine ignorance. Sermons at the parish level railed against three evils: divorce, abortion and artificial birth control. This last was the term commonly used in an era when there was considerable reticence in speaking about sexual matters. Inclusion of the word 'artificial' led many Catholics to believe that it was the use of devices such as condoms and caps which constituted the evil element in birth control. Natural methods such as withdrawal and the use of what was then called the safe-period were not thought to come under the ban. That this ignorance was genuine was very apparent in the 1950s when talking to couples who, dissatisfied with withdrawal, were seeking help with NFP.

Not all couples were in blissful ignorance. How did they fare? Evidence is of necessity anecdotal but is, nevertheless, compelling. At the time of the publication in 1968 of the encyclical *Humanae Vitae* of Pope Paul VI, reaffirming the ban on contraception, many priests found it difficult to accept this teaching and made public protest. An old priest who had served a parish in Wigan during the years of the depression expressed surprise that they found it such a problem. How, he asked, did they think the priest got through the years of the depression when people were living at bare subsistence level in overcrowded conditions. The first priority, he said, was to keep people close to Our Lord. Clearly, he had not allowed difficulties over the teaching of the official Church to interfere with this. In the same vein, another old priest who had spent his life in an inner city parish where living conditions were bad said that he had never in the whole of his priestly life refused anyone absolution. The frightening warning to priests in *Casti Connubii* that a confessor 'will have to render to God the sovereign Judge a strict account of this betrayal of his trust' (1930: 26, §57) by failing to admonish people about the evil of contraception had not deterred him from what he saw the pastoral situation demanded.

Not everyone was so fortunate in their pastor. Again, at the time of *Humanae Vitae* (Paul VI, 1968), an old lady confided how many years before she had been refused absolution. When asked what she did about it she replied, 'Nothing, I knew I had to keep my man happy for the sake of the family and no priest was going to come between me and Our Lord.' And so she carried on going to Mass and communion and keeping her man happy.

This anecdotal evidence suggests that the reduction in the size of Catholic families was achieved largely by means condemned by the official Church and that this contradiction was accommodated in a number of ways. Some were genuinely unaware that the method they employed, namely *coitus interruptus*, came under the ban. Others were helped by priests who took a broader view of their pastoral responsibilities than securing adherence to the official teaching on contraception. Yet others made their own moral decision as to which was more important, following the official teaching or preserving the well-being of the family. Some endeavoured to live as 'brother and sister', enduring great stress in so doing and some ceased to practise their religion because of this teaching.

The Pontifical Commission

The 1960s saw a change. The permissive society which emerged during that decade led, as one of its many consequences, to more openness about sex and sexual behaviour. This affected Catholics along with others. In 1963, Pope John XXIII established a Commission on Birth Control with a membership, not only of clergy, as had always been the custom, but including laity. These were not merely one or two token members but included men and women, married and single, in equal numbers to the clergy making a Commission of 64 members in all. The spur to this initiative by Pope John XXIII was not the difficulties encountered by married people in following the official teaching of the Church on contraception, but the move by the international organizations such as the United Nations and the World Health Organization to put the question of population growth on their agenda. The Holy See was seeking guidance on how best to respond to this situation.

It soon emerged in the discussions of the Commission that some pastors had been concerned for some time about the impact of the official teaching on the lives of many families. It also became apparent that the theologians of standing were unhappy about the basis of the teaching. Scientific study had established that conception was only possible during a limited number of days in the menstrual cycle around the time of ovulation; hence, when intercourse was taking place throughout the cycle most acts of intercourse were infertile. Coupled with this was the increasing testimony of married people that intercourse was not just about conception but was an important means of expressing and fostering love. In the light of these developments, the traditional view of the nature of intercourse held by the official Church was seen to be inadequate. Intercourse was not solely an act oriented towards procreation; it was a personal encounter between husband and wife from which procreation might or might not flow.

The deliberations of the Commission lasted for three years, at the end of which the majority conclusion was that the traditional teaching on contraception could not be sustained by reasonable argument. The conclusions of the Commission were never published by the Holy See, nor was the vast collection of supporting papers, but an accurate leaked version of the final report was published by *The Tablet* in the United Kingdom and in *The National Catholic Reporter* in the United States. Pope Paul VI, who had succeeded Pope John XXIII, did not accept the majority view and published, in 1968, his encyclical *Humanae Vitae* (Paul VI, 1968), which reaffirmed the traditional condemnation of contraception, though in less fearsome language than that of *Casti Connubii*. (For an authoritative account of the Commission, see Kaiser, 1987; see also Stourton, 1998: 41–59.)

Despite attempts by the Holy See to maintain secrecy, the existence of the Commission became public knowledge during the first year of its three-year existence. After it had concluded its work there was a delay of eighteen months before the publication of the encyclical. During this long period of gestation there was much public debate on the issue, so much so that, towards the end of the time, Cardinal Heenan, who was always in touch with the grass-roots, said, in private conversation, 'It does not matter now what the Pope says, the people have made up their minds.'

This was borne out by the unprecedented reception given to the encyclical. *The Times* newspaper received more letters than it had ever had on any previous subject; public meetings were held; 55 priests in the UK signed a letter of protest to *The Times* on 2 October 1968 and in the same week 75 prominent lay people wrote in a similar vein to *The Tablet* (Hastings, 1986: 576, 698; Dalrymple, 1995: 37). Though no hierarchy rejected the teaching, several in their pastoral letters put a gloss on it which a strict analysis would find difficult to reconcile with the essence of the teaching.

Catholic Experiences

Basal Body Temperature Method

Meantime, what had been happening in the lives of ordinary Catholic families? About this there is better evidence, because greater openness about sexual behaviour in general had made surveys possible. The uptake of Natural Family Planning had increased though it still constituted only about 5 per cent of the methods used by the population in general. In 1968, the results of a prospective field trial of the basal body temperature method of regulating births was published in the *Lancet* (Marshall, 1968). The trial involved 502 couples over two years. In 269 couples both husband and wife were Catholic, in 52 they were of mixed religion and in the remainder religious affiliation was not known. The result, as far as conception avoidance was concerned, was that the basal body temperature method was more reliable in avoiding conception than the condom or diaphragm but was not as reliable as the oral contraceptive.

Following the conclusion of the trial, the participants were invited to take part in a survey in which the husband and wife completed separately an anonymous questionnaire. Although the questionnaire was anonymous, husband and wife shared a respondent code number so that their responses, returned separately, could be matched. A good response was obtained, 410 of the 502 couples (82%) returned the completed questionnaire; in addition 50 were received from husband or wife alone; these latter were not included in the analysis. In all 36 questions were asked. The results of the survey were subsequently published (Marshall and Rowe, 1970).

A vast amount of data were obtained and analysed. In this chapter a brief synopsis of the data relevant to the present subject of Catholic family life is presented. The basal body temperature method (BBTM), as indeed do all natural methods of family planning, entails periods of abstinence from intercourse during the menstrual cycle; unsurprisingly, 93 per cent of men and 78 per cent of women found abstinence 'often' or 'sometimes' difficult. This led in 25 per cent of men and women to a 'bad' change in their relationship with one another and caused 45 per cent of the men and 27 per cent of the women to be 'more inclined to temptation'. Nevertheless, 47 per cent of the men and 48 per cent of the women felt they could express their love adequately during the periods of abstinence whereas 36 and 37 per cent, respectively, felt that they could not; 69 per cent of the men and 61 per cent of the women had a greater appreciation of intercourse after the periods of abstinence.

Exploration of sexual behaviour during the periods of abstinence from sexual intercourse showed that 88 per cent of men and 90 per cent of women said they had some degree of love-making, which led to a climax 'sometimes' or 'often' in 62 per cent of the men and 57 per cent of the women. Among the men, 33 per cent found it better to avoid all sexual contact during the periods of abstinence, whereas 42 per cent found it worse; the figures for women were 46 per cent and 34 per cent, respectively. Despite these difficulties, 66 per cent of the men and 75 per cent of the women thought that the BBTM was satisfactory and 75 per cent of men and women thought that it helped their marriage.

There are no data about the experience of other methods of avoiding conception with which to compare these results, as studies like this have not been carried out in relation to them. Anecdotal evidence indicates that donning a condom is sometimes found to be disruptive to the process of love-making as is insertion of a diaphragm at this stage; insertion beforehand may introduce an element of premeditation inimical to spontaneity.

The interesting feature of the data from the point of view of Catholic family life is the frequency with which orgasm apart from intercourse occurred. Strict Catholic moral teaching would rate this as much a sin as use of a contraceptive. It would have been interesting to explore the reasons which led couples to accept an illicit orgasm but not the use of a contraceptive.

CMAC Correspondents

Surveys, though valuable in providing an overall picture, are limited in exploring the reasons for, and feelings behind, behaviour. In the present instance, evidence from the survey was complemented by evidence from another source. The Catholic Marriage Advisory Council (CMAC) had for many years conducted a correspondence service to instruct couples who could not, or did not wish to, contact a personal instructor in NFP.

During forty years I was engaged with over 10,000 correspondents; sometimes the correspondence would be brief, terminating when they had learned the method; in other instances the correspondence extended over many years as different phases of experience, initiation, child-birth, the menopause, demanded. Many of the letters dealt only with technical matters such as the significance of a particular type of temperature shift or of change in the length of cycles; others were more revealing, recounting personal experience and raising personal questions. The letters were kept, making a formidable dossier, the essence of which was published in the book *Love One Another* (Marshall, 1995).

It is difficult to summarize so vast a correspondence; each letter is an individual testimony, but some general points can be made. The first is that the use of NFP was, for some couples, a great release, not only from troubles of conscience, but in opening up to them a new dimension in their relationship. 'I still think of it as family planning, when it's really *our way of life*! Something now, quite naturally integrated into our happy relaxed relationship' (ibid.: 29), was a typical comment. For others, this was not the case. 'We have tried to keep to these rules, with as I believe, a bad effect on the development of our marriage, our sex relations, my temper and our treatment of our children' (ibid.: 31) illustrates this.

A second theme was the way in which matters of conscience dominated the lives of some Catholics. 'It seems that self-denial because of the temperature method can lead to sins as grave in every way as is the sin of unnatural methods of birth control' (ibid.: 87) expressed this. But it was also apparent that some couples recognized that the exercise of conscience involved more than simply keeping a rule of the official Church. 'What the Church does not realize is that people have consciences towards other things than just the Church' (ibid.: 86). She was referring to the high probability that a child she conceived would have a serious genetic condition.

The correspondence was not limited to issues surrounding NFP; broader themes emerged. One was concern for others, husband, wife, children. There was clearly a great deal of selflessness and devotion. The other was the importance of the spiritual dimension in people's lives. 'Our love for one another and our mutual understanding has become indescribably precious and much too intimate to even try to describe. I am sure that this spiritual union has resulted in large measure from relief from anxiety both physical and economic' (ibid.: 84).

A panorama of human experience was revealed by this correspondence, particularly as it involved so many people and extended over so long a period of time. To evaluate its 'Catholic' dimension is, however, difficult as there are no comparable data from non-Catholic couples. Clearly, the issue of the morality of contraception was peculiar to Catholics but, for example, what effect dislike of one or other method of contraception, for what are called 'aesthetic' reasons, has on relationships in non-Catholic marriages is unknown. There is clearly a danger in attributing stress in family life to the fact that the couple are Catholics, endeavouring to follow a particular code of behaviour, when factors common to all marriages might well be at work. Likewise, it would be a mistake to think that the obvious spiritual dimension present in the lives of these correspondents might not be present in a different form in the lives of others.

New Perspectives on Marriage and Sexuality

The data presented here, because of the way in which they were gathered, have, of necessity, focused on the issue of family planning. But other influences were at work in the Catholic community; these are exemplified by the work of Dr Jack Dominian, a Catholic psychiatrist who has endeavoured to make a synthesis of knowledge gained by scientific studies in psychology and psychiatry and that obtained from religious sources, particularly from the scriptures (see e.g. Dominian, 1975; 1977; 1981; 1991). He considers that the emphasis placed by the official Church on the procreative element in sexual intercourse and its negative attitude towards sexual pleasure has distorted the true nature of marriage. This he sees as a personal and permanent commitment of husband and wife to each other, a commitment which is uniquely expressed through sexual intercourse, the pleasure of which is integral to the act and is to be enjoyed. He described sexual pleasure as 'an instrument which brings about a communion in which two people, a man and a woman, acknowledge, invite and accept each other as objects of love'. He has shifted the focus on Catholic marriage away from sin and contraception to personal commitment and love through numerous books, articles and lectures (see, for example, Dalrymple, 1995).

What we have to offer in terms of data on Catholic marriage and family life cannot be described as abundant. Nevertheless, there are more data than exist in relation to other religious denominations, sects or secular groupings. Without information about other groups, it is difficult to interpret the data relating to Catholics. To what extent does the behaviour of Catholic couples stem from the fact that they are Catholic and to what extent is their behaviour part and parcel of their being human? More research is needed to answer that question.

5

Have We Seen the Death of Dialogue?

Philip L. Daniel

Dialogue Within the Church

My main thesis is that authentic dialogue, by which I mean a sustained and practised relationship at all levels within the Church, from the international to the local, has not really been genuinely attempted and persisted in through the creation and maintaining of stable institutional forms. It seems to me, therefore, desirable that those who have experienced in their lives the Second Vatican Council and its consequences should seriously attempt at this time to evaluate the various aspects of that journey in faith and hope and with charity. Still confident that the Holy Spirit will continue to guide and, if necessary, intervene to readjust, I hope that such an exploration will reflect fairly the joys and hopes, the griefs and anguish not of the Church of 1965, which so strikingly portrayed them in the great document *Gaudium et Spes* of December 1965 (Abbott, 1966: 199-308; Flannery, 1996: 163), but of the Church of today, over thirty years later.

I have chosen to concentrate on dialogue within the Church, as a key element which emerged from the Council, and as a concept which has now entered into the common language of everyday diplomacy and negotiation. I may in consequence be accused of elevating a concern for mere process over content; confusing perhaps the medium with the mission. I am just as concerned with the authenticity of the message, the proclamation of the Word, which the assent of the whole Church indeed authenticates. But, after a lifetime of commitment to the institution, I am convinced, and have for some time expressed my concern, that a major part of the dynamic and continuous process needed to create and foster an authentic, living community from local to international level, namely genuine co-responsibility based on mutual respect and maintained through continuous, ordered and structured dialogue, as it emerged from the Council and is implied as a necessity in the major documents, has become sidelined to a degree that seriously impoverishes the institution and devitalizes most post-conciliar structures. The situation has reached the point that now a new generation, unaware of the labours which predated the Council, often questions the effectiveness of the institutional Church to bind together its adherents in a living community.

In recent days we have been told of 'new traditionalists' who, while not wishing to put back the clock completely, seem to be striving for a past and mythical Church of pious docility, rather than one of joint adventurous encounter, 'firm in the faith and Christian teaching' (*Apostolicam Actuositatem*, §14, in Abbott, 1966: 505; Flannery, 1996: 422) which was the model for the post-war enthusiasts of my generation. That was a world which might in different places be receptive, indifferent or hostile, but where a quietist Church, necessary as periods of quiet retreat are for what the French call *les responsables* to recharge their batteries, could not be the manifest New Israel, the Church of all the people of God on their journey described in the first great decree of the Council, *Lumen Gentium* (in Abbott, 1966: 14-101).

What there now seems an urgency to strive for is the reclaiming of the central message of the Council anew through a fresh affirmation of genuine collegiality at all levels. As a layman, my view is, of course, necessarily partial, but my conviction is not that co-responsibility or, to use a newer phrase, collaborative ministry, has failed but that it has been tried, found difficult and, to all intents and purposes, largely abandoned. What has supervened and threatens to obscure it is a form of *ad hoc* consultation which tends to be partial, even haphazard, and which though it may at times be valuable to the initiators does little to enable those consulted to prepare successors in the light of their own experience. No real tradition of continuous consultation has been established.

A Curriculum Vitae

What I have been for most of my adult life is a 'committed layman', that is a layman who early decided that a vocation in and to the world was the life proper to me, and should be lived in ways in which such talent as I seemed to have for a successful professional career should be devoted in at least equal part to the building up of the kingdom of God. This required that I should seek, within my competence, to impress 'divine law on the affairs of the earthly city' (*Gaudium et Spes*, in Flannery, 1996: 212) but also entering into true dialogue within the Church to inform the pastors so that their guidance might be that much more sure-footed.

As a staff officer at a major headquarters during the Second World War, I saw, sometimes at very close hand, how great and irreversible decisions had sometimes to be taken by those in authority in almost an instant, relying at a critical moment on the trusted advice of a very lowly subordinate, while in no way avoiding personal responsibility for the outcome. Years later as a public servant in a key department, I saw how dependent those in authority could be on advisers whose word had to be trusted because time allowed no second chance. This impressed on me the value of integrity in small things, of thoroughness in consideration of the implications of giving advice, and of consistency in its application. Throughout my life I have found not only parallels in the handling of business for the benefit of Church and State but also how closely fidelity in one sphere can illuminate the way to handle tasks in the other. A proper evaluation of the layman's vocation in the Church displays a requirement for precisely those virtues of which the world itself stands most in need.

Much has yet to be written of the processes which led up to Vatican II, and of the work for nearly a generation before in the 'apostolic organizations', often of a laity influenced by charismatic priests, but free of any direct episcopal promptings, to the events behind the drafting of the key documents, and to the subsequent analysis and debate. The prophet is found at all levels within the Church. Much is likely to remain forever in the archives. What I can give is the testimony of a person who has followed events in the Church closely, especially since 1951. Since then I have been in a variety of roles close 'to the centre' at national level, and often considerably involved internationally, sometimes through association with movements of international character, such as Pax Romana (the International Movement of Catholic Intellectuals), or even at times by invitation to take part in *colloquia* organized directly by the Holy See.

I have in consequence never been far from decision-makers. In 1951 after the first World Congress of the Laity I was invited to represent the Catholic Social Guild (CSG) on the continuing Committee which had been formed largely under the influence of Fr (later Archbishop) Derek Worlock, then the Secretary to Cardinal Griffin, to provide national continuity, in relation to a new Roman permanent office. This was established to forge a world-wide lay voice, as COPECIAL (the 'Permanent Committee for International Congresses of the Lay Apostolate'). The English and Welsh corresponding group, the National Council for the Lay Apostolate (NCLA), had an elected lay chairman, and a freely nominated membership from the participating organizations. It had provided a wide spectrum of developing lay opinion well before the Council, and clearly had the confidence of the Archbishops of Westminster, and their most trusted colleagues.

I was a member of NCLA until the early 1980s, as the representative of either the CSG, or later the Newman Association, and then as an invited 'expert'. When the provisional Laity Commission was set up in 1968 to begin the implementation of Vatican II, I was nominated to it from the NCLA's quota of five, and I remained a member from then, through the lifetime of the more 'permanent' Commission, without in any way lessening my commitment to the Newman Association which provided an intellectual stimulus to ensure that I was keeping abreast of new developments over a range of disciplines. In this role I served as its President at a time when the Cold War was probably at its most acerbic, and I was in my professional life most acutely aware of some dire possibilities. I was a close defence adviser in the Wilson era to George Brown, as First Secretary, and had to be at one stage 'Atomic Cleared' for the knowledge to which I was party; and was from then on circumspect about all foreign travel and association.

Shortly afterwards I became aware of the potentiality for advice to the government of the day which could be furnished through a revived Catholic Union, and began a different form of apostolic activity proper to a layman, and one unable to be performed by any ecclesiastic, however eminent. This led to the Review Committee of the Catholic Union of 1975, and the appearance of the Issues Committee, which I stewarded for 21 years (Daniel, 1998).

During all this time, and engagement through the period of the National Pastoral Congress of 1980, and the papal visit coinciding with the Falklands War, I was acutely conscious of the distancing effect of national involvement from parish life, and the views of the 'persons in the pews'. Nevertheless I strove also to keep my feet on the ground at that level, which was by no means easy since time is always limited, and to most Catholic parish priests willing and anxious to make use of 'talented' parishioners, those involved with esoteric national activities are just undependable, and somewhat stand-offish irrelevancies!

The rather special alienation from the generality of the laity which involvement with national structures entails can be paralleled with that wariness with which professional colleagues regarded someone who pursued openly what for them was an irrelevant 'holy hobby'. In the Army of my time attachment to the Roman persuasion itself could by some commanding officers even be regarded as a sort of disloyalty, and I found traces of this even in the public service. At a crucial promotion board in the 1970s a senior colleague remarked sneeringly and unnecessarily, 'Philip is, of course, a dedicated Roman Catholic.'

I was determined in my official career that I should not be identified with any Catholic exclusivity, and tried to make my social and voluntary life at least equally shared between 'Catholic' and other contacts. A desire for the reconciliation of 'the opposites' has predominated in my personal approach since I have never found the confrontational congenial. This makes single-mindedness, which is often the key to acknowledged success, difficult. 'Whitehall wars', once the stock-in-trade of colleagues, left me singularly disinterested and sometimes accused of not following closely enough the departmental interest! The focuses of my attention have included Poland, and the former Soviet world which at one time engulfed it, and where I felt a debt of honour still unpaid since 1939; the German-speaking world, which led me back to family ties and ruptured friendships of the First World War; Christian responsibility for the myths which led to the Holocaust, the Holy Land, and the rights of all three peoples of the Book; and last but not least, Anglo-Japanese reconciliation, since it was in Burma that I encountered the realities of war at its beastliest.

I mention these aspects of my own life because harmony within the Church and a unity of purpose and process seem to me as essential there as in society at large, and much of the current *malaise* stems from reluctance to part from pretensions to power which ignore the primary duty of service.

Five Dramatic Decades

I set out the previous account to provide a backdrop against which to reflect on the five momentous decades since the end of the Second World War during which the Church has itself come through many transforming experiences. It is useful when reflecting on changes in the visible aspects of the Church to recall events in the wider world, because the coincident interpenetration of secular developments had so often a crucial influence. In setting out recently the experiences of the Catholic Union in seeking to have an influence on the course of public and especially parliamentary affairs in this country I found it useful to give as chapter headings the six Parliaments of the period (Daniel, 1998). In looking at the concept of co-partnership in the Church, the manner in which consciousness of it came about, I find it convenient to think in terms of the five decades, from the 1950s to the 1990s, each of which saw major events in the world, and in the Church, and each of which has in retrospect a particular stamp and resonance.

Fifty years, however, is a long time, more than the productive period of most men's lives, and I can do no more than allude to some of the events in the world and the Church which have moulded my view of today. Undoubtedly the emphasis will seem to some wrong, but while anxious or even critical of some present-day directions the Church has taken I am content to believe that nothing is irreversible and that sometimes the will of God is reached by men following circuitous paths.

The Fifties: A Decade of Anticipation

The decade before the Council was not a period in which the Church slept, but one of extraordinary liveliness and expectation. There was a sense of relief from the end of major hostilities, but also of exhaustion, and the need in the main combatant countries to recover. At the same time there was an uneasy peace shortly to be disturbed by the realization of the nature of the Soviet and the nuclear threat, the Berlin airlift, the Korean War, the tumultuous upheavals in China, and much beside. In the young and post-war European Church of my time there was much stirring. The word 'renewal' was heard all around and particularly among the young ex-servicemen who were resuming studies or beginning careers. There was an excitement in what increasingly were called the 'movements of the apostolate' and there was a genuine *camaraderie* between young clerics and young people which was manifest when we met.

Frequently we met on a European basis, and often in places which bore the signs of recent conflict. The pontificate of Pius XII, and from 1958 that of John XXIII, seemed to welcome in particular those movements which preface their description with the adjective *jeune*, and whose influence was to be widely felt from the very beginnings of the Council. The so-called Cardijn dialectic of 'See, judge and act' became widely accepted in those years, and provided a way through the subtleties of Soviet propaganda which sought to exploit the universal longing for international harmony and reconciliation, particularly among young people.

In the Church of the Fifties there was a notable harmony of relationships across the whole spectrum of Church membership which became manifest in the degree to which discussion led to new ways of working together. The international consensus which in civil society upheld the United Nations, and other international bodies such as the nascent European community, stimulated Church 'internationals' such as the Conference of Catholic International Organizations (the CIOs), and all the multifarious international Catholic specialized organizations which were recognized within it. It was the period, encouraged by easier air travel, in which attendance at some kind of international gathering became an expected part of the summer vacation. But there was more to it than that. An ease came over relationships between bishops, priests working with organizations, and the laity, which laid the foundations of the realization of co-responsibility including the laity, a partnership which was to be so eloquently set out by Cardinal Suenens (1968) following the Council.

This was the period in which the Vatican called the first of the World Congresses of the Laity, and set up a permanent office to prepare for future such events, and it was the success of the first event (1951) and its successor (1957) which brought into existence the NCLA in England and Wales to provide a permanent means whereby the bishops collectively might consult the laity. There was a downside, of course, and it was that the effective organizations were rarely parish-based, so that the activists tended to form separate but quite distinct communities, and in doing so provoked some hostility.

The Sixties: The Decade of the Council

The decade of the Council brought throughout the Church a vivid realization of the interdependence of pastors and the faithful because increasingly the bishops found themselves under the necessity of knowing in an intimate way what the people really were thinking. The Council forced its own dynamic on them, and the use increasingly made by senior

Churchmen of the advice of trusted lay counsellors influenced in particular those passages in the major documents that bore on lay responsibility. Paul VI, while always careful, as in *Ecclesiam Suam* (1964), not to upstage Council conclusions yet to come, had made known his view of the paramount need in all dioceses of a pastoral council. Not a great use of them was made at the time of Paul VI's injunction, though one of the features of the Sixties was the convening of a few diocesan synods as part of the growing sense of renewal.

For the most part the influence of Vatican II was felt in the sharpening up in the organizations of awareness of the Council's progress, and in the approval felt by the laity as a whole of the public acts of Pope John XXIII, his international impact as a personality, and particularly in the great encyclicals *Princeps Pastorum* (1959), which stressed lay participation, *Mater et Magistra* (1961) on social progress, and *Pacem in Terris* (1963) on peace. These had an impact which even percolated to the Soviet world, and in particular the 'occupied' Eastern republics. The reverberations were to be noticed in the Council documents, such as *Gaudium et Spes*, on the Church in the Modern World, *Apostolicam Actuositatem*, on the Apostolate of the Laity, *Inter Mirifica*, the decree on the Mass Media, and above all in the declarations on religious liberty, and attitudes to non-Christian religions.

Preparation went on in the period of the Council for the third World Congress of the Lay Apostolate, under the title of 'The Laity in the Renewal of the Church' scheduled for 1967. The chosen instrument for the English and Welsh delegation was the NCLA, chaired at that time by the late Dr Kevin McDonnell. Great efforts were made to bring in the element of the 'non-organized', essentially parochial, laity since the accusation was made, often in the correspondence columns of the Catholic press, that such bodies as the NCLA or the NBCW, were self-selected zealots responsible to no one but themselves and that they were unrepresentative of people in the parishes. Such dialogue as existed, it was suggested, was between certain prelates and unrepresentative laity who were already too much in each other's confidence. This, it was claimed, represented a wholly undesirable influence on the traditional Church. What clearly was already in train was something of the backlash which became apparent following the Council.

The flavour of the NCLA of that time, which was in fact a broad cross-section of actively minded lay people with understanding chaplains, was perhaps best conveyed by Kevin McDonnell in an article which appeared in *The Laity Today (LTD)*, the bulletin of the Consilium De Laicis, the Roman successor office to COPECIAL towards the end of the decade. In his article McDonnell took on the objections to the narrowness of the NCLA as a true reflection of the English laity as a whole, briefly sketching its history and its origin in 1951 following the first World Congress and the uniqueness of the appearance with ecclesiastical approval of a freely elected delegation to represent the country in Rome. 'Never before had the laity in England been represented abroad by delegates chosen by free choice from constituencies democratically controlled. The Catholic aristocracy ceased at that moment to be the "leaders" of the laity' (McDonnell, *LTD* 1969: 128).

From then onwards the NCLA sought ways of establishing diocesan constituencies to balance the national associations of committed laity; and it was generally agreed that these ideally should and were confidently expected to emerge from pastoral councils at diocesan level.

The World Congress produced a gratifying and coherent series of recommendations, but ominously certain Roman circles opined that the laity had grown too big for their boots (see Vaillancourt, 1980). Cardinal Ottaviani in particular had given a negative view of the World Congress, in sharp contrast to Cardinal Suenens's positive one, and there was some satisfaction in curial circles, and dismay in lay ones, when the COPECIAL office was abolished, and a new Consilium De Laicis established by Paul VI in January 1967 to implement §26 of the Decree on the Laity, and §90 of the Church in the Modern World which called for a new International Secretariat to cover lay activities. It had been remarked in the course of the World Congress that a Council whether for, or on behalf of, or respecting the laity, however *de* was interpreted, was not that Consilium Laicorum which had been hoped for, and some dismay was expressed that, as first constituted in a membership of 40, eleven, including the President, Vice President and Executive Secretary and eight 'Consultors' were clerics. It was not a propitious beginning.

A pontificate which had included an encouraging encyclical *Populorum Progressio* (1967) in the line of the great social encyclicals, which had more than anything else engaged the active collaboration of the laity and embraced the World Congress, produced as its last significant document *Humanae Vitae* in 1968, which proved divisive in the Church, and coincided with the Russian invasion of Czechoslovakia, which seemed to freeze into immobility the Iron Curtain. For the last ten years of the pontificate there were no further pronouncements, and while the new

Consilium de Laicis was producing some interesting documents and mounted numerous *colloquia,* much of the excitement generated by the Laity Congress internationally began to evaporate. The received opinion was that Rome was unlikely to sponsor another World Congress of the Laity for the foreseeable future.

The Seventies: The Decade of Implementation

Although I have called this the decade for implementation it was a decade of some disappointment. What started fair concluded somewhat differently. So far as the conclusions of Vatican II were concerned there was a sense of both gain and loss.

Internationally, the volumes of *The Laity Today* (*LTD*), the Bulletin of the Consilium de Laicis which succeeded *Lay Apostolate*, the bulletin of COPECIAL, following the Congress started on an upbeat from the Congress and an encouraging message from the new President, Cardinal Roy. The earlier issues reflected from both ecclesiastical and lay contributors the atmosphere of close companionship and collaboration which had led to *Apostolicam Actuositatem* and the Lay Congress. Personalities featured in the pages were generally familiar from the Congress years. The earlier issues reported factually national responses to the Council's decrees affecting the laity, and to developments in various parts of the world seeking to implement both them and the recommendations of the Congress. It was not till the third year that the Bulletin began to devote whole issues to single topics in the form of instructions.

In 1971 the Council had sponsored a symposium on 'Dialogue Within the Church', the whole context of which suggested that though its practice at international, national and local diocesan level was far from perfect, its place within the Church was now assured. Issues 9/10 of the Bulletin were totally devoted to this subject, which in particular highlighted the reference in §26 of *Christus Dominus* (The Decree on the Pastoral Office of Bishops, 1965) stressing the desirability of a pastoral council in each diocese.

In England the NCLA had welcomed with great enthusiasm the setting up of first a provisional Laity Commission, and shortly afterwards Commissions for Justice and Peace, Education and Ecumenism. In each, while there was a strong element of episcopal appointment, the majority of participants were expected to consist of persons nominated by self-governing, and largely lay-controlled, Church bodies. In the ensuing decade the Laity Commission had two periods of office under outstanding chairmen: Dr (later Professor) Paul Black and Mrs Eleanor Barnes. Paul Black showed that skill in presiding over educational bodies within the University of London, and for government assignments, could equally be deployed effectively in Church roles.

The Reports of the Provisional Laity Commission and its successor on *The Church: Joint Venture of Priests and Laity* (Brech, 1972*)*, an enquiry initiated by the Provisional Laity Commission, and *Church 2000* (1973*)*, a report produced by a Joint Working Party on Pastoral Strategy directly sponsored by the Bishops' Conference, were among the most important leading up to the National Pastoral Congress of 1980. In both Chairmen's Reviews, i.e. that of Paul Black in 1971 and that of Eleanor Barnes in 1976, the theme of co-responsibility looms large. In the first Report recommendations were made to increase the number of elected members from the associations now grouped into recognized national consultative bodies, and to strive for at least one lay person appointed from each diocese from either the diocesan pastoral or laity commission. In the course of the consideration of the Reports it had been noted that by the end of 1971 seven dioceses reported the existence of one, occasionally both, of these bodies. The second report in 1976 made no proposals in respect of membership but stressed that the nature of representation seemed itself to be imperfectly understood: e.g. 'representatives from dioceses are uncertain whether they are meant to be giving their own views or reflecting the views of the body they represent'. Clearly the difference between delegate and representative, the basic distinction for the British MP, had not then become clear to some lay participants. However, the Laity Commission published a number of useful studies in the series of Living Parish Pamphlets sponsored by Ealing Abbey.

At a very early stage in the life of the new commissions some alarm at their reported independence of mind had been voiced in the episcopal conference and a Bishops' Review Committee set up in 1971 sought to allay such fears, not dissimilar to those voiced by the more conservative cardinals over the World Congress of 1967. Giving its views on the now impressive tally of twelve commissions the Report requested that the consultative nature of the commissions be fully stressed. 'No executive task is to be undertaken by a commission except by authority granted by the Conference directly or through the episcopal member' (Review Report, 1971, §22 (b)). Other *obita* in this significant document were that their 'work will never be fully effective until the appropriate councils are established at parochial and diocesan level' (§20) and 'it would be useful to arrange occasional national Pastoral Congresses to discuss aspects of the mission and pastoral strategy of the Church' (§21).

Nothing had been said in the Report about any organic link between the commissions and the Bishops' Conference as such, and the general practice was that any report of a commission's proceedings and recommendations was made by the bishop concerned, even where the chairman was a layman and maybe a person of some stature in his own right. Consultation within the Church, as a matter among equals, was still a delicate subject. As a 'not for publication' report of the Laity Commission circulated in 1974 to the other national and diocesan consultative bodies explained, 'the Church has a tradition of "downward" communication. Persuading, warning, comforting, enthusing come easily. There is no corresponding "upward" communication.' Pointing out that such continued practice was somewhat contrary to the plain message of Vatican II, the document asked how some better approach to consultation could be achieved.

Around the same time the Consilium de Laicis in the 1975 Bulletin 19/20 of *LTD* reported under 'New Trends' in a style remarkably different from its earlier informative manner, and notified readers that the Council had now extended its 'juridical competence' to the Catholic organizations for the 'apostolate and spirituality'. The precise meaning of this seemed somewhat unclear and its significance never came through to the national bodies. It is from about this time that a number of Roman communications meant for the laity employ a kind of Vatican 'nu-speak' which lessens their impact. Certainly they are in marked contrast to the plain speaking of Ronald Brech's Report (1972), which brought together the experiences of 112 working groups, and faced squarely such questions as lay attitudes to the possibility in the future of married priests.

The Eighties: A Decade of Confusion

The Eighties internationally saw the crumbling of the Berlin Wall, and with it Soviet power; the lifting in civil society, even in China to a great extent, of the active menace of the 'thought police'; and in Britain an economic revolution, not entirely acceptable to those with a social conscience, through the years of Thatcherism, certainly a new, and somewhat rougher, society suggesting a 'survival of the fittest'. Only in the Roman Church and for its own adherents was a 'command structure' even over lateral thinking retained and even reinforced. That came with the new Pope, often applauded for his openness to the world, but seen within the Church as reversing completely the styles of John XXIII and Paul VI. For the laity much of what they had come to expect, and in which a new generation had been fostered since the Council, seemed to be in the course of being set aside. Caution was the note of the day. Communication, consultation, conferring, conversation were no longer in the forefront of Church activity, or at least not in the pattern which assumed an equality of contribution from all the 'People of God'.

In England the decade started well with the enthusiasms generated by the Council, and the new array of national, and in some dioceses local, councils and commissions. The National Pastoral Congress, splendidly presented and choreographed by Archbishop Derek Worlock, gathered bishops, priests and people in an enthusiastic manifestation and suggested a vibrant future. The resulting document *The Easter People* (in Anon., 1981) was the bishops' response to the collected reports of the working parties, but to some it seemed as though important emphases, as compared with the *Congress Report* (CTS, Do 521, 1980) had been edited out. Very little was said, apart from thanks duly given, on the contributions made in the preceding decade by the commissions, and proposals relating to future structures for dialogue were limited.

It was with some surprise then that the laity heard in the course of 1982 that a new review of the national structures had been undertaken and was now presented under the title *In the House of the Living God*. A defensive introduction suggested that some might find the proposals 'an implied criticism of a decade of effort'. The Report, therefore, claimed that it stemmed from reflections from the experience of the Pastoral Congress and doctrinal conclusions on the role of bishops. The Report 'was primarily about the collegiality of Bishops and secondarily about the co-responsibility of all the faithful for the mission of the Church' (para. 4). In its examination of the deficiencies of the commissions the Report suggested that the element of so-called conciliar or representative membership had 'swamped' the value of the 'expert' element! Given that apart from the Laity Commission all the commissions depended upon episcopal nomination this was surprising. The commissions, the Report added, had no national credibility; they remained largely remote and unknown 'despite a policy of drawing upon all parts of the country for membership'. In future, therefore, all national work would be grouped into three functional commissions, entirely composed of bishops, but assisted by experts, and served by an enlarged (and salaried) secretariat. In the accompanying briefing document, launched as a discussion document on what had as a provisional report already been in principle accepted by the bishops, the thinking behind the proposals as regards the laity was presented as follows:

> the laity will contribute nationally as experts in the secretariat and Commissions, and in the *ad hoc* working parties to be set up by the Commissions. They will have their voice nationally through the lay liaison groups and in the agencies. But like priests and religious the laity are the Church primarily when they are gathered round their bishop. (*Briefing* 12/39: 10 December 1982)

In this astonishing, and completely unexpected upsetting of all that had transpired in regard to lay participation since the beginning of planning for the first World Congress of the Laity in 1951, no role was allocated to or credit for past service given to the national bodies such as the NBCW, or the NCLA, or the apostolic organizations such as the YCW, the UCM, or the Newman, which had largely provided the personnel. A footnote relegated them from constituencies serving the Laity Commission to 'liaison bodies' which might or might not be 'consulted' on advice from the Church employees who would provide the salaried secretariats for the episcopal commissions. What had happened was that almost overnight the experienced cadres which had fostered lay co-partnerships since the first Lay Congress were dispersed, and their collective witness abandoned. For the generation which had eagerly followed the Council and taken part in the World Congresses and the European Forums this outcome was seen as a rebuff from which quite a few decided that they had no wish to play any further part in official Church relationships.

A crisis working party of the three major lay consultative bodies approached Archbishop Worlock and were somewhat incredulously assured that their position would be 'even stronger' than it had been in nominating representatives to commissions since they would have immediate access through their liaison bishop to the Conference. He said that he had been obliged to insert the critical paragraphs in the Report by strong representations made to him by several bishops about the undue prominence assumed by forceful lay personalities associated with particular commissions, and the remoteness of such spokesmen from parish life. It was clear that what amounted to a *coup d'état* had taken place behind the scenes. At a later stage and before the Review Report was issued in final form, the following rubric was inserted, and appears in the *Catholic Directory* today in relation to the six national consultative bodies (three of which are clerical) listed: 'The Bishops' Conference undertakes wherever practicable to enter into formal consultation with these bodies on matters of particular concern to them. (Review Report, para. 50 (vii)).'

Much had been made in the Report of the primacy of the diocese, and the need for a full coverage of diocesan councils was stressed. That need was set out in the revised *Code of Canon Law* (1983) and it is the only such body to which the laity have a legalized right of presence. The existence of such councils is in fact rare. Currently less than a third of English dioceses have one, and the phrase in Canon 511 'so far as pastoral circumstances suggest' seems somewhat overused to explain their absence. In an early Report of Commissions the need for adequate preparation for the introduction of diocesan councils expressed the view that parish pastoral councils should come first. For this reason the provisional Laity Commission concentrated on the parish, inspired among other things the Living Parish series, and sponsored in a number of dioceses the setting up of parish councils as 'models'. A rough survey suggests that today only an insignificant number of parishes countrywide have pastoral councils, as distinct from administrative bodies, and that the number of active ones has been declining, even since 1980.

The 1987 Synod on the Laity was mounted by what had now come to be called the pontifical *Consilium Pro Laicis*. The word *Pro* suggested an even further distancing than *De*, and aroused little discernible enthusiasm among lay activists. Under the title 'Christ in the World' it had been announced as the first update since the Council of the documents on the Church in the World and on the Laity. It was of course an episcopal gathering, and it resulted in *Christifideles Laici* (John Paul II, 1988), a post-synodal apostolic exhortation. Considerable stress is laid on the secular character of the layman's role in the mission of the Church, almost to suggest that any interest in the functioning and management of the institution itself is not his business.

The Approach to the Millennium

I have dared to suggest that true dialogue is almost dead. It is certainly a devalued concept and the Nineties have shown no significant movement in the building of genuine community within the Church. At international level there is almost universal despondency, at least among the Council generation, about the recent years. The *Concilium Pro Laicis* and its publications have not been greatly influential, and the great lay internationals, largely located in Switzerland, feel, at the best, 'detached'. Nationally there has been since the early Eighties no direct and assured access to the bishops and opinions about the reality of the consultation assured by the last Review Committee are certainly divided. I can recall only one formal consultation of substance, that on the 1987 Synod, and even then there was no report back, or chance to evaluate what had happened. The story of *The Common Good* (Bishops' Conference, 1996a) is itself a little object lesson in missed opportunity. At diocesan level the situation remains much as it was in the Seventies.

This, of course, does not mean that the lessons of the Council have been entirely discarded. There is, for example, much to commend in *The Sign We Give* (1995), the product of a working party from within the Bishops' Conference at the suggestion of the National Conference of Priests. The document stresses the role of collaborative ministry and calls for a revolution in the way in which we live and work in the Church today. Its message is incontestable, but it has to be said that most of the practice suggested had been advocated as far back as the publications of the Provisional Laity Commission, and even in documents arising more directly from Vatican II. New perspectives for the place of collaborative ministry stem partly from the expected shortage of priests, and in discussing the diocesan level there is a welcome reminder of the place of the pastoral council, but no reference to canon law, which requires each diocese to establish such a body and lays down that it should meet at least once a year.

A Retrospect and a Conclusion

I come back to my starting theme, the necessity to create the conditions at all levels in the Church for true dialogue. I recall that I had not only been the discussion leader for the Anglo-Spanish Workshop on 'Dialogue in the Church' but had been the author of the General Report to the 1967 World Congress on this theme and the speaker on it at the closing session. A major theme had been the equality of all parties to dialogue, an equality of esteem not function. True dialogue, said one summary, was not a safety-valve for 'real authority' to obtain advance assent but a positive, dynamic and creative means essential for the well-being of the Church in changing situations. A footnote in the record of the third Congress noted:

> When he described the work of the five language groups in broad terms to the Plenary Session Mr Daniel remarked, 'We didn't like the word "dialogue" very much. It has already become a jargon word. We prefer the word "encounter" because this gives the idea of reciprococity and the transforming function of it.' (*Laity in the Renewal of the Church*, vol. III: 78 n. 3)

Clearly in this sense we did not consider that 'encounter' embodied the idea of opposition, although I remember the shudder in my workshop when I introduced from our parliamentary experience the idea of 'Her Majesty's loyal Opposition'!

The conclusions which the combined workshops set out for authentic and effective dialogue are worth repeating in full, because they have often been restated when the modification of structures for service to the Church as a whole, or locally, has been under consideration, and have for the most part been as consistently ignored. They were certainly restated by the Catholic Union in memoranda to the bishops over the years whenever the question of structures for implementation were under discussion. They were, in abbreviated form:

1   There is no opposition between the hierarchical character of the Church and the adoption of democratic structures representing Church communities in their historical and geographical contexts.
2   Tension is necessary for the dynamism of the Church's life. It is not to be identified with systematic opposition.
3   It is of primary importance to recall that dialogue is experienced at grass-roots level in the midst of concrete realities. However excellent the system that is set up, there is the risk of our deceiving ourselves as regards the Church's ability to understand our contemporary world from within.
4   Formation for dialogue is basic, and it would be a good thing if more lay people took degrees in theology. Both men and women religious should take their place in the structures for dialogue.
5   The Church has one single mission. We have to rethink the specific function of each person in relation to the mission (*Lumen Gentium*, §13).

6 The whole People of God should take part, through appropriate structures, not only working out the ideas but sharing in pastoral activity. The whole People of God at all levels should have a share in choosing the leaders, including bishops.

7 Councils at diocesan level should include not only representatives of apostolic organizations, but also of the unorganized laity and of religious men and women.

8 Local churches should be trusted to decide on the structures which are to be set up. In this way, local conditions will be taken into account and the Universal Church will gather up the experiences of the local churches, while recalling the principles involved and discerning the signs of unity through a normal pluralism.

9 It would be to the Church's advantage to recognize the specific contribution of women and to make more room for them at all levels.

10 The unity of Christians resides in the aim to be pursued. It is normal that there should be pluralism in action (*Gaudium et Spes,* § 92.2).

What these conclusions suggest, for they are themselves the result of compromise and an attempt faithfully to reflect five bilingual group discussions, is a consciousness that dialogue, or loving encounter, requires an equality of esteem among the parties, and this can only be expressed through structures which, though necessarily reformable by experience, are stable, predictable, regular, and of freely consenting participants. The pastors cannot with any credibility be content with 'pick and mix' assemblies where the choice of membership is determined by the convenors. In a notable passage in his book on the fourth session of Vatican II, the author Xavier Rynne drew attention to the insistence of Pope Paul VI, in his comments following the Council, on using the word *rinnovamento* (renewal) in contrast to his predecessor's use of *aggiornamento* (bringing up to date) and linked this to the expression *ecclesia semper reformanda*, as indicating that the Church needed continual revitalization, and that such revitalization was the business of the whole body (Rynne, 1965: 251). Significantly he left his readers with the image of the open door from Revelation: 'Now I have opened before you a door that nobody will be able to close' (Revelation 3.8).

It follows, then, that the means must be found, at all levels within the

Church, of listening to the faithful in their role as co-workers, and that this is a requirement, not an occasional option. Without the instruments to ensure it, it simply cannot exist as a living and continuous reality. As Suenens said, the Church makes its way towards the future in living continuity with the past, but this continuity is neither conservatism nor servility, it is fidelity. 'The sense of co-responsibility must be the soul of the apostolic activity of the 20th century, and of the centuries which follow' (Suenens, 1968: 212).

Given the insistence which Paul VI himself placed on dialogue several times in *moto proprios* before and after the Council, (such as *Christus Dominus* and *Ecclesiae Sanctae*, and especially in his first Encyclical *Ecclesiam Suam* (1964) before the Council ended), and on the means necessary to ensure it, it seems astonishing that as soon after the Council as 1971 a Roman seminar held on the initiative of the Laity Council, and presided over by Cardinal Roy, and which was directly addressed by the Pope, in discussing the situation then about dialogue in the Church came to the view that it was widely held to be disappearing, to be dying out, was finished and was out of date. That was not of course the seminar's conclusion, for the Pope himself in addressing the participants said: 'Dialogue in the Church is human action, but also divine action. In the Church when two persons engage in dialogue there are always present more than two. The Three Divine Persons are there, sharing in the exchange of views, just as they are present in the dialogue carried out by diocesan bodies, by individual Churches, by the Holy See, and by the various Christian communions among their own members and with the world' (Paul VI, 20 March 1971; *LTD* 9/10 (1971): 16).

Yet it was at that same seminar, at which the only English delegate was Archbishop Worlock, that the Chairman put the opening question, answering a prevailing view which had occasioned the seminar, that dialogue was, within six years of the end of Vatican II, already dying out, was finished and out-dated ('What Has Killed Dialogue?', *LTD* 9/10: 13). Perhaps my posing of the same question ten years later, at the end of my service with NCLA, when I invoked the image of the Roman courtyard with the dove vainly fluttering outside the closed jalousies, was not so outrageous?

Dialogue, then, is not a 'process' which can be switched on and off when required but a necessary condition, a fundamental element towards achieving that dynamism which alone can generate a Church which while always engaged in evangelization has also always to be examining its own need of renewal. This is the affirmation of its own authenticity about which Newman was speaking when he stressed the reality of the *sensus fidelium* (1961). Because of the presence of the Holy Spirit deep within, the Church always senses when the guidance is faltering, but to ensure that heart always speaks to heart the necessary means must always exist for the voicing of opinion. There cannot be 'closed conditions' insofar as the *rationale* always needs updating for the language of the time.

Structures are not to be created for their own sake, but for training in service, so that the laity can be integrated into the Church as adults who have responsibilities to it. In *Ecclesiam Suam* Paul VI had likened dialogue to the conversation of Christ among men: 'a family conversation which would render the Church sincere and sensitive in genuine spirituality, ever ready to give ear to the manifold voice of the contemporary world, ever more capable of making Catholics truly good, wise, free, serene, and strong; that is what we earnestly desire our family conversation to be' (*LTD* 9/10: 107).

Where then, 34 years on from the end of the Council, is that opportunity for sustained dialogue at all levels of the Church to be found? Surely by now the required instrumentation should be firmly and recognizably in place? At international level by recognized channels linking the nations with Roman offices with a ready and practised ear? At national level with the bodies serving Bishops' Conferences? At diocesan level in a recognized and regularly consulted partnership directed towards the pastoral objectives of the diocese as a whole, which I suggest means a regular meeting of a pastoral council? At deanery or parish level in councils where administrative and financial aspects are the secondary concern, or appropriately delegated to an executive sub-committee, so that the real business of the parish, that is the evangelization of the location which it serves, can be proceeded with as the core of its parish mission?

Is this in fact truly what we find? My conviction is that somewhere along the way the impetus has flagged, if not been entirely lost, and that the vision has become misted over. The high-point in our own land had probably been reached with the National Pastoral Congress of 1980, and since then much of the excitement, the inspiration of that event has ebbed away.

I conclude with one last thought on the subject of participation, leading to co-responsibility, and from there to collaborative ministry. In my secular profession I was seriously concerned with the process of public participation, and became well aware that however conscientious my attention to duty I would not be able to convince the man in the street that 'the man in Whitehall knew best'. How in the Church can that right and duty of the laity which is set out in *Lumen Gentium* (ch. 4, §37), i.e. to make known to their pastors their opinions on matters that pertain to the good of the Church, be properly fulfilled without recognized and stable channels for timely communication at the appropriate levels?

6

The Changing Nature of Catholic Organizations

Mildred Nevile

Prologue

This chapter offers a series of informed reflections on the work of Catholic organizations based on my own particular experiences. I was for seven years a full-time worker for the Young Christian Students (YCS) and, following this, a staff member and General Secretary of the Sword of the Spirit/Catholic Institute for International Relations (CIIR) for a further 28 years. I was Secretary for several years of the Lay Apostolate Committee which prepared delegations of English Catholic organizations for the Laity Congresses in Rome in 1951, 1957 and 1967 (see Vaillancourt, 1980). I was acting Secretary to the Episcopal Commission for Justice and Peace when it was established in 1968 and a member of the Commission for many years. Recently I retired as Chair of the Churches' National Housing Coalition (CNHC). I am a Trustee of the Catholic Fund for Overseas Development (CAFOD).

My concern throughout these years has been, and remains, the apparent gap between the model of Church led by the hierarchy and clergy which we experience at parish and diocesan level, and the model of Church as instanced in the response to the 'joys and hopes, the griefs and anxieties of the world, and especially of those who are poor' (*Gaudium et Spes*, §1, in Walsh and Davies, 1984: 81) which has been developed by lay-led Catholic organizations since Vatican II. The question for me is: whether and how such lay-led initiatives will want to and be able to maintain their Catholicity in the years ahead, and whether it is important for the Church and for the world that they should do so.

In April 1974, Cardinal John Heenan wrote to the General Secretary of CIIR telling her he had received an indignant letter from the Portuguese Ambassador in London about the political slant of CIIR's literature on Portugal and Portuguese Africa (*Comment 14* and *Comment 17*): literature which the Ambassador described as having been distributed 'in the name of the Catholic Church' (Walsh, 1980: 32). As Cardinal Heenan felt he had to bring this complaint to the Low Week Meeting of the Bishops' Conference, he wanted to know what CIIR had to say about the matter. CIIR replied that the information contained in the publications had been provided, at least in part, by people from Portugal itself and confirmed independently by religious orders. 'But', the General Secretary replied, 'we do not speak for the Catholic Church and have never claimed to do so. The CIIR is an independent lay organisation.'

A year later, at CIIR's 1974 Annual General Meeting, Cardinal Heenan (who was President of CIIR and a long-standing supporter and friend since its inception in 1940 as The Sword of the Spirit), made public this exchange of correspondence. He said CIIR's reply had been received with no voice raised in objection by the bishops (the stance taken by CIIR had been confirmed shortly before the Low Week meeting by the peaceful revolution in Portugal which overthrew the Caetano regime and paved the way for democratic elections), and he went on to say:

> It is an excellent thing that this organization should exist, which can say what it likes, can give a Catholic point of view. It is up to a bishop, if he thinks it is not the Catholic point of view, to denounce them. The fact is that it is very good indeed to have an unofficial voice and a voice of the laity which is not stamped with the official approval of the Church; most valuable to the public; most valuable to the Church at large ...' (ibid.)

Background and Context

To understand anything about Catholic organizations in England and Wales it is necessary first to remind ourselves of the world in which they came into being and the Church to which they belonged. For the majority of the Catholic population, which was of Irish descent, belonging to the Church was very much a family and a communal affair. Being a committed Catholic definitely marked one apart and most Catholics accepted this separation from the rest of society 'as being an integral part of their faith' (Hickey, 1967: 169). Indeed, in some ways it was, because the Church still conceived of itself as the 'perfect society', apart from the world, having its own beliefs, laws and institutions.

While membership of the parishes was largely working-class, with some notable exceptions, the Church seldom championed working-class issues or causes. Its concerns were largely to do with religious practice, the maintenance of the Catholic community and sexual morality. It was widely accepted that the Church and Catholic organizations should not be 'involved in politics'. (An important exception was the Church's massive and highly successful campaign in 1943–4 to retain a state-supported segregated Catholic school system under the 1944 Education Act, in which all Catholic organizations and the entire Catholic community were involved.)

Before Vatican II most Catholics equated the Church with what they understood to be the Kingdom of God. Indeed, many textbooks on ecclesiology used the terms 'Church' and 'Kingdom' interchangeably (Winter, 1985: 29). This understanding of the Church as the Kingdom of God is amply illustrated by a letter from Bishop Beck to *The Times* in 1949, in which he explained 'why it was that Roman Catholics could not rightly even say the Lord's Prayer with other Christians':

> United prayer, if it is to mean anything at all, must be an expression of united minds. But a Catholic and a non-Catholic saying the Lord's Prayer could not have united minds or mean the same thing. The Catholic saying for example, 'Thy Kingdom come', would be praying for the conversion of all men to Catholicism; the non-Catholic evidently would not subscribe to this petition. ... To look for 'reunion' in religion except on the conditions explained by Pope Pius XI in the encyclical *Mortalium Animos*, is to look for a will-o'-the wisp. (Quoted in Hastings, 1991: 488–9)

The 1950s have been represented as the high-point of English Catholicism, but a high-point which was characterized by a supernaturalist view of religion, uncompromising, neo-traditionalist and triumphalist (ibid.: 482). 1950 was not only a Holy Year for the universal Church, but the centenary of the restoration of the Catholic hierarchy. Catholics were urged to turn out *en masse* and fill Wembley Stadium for an Episcopal

Mass. There was also the Family Rosary campaign, and the massive '*Put Christ back into Christmas*' campaign; and other rallies too marking the Marian Year in 1954. Catholics generally felt more at ease within British society and gladly participated in explicitly religious events of this kind.

At the same time, improved education combined with increasing affluence made for more independent-mindedness. Jobs were plentiful and, for the first time, young people had money of their own. Attitudes to authority were changing and this was reflected in the Catholic community as well. Although on the surface there was apparent conformism, in the minds of Catholic teenagers there was a sharp division between religion and life. In 1957, a report from the Young Christian Students (YCS) found that for Catholic secondary school girls, life meant 'having fun, friends, successes and failures, school life, future jobs or career, cinema, dancing etc.,' while religion represented 'rules, prayers, Mass, being good, doing their duty, setting a good example and avoiding occasions of sin' (World Congress, *Apostolic Training in Schools*, 1957: 5).

Catholic Organizations Before Vatican II

Membership of Catholic organizations was always a small proportion of the Catholic population, perhaps 10 per cent of regular Sunday Mass attenders, including altar servers, members of the choir, fund-raisers, readers, organizers of parish events and so on. Of these, perhaps 2–3 per cent were active members of organizations concerned with the apostolate of lay people (*The Church 2000* (1972): 104). Many of these organizations had been started by lay people themselves with the permission and/or encouragement of the bishops. Although not 'mandated' in the sense in which Catholic Action had been hierarchically mandated by Pope Pius XI in 1930 (Congar, 1965: 366, 370; *Apostolicam Actuositatem* §20 in Abbott, 1966: 510–11), their existence depended (as it still does today) on the approval of the bishop in each of the dioceses in which they operated. Individual members may have grumbled about episcopal or clerical control, but all were intensely loyal to the Church and expected to have to get 'permission' for their work.

In the mid-1950s, some eighty organizations were listed in the *Catholic Directory*. The parish and locally based organizations – Catholic Womens' League (CWL), Union of Catholic Mothers (UCM), Knights of St Columba (KSC), Society of St Vincent de Paul (SVP) and so on, undertook a great deal of practical work for the Church. But beyond the many mundane services, which have been described as 'cleaning, catering and catechetics' (a general catchphrase which in no way does justice to the committed and loving service and involvement of so many people), other more specialized programmes were established in response to requests from the hierarchy or to pressing needs of which the organizations themselves were aware. The CWL, in particular, had a notable record in establishing a variety of other groups and services beyond its own and, jointly with the National Board of Catholic Women (NBCW), in making an overall contribution to public welfare and national life (Ryan, 1981; Noble, 1991). In 1960, the CWL, the UCM and the NBCW launched a national Family Fast Day. When in 1962 the hierarchy established the Catholic Fund for Overseas Development (CAFOD), Family Fast Day became the centrepiece of CAFOD's annual collections.

What characterized most of the Catholic organizations at this time was what characterized the Church: loyalty to Rome and devotion to the Church; concern with the needs of the Catholic community; determination to protect Catholic 'interests' in the public domain; desire to educate their members in Catholic teaching and in the apostolate; acceptance of hierarchical and clerical authority; acceptance of a hierarchically structured way of doing things within their own organizations. Some organizations had it within their objectives to foster vocations to the priesthood and religious life; others tried explicitly to support Catholic family life. Most encouraged religious devotions and personal piety through special services, prayers and pilgrimages. All tried to nourish and sustain their members' faith.

There was a cluster of organizations which in one way or another promoted Catholic social teaching, the most significant of which, the Catholic Social Guild (CSG) (1920–65), was closely linked to the Plater Catholic Workers' College (1922–present). Then there were two much smaller organizations: the Association of Catholic Managers and Employers, which aimed to improve human relations between managers and workers in industry, and the Association of Catholic Trade Unionists, whose purpose was 'to provide moral leadership for the Trade Union Movement'. All three organizations closed down in the late 1960s.

There were also the 'vocational' organizations, such as the Guild of Catholic Doctors (1910–present), the Catholic Teachers Federation (1950 present), the Guild of Catholic Professional Social Workers (1950–present), the Catholic Nurses Guild (1920–present), the Catholic Police Guild (1925–present), as well as many others which provided specialized services or catered for social and spiritual needs: support for the missions, apostolic groups, devotional societies, groups for Catholic intellectuals, and so on.

The Jesuit Sodalities (now Christian Life Communities), under the leadership of Father Bernard Bassett SJ, which previously had been concerned exclusively with the spiritual life of its members, in the 1950s adopted the Cardijn 'See, Judge, Act' methodology and became more actively involved in public issues.

Some organizations were more outward-looking than others. The Sword of the Spirit, which was not parish-based, worked in the wider inter-Church and secular sphere. Established by Cardinal Hinsley in 1940 as an anti-fascist and anti-totalitarian 'crusade', it was intended from the first to be ecumenical. When Rome withdrew support for this, in spite of many difficulties, it nevertheless continued throughout the war to work with the other Churches and with the Council of Christians and Jews (Walsh, 1980: 2–17). From the mid-1950s onwards The Sword extended its objectives to include the creation of an informed and active Catholic opinion on international affairs.

The organizations which had a different genesis and history to the above were the specialized youth movements – the Young Christian Workers (YCW), the YCS, and the Young Christian Groups (YCG). These took their inspiration from the international Jocist Movement which was started in 1924 by a Belgian priest, Joseph Cardijn. The young Cardijn, returning home for the first time from the junior seminary, was deeply shocked by the dehumanizing and de-Christianizing effects of industrial conditions and working life on the young men and boys with whom he had recently been at school. In addition, they no longer regarded him as one of themselves and felt he had opted out of the working class and had joined the 'bosses'. Cardijn saw that if there was to be any hope of bringing such young people back to Christ, the environment of their working lives had to be transformed. This would only come about through the action and involvement of the young workers themselves, in other words, through 'the apostolate of like-to-like' (McGuinness, 1986: 42ff.; Maccagno, 1971; see also YCW archives; archives for YCS are with the Salford Diocese). YCW, therefore, was intrinsically outward-looking and concerned with the needs and realities of all young workers within their social, cultural, political and economic environment.

Although the hierarchy of England and Wales in 1934 decided to coordinate Catholic lay organizations into a united Catholic Action Movement, and although the Archdiocese of Liverpool established an Archdiocesan Board of Catholic Action at about the same time, the only strictly 'Catholic Action' organization was the Catholic Action Girls' Organization (CAGO) which the hierarchy invited a Miss Carmelita Greville to establish in 1937 (Maccagno, 1971: 31). CAGO was charged with the responsibility of organizing the 'specialized movements' of Catholic Action, the YCW, YCS and YCG, for young women and girls. It succeeded in establishing a widespread network of YCS groups, mainly in convent secondary schools, although it was not until the mid-1950s, when CAGO no longer existed, that YCS became a genuine student movement based on the apostolate of like-to-like. The YCG existed in small numbers, but never really got going and was abandoned in the early 1950s. The girls' YCW objected strongly to being part of CAGO which they saw as a middle-class imposition, with no real understanding of working-class realities and needs. Instead, they identified with the boys' YCW which was started at much the same time in various parts of the country and was a genuine movement of young workers (ibid: 42ff.). From 1942 onwards the influence of CAGO within the girls' YCW declined, and from 1952 CAGO as such ceased to exist.

Bishop Butler gives a flavour of the issue at the heart of the CAGO–YCW conflict: namely that the genuine apostolate of like-to-like cannot be imposed either from 'outside' or from 'above':

> The papacy, under Pius XI and Pius XII, was a promoter of what was called Catholic Action, which sought to make an organized laity into an instrument of hierarchical policy and the subject of a hierarchical mandate. But movements like that of the Young Christian Workers sprang up from the grass roots of the Church's local pastoral anxieties, and were far more suitable, in most countries, than Catholic Action could ever be as a stimulus of genuine lay initiative. (Butler, 1981: 14).

In Europe, among the important factors contributing to the reforms of the Second Vatican Council, in addition to the ever-present threat of Communism, were the growing recognition of the Church's loss of the working class and the emergence in France of the priest-worker movement. The publication in 1944 of Pius XII's encyclical *Divino Afflante Spiritu*, which promoted a significant revival of Catholic biblical scholarship, bore fruit in what was known as the 'new theology'. Led by men like Karl Rahner SJ and Joseph Ratzinger in Germany, and Henri de Lubac SJ, Jean Danielou SJ and Yves Congar OP in France, the new theology opened the Church to dialogue with the world. The combination of pastoral movements and the new theology spearheaded a whole new perception of Catholicism which was to lay the foundations for what later emerged in Vatican II.

In 1950, Pope Pius XII convened the first ever Congress of the Laity which took place in Rome in 1951. Delegates from 72 countries and 38 international organizations took part and, although this was all very new to many of the twenty-odd delegates who attended from England and Wales, the Congress was considered a success. Many were astounded by the 'electric atmosphere' and the 'strong sense of the presence of the Holy Spirit' which pervaded the Congress (see Minutes and Reports of the Lay Apostolate Committee, 1955–59 in YCW Archives; documents for the earlier period are in the Archives of the Westminster Archdiocese). Not only did the occasion bring together organizations in this country which had had no previous contact with each other, but for most of them it provided a unique opportunity to meet with their counterparts in Europe and the rest of the world and to experience the new thinking, the sense of urgency and movement emerging from the Church in Continental Europe and elsewhere. New understandings of the role and importance of the laity in the Church continued to be transmitted after the Congress through regular meetings of the co-ordinating body, known as the Lay Apostolate Group (now, the National Council for the Lay Associations).

Catholic organizations were not of one mind in their experience of reality and their understanding of the Church. There was a wide divergence of political views. If the Church presented a united front, it was because there was little questioning of the *status quo*. Class analysis within the Church was unheard of and loyal criticism was in its infancy. The Lay Apostolate Group was one of the fora in which Catholic organizations, many of them for the first time, began to confront the realities of daily life for the ordinary Catholic outside the confines of the Church.

In 1956, with the assistance of the Newman Demographic Survey, the YCW conducted its most extensive survey on the religious practice of young workers – *Youth and Religion* (in *New Life* 14/1–2 (1957)). Such information had not been available before in any comparable form. The struggle had been centred on maintaining Catholic schools, not on questioning what happened to young people after school. The YCW showed that the shock of transition from school to the work-place at this critical stage in their lives meant that many young people lost their Christian bearings altogether. The utter lack of self-confidence, the desire to appear mature, not to seem different from other people, and above all their subjection to a wholly unchristian atmosphere in matters of sex, together put too great a strain on the average Catholic school leaver (World Congress Report, 1957: 6).

Many of the themes which were researched and debated within the Lay Apostolate Group from the early 1950s onwards were later to be the key themes of Vatican II and, particularly, of the Pastoral Constitution on the Church in the Modern World (*Gaudium et Spes*): the meaning of work in God's plan of creation; the responsibility of the international community; a spirituality for lay people; Catholics in public life, and so on.

Consequences of Vatican II

Nevertheless, much of the English Church was unprepared for the total change in the ecclesiastical atmosphere which resulted from Vatican II and was ill-equipped to respond (Hastings, 1991: 529). The results of the Council were very divisive. For the traditionalists at one end of the spectrum, the *raison d'être* of the Church, which had suffered since the Reformation and which previously had attracted and sustained loyalty, seemed to have been abandoned, and people felt betrayed. For these, 'the witness of the Church largely depends upon her changelessness ... What need has the Church, – one, holy, Catholic and apostolic – of planning and adaptation' (Miles Board, 1980: 1ff.). At the same time, those at the other end of the spectrum, whose ideas had really presaged Vatican II, felt vindicated by the Council. They thought the Church had finally 'caught up' and were bitterly disappointed by the lack of implementation of Council teaching. What they expected to happen, of course, was that Council teaching would be implemented through the Church from the hierarchy downwards. When this did not happen there was considerable disaffection and despondency (Hastings, 1991: 631; Winter, 1985). The publication of *Humanae Vitae* (Paul VI, 1968) further divided the Catholic community and caused a crisis of authority which has still not been resolved.

It should be recognized, however, that the Church's transformed self-understanding which resulted from dialogue within the Council (Abbott,

1966: 10) was, perhaps, no less dramatic or unforeseen than the early Church's decision 'to move out from the limits of Judaism to a genuine universalism' (Butler, 1981: 211). And that was not an orderly or peaceful passage.

No account exists of what was happening to the traditional Catholic organizations or to the specialized youth movements from this time on, but by the 1970s much of the world, and Church world to which they belonged, had gone for good. Today, the membership of the 'big three', the CWL, UCM and KSC, is about one-third of what it was twenty-five years ago with at least 61 per cent of members over 60 years of age (Noble, 1991: 34–5). There are clearly many different reasons for the falling membership in the traditional Catholic organizations. Among them are the break-up of the old communal structures of Catholicism; increased levels of education among Catholics and their consequent identification with wider-than-Catholic organizations and causes; greater affluence and mobility leading to multiple choices in leisure; the desire of Catholics after Vatican II to join with ecumenical and secular causes; the inability of some Catholic organizations to adapt to new situations and needs, often retaining outmoded titles, structures and devotions. More positively, as suggested by the bishops, the renewed emphasis on parish and diocesan structures since Vatican II and the emergence of lay ministries may also have been a cause for their decline (*Easter People*, §149, in Anon., 1981: 370). This is borne out by research undertaken in the Archdiocese of Birmingham, where Ryan found that the old style 'hierarchical' Catholic organizations had frequently given way to local parish-level initiatives (1996: 195).

As far as the specialized youth movements are concerned, these too were largely overtaken by events, although the YCW movement is carrying on and a small number of YCW sections still exist. It has been suggested that it was harder for YCS to flourish in the larger, lay-run Catholic comprehensives than it had been in the more intimate environment of secondary schools run by religious orders. Moreover, money was always a problem as neither organization was adequately financed by Church funds. In the case of the YCW, many of the potential leaders benefited from the 1944 Education Act and effectively moved into middle-class jobs and professions.

Yet YCS and YCW were among the organizations most in tune with Vatican II. Both movements were certainly advanced in liturgical celebrations – the first Mass facing the people was said at a YCS summer school; para-liturgies based on biblical reflections were regularly prepared and presented by the students. Both worked with priests, teachers and religious to awaken them to the young peoples' own responsibilities as the People of God (1 Peter 2: 9–10). The whole basis for YCW's work was the dialectic between the reality in which young workers were obliged to earn their living and the vocation to which they were called as daughters and sons of God. YCS, at its annual conferences for religious, emphasized continually that it was not the 'permission' or the 'authority' of the religious superior or staff at school that empowered students to carry out their apostolate of like-to-like, but the power of the Spirit conferred on them by baptism and confirmation. Perhaps, when the Council authoritatively confirmed so much of what these movements had struggled for within the Church, their momentum was lost. It may have been, too, in common with other stronger and better-established Christian groups, that they were overtaken by the events of the 1960s and swept away in the headlong rush for *communitas* (Hastings, 1991: 584–5).

By the mid-1970s the world and, consequently, the agenda had moved on. In what appeared as a spontaneous world-wide phenomenon, there was an instinctive move away from organization and structure to issues and causes; from the denominational to the ecumenical; from the religious to the secular; from what was *permitted* in terms of hierarchical consent to what was *assumed* in terms of lay leadership and responsibility.

New Models of Catholic Organization

From the early 1960s onwards, a momentum was developing among Catholic groups which were not parish-based, particularly those whose work related to current national and international issues and concerns. Prominent among these were: the Sword of the Spirit (1940), which changed its name in 1965 to the Catholic Institute for International Relations (CIIR); Pax Christi (1971); the Catholic Housing Aid Society (CHAS) (1956); the Catholic Fund for Overseas Development (CAFOD) (1962). Later, there would be the Justice and Peace (J&P) network (distinct from and additional to the Commission for International Justice and Peace established by the hierarchy in 1968), and the Catholic Association for Racial Justice (CARJ) (1984).

All of them effectively 'do theology' when coming to a judgement about their particular stance or response to a situation. The model of Church to which they work is the Vatican II understanding of the Church as the People of God, struggling to bring to birth the fulfilment of God's plan for creation – which is the Kingdom of God (*Lumen Gentium*, §§ 9–19, 36ff.; in Abbott, 1966: 24-37, 62ff.). They would understand this too in terms of evangelization or pre-evangelization (*Evangelii Nuntiandi*, §§ 30ff.). Once engaged, their agenda is frequently defined by the position they take on particular issues. They are led by the desire to respond to immediate needs in the short term and, in the longer term, to address their causes.

The Catholic Housing Aid Society (CHAS)

The work of the Catholic Housing Aid Society (CHAS), which was established by Maisie Ward, Molly Walsh and a group of friends, will serve as one example (Howes, 1996). CHAS came into being in 1956 in direct response to the difficulty families with children had in finding decent accommodation at an affordable price. Initially, it was a small-scale voluntary effort through which families in need, many of them Catholic, were enabled to purchase a house with the help of loans and guarantees from CHAS, or were housed in rented accommodation purchased or acquired by CHAS itself – much of the money being donated by the founding members and their friends.

Later CHAS had some 63 branches throughout the country, most of them started by Catholic parishes. Initially, they offered housing advice, and many of them also acquired properties from local authorities or raised money to take out a mortgage on houses in which to settle homeless families. Although initially the majority of those CHAS helped had been Catholics, from this time on, CHAS's services were available to all. Subsequently, the groups, which were housing providers, merged to form independent housing associations in order to get financial assistance from local authorities and, later, from central government through the Housing Corporation (as with the South London Family Housing Association, which currently has around 10,000 tenancies, the Family Housing Association and the Birmingham Family Housing Association).

In 1966, under the dynamic and imaginative leadership of CHAS's Director, the Revd Eamonn Casey, SHELTER was established jointly with the Notting Hill Housing Trust, the National Federation of Housing Societies (now the National Housing Federation), the British Churches' Housing Trust and Christian Action, with the aim of raising money for bodies such as CHAS, and of campaigning at the national level for changes in housing policy. Three years later, in 1969, CHAS and SHELTER jointly established the one-stop London housing advice centre, SHAC. A decade later, in 1979, CHAS turned its attention to research into national housing policies, both to inform its own housing advice work and also to enable it to comment and make representation to government on housing policy.

As the only denominational agency working exclusively in the field of housing policy and advice, CHAS has been drawn increasingly into working with other denominations. Indeed, its services are now perhaps more widely used outside the Church than in it. In 1980, CHAS initiated a joint pastoral letter on the needs of single homeless people in London for the dioceses of London and Westminster. In 1981, it helped to establish UNLEASH (the United London Ecumenical Action for the Single Homeless), to campaign and offer advice and practical assistance to the Christian organizations working with the single homeless in the London area. From 1982 to 1985 the Director of CHAS was the only Roman Catholic and housing specialist invited on to the Archbishop of Canterbury's Commission on Urban Priority Areas which published the report *Faith in the City* (1985). CHAS is also consulted by the Anglican Board of Social Responsibility when briefings are required for Anglican bishops in the House of Lords.

From 1991 onwards, CHAS established its own education programme, directed primarily at the Christian community but also offering information and analysis to a much wider constituency. The organization was the key player, with Church Action on Poverty (CAP), in establishing the inter-denominational Churches' National Housing Coalition (CNHC), set up to help churches and church-related housing groups to find ways of making a more strategic response to the problems of homelessness (Nevile, 1995). In 1985, at the instigation of CHAS, the Catholic bishops issued a statement, *Housing is a Moral Issue*, calling for a radical change in government housing policy. In 1990, they invited CHAS to help in the preparation of a further report, which was published under the title *Homelessness: A Fact and a Scandal*.

CHAS is active too in the political field, in the 1970s being a key member in the coalition of housing organizations responsible for drafting the 1977 Homeless Persons Act which for the first time provided homeless people with the statutory right to be rehoused by local authorities. Since 1989, CHAS's Director has acted as Clerk to the All Party Parliamentary Group on Homelessness and Housing Need, which CHAS helped to found.

The Catholic Institute for International Relations (CIIR)

The work of CIIR, although very different in content to that of CHAS, has developed in a not dissimilar fashion (Walsh, 1980). Because of The Sword's interest over the years in the work of the Food and Agricultural Organization (FAO) of the United Nations, when the inter-governmental Freedom from Hunger Campaign was established in 1962, The Sword was invited to join the UK National Committee. At the same time, because The Sword had responded to Pope Pius XII's Encyclical *Fidei Donum* (1957) in a variety of different ways (Walsh, 1980: 20–2), it was encouraged to professionalize its personnel recruitment service to Catholic schools in Africa by setting up a Catholic Overseas Appointments Office.

These two involvements in the early 1960s laid the foundations for a radically different response to the needs of developing countries which CIIR pioneered in the next two decades and beyond. What progressively moved CIIR from its previously neutral stance on international affairs, and from its assumption of doing something '*for*' the poor, was the recognition that many of the problems it sought to address were frequently the consequence of UK and other rich country policies towards the Third World. Rather than offering charity, therefore, CIIR came to side with the poor countries themselves in their demands for justice.

What came to characterize CIIR was that it based its work on social, political, economic and theological analysis and took a moral stance, the 'Option for the Poor', on specific issues of justice and injustice in solidarity with those in need. It worked in direct partnership with groups struggling for liberation in their own communities and countries overseas, acting as their advocate in this country, in the European Union and elsewhere in the developed world (CIIR now has Consultative Status at the UN). Many of these partnership groups were church groups, like Justice and Peace Commissions, or action-research groups set up by the local church, as well as Secretariats and Commissions of national Episcopal Conferences. CIIR's strategy was to work in whatever networks and partnerships would be most effective in terms of achieving long-term goals both here and elsewhere in the world.

While remaining a Catholic organization and working with and within the Church as and where it could, CIIR became progressively more open to working with people of all faiths and none who shared its goals and wanted to work with it. Implicit, rather than explicit in all that CIIR does, is its understanding of what the Church is, and of what model of Church it is witnessing to and promoting. Pope Paul VI's exhortation to lay people in *Populorum Progressio* (1967), reiterating the teaching of Vatican II that the laity should 'infuse a Christian spirit into people's mental outlook and daily behaviour, into the laws and structures of the civil community ... without waiting passively for directives and precepts from others', but 'using their own initiative and taking action' themselves (§81, in Walsh and Davies, 1984: 162–3), became CIIR's blueprint for action.

Catholic Association for Racial Justice (CARJ)

CARJ is a tiny organization in comparison to CHAS and CIIR and it aims to work closely within the Church. CARJ came into being in 1984 when the Catholic Commission for Racial Justice (CCRJ), established as an advisory body to the bishops in 1970 at the instigation of CIIR (Walsh, 1980: 25–6), was reorganized as part of the restructuring of the Bishops' Conference. Its work was then undertaken by the newly formed Committee for Community Relations (CCR), which included in its remit racial justice, urban poverty and community development (CARJ, 1997). But the work of the original Commission had fulfilled a wider role (inside and outside the Church) than simply advising the Bishops' Conference, and lay members wanted to see this continued. At the same time, some members of the Commission interpreted the restructuring not as a diminishment of episcopal commitment to racial justice issues so much as a way of taking power from the laity. Consequently they convened a forum of other black Catholics and leaders in organizations concerned with racial justice, and together founded a new, 'independent' but authentically Catholic lay organization (100 names are on the list of CARJ's founding members). CARJ was approved by the bishops and a member of the Episcopal Conference was appointed as Ecclesiastical Adviser.

CARJ is a black-led lay association which works for racial justice in Church and society and for the empowerment of minorities and marginalized groups in Britain. It has a membership of several hundred, which includes individuals, groups, parishes and religious societies. From the beginning, its focus has been on black people and the Church; struggling to have the place and role of black people fully recognized in regard to their contribution to Church life, whether it be in religious life, parishes or schools. CARJ continues to work closely with the CCR, but also directly within the Catholic community, helping to support and resource (among others) youth work, schools, Justice and Peace groups and the National Conference of Priests. It organizes race awareness training for Catholics. From the first, CARJ established links with the black majority churches (cf. *Building Bridges*, CARJ, 1987). In 1990 it organized the first-ever Congress of Black Catholics. In 1996 CARJ appointed a Youth Development Worker with the Catholic Youth Service.

When the Council of Churches for Britain and Ireland (CCBI) first suggested the possibility of a national Racial Justice Sunday, the bishops of England and Wales invited CARJ to assume responsibility for this. Some four to five hundred parishes of different denominations are now involved each year.

Pax Christi

Pax Christi, too, is a membership organization. Founded in France in 1945 to reconcile France and Germany after World War II, the English branch was established in 1971 in a merger with the Catholic pacifist movement, Pax (Flessati, 1991). Its present purpose is to encourage Catholics and all people of goodwill to become involved in prayer, study and action for peace. It acts as a bridge between the Church and the peace movement – which is generally 'very secular and quite anti-religious' – interpreting the one to the other on issues such as the Church and militarism, Catholics and the arms trade, non-violence, peace education and so on.

Pax Christi sees great strengths in networking and in subsidiarity. It was one of the organizations responsible for setting up the non-denominational Campaign Against the Arms Trade (CAAT). It is a member of the Churches' Peace Forum of the CCBI. Since the other denominational peace groups are generally linked to the issue of conscientious objection, many of them make use of Pax Christi's materials which deal with wider peace issues.

The organization's membership is almost entirely Roman Catholic. Great emphasis is placed on prayer and liturgy as the source and expression of faith. Membership of Pax Christi provides a framework which 'nourishes and cultivates a way of life'. It empowers its members to be as active as possible on peace issues, wherever they find themselves.

Pax Christi is more explicitly religious than some other organizations and all its material contains the three elements of prayer, study, action. A distinctive feature of Pax Christi's Christian witness is its public peace liturgies. These are devised by members and emerge from the heart of their involvement with issues of non-violence, peace and disarmament. The best-known of these is, probably, the symbolic act of public penance which Pax Christi performs each Ash Wednesday on the steps of the Ministry of Defence, in Whitehall (for which Pax Christi members have several times been arrested). Pax Christi say that these liturgies are greatly valued by CND and the wider peace movement; they offer 'uplift' to non-believers and are seen as maintaining the dignity and tone of non-violence.

The Catholic Fund for Overseas Development (CAFOD)

CAFOD, which is the official overseas development and relief agency of the Catholic Church in England and Wales, is in a different category. Although lay-led, its governing body is chaired by a bishop appointed by the Episcopal Conference. The appointment of trustees is also in the hands of the hierarchy. CAFOD's goal is to promote human development and social justice in witness to Christian faith and gospel values.

CAFOD acts as a bridge between the Catholic community (all parishes have a twice-yearly collection for CAFOD) in this country and its partners and projects in the Third World. Its primary task is that of fund-raising and awareness-raising within the Catholic community, but its radical campaigning and advocacy work are also directed towards changing attitudes in the wider community, as well as changing policies (governmental, inter-governmental and commercial) which perpetuate poverty and injustice in the Third World. Its current three-year campaign in the run-up to the Millennium is directed towards persuading UK companies trading with Third World suppliers to establish voluntary, independently monitored codes of conduct on working conditions in Third World export industries, and persuading rich-country governments and the international community to remit the debts of the Third World as a mark of the Millennium Jubilee (*Fair Deal for the Poor*, CAFOD, 1997).

The Justice and Peace Network

The term Justice and Peace is used rather loosely to describe diocesan commissions, local J&P groups and the National Liaison Committee of

Justice and Peace groups (NLCJP). At present, only the four dioceses of Menevia, Portsmouth, Wrexham and Westminster do not have any Diocesan Justice and Peace Commissions. Of the nineteen dioceses which do have commissions, nine employ a part-time or full-time fieldworker. There are several hundred groups with which the NLCJP is in touch at any one time. The number and types of activities in which they engage varies according to many different factors – personal enthusiasms, diocesan leadership, availability of resources, facility of communication within the diocese, urgency of current issues, pressures from outside, and so on. Although predominantly Catholic, many J&P groups are ecumenical in membership and work with a wide variety of other groups inside and outside the Churches.

Local groups are independent and self-managed and work on whatever issues the groups themselves choose. The bias is still probably towards Third World issues, since the Pontifical Commission for International Justice and Peace was the initiative that inspired national and local J&P. But, increasingly, commissions work on issues of domestic poverty and injustice from, for instance, unemployment in Middlesbrough, to home-lessness in Arundel and Brighton.

Characteristics of Post-Vatican II Organizations

Allowing for the difference in status between CAFOD and the rest, these organizations have certain characteristics in common. They are recognized by the Church as authentic Catholic organizations; they are lay-led; they are 'issue specific'; they represent a particular option or stance in terms of what they understand as gospel teaching and gospel values; they work to bring about changes in attitudes within the Church and wider public opinion, as well as in social, economic and political policies; their work is concerned with social, political and cultural issues in the world (which is properly the responsibility of lay people) and is not governed within parish or diocesan pastoral structures; they work in collaboration with other Christian or secular groups as effectiveness demands; they are generally not concerned with strictly *ecclesial* questions; they interconnect with the Church in a strategic sense and at different levels in order to achieve their goals.

Some Tentative Conclusions

In this short review it is impossible to do more than suggest some tentative conclusions and raise some further questions about the future of lay organizations. In many ways they are the vanguard of the Church. For many, they represent the only contact they will ever have with the Church. They act as a bridge between the Church and the world. They witness to gospel values in the public and secular arena.

They are frequently much envied by other denominations. In 1980, the International Secretary of the (then) British Council of Churches, in an article to *The Times* of 25 April, expressed his regret that the Church of England had 'nothing half as professional and prophetic as the Catholic Institute for International Relations' (Walsh, 1980: 38). Quoted in *The Tablet* of 19 July 1997, the retiring Apostolic Delegate, Archbishop Barbarito, said 'CAFOD is one of the best organizations of its kind in the Catholic Church. English Catholics should be proud of it.' As far as the non-Church world is concerned, previously, when it was less common for Catholics to be working co-operatively with secular (particularly, radical) groups, such co-operation was taken to mean that 'the Church' had come on board. Even now participation by, say, a Justice and Peace group in CNHC will be taken as a sign of 'the Church's' involvement and approbation.

In fact, CAFOD, CIIR, Pax Christi and CHAS are sometimes referred to as 'agencies'. This is helpful as it suggests what they are: agents for the Church and of the Church; running specialized services on behalf of the Church, while at the same time being Church in and to their particular world. With the exception of CAFOD, however, (and, in some dioceses, also Justice and Peace) it cannot be claimed that their relations with the institutional Church are as clear as this. Pax Christi has found that their work is often more appreciated outside the Church and that sometimes 'distance enhances respect'. CIIR would also claim that in some ways they are better known outside the Church than in it. Also for CIIR and, to a lesser degree, for CHAS, the professionalization of their work in recent years has changed the nature of their relationship with the Church.

Although members of the hierarchy are still consulted, the professionalization which has been demanded of an organization like CIIR working within an almost totally secularized society makes it difficult for the bishops to make a contribution, unless the institutional Church is of particular or strategic importance – as it was in the struggle for independence in Zimbabwe, or in the ongoing struggle for human rights in Latin America and elsewhere. The same is true for 'ordinary' Catholics, except in their very important role as supporters and constituents on the side of social justice.

CARJ, Pax Christi, CAFOD, Justice and Peace and CHAS, most of which serve and depend on a network of local groups (parish, deanery or diocesan), are more closely connected with the Church at the local level than is CIIR. In a recent survey, CIIR found that its membership was 85 per cent Catholic and, overall, 92 per cent Christian. The Cardinal Archbishop of Westminster is the President and CIIR also has an Episcopal Adviser and a Chaplain. The Chairman and most members of the Executive Committee are Catholics, but there is a decreasing proportion of Catholics on the staff. Since 1965, when CIIR opted to launch what was effectively a secular Overseas Volunteer Programme (now International Cooperation for Development (ICD)) as part of the British Volunteer Programme, it has maintained an open policy of staff and overseas worker recruitment. At the same time, its advocacy and educational programmes in this country are now so specialized that, from a strategic point of view, the Church is less involved.

The same applies in some senses to CHAS, which has the Cardinal Archbishop of Westminster as President and a Catholic Executive Committee. CHAS has ten local advice groups, most of which use the name in their title, but none of which is Catholic in any sense (Howes, 1996: 12). On the other hand, because CHAS's areas of concern are something with which many Catholic parishes and parishioners are only too familiar, and because its support comes largely from the Church, it is in touch with all parishes two or three times a year, informing them of CHAS's work and soliciting their help.

It is still unclear as to whether and how these organizations, and the contribution they make, could and should be more integrated into the overall life of the Church and what expectations they themselves have of and for the Church in this regard. It may be in the future that such organizations will take their place among the honourable list of institutions which have been started (and are still being started today) by the Christian Churches or by individual Christians and Catholics, such as Amnesty International, the hospice movement, the Cheshire Homes, the Children's Society, the Samaritans, and many others, which count on Church constituencies as among their most committed supporters but are no longer exclusively identified with them. If this seems a loss to the Church, may it nevertheless be where the Kingdom is to be found?

It would seem that the bishops have been happy for lay organizations to develop their own initiatives and to call these *Catholic*, provided they do not expect the Church to finance them and provided they do not necessarily expect the hierarchy to support their work publicly, or even to be identified with it. In the case of the peace movement, for instance, while Pax Christi is recognized as a Catholic organization and its President and Vice-President are both bishops, it is never consulted in a formal organizational way by the Episcopal Conference. At the same time, one of Pax Christi's lay Vice-Presidents is a member of the International Commission for Justice and Peace and has contributed to the preparation of Church statements and episcopal deliberations in a personal capacity (though his point of view has not always been acceptable to the bishops). This way of working through chosen individuals rather than through formal representatives, of course, gives the bishops greater freedom to select their own advisers and to choose whose advice they wish to hear. The decision as to whether or not they take this advice rests entirely with them.

The same applies in regard to the use of central Church funds. Recently Pax Christi, which had come to rely on parish donations from Peace Sunday for a third of its annual income, was badly affected when the bishops, in spite of representations to the contrary, decided that Peace Sunday should be moved from the last Sunday in January to New Year's Day. From 1996 to 1998, collections for Pax Christi dropped from £20,000 to £4,000, a huge loss of income for a small organization. By the same token, when approval was given for an inter-Church Racial Justice Sunday in 1995 (this is run jointly by CARJ and the Churches' Commission for Racial Justice of the CCBI) CARJ, for the first time, was enabled to raise funds for its work from within the entire Catholic community. In the words of the current Director of CHAS, the bishops are proud to have CHAS within the Church, and proud to say they have it, as long as they don't have to be responsible financially. In fact, 98 per cent of CHAS funding comes from 'Church sources', that is individual Catholic donors, religious orders, parishes, legacies and so on, but only 0.35 per cent from the National Catholic Fund.

Within the broad parameters of what is accepted as Catholic teaching and practice, it would appear that Cardinal Heenan's dictum about the role and responsibility of lay organizations has become the norm, provided these are considered by the hierarchy to be within the sphere of lay competence. This approach is in keeping with modern realities and with the Church's recognition both of the limits of episcopal authority and the 'distinctive role' of the laity (*Gaudium et Spes* §43.1, in Walsh and Davies, 1984: 105). This style of leadership on the part of the hierarchy has created an openness within the Church which is greatly to be welcomed. While lay expectations of pre-Vatican II style hierarchical leadership still exist, however, such openness can be interpreted as indifference. If the apparent self-sufficiency and professionalism of lay organizations on the one hand, and their genuine acceptance by the hierarchy on the other, were to make either feel they had no need of the other, this would surely be a loss for the Church.

At the same time, it is a source of confusion, and one which perhaps adds to the general expectation that the hierarchy will continue to dictate as well as to provide, when this apparent openness on the part of the bishops is contradicted in matters which are considered to be strictly under ecclesiastical jurisdiction. A case in point is the strictures which have sometimes been imposed on Justice and Peace, in regard to its freedom both to operate within a given diocese and to work on particular issues, as well as the limitations imposed on the Standing Conference (now the NLCJP) in regard to any proactive programme at a national level, or any initiatives which might amount to it becoming a genuinely national movement.

Although there is development in the Church, what we are seeing now is different models of 'Church' in operation at the same time. At parish level, what the Church in this country has still been unable to do (though there was much hope for this at the time of the 1980 National Pastoral Congress), is to develop a pastoral strategy or praxis which would empower ordinary people and parishes to assume their responsibilities in line with the teaching of Vatican II. The 'sacramental' Church is still struggling to maintain practice, to instruct and encourage belief and devotion, to strengthen Catholic family life and Catholic values for the individual (all of which is necessary and good), without much explicit connection with witnessing to Kingdom values in the world. In effect, this is not so different from the Church's concerns before Vatican II. The apparent gap which exists between the world of Catholic professional lay organizations and the world of the *ecclesia* is one of the factors which makes it harder for organizations to relate to the Church as they would wish. It is also difficult for them to remain Catholic in more than name.

At the same time the Church is less confident, more open, more fragmented, less regimented, all of which makes change more possible and more likely. The dying of the old is almost certainly a *sine qua non* for the birth of the new and it may well be that Vatican II is unfolding before our eyes, though we have difficulty in seeing it in these terms. Undoubtedly, the challenge both to the institutional Church as well as to the lay organizations is whether they will be 'strong enough to provide coming generations with reasons for living and hoping' (*Gaudium et Spes* §31.2, in Walsh and Davies, 1984: 97).

7

Catholics and Public Policy

Michael P. Fogarty

Catholics and Policy in Retrospect

'The fox', the saying goes, 'knows many things, the hedgehog only one, but a big one.' So it has been with the influence of Catholics on public policy in Britain. We have been present at many points and contributed in many useful ways, but when one adds it all up the 'big one' has been missing. We cannot honestly claim to have led in setting the agenda on the practical issues which have been central to public policy. There is a range of what our bishops in their briefing before the 1987 General Election (*Briefing*, 29 May 1987) once called 'minimalist' issues, directly affecting Church interests, like Catholic schools, or in fields like abortion, euthanasia, bio-ethics and sexual morality, where we have set out to give a lead and have done so, though not always with great success. As the bishops pointed out in that same message, however, the Church has no business to confine itself to 'minimalism'. It has a message to deliver across the whole broad field of politics, including practicalities as well as principles, and in that broader field we have cast only a modest shadow, following where others have led, commenting and criticizing, dotting i's and crossing t's, filling a gap here and there with practical action, but, overall, marching to the beat of others' drums.

The question here is not, of course, only for Catholics. When John Patten was Minister of Education and had to reply to a House of Commons debate on '*moral values*' (*Hansard*, House of Commons, 13 February 1980, col. 64), he hit the nail precisely on the head. Neither the Church nor the Churches, he said, had yet found 'a theology, a rhetoric' appropriate for talking to a nation in the state of Britain today. Care for 'the unfortunate, the downtrodden, and the under-privileged' had been and remained one of the Church's essential roles, but more needed to be said, and as yet was not being said.

Looking back at my own experience through sixty years of political involvement – at all ages from chairing the Oxford University Labour Club in the days when we had a quarter of all undergraduates in paid-up membership to the last years, when one becomes honorary (but still not necessarily inactive) this or that; at all levels from the doorstep to chairman of my county council and vice-president of my party and trade union; and at all three levels of local government – I can honestly say that, like Patten and many others, I did my best to apply the principles of Catholic social teaching as I learnt them from Leo O'Hea SJ, in what is now Plater College. I have fought the good fight and kept the faith. But it could be lonely; for I never felt, as I might have done in other European countries, that I was riding on the shoulders of a Catholic, or ecumenical, movement with the ability to shape and dominate events. We are no longer even, as we were in the nineteenth and early twentieth century, visibly a peculiar people, and non-discrimination has its price. When I was chairman of my county council one of our town councils invited me and the chairman of their district council to their annual dinner. A historic occasion, as it happened, such as had not been seen in Oxfordshire since the Reformation, for here were two Catholic civic leaders, one from one of the old Catholic families and the other from Ireland, slung round with the jewellery of office and taking the places of honour in a part of the country where on into the nineteenth century the Squire Browns, as in Tom Brown's Schooldays, could rally *en masse* against allowing people like us to be elected to anything at all (Leys, 1961: 150). But not only did no one, including ourselves, notice this historic event at the time – one does come to take emancipation for granted – but neither, to come to the really significant point, did anyone expect these representatives of our no longer so peculiar denomination to have anything peculiar to say. So far as the general political scene is concerned we Catholics of the English diaspora have merged into the mass.

Take the case of the rise and decline of the welfare state. When it took shape at the end of the Second World War Catholics had a great deal to say about it. Many protested because they saw subsidiarity neglected, the prospect of Belloc's or Hayek's *Servile State* – a few even drew parallels with Nazism – and specific risks to Catholic education and the right of doctors, nurses and patients to follow their Catholic conscience (Coman, 1977). Except in the case of the financing of Church schools, however, protests like these were far from unanimously supported even within the Church, and did not make a significant impact in the general public debate. Presently they died down and most Catholics joined the welfare state consensus if only, for some of them, as a tolerable second best, leaving only isolated voices – Colin Clark, Douglas Woodruff, Paul Crane SJ – still challenging the trend.

Over time, many of the objections originally put forward by Catholics did in fact begin to be met. General practitioners bargained for professional freedom rather than a salaried state service. LMS ('local management of schools') came in along with other moves towards schools' autonomy. In industry state monopolies were dismantled. Personal ownership was vastly extended: homes, consumer durables and cars, new vehicles for personal saving. Non-state pensions, occupational ('social partnership') or personal, came in alongside National Insurance. Presently the idea gained ground of returning to the concept, considered but rejected by Beveridge, of 'statutory indirect' provision: pensions delivered under state guarantee by agencies in the 'middle field', a classic example of subsidiarity. Once again, however, it was others who drove these changes. It cannot be claimed that thinking and action by Catholics were at their cutting edge, any more than in the original shaping of the welfare state.

Did that matter, so long as the right changes were made? Yes it did. First because the changes made were not always the right ones. They could be perverse: think of the abortion explosion after 1967, the widening of the gap between rich and poor in the 1980s, the scandal of the mis-selling of pensions, and the progressive extension of means-testing, the purest and most dependency-creating form of welfarism. Or chances to promote positive change in line with Catholic thinking might be missed. The canonization of the market in the 1980s was commonly presented as victory for the market over state control, but that could too easily mean being shut into the straitjacket of what the Dutch call 'state–market thinking', as if state and market were the only choices. It has taken time to gain a new appreciation of the role of intermediate agencies, of co-operation between the social partners, of communities and 'civil society'. Of course that role has needed to be rethought in a new and changing context, and is being so, but again there are rather few English Catholic names among those who have led the process of rethinking (though see

Boswell, 1994; Boswell and Peters, 1997). It is no accident that it is countries where Catholic thinking has become particularly embedded in practice, as in the Netherlands with their 'polder model' and Ireland with its national partnership agreements, which to their own profit have led the way out of that straitjacket.

Second, Catholic social teaching is not merely about cherry-picking measures from a menu laid out 'like items in the catalogue of a department store' (Pütz, 1985). Its point is that it proposes, not just this or that change in society but a coherent social order whose distinctiveness lies precisely in its coherence and the way its elements reinforce one another. That *Ordnungspolitisch* coherence needs to be explained and made visible in practice. Kees van Kersbergen (1995) has shown how in the parts of Western Europe where Christian Democracy is strong the creation of the welfare state was the joint work of Christian Democrats and Social Democrats and the Christian Democrats were able to put their own distinctive stamp on it, particularly in matters like subsidiarity and use of agencies in the 'middle field'.

So could we do better in the new millennium? I suggest three roads to follow: leveraged discussion of selected current issues, with a special role for the bishops; long-term and radical thinking, think-tank style; and more tentatively, but not entirely so, direct political action.

Leveraged Discussion: Bishops' Move

In a memorandum accompanying their message for the General Election of 1987 the Catholic bishops of England and Wales pointed out that they had a right and duty not only to proclaim the principles of Catholic social teaching but to point to specific practical applications; but 'there are very few specific applications' where they could give unambiguous guidance unless the Church at large came to their rescue. That 'depends in part on development of the consciousness of the Church at large to the point where there is something like a substantial consensus', for it is 'the absorption and reflection by the whole body of the local Church' of the Church's developing social teaching which makes it possible for general principles to be more specifically and confidently applied, so that Patten's 'rhetoric' can be delivered from the Church whether by its official leaders or by its lay members acting in their own autonomous sphere. For this purpose the Church should provide a space, a forum, within which people can, in the light of their common commitment to the teaching of the

Church, 'discuss and deal with problems', economic, social or political, which might otherwise seem overwhelming.

This discussion, the bishops said, should not be confined to current issues, for the roots of social change run far back, and those whose thinking and action is shaped by the principles of Catholic teaching need to take a 'long-term and radical view'. I come back to that below. But let me start with the discussion of current issues, for one thing which the bishops did not bring out was the part which they themselves might play in stirring the pot of discussion at that level. They were rightly careful about proclaiming 'specific applications' until discussion in the Church at large catches up. But the example of certain other countries shows that bishops have a status which gives them, on their own or along with leaders of other Churches, leverage to mobilize discussion on selected issues of major practical importance in such a way and on such a scale as not only to develop the Church or Churches' consciousness but to generate a word of power of which the nation has to take note.

The pioneers, in the 1980s, were the National Conference of Catholic Bishops (NCCB) of the United States in preparing their pastoral letters on *The Challenge of Peace* (1983; see Reid, 1986) and *Economic Justice for All* (1986; see Houk and Williams, 1984; Gannon, 1987; Foster, 1989). The American bishops had a long though irregular tradition of commenting on public policy. What was new this time was that the pastorals were not simply handed down but the outcome of wide consultation in and out of the Church, and were addressed to the nation as a whole, not only to Catholics. The steering committee preparing the Economics Pastoral held 117 hearings and published a first and then a second discussion draft before finally revising their text. The interpretation given to Catholic social teaching in that text was not unanimously approved even within the Church. A lay commission of new-right Catholics led by Michael Novak and William Simon agreed with Milton Friedman (Gannon, 1987: chs. 7 and 16) that it tended, in America of all places, to undervalue market competition. Nevertheless, consensus was 'substantial' enough and widely enough based to ensure that what Thomas M. Gannon called *The Catholic Challenge to the American Economy* was taken seriously. Who, even a few years ago, wrote one insider, would have expected directors of Fortune 500 companies or the Joint Chiefs of Staff to take a Church pronouncement seriously? (J. P. Langan, in Gannon, ibid.: 257–8.) The Church had delivered a word of power.

The American example led the Austrian bishops to do likewise in preparing their Social Pastoral of 1990. Its accent was to be on work and social solidarity, and publication of its opening discussion document on *Meaningful Work: Living in Solidarity* touched off wide and intense discussion in and out of the Church, with political parties and interest groups, and in the media, including the specialist economic and political press: 2,400 written submissions were received. The opening document was reworked in the light of them, for example by strengthening its reference to ecology, correcting what many respondents saw as its hostility to business and deleting certain perhaps offensive sound-bites. The process of smoothing and conciliation may, however, have been overdone, and the price was some loss of forcefulness. The fact that the American bishops left rough edges in their economics pastoral helped to win attention and give bite to discussion. The Austrians made their final text too bland. It trod on nobody's toes and happened also to be published in the run-up to a general election in which neither of the main parties wished to be seen as critical of the Church. The result was that the sharp impact of the initial discussion document was not repeated. The final version was welcomed with suspiciously unanimous enthusiasm and 'hugged to death'. Beware when all speak well of you!

The Germans in turn were inspired by the Austrian and American examples to see what use they could make of this method. Could we do something similar? We could, they decided, though they admitted afterwards that they had not realized 'what we were letting ourselves in for'. So, accordingly, they did in preparing the 1997 joint 'word' of the German Catholic Bishops' Conference and the Council of Evangelical Churches on the economic and social situation in Germany. That 'word' is well worth reading, but the main lesson, as the Germans themselves insist, was again about procedure. In the slogan which they used at the time, *Der Weg ist das Ziel*, the road is the goal. What matters most is the consultative process itself (Katholisch-Soziales Institut, 1996).

Once again a discussion document was published after a preliminary round of consultation with experts, politicians of all parties and interest groups, and within the two Churches themselves. It attracted approaching 3,000 formal comments, which the enquiry team analysed into fourteen major themes. It was subjected to the 'unflattering' comments of a major conference of experts, and debated at four thousand other events and meetings up and down the country. Provisional findings were checked at a conference of four hundred top representatives from Churches and the community. Respondents showed themselves aware of the need to avoid the Austrians' mistake of excessive blandness. Let the churches, one said, give us 'the salt of the earth, not *Maggi*'. They must, another said, conciliate prejudices on neither the left nor the right but tread equally on the toes of both.

What was specially distinctive in the German case, however, was the immense effort which went into ensuring that the collection of data and ideas should be not only comprehensive, from all interests and levels – we English, too, can sympathize with the problem that questions addressed to parishes may stop at the parish priest's desk – but more than a one-way flow for the use of the project's organizers and for its immediate purposes. Its 30,000 pages of documentation were made available to all comers, data-banked and cross-referenced with contributors' names and addresses – a CD-ROM comes with the report – so as to promote and facilitate a continuing cross-flow of ideas, leading in whatever directions participants might choose. Transparency, networking and open-ended discussion were of the essence. By the Millennium half of all German households were expected to have a PC with a CD-ROM drive, and great efforts were made also to meet the needs of those less well equipped. Among those who made most use of this service, unsurprisingly, were students, in schools as well as colleges.

Here, then, were three 'words' of real power such as we in Britain might well envy. We have had some modest beginnings towards that sort of approach, but with nothing like the same intensity of consultation, and with marginal Catholic involvement rather than Catholic initiative: think of *Faith in the City* (1985) or *Unemployment and the Future of Work* (1997). The bishops' statement, *The Common Good* (1996), was an excellent document and generally well received, but prepared in haste from one year to the next, without time to put a significant weight of consultation behind it. The one episcopally organized consultation of Catholics in England and Wales on a scale comparable to the American, Austrian and German cases was the National Pastoral Congress of 1980 (Anon., 1981), but that was a different animal, an inner-Church occasion, the Church talking primarily to itself and about its own problems rather than generating a message to the nation. Media reactions at the time showed that it was precisely the NPC's inner-Church issues which tended to attract attention. Even as an inner-Church project, in any case, many participants, looking back eighteen months later, were dissatisfied with the way its consultative process had worked (Hornsby-Smith, 1987: 139–53) and it has not been repeated.

If we English Catholics, on our own or with other Churches, do go down the same road as the Americans, the Austrians and especially the Germans, there will of course be a major practical problem: money, for which we laity will have to dig deeper into our pockets, since our bishops do not have it. As one of them pointed out to me, the budget of the American NCCB simply for publishing and diffusing their Economics Pastoral was equal to the whole annual budget at that time of the Catholic Bishops' Conference of England and Wales. Operations on that scale do not come cheap.

More important, however, would the effort be worth it – would we be listened to? The Americans had the advantage of an exceptionally large constituency to which to make a direct appeal. In 1990, 41 per cent of American adults were 'core' members of Churches, not only regular attenders but 'actively engaged in activities of and for their Church' (Ester *et al.*, 1993: 43–4). No European country, not even Ireland, could match that. In Britain there were 13 per cent 'core' members alongside a very high proportion (42 per cent) of 'unchurched' people, half of them at least second generation (ibid.; see also Ashford and Timms, 1992: 45). In Germany the 'core' was only 12 per cent. The importance of mobilizing the 'core' should obviously not be underestimated. Britain's 5 or 6 million 'core' Christians are a considerable constituency, and one whose political and social attitudes as well as their Church commitment do predispose them, if in some areas only marginally, to hear and act on a message from their Churches.

Another finding from the European Values studies is that readiness to hear a voice from the Churches on many issues of practical politics is considerable even among the 'unchurched'. In Britain in 1990 between 58 and 83 per cent of 'core' Christians answered 'yes' to the question whether it is 'proper for Churches to speak out on' a range of issues, and the proportions were between 37 and 70 per cent even of the 'unchurched'. Neither group showed great enthusiasm for Church pronouncements on general 'government policy' – 31 per cent among the unchurched, less than half even of the 'core' – but the proportions were much greater on specific issues such as the problems of ecology, the Third World, the arms trade, race, unemployment, or issues of life and death. Leveraged discussion of selected issues of current importance, if pursued with skill and determination and with the special features of the German approach – transparency, networking, and open-endedness in addition to compre-hensiveness – would have every prospect not only of raising and focusing consciousness among the faithful but of generating a 'word' as powerful as in the three cases I have quoted.

The Long-Term and Radical View: Think-Tanks

Leveraged discussion is a way to activate the Church and deliver a weighty and well-debated message to the nation, but that message will not necessarily reflect the 'long-term and radical view' for which the bishops called in 1987. Taking the lead in setting the nation's agenda calls not only for promoting debate and mobilizing the power of opinion round issues already recognized as important but for entering into discussion, and continuing to influence it, from the far earlier stage when those issues begin to be defined and the first stirrings of change become apparent. That is characteristically the work of a long-range think-tank.

Think-tanks are not new either in the Catholic world or in secular politics and social affairs, where in recent years they have mushroomed (Kandiah and Seldon, 1996). They may work in any of several modes: scholarly research, contract research, non-partisan or as advocates of a cause, to time horizons which may be short, up to say 5 years, or 30 years or more. They may be independent or under the wing of government, a political movement, a business, or in the Church a religious order such as the Jesuits or the Dominicans. A large part of my own working life was invested in two of them, one, in Britain, independent, non-partisan, and engaged in contract/scholarly research (the Policy Studies Institute) and the other, in Ireland, governmental or more precisely semi-state (Economic and Social Research Institute).

The variety of think-tanks is immense, but in the light of the bishops' call for 'long-term and radical views' I have in mind one particular type, of which the best example in the secular world in Britain is the Institute of Economic Affairs (IEA): long-range, so of necessity to a degree speculative, yet also scholarly; committed to a cause, a vision, but free to pursue it independently in its own way (Muller, in Kandiah and Seldon, 1996: vol. I). One of Keynes's most famous sayings is that 'practical men who believe themselves to be quite exempt from any intellectual influences are usually the slaves of some defunct economist', of some 'academic scribbler' years ago (Keynes, 1936: 383). IEA was founded in the 1950s, on a suggestion from Friedrich Hayek, to promote understanding of the importance of competition and the market, and Ralph Harris, its first Director, set out to be that scribbler. In the face of the overwhelming consensus at that time in favour of the welfare state and the managed economy he and his colleagues began to 'think the unthinkable' (Muller, ibid.). For a quarter of a century they battled on to undermine the consensus and turn the tide from state to market thinking, assembling a network of collaborators, turning out a stream of high quality though by definition slanted publications, and making friends and influencing people in their small but convenient and welcoming centre in Lord North Street, until at last their thinking broke through and merged into Conservative government policy.

Was it facts or ideas that mattered most in the end? Both, in proportions about which I am not going to argue. But I do underline from much wider evidence (Fogarty, 1963) that IEA's 30-year time horizon is actually the minimum for which it is necessary to look ahead if one is hoping to influence a major social change from its start. There is no iron law of social development, Marxist or other, which says that change must proceed in this direction or that. But there is one which says that innovation, whatever its direction, is likely to come in by successive steps in a predictable decision process, from initial unease about a *status quo* to final decision on accepting and implementing new policies. These steps take predictable time, and the larger and the more complex the group or society involved the longer this time will be.

Take again the case of the welfare state. The first stirrings of revolt against mid-nineteenth-century liberal orthodoxy came in the generation to around 1890, but the agenda of British politics still remained much as it had been. By around 1920, however, debate had gone further and a new agenda took shape. When in the 1940s I was assigned to read back over the documents of that period, I saw that this agenda was very unlike that of the mid-nineteenth century but remarkably like what I saw being currently followed in the years when the welfare state finally crystallized. It was still, however, only an agenda, one might almost say in note form, and as yet there were still only fragmentary results to show. A further generation was needed for its full-scale implementation. I have used that type of analysis many times since, when looking at change, whether in a large and complex society or in smaller groups such as a firm, and found it a reliable guide.

Blessed, one might say, are those like IEA whose interest in long-term and radical analysis leads them to lock on early to a vision, pursue it, and bring it progressively down to earth, for theirs in the end is the agenda, provided, of course, that they have got it right, for there are warnings to observe. Looking a generation ahead need not be wholly a matter of guesswork, but is certainly speculative, a matter of seeing through a glass darkly: and thinking of that sort does not sit easily with a regular bureaucracy. It is no accident that the think-tanks which contributed so much to the rise of the political right wing from the 1970s through the 1980s were never part of the official machinery of the Conservative Party, any more than the Institute for Public Policy Research or the Fabian Society are run today by the executive of the Labour Party. Free-floating independence is of the essence.

Let me apply that to the Church. The Catholic Bishops' Conference of England and Wales learnt a lesson about the problems of trying to contain free-floating agencies within its bureaucracy in the first years after its constitution in 1968. At first the Conference's machinery grew like Topsy. By 1982 it had nineteen commissions to advise it from a combination of expert knowledge with representation of 'the so-called man in the pew'. Representatives and experts did not always mix well, but the key point was that the commissions were largely autonomous in their agenda and publications. As they got into their stride and began to push their thinking into new fields the flood of material coming forward from them deluged the bishops' agenda. Though their publications were not actually very speculative and never went beyond the limits of Catholic orthodoxy, they seemed at times to be putting a stamp of episcopal authority on formulations which the bishops had had too little time to consider. Autonomy and bureaucracy did not mix. Accordingly a review committee was set up and the Conference's machinery was reorganized as a civil service more directly under the bishops' control, more manageable and with less autonomy and scope for wide-ranging thought and leadership. (See for Report and documentation, *Briefing*, 1982; Hornsby-Smith and Mansfield, 1975; Mansfield and Hornsby-Smith, 1975; McHugh, 1982.)

Some years earlier there was a similar experience in the Catholic Social Guild, for many years the official agency of the bishops for education in Catholic social principles. The CSG was an educational agency and never formally authorized as a think-tank, but similar difficulties nevertheless arose as new insights into the implications of Catholic social theory began to be introduced into its work from social and management research (McHugh, 1982). The Guild also became a somewhat embarrassing battleground between supporters of the welfare state consensus and those (notably Paul Crane SJ) of the new wave of market thinking.

And yet we do in the English Catholic world need, as the bishops said, 'long-term and radical' thinking about the practical application of Catholic social teaching, and therefore institutes in which to do it. Those institutes could be of several kinds, provided that they meet the essential requirement of free-floating independence: academic, within a religious order, or perhaps a free-standing trust. What we could do with, as I said in a Westminster Cathedral centenary lecture (in Stourton and Gumley, 1996: 46), is 'a think-tank full of lunatic but professionally competent Christians of whatever denomination, thinking the unthinkable and conducting radical and long-term analysis of the economy as it may develop or be made to develop over the next thirty to sixty years'. 'Long-term', of course, implies a need for continuing support, for as the example of IEA shows, success in this type of work depends on persistent effort over many years. That, once again, will not come cheap. It is possible to economize, as IEA has done, by out-sourcing research and publications, but for a full-grown and well-staffed think-tank like the Policy Studies Institute or Chatham House, budgets start in seven figures.

There are or might be short-cuts, for example by linking in to similar thinking in the Church or the Churches elsewhere in the world, given that so many of the problems to be considered are global or at least cross-national. One of the most useful services of the early leaders of the Catholic Social Guild (Cleary, 1961) was to build a network of contacts with Catholic centres and movements across Western Europe and draw on their thinking and experience. This traffic was never entirely one-way. At the end of the Second World War, for example, there was great interest in the new British welfare state, and I found myself invited to speak on it in Austria, at the Semaine Sociale de France – in, the local press said, a 'délicieux accent Londonien' – and at the Deutscher Katholikentag. Or it might be a matter simply of delivering a dose of down-beat Anglo horse sense. Once more, a French Jesuit colleague whispered on one rather high-flown occasion, the British have brought us back to common sense. The fact remained that in the first half of the twentieth century the leading edge of Catholic social and political activity was across the Channel, and we had more to gain than to give.

That may no longer be so, for in the matter of long-term and radical thinking the Continental colleagues have in recent decades been in trouble. Support for Christian democratic action, political or social, in most of its classic centres in Western Europe fell away sharply from the 1960s. The essential reason, as shown in electoral studies and in analyses of Christian Democracy by Roberto Papini (1997), Thomas Jansen (1989), and myself (1995), is that from lack of long-range and radical thinking Christian Democracy became boring. By contrast with the years just after the Second World War, voters no longer looked to the CD parties for new and inspiring ideas.

They were not reactionary. When new issues emerged, for instance on the environment and on the family and women's opportunities, the Christian Democrats presently caught up, but it was others who led, as again they did on the general movement towards 'post-materialism'. So, for example, the European People's Party, the Christian Democratic parties' umbrella organization for the purpose particularly of European elections, has tended under German leadership to turn away from adding to and rethinking its ideological capital and to focus instead on extending its power base by becoming a rally of the centre-right, bringing in a lengthening list of moderate conservative parties which accept EPP's policies but have little or no foundation in Christian Democracy's traditional ideology.

I must not exaggerate. EPP's new trend led by 1998 to a counter-attack by some of its smaller affiliates, the Benelux parties, the Irish, the Catalans and Basques, the Italian Popolari. They formed their own Athens Group to defend and develop from basic Christian Democratic principles. The type of new thinking to which this could lead is illustrated in a series of articles in 1996 by J. J. A. M. van Gennip, the director of WI, the Dutch CDA's research institute, appealing for collaboration in long-range and radical thinking right across the CD world. In so far as that tendency develops there will again be a body of radical and far-from-boring thinking on the practicalities of Christian political and social action from which we too will be able to learn. But unless and until that happens we, if we develop our own long-range and radical thinking, could well find ourselves giving a lead not only in Britain but to our colleagues in Christian-based social and political movements in the rest of Western Europe.

Direct Political Action

For well-known reasons, direct political action in its most obvious sense of putting up political candidates or running our own political party has not for British Christians, Catholic or other, been an attractive or even an interesting option. We never had to face the sustained hostility to religion and religious institutions by radical liberals in the tradition of the French Revolution, or Marxist or other socialists, or the Erastian enthusiasm of a Bismarck for bringing religion under political dominance, which drove believers elsewhere in Western Europe to rally behind fortress walls and build their own parties and social movements. There have from time to time been loose links between British parties and Churches: Liberals with nonconformity; Labour, as Tawney said, owing more in its early days to Methodism than to Marx, Catholics and Irish nationalism; and, of course, there is the old joke about the Church of England being the Conservative Party at prayer. We might carry our religious disputes into the political field, as happened over Church schools and 'Rome on the Rates'. But these were, precisely, disputes between Christians, not for and against Christianity. None of our mainstream political parties has been closed to Christianity, and even when, as in the nineteenth century, Catholics were marginalized in British society, what they wanted was to get into the mainstream, not to contract out and go it on their own.

There were considerable advantages for Catholics in life behind the walls of the ghetto: excuse the term, but the standard history of Christian democracy in Switzerland is *Swiss Catholics' Road to the Ghetto* (Altermatt, 1972). It meant the preservation of the faith, for one thing, in closed worlds, 'pillars', or camps, where religion and action on day-to-day interests were knitted closely together. Working together in the 'pillars' made it necessary to hammer out the distinctive inter-class ideology which is the mark of Christian Democracy to this day, and facilitated the acquisition of power and influence as the leaders of the respective camps, with their massed forces behind them, negotiated across their fortress walls under 'consociational' democracy. But the ghetto is not where English Catholics have ever wanted to be. Even 'core' believers in Britain are a political diaspora, spread across the electorate in much the same proportions as everyone else, and Catholics, in particular, tend to draw a sharp line between their religious and political commitments. The national survey of *Roman Catholic Opinion* found in 1978 that only 7 per cent of Catholics, and 3 per cent among young adults, saw 'being politically aware and active' as one of Catholics' identifying characteristics (Hornsby-Smith and Lee, 1979: 195). And, anyway, even in those countries where 'pillarization' was once the norm, it is on the way out (see, e.g., Dobbelaere, 1988; and Special Issues of *West European Politics* on the Netherlands, 1989, and Austria, 1992).

In spite of all this I raise, at least tentatively, the question whether for two reasons the position in Britain might change, at least gradually and to a degree. First, political parties are defined at least as much by what they are against as by what they are for. They need clear blue water between themselves and the enemy, and one area where clear blue water is opening between 'core' Christians and others is Life and related 'moral' issues of the kind which our bishops once called 'minimalist'. In recent years these issues have been moving further into the centre of politics: though Life for this purpose must not be understood too narrowly. In the British General Election of 1997 Pro-Life candidates presented themselves essentially as a single-issue party and were slaughtered; none polled more than 2.5 per cent. By contrast in Norway the Christian People's Party (CPP), which also began, in the 1930s, as a niche party concerned mainly with 'moral' issues, went into the General Election of 1997, without abandoning its Evangelical pro-Life views, with a wide social programme – one might call it, in Life terms, 'life is for living' – and emerged with 15 per cent of Storting seats, opinion poll results now rising to nearer 30 per cent, and the prime ministership in a coalition government (*West European Politics*, Election Report in 21/2 (April 1998); see also chapters by L. Karvonen and J. Madeley in Hanley, 1996).

A rise like that of the CPP was made possible by proportional representation, and there is the second reason why change in Britain may be on the way, since proportional representation is now enacted for Scottish, Welsh and European elections and may go further. PR does not guarantee a quick rise for a new party, in Britain any more than in Norway, but it leaves the possibility of getting a foot in the door, and it is likely that there will be Christian Democratic candidates in 1999, under a label still to be determined, for Scotland and for Europe.

Meantime there is another road to direct political influence by extending into general politics cross-party advocacy and pressure-group work of the kind developed by the Catholic Union and a number of our special-interest groups. That is what the Movement for Christian Democracy (MCD), of which I am honorary president, has set out to do since David Alton founded it in the early 1990s. There are other possibilities, like the idea of a consortium of 'all Christian bodies committed to achieving a more truly human society' – 'Towards a New Christian Partnership in Public Life' – on which Christians in Public Life has been working. Work of that kind is slow, and yet it moves. MCD is cross-party, designed for a country where Christians are a political diaspora. In 1998, as the introduction of proportional representation brought the possibility of at least the beginnings of a distinctively Christian Democratic political party in sight, MCD had to decide whether to identify itself with that trend. Its Council's conclusion, however, was negative. For an indefinite time to come, we have still to live with the Christian political diaspora, and MCD accordingly remains cross-party.

And again, international links? After the Second World War a small British group, mainly of Catholics, set out to build bridges between British political parties and the CD parties which were beginning to reshape the political scene in Western Europe (Papini, 1997). It had, frankly (I was part of it), only limited and one-sided success in Britain, but played an active and, for the Christian Democrats, welcome part in the formative years of the Nouvelles Équipes Internationales, the predecessor of today's European Union of Christian Democrats (EUCD) and European People's Party (EPP). By 1961, however, the Liberal and Labour members of the British Équipe withdrew, and presently it was absorbed into the machinery of the Conservative Party. When MCD was set up it, in its turn, established informal contacts with a number of European Christian Democratic politicians and received considerable help, but formal links became impossible as the European People's Party developed towards an association only of political parties, which of course MCD is not. EUCD, which constitutionally could have offered an opportunity for a movement like MCD to affiliate, was merged with EPP in 1998. The Athens Group might be more accommodating, and in June 1998 the Council of MCD wrote to applaud the Group's formation and defence of Christian Democratic values, and to

> advocate and promote the setting up of a support group to be known as Friends of the Athens Group, to which like-minded parties and organizations which do not have representation in the European Parliament can belong.

If a Christian Democratic Party, under that name or another, regional (for example in Scotland) or national, were established durably in Britain and reached the threshold of support laid down by EPP – 10 per cent of the vote in the last relevant election or 5 per cent in each of the last two – it could without further ado affiliate to EPP. But the question whether to support the Athens Group's insistence on traditional Christian Democratic values or the German policy of a centre–right alliance would remain.

Into the Millennium

The Catholic fox does indeed know and do many things in English and British public life, and very useful ones. I am the last person to underestimate the value of that piecemeal and problem-by-problem activity. After all, through a long and active life I have been part of it. But the hedgehog's 'big one', the capacity to lead the agenda in general politics, has still been missing. I have suggested three ways in which we could set about making a bigger *figura* in general politics in Britain and setting its agenda. In all of them we should beware of being too modest and shooting short. If, for example, I ask myself why the British group of the Nouvelles Équipes Internationales made so small an impression on British political parties, one answer is that we did not aim for influence in the parties at a high enough level or go for the jugular. My fault, among others, because I am that kind of person, but in the end one learns from one's mistakes.

In the case of long-term and radical thinking it is no use just nibbling at the edges. If we are to have our own think-tanks, then let us go right in and be prepared for an effort which continues and is financed over decades. If the organization of leveraged discussion is to have its full impact its scale needs to be adequate, for there are thresholds of effectiveness, if you like economies of scale. Time is needed as well as resources, for when setting out on a course such as I have been discussing, full and definitive results cannot be expected overnight. The time-scale and succession of decision steps which I described in talking about think-tanks applies. As I once told an MCD conference, with reference to the time horizon of MCD's own work and to the century which it took for West European Christian Democracy to reach its peak, when the saints come marching in the road is paved with the bones of their predecessors: and we, I reminded them, are those predecessors.

8

Social Justice in Historical Perspective

Ian Linden

The Preferential Option for the Poor

Did the teaching of the Second Vatican Council signal the dawning of a new epoch in the life of the Church? Did something radically new happen during the 1960s? At the level of the development of doctrine obviously not. The practice of the early Church, the teaching of Patristics, the mendicant orders in the Middle Ages, the insights of Bartholomeo de las Casas, the nineteenth-century religious orders working amongst the poor, all testify to the continuity of a clear tradition that has generated a variety of social forms.

The Church has always had in mind what came to be known as 'the preferential option for the poor' after the 1968 meeting of the bishops of Latin America at Medellín, Colombia. Only, having kept it in mind and wrestled with its implications for centuries, the Church – though never all the Church – often forgot about it or found it more comfortable not to remember.

The growth of Catholic social teaching (CST), from its beginnings in the 1890s as a self-consciously coherent and organic body of thought, marked a new stage in this tradition. For, whatever else it imparted, CST consistently recommended the protection of the poor and marginalized, albeit first seen through the European prism of the industrial revolution and its dire social consequences. CST set out principles, denounced aberrations and sought to define human values that should be enshrined in social structures, in relations between nations, in war and peace, and in the conduct of individual states. Underlying this body of teaching, for example in the acknowledgement of the right of workers to associate and the idea of a 'just wage' (Leo XIII, (1891) 1949; Pius XI, (1930) 1951; Dorr, 1992; Linden, 1994), was a fundamental concept of a just social order. This vision did not call in question active Christian charity as a normative mode of relating to poverty for individuals and organizations – many of the nineteenth-century religious orders had incorporated charitable themes into their rule and charism – but it provided guidance for Catholic political action through lay associations, trade unions and political parties.

The Catholic quest for social justice was strongly influenced and channelled by its opposition to communism and it was only in the early 1960s, with the Khruschev reforms in the Soviet Union, that any thaw took place. What characterized the 1960s was growing support for a vision of the Church's mission that went beyond charity, understood as unconditional love expressed in charitable activity, towards the concept of working for structural change implied in the Catholic term social justice. A movement away from what might pejoratively be called an 'ambulance' ministry, for example coping with the collateral damage of advanced capitalism by relief work, towards different forms of political engagement in social movements seeking structural change, had begun.

This change in emphasis seemed new because the Church's flirtation with, then belated rejection of, fascism, and its persecution by Marxist-Leninism, had thrown up only Christian Democracy as a terrain for 'legitimate' Catholic political action. Moreover, with the CIA pouring money into Christian Democrat parties around the world, such parties did not seem a plausible means of bringing about profound structural change in the interests of the poor. It was in this context that liberation theology began to emerge in Latin America giving Christians a powerful theological legitimation for radical social action often in opposition to Christian Democrat strategies. Meanwhile in Europe, Catholic development agencies such as the Catholic Fund for Overseas Development (CAFOD) were created and others, such as the Catholic Institute for International Relations (CIIR), felt a new wind in their sails.

Perhaps one of the most surprising features of liberation theology was how little CST provided a template for its development and how minor was the Vatican Council in its inspiration. This hiatus between the different bodies of thought was not total, of course, and only trivially explained by geography. The Vatican Council's main intellectual inputs had come from French and German theologians. But most of the Latin American liberation theologians had at one time or another studied in Europe, and might have been expected to have looked to their former teachers for theological themes. Leonardo Boff was famously Cardinal Ratzinger's student. There were other notable links too. The Cardijn movements, Young Christian Students (YCS), and Young Christian Workers (YCW), spanned Europe and Latin America, and played an important role in Brazil.

The principal social form from which liberation theology emerged, the base Christian communities, had grown up and flourished in Latin America since the late 1950s. Unlike CST which had arisen in response to a specific set of problems arising out of European economic, social and political change, liberation theology was asking how to preach the gospel in the context of the 'underdevelopment', gross injustice and military dictatorships of Latin America. CST showed the Church as, at best, interlocutor for the European worker; the liberation theologians were interlocutors for the Latin American peasant or the first-generation shanty-town dweller. To express things in a more Latin American way, in each instance the primary subjects of salvation history were different.

But this was not the only difference in emphasis. The liberation theology tradition was Christological, prophetic and denunciatory and essentially preoccupied with evangelization. CST was implicitly prescriptive and, at least until the 1970s, strongly underpinned by a concept of natural law that believed with Aquinas that we all had the 'light of understanding infused in us by God, whereby we understand what must be done and what must be avoided'. This applied to the 'autonomous' spheres of economics, politics and sociology.

Liberation theologians were not attracted by CST because they were asking different questions, saw it as a Eurocentric discourse, and, worse, as a generalized and abstract prescriptive tradition that did not start out from the perspective of the poor. It was likewise too rooted in natural law rather than in Scripture, theology or in the quest for solutions to the problem of evangelizing societies whose structures dramatically belied the love of God.

Because liberation theology was not in the business of devising a prescriptive theory of society, it was open to borrow uncritically from ideologies that did. The choice of Marxist social theory as a tool for analysing the societies of Latin America in the 1960s-1970s was hardly surprising. Many were marked by obvious class conflict between rich landowners and landless peasants. Liberation theology was most compelling in its account of the plight of the poor in Latin America and of US 'developmentalism' with its foreign control of wealth and supposed 'trickle-down' benefits. Liberation theology was first and foremost a theology, a proclamation of the Reign of God, an annunciation of the salvific role of the martyrs in the context of the theme of resurrection and the way of the Cross. Its Christocentric themes made it attractive to Christians involved in development for whom it articulated a usable theology and spirituality for their work and action amongst the poor of many of the least-developed countries. It spoke intentionally in the indicative not the imperative mood.

Moreover against a creeping liberal Protestantism which had moved God from Lord of history to ground of being, and against a secularism which demythologized the divine intervention of the person of Jesus, it presented a narrative that marginalized the secular as another and alien postmodern story. What made the 1960s exciting was that alongside *Populorum Progressio* (Paul VI, 1967), giving an unequivocal mandate to Christians to work for international economic justice and human rights, came the first stirrings of liberation theology, offering a usable theology and spirituality for the resulting struggles for justice.

Development Agencies after the 1970s Synthesis

If liberation theology is seen as a large river emptying into the sea of Catholic social teaching, the 1970s was a time when the confluence of the two produced considerable richness and movement. One of the consequences of this confluence, or at least related to it, was the decline of natural law arguments. This was partly because the pre-Vatican II Church had so distorted the understanding of natural law as to make it a chronic liability. Instead of offering a training guide to virtue, on how to live – its original function – it had become transformed in the nineteenth century into a rigid rule book. This had proved damaging in the realm of understanding human sexuality and threatened to undermine the Church's teaching authority.

Evangelii Nuntiandi sums up the confluent vision of the 1970s beautifully: 'One cannot dissociate the plan of creation from the plan of redemption. The latter plan touches the very concrete situation of injustice to be combated and of justice to be restored' (Paul VI, 1975, §

31). The answer to Aquinas's, and – for John Paul II – Lenin's question, 'what must be done' and 'what must be avoided' was to be found in the gospel rather than in any more universally accessible 'light of under-standing'.

As the bishops told the Church in the 1971 Synod (see Walsh and Davies, 1984: 188-203), evangelization to be authentic had to contain work for social justice as a constitutive dimension. So, in short, there were a set of gospel imperatives that defined the mission of the Church and one of these was social justice; this meant, amongst other things, working for international economic justice and the protection of human rights. The 'option for the poor' was not primarily the demand for the rich to be just, nor charitable, nor even for the poor to make themselves the subjects of history rather than its victims; it was God's choice expressed in the life and teaching of Jesus of Nazareth, in Scripture and Patristics, and the tradition of the Church. In many places around the world following this option qualified people for prison.

This was the context in which the Catholic Institute for International Relations (CIIR) began supporting Christian groups and organizations working within national democratic struggles for justice in Latin America and Asia in the mid-1970s, and played a role in speaking out against human rights violations and supporting decolonization in Africa. CIIR championed the cause of Archbishop Oscar Romero of San Salvador, worked with the Chilean Church to end the human rights violations of the Pinochet regime and restore the country to democracy, exposed the Wiriyamu massacre in Mozambique and worked effectively with the Rhodesian Catholic Commission for Justice and Peace on documenting and publicizing the human rights violations of the Smith regime. CIIR was issued with a direct warning from British intelligence agents during a visit to London of the Portuguese dictator, Caetano, and its staff were threatened with deportation from Rhodesia by the interim British administration under Lord Soames.

So, by the beginning of the 1980s, members of the staff of CAFOD, CIIR and the Scottish Catholic International Aid Fund (SCIAF) could interpret their work as an attempt to fulfil the mandate of *Populorum Progressio* and, in addition, as being an integral part of the Church's mission of evangelization. Their quest for a Christian sociology and practice of international relations was the Church's quest. But the impression given by many, not least by some bishops, was that this was a commendable – or dangerously political – *lay activity* while 'the Church' got on with the important activity of administering the sacraments and the *real* work of evangelization. This was a perfectly logical and tenable position. But it seemed to bear no relation to the ecclesiology of the Second Vatican Council, nor to the synthesis reached in the 1970s that had *de facto* marginalized natural law.

The downside of this shift was soon to be apparent in the thinking of Pope John Paul II, who, on the whole, abandoned the analysis of concrete economic, social and political situations which Pope Paul VI had begun tentatively to explore. With his back to bureaucratic communism, the Polish Pope had little faith in the relative autonomy of political science, sociology and economics. His early thinking was dominated by an almost mystical Christocentric personalism coupled with a profound pessimism about 'human progress'. But whether it came from liberation theologians in Latin America or the Pope's cohorts in Poland, the tendency was increasingly to confront secularism with a language and praxis that had arisen in Catholic cultures.

The 1980s: A 'Second Cold War'

The USA, the Soviet Union and, to a lesser degree, China chose to fight a Second Cold War in the 1980s, largely by proxy in the context of national democratic struggles in the Third World. This made technocratic strategies for development, that neglected social transformation in favour solely of building up technical competence, both questionable and dangerous. Whether in apartheid South Africa, the Philippines or El Salvador, the choice of not taking sides was illusory. 'Communist' was used as a catch-all word to describe everyone from Christians involved in work for social justice to Maoists, feminists and national democratic guerrilla forces. Liberation theology made Christian sense of such conflict situations and rapidly drew down the wrath of the Vatican and CIA.

For Catholic organizations committed to justice and development, this was a challenging time. Since the membership of Churches is heterogeneous as regards social class and political viewpoint – not to mention race and ethnicity as regards Zimbabwe, Guatemala, Mozambique and South Africa – churchgoers chose different sides in the decade's major conflicts over social justice. European Catholic development agencies who claimed to be 'working through the local Church' often had a conveniently different model of the Church from many of their donors, who despite *Lumen Gentium* (in Abbott, 1966: 14-101) might still think this meant working through the bishops and their commissions. Alternatively, such agencies indeed were doing what they proclaimed, thereby funding some politically questionable organizations who were either passively or openly supporting an oppressive *status quo* (one in which radical Christians were often tortured or killed).

If they were lucky, Catholic development agencies found a bishop or two to work through who actively shared the vision of social justice set out in CST, rather than giving it perfunctory intellectual assent. The problem was further aggravated by Pope John Paul II's attempts to eliminate liberation theology by the selection of new bishops who opposed it. Unlucky development agencies could become the focus of ferocious political assaults from the right; a running campaign in *Le Figaro* against the leading French Catholic development agency, CCFD, cost it income and resulted in staff redundancies in the early 1980s. The German and Dutch agencies, Misereor and Cebemo, with their government funding and consideration of their conservative constituency in mind, for example, felt it prudent only to relate to the African National Congress through the CIIR. The British agencies, protected by the good offices of Cardinal Hume, a more liberal Bishops' Conference, and somewhat 'offshore' in the eyes of Rome, were afforded a degree of protection from a less organized religious right.

This therefore became the era of 'development education' as Catholic organizations struggled to close the gap between their staff, stakeholders, donors and beneficiaries. If the hierarchy were not going to articulate a Christian vision of social justice, or even promote CST actively, lay organizations would do so instead. But 'development education' and 'campaigns' no less than any other activity that challenged quietism or passive support for the *status quo*, could be, and sometimes were, interpreted as an instrumentalization of the Church for 'political ends'. This quaint idea prescinded from the question whether anything plausibly described as the Church could exist without 'political ends', and would have gained in honesty and clarity by inserting the words 'the wrong' before 'political'.

When CIIR published a small pamphlet by the South African Dominican theologian, Albert Nolan, called *Taking Sides* in 1981, it rapidly sold thousands of copies and clearly spoke to the condition of many Christians during what Hobsbawn (1994) has called 'the Second Cold War'. How was it possible not to take sides in struggles for social justice if the preferential option for the poor was to mean anything? A similar reception was given to the South African *Kairos* document (CIIR/ BCC, 1985) and the international *The Road to Damascus* document four years later (CIIR, 1989) for which CIIR acted as a central secretariat. Each of these in different ways came out of a contextual theology that reacted to the violent repression of those working for social justice.

The problem was translating the option for the poor into the organized political domain, and finding a satisfactory relationship of critical solidarity with those social and political movements that were widely seen as giving political expression to the needs and demands of the poor and oppressed. For it did not make much sense to talk of an abstract liberation without formulating some strategy towards relationships with liberation movements, trade unions and political parties of the left that materially might be expected to bring about change. It was, of course, this necessity to enter on to morally equivocal terrain that created a costly form of discipleship and condemned liberation theologians to accusations of creating a 'political Christ'.

So Christian development education was not essentially about teaching people how to use solar panels to power water pumps in the desert, but about changing hearts and minds over the implications for discipleship of 'social justice'. In countries whose mass media were playing a growing role in shaping opinion, this was no easy task. It was made virtually impossible by entrenched views about the content of 'religion', namely the core sacramental life of the Church and certain moral themes. When, for example, the Pope spoke out strongly in Nigeria in March 1998 about human rights and democracy, the visit was described as 'one of his most political'. Had he advocated frequent confession and condemned abortion it would have been called 'spiritual'.

For many Catholics as well, a Catholic – religious – organization could either be about 'spirituality', which directed people back to the sacraments, or about charity, understood as a 'corporal work of mercy', some form of giving to the poor. Almost by definition Catholic organizations that talked about – and did – something outside these narrow parameters were 'political'. And 'political' was a bad word in the political culture of the UK in the 1980s, as it was elsewhere.

If giving to the poor resulted in them taking their history into their own hands, seeking power and confronting the powerful, this also meant that support for them would no longer be described as 'charity' but 'politics'. In short the poor could build latrines, schools and form sewing circles, but not women's organizations that sought gender equity or political formations that challenged what was then called the military–industrial complex, elites and oligarchies. Outrage had been expressed by conservative Christians when the World Council of Churches gave money for humanitarian purposes to liberation movements. In short, whatever Catholic social teaching might say, the development agencies had permission to change hearts, minds and lives but not structures.

In Britain the constraints were reinforced by Charity Law that did not permit 'political action' – though what this constituted proved to be vague at the edges and subject to interpretation – and was activated against radical development agencies by letters of complaint usually stage-managed by the political right. OXFAM and CIIR, in different ways, both fell foul of the Charity Commission over their advocacy of sanctions against the government of South Africa.

Development Education versus Emergency Aid

A period of development education slowly merged into a decade of 'emergency aid' that had begun in earnest with the 1984 Ethiopian famine and, subsequently after 1991, attained the lofty title of 'humanitarian intervention'. CAFOD was chairing the Disasters Emergency Committee, a grouping of non-governmental organizations (NGOs) that included the Red Cross, as the Ethiopian famine became news.

Emergencies and – usually man-made – disasters were brought into the living room by television. Only massacres and civil wars could get camera crews on to a flight to countries that otherwise received zero coverage. Cardinal Hume kneeling before an emaciated Ethiopian child had considerable 'iconic' clout. Governments were forced by the pressure of public opinion to react by allocation of funds to the 'disaster area', the Minister of State for Overseas Development would answer journalists' questions and be filmed with malnourished children, whilst development agencies fund-raised on the back of subsequent appeals. But the overwhelming message of the media was that the least-developed countries were home to passive victims of 'disasters', their economies were basket cases, and an 'ambulance ministry' served the needs of the hour.

The concept of 'profile', being seen in action as a spur to charitable donations, meanwhile became more critical. Agencies that were 'operational', in other words put staff 'on the ground' during emergencies, got profile as television crews talked to them against a background of human misery, refugee camps, feeding centres and village massacres. CAFOD, which worked through Church organizations, particularly local CAR-ITAS groups for principled reasons of building up the local Church, could not benefit from publicity in this way. The only other path to 'profile' was campaigning that brought development agencies to the public attention as defenders of pro-poor policies and interlocutors for marginalized groups around the world.

Once the big 'humanitarian interventions' of the 1990s, Bosnia, Rwanda, Somalia, got underway, the ideological onslaught against radical analysis of the root causes of poverty and social disintegration gained in strength. Development education faced an impossible task against such odds. CAFOD, for example, faced perennial questioning from powerful members of its Board about the justification for monies not being sent directly to the poor of the Third World, but persevered. CIIR found it increasingly difficult to enlarge or sustain the budget of its education department, but its other work of sharing skills in the world's poorest countries grew steadily.

For many of the big development agencies, beneficiaries of several years of growing emergency aid, the main problem was dealing with the rapid expansion in staffing that it stimulated. CAFOD's budget almost doubled as a result of increased emergency aid, and staffing rose from around 50 to 80 during the late 1980s. A similar growth could be found at Christian Aid.

Enter the Master's Degree in Business Administration in the Voluntary Sector and a major outbreak of modern management theory and practice. This sharpened NGOs' 'performance', their definition of objectives and thinking about strategies, and, not least, was useful in dealing with the consequences of subsequent cut-backs in emergency aid provision that inevitably came in the mid-1990s as governments lost the will to keep up with demand. The nascent 'compassion industry' thus became surreptitiously competitive; it was soon restructuring, downsizing and lobbying government for its sectoral interests.

Catholic development agencies, of course, had their own understanding of the root causes of poverty and man-made disasters based on theories of structural injustice. But even in the face of increasing numbers of emergencies, this approach found it difficult to win adherents. The dominant story about emergencies was that the cavalry needed first to come over the hill, then the experts and World Bank officials, bearing liberal democracy to the benighted races. NGOs could either join in the charge or sulk in the corner ... and lose out on large grants-in-aid, media exposure and public acclaim. Whether or not African countries were in any meaningful sense on a trajectory towards liberal democracy, or, in many cases, were showing their acute distress as marginalized actors in a globalized economy in ever more dysfunctional and violent political forms, was a moot point.

Arrayed against this ideological block to the furtherance of sustainable development and genuine evangelization were returned missionaries from Latin America, men and women religious seeking new forms of social apostolate, the Catholic peace movement, CAFOD and CIIR staff, and Justice and Peace groups. It was a mass of people small enough on the whole to know each other but big enough and too scattered amongst disparate institutions to find it easy to think strategically as a discrete constituency.

The religious orders were significant but often were represented by individuals who did not easily carry their small Catholic institutions with them, and had to deal with their organizations' declining size and energy as their communities aged. This informal grouping never became a critical mass able to bring about dramatic reform disproportionate to its numbers. Though, over a twenty-year period, it did bring about significant change in the local church. The bishops' statement on *The Common Good* (1996), for example, would probably never have seen the light of day had the work of these loose congeries of individuals and groups, coupled with that of those organizations working on race, housing and domestic poverty, not existed and lobbied for change.

In the event, development education not surprisingly failed to change enough hearts and minds for several large development agencies – for example Christian Aid – to continue making it a priority in the financially constrained conditions of the 1990s. The general public clung to views that were reinforced by the mass media. An image of the 'bottomless pit' had gained in credibility as the volume of emergency aid grew almost exponentially throughout the late 1980s. Indeed, by the early 1990s the Tory back-benches and, as Gore Vidal calls it, that single political party which rules the USA, with its two major factions, the Republicans and Democrats, had almost won the policy argument against governmental development assistance.

Flows of foreign direct investment (FDI) were now considered the universal panacea. By 1997 they had reached a peak of $256 billion to low- and middle-income countries – though highly focused on a handful of middle-income ones. Total official aid declined by 1997 to $37.3 billion, a third lower than a decade earlier, and only one-sixth of FDI. But FDI could and did – Mexico in 1994, South-East Asia in 1997 – flow out just as fast as it flowed in. A strong rearguard action by the development lobby had failed to hold the line. The USA halved its development assistance between 1986 and 1996 and the British development budget also declined as a percentage of GDP. Aid had become increasingly the business of NGOs, championed by them and channelled through them.

The Post-1991 Consensus on Advocacy

The new international disorder that emerged from the apparent symmetries of the Cold War and the defeat of communism further benefited organizations with centrist politics and technocratic methodology, and penalized radical groups committed to structural change. The former could carry on as normal. The latter had to go back to the drawing boards.

For the poor of the developing world, Cold War symmetry had led to the cemetery. But the new international disorder which included the collapse of states in sub-Saharan Africa, ethnic conflict and the globalization of crime led to the cemetery as well, or at least to the mass grave bulldozed over hastily as irregular troops moved on. The problems of the least-developed countries did not get any less, and, losing any geo-political significance in a world where geo-economics was primary, their prospects deteriorated. The Clinton whistle-stop tour of Africa in March 1998 ended a twenty-year absence of US Presidents from the continent, a fair measure of the USA's strategic interests.

The global war on the poor continued by other means. For radical development agencies, the structures to be changed increasingly took on a global dimension and involved multilateral financial institutions, trade organizations and transnational corporations. Moreover, there had to be a painful paradigm shift from a discourse primarily about alternatives – which Christians were able to hold on to in an eschatological future of the Reign of God – into a dialogue primarily about feasible reform. So new approaches had to be adopted and new ways of working. It became more a matter of changing policies than changing structures. This was pre-eminently the era of the NGO policy department and what became known by the American term, 'advocacy', i.e. lobbying for policy change, proposing other ways forward than those imposed by the contemporary 'principalities and powers'.

CIIR was unusual as a Catholic organization in that it had pioneered 'advocacy' approaches for over three decades, lobbying over a variety of issues, for example decolonization in southern Africa, the arms trade to Latin American dictators, and European Union policies that affected primary producers in the least-developed countries. Advocacy was seen as an integral part of development, 'good news for the poor', that other ways were possible instead of beggaring your neighbour and passive acceptance of economic injustice.

The end of the Cold War 'depoliticized' much of the activity of development agencies in the eyes of the beholder; it could no longer so readily be measured against a calculus based on the conflict between 'communism and capitalism'. At about the same time official interpretations of British Charity Law gave development agencies the green light for advocacy provided it could be shown to stem from their experience 'on the ground'. CIIR was soon being overhauled by the richer, larger agencies who had come to see in expanding their advocacy work an appropriate response to the new geo-economic situation, not to say a way of catching the headlines in the competition for charitable giving between different agency 'brand' names.

CAFOD came to creating a policy department relatively late, building up a small unit after Christian Aid and OXFAM had begun fielding an impressive array of lobbyists. This was partly because some of CAFOD's key stakeholders retained a firm conviction that its mandate for development was to use money collected in the Catholic community primarily in 'overseas' projects – though the insights and instincts of some of the staff was to see policy change in the UK and Europe as no less essential for any coherent 'preferential option for the poor'. In this they were no different from the stakeholders of most of the other European and North American Catholic agencies – Trocaire in Ireland would be an exception – who on the whole also did not prioritize advocacy work.

But this was partly because CAFOD had persevered with its development education, and had taken a significant part of its constituency with it, so was cautious about alienating them. CAFOD made a distinctive Christian contribution to development education, rooting development in biblical sources and CST.

CAFOD moved on in the mid-1990s to link campaigns with its development education in annual themes. Growing out of a theme on the needs of refugees came involvement in the land-mines campaign. From a broad theme focusing on international economic justice came the debt campaign. These campaigns were able to mobilize even the more conservative Catholic organizations, and link up with wider secular and ecumenical campaigns. They were reinforced by high-level interventions from bishops, the Pontifical Commission for Justice and Peace, and the Pope. Meanwhile, alongside its expanding skillshare programme, CIIR was pioneering work on the supply-side issues of the international drugs trade, studying peace processes and exploring ways of tackling in monitored codes of conduct the overwhelming power of the transnational corporations as economic actors.

A decade of advocacy associated with a quest for more effective ways of working, and latterly 'performance indicators', made a significant impact on all Catholic development agencies. In order to present cogent arguments against complex policies, a higher level of expertise was required. Recruitment of this expertise from within the dwindling Catholic community became more difficult.

For all development agencies, the complexity of the issues confronted has made the arguments increasingly inaccessible to the vast majority of the membership and supporters. Skilful simplification and popularization into a campaign format, as in the Jubilee debt campaign, can sometimes, but not always, overcome these difficulties. CIIR publications increasingly were tied to advocacy objectives and reflected the complexity of the issues. Popularizing broader issues and concerns continued, but exclusively in CIIR's *Comment* series.

So, while in the 1980s the problem had been the gap in political – and to some extent theological – understanding between stakeholders, staff and beneficiaries of development agencies, by the late 1990s it was more a question of a difference in expertise. There was a world of difference between lobbying on issues arising out of apartheid or the sale of landmines and attempting to involve people in development agencies' advocacy work about the multilateral investment agreement (MAI).

There was a point at which popularization of the issue, or its presentation in a dramatic and arresting form for a campaign, could amount to a distortion of what the lobbyists were saying in the Department of Trade and Industry. The risk grew that a development agency's constituency could be subtly manipulated. Correspondingly the successful practice of advocacy, going for small gains, does not lend itself to championing the kind of clear moral distinctions that arouse people to support a major campaign.

To say this is only to spell out to what degree it might be appropriate to describe the Catholic agencies' living-out of a preferential option for the poor as moving from a prophetic to a professional approach. Is it possible to maintain a prophetic simplicity in the midst of the professional demands of advocacy and other forms of development work? Perhaps up to a point. At a practical level, the land-mines and debt campaigns would suggest that this is still possible even if pre-selection of themes is more than part of the battle. The exciting and innovative role of NGOs in human rights monitoring, peace-keeping and peace-building is another.

The question follows: is this setting the 'professional' against the 'prophetic' a justifiable distinction? Is prophetic utterance necessarily simple and direct? This cannot entirely be true as *The Common Good* (1996) was, in the context of Britain in the late 1990s, a prophetic document though it was far from simple. Advocacy on debt alleviation required detailed research. If it is not to be merely rhetorical, repentance worked out in practice is often complicated. The debate about debt relief with governments is now focused on concepts such as the 'sustainability of debt', involving complex economic calculations, but the outcome of the debate will be measured in perinatal mortality and a calculus of human suffering that has a biblical simplicity.

There is a danger if 'professional' comes to mean routinized, lacking in imagination, spontaneity and creativity, and bounded by rules benefiting largely a closed elite. Such professionalism has always to be challenged by the voice of those who experience material poverty and political oppression. Catholic development agencies have striven to encourage these challenges as an integral part of their examination of conscience and witness. CIIR, for example, is developing a new programme to build the capacity of its partners in advocacy at local, national and international levels.

If liberation theology gave the spiritual underpinning of an incarnate spirituality for the last years of the Cold War – and for many it did – what did it have to say to the professional world of impact assessment, performance indicators, and coalition-building for advocacy into which Catholic development agencies were being drawn? Clearly, in its early-1970s form, not directly a great deal. The skills, knowledge and experience needed to bring about integral development, like those informing good political science or economics, cannot simply be learnt in, or derived from, the Gospels. Such skills are unlikely to be the special prerogative only of Christians. Even so in a Catholic agency their practice might be expected to reflect a vision of redemption or 'right relationship' – political, economic and ecological – and be applied to the 'concrete situations of injustice to be combated and justice to be restored'. In this sense, as a spiritual formation, liberation theology retains its importance in advocacy and other development work and will find new social expressions in the future.

Christian Development Agencies into the Twenty-First Century

In a globalized economy in which nation-state governments vie with transnationals, drugs barons and multilateral financial institutions for control over the economic activity of their citizens, development agencies today face exceptional challenges. Their constituencies, on the whole, lag behind their staffs in their understanding of contemporary geo-economics and its implications. And, however much development education has, or has not, achieved, these are issues that require a thoroughly professional approach. The fund-raising model of 'us' helping 'them' by sending money through development agencies for projects overseas remains dominant except amongst a minority of donors drawn from the churchgoing general public. Yet it seems increasingly anachronistic.

Both the 'us' and the 'them' experience similar economic forces and suffer forms of marginalization even if the richer industrialized nations have incomparably larger social safety nets to deal with them. Social exclusion and structural poverty form a global patchwork whose reality is violated by any simplistic division between 'domestic poverty' and 'Third World poverty'. The least-developed countries, of course, have gross additional problems, such as unsustainable debt, dependence on a few low-value agricultural exports and high birth rates. But they are in the same queue for foreign direct investment, sell their products in the same unfair trading system, and face similar environmental threats to our own; what is different is their drastically limited capacity to deal with crises and with the growing problems created by the globalized economy.

Catholic development agencies are well situated to tackle the threatening processes of globalization which now claim attention. They are *theologically* internationalist, rooted in civil society, and have an almost universal capacity for working at the grass-roots and giving voice to the poor to speak truth with power. They grow out of a resource-rich organization that can mutate according to need to be an NGO or a nation-state; the Vatican has played an effective but highly contentious role as a state-body in international governance bodies, particularly in the recent wave of UN special conferences, while Catholic NGOs could be found lobbying in alternative summits outside. This seat both inside and outside the councils of state is, of course, a double-edged sword but it is worth noting. Human rights groups working through the Pope have achieved some remarkable results in Cuba and put the heaviest pressure on the Abacha regime in Nigeria.

Given this comparative advantage, it is a growing problem that large sections of the constituencies of development agencies still retain a theology of solidarity that has moved little beyond compassionate giving for a narrow range of small-scale emergency and self-help projects, preferably run by fellow Catholics. Catholic agencies could be doing so much more for the poor, so much more effectively, if more of their constituency would only share their analysis – and their theology – of what it takes to eliminate poverty.

With government, business and NGOs in the UK beginning to break out of knee-jerk antagonisms and misunderstandings, the late 1990s is a time of great opportunities and corresponding dangers. The emerging redefinition of the 'consumer' as a moral agent with choice, defined by ethical rather than emotional need, has significant implications for the Church and for development agencies. To what extent has the Church followed up the lead of NGOs and government to make the new 'ethical initiatives' a subject central to moral teaching? To what extent will the consumer be co-opted into the cosy niche market as an 'ethical investor, purchaser, pensioner'?

Likewise the different structures of the Church offer great potential for advocacy, across frontiers and North–South – more so than those of the trade unions – as the Jubilee debt campaign has illustrated. The Church can uniquely work at local, national and international levels if it sets its mind to do so. But Church structures are only weakly being co-ordinated or utilized. At best European and North American Catholic agencies get together for limited joint action in the Brussels-based association for co-ordination, CIDSE ('International Co-operation for Development and Solidarity'). A modicum of co-ordination across the usual boundaries has been achieved during the Jubilee campaign, though the top levels of the Church hierarchy have tended to act independently and are not easily drawn into co-ordinated and strategically planned action.

A related problem is how to dissuade Church leaders from speaking on behalf of people who are more than capable of speaking for themselves if only they were given a platform. CIIR has left behind its 'voice of the voiceless' claims of the late 1970s, and is undertaking joint advocacy with Southern partners, and responding to requests for training in advocacy by Southern NGOs with whom we work. A similar shift in emphasis has occurred in several other development agencies. It offers a tangible expression of the amorphous concept 'international civil society'.

The model prevailing today is one of coalition, groups of Northern and Southern NGOs working together, often with great difficulty because of the difference in cultures and expectations, to call for changes in the policies of governments or inter-governmental bodies in the interests of the poor. Such coalitions embody a concrete, not an abstract universality, bringing local, differentiated and rigorous analysis to problems of the global economy. CIIR hosted a remarkable meeting of Asian and European civil society groups at the end of March 1998 at a conference on 'people-centred' development, the 'Asian Peoples' Forum' to coincide with the Asia–Europe Meeting of heads of state in London. It pressed governments to take seriously the human impact of rapid economic collapse in South-East Asia. The possibilities for effective co-ordination within such international coalitions is enhanced by the revolution in information technology. Similar groups are increasingly able to meet transnationals and governments, sometimes coming the other way, in negotiations for codes of conduct and their monitoring.

It seems likely that these complex interactions will continue to flourish into the twenty-first century. But there remain dangers for development agencies. In order not to become elite organizations clothing their elitism with a fraudulent populism and manipulation of their constituencies, they need to nourish their roots and base. CAFOD, with its area offices and outreach, CIIR with its membership and eleven country offices in the poorest countries of the world, both have the capacity to do so.

The story of the Catholic development agencies during the last three decades has been a remarkable example of the working-out of one expression of the lay vocation which Congar (1965), for example, first explored theologically in the 1950s. The model of the Church implied by this vocation for justice, committed to the option for the poor, open to the world, reading the signs of the times, discovering and nurturing values of the Spirit both inside and outside the Church, is inherent in the thinking of the Second Vatican Council. Yet there is little sign that the broad acceptance and support amongst the general public for the work of the development agencies is about to become dominant and transform parochial and diocesan life and structures.

So a final question needs to be asked. Under these circumstances, to what extent will Catholic development agencies in the twenty-first century be able to act as a leaven for the Church while continuing to play a significant role in civil society in a secular Britain? With a usable theology, an adequate Christian anthropology and Christian hope, Catholic agencies should be able to plough this difficult furrow. But it remains to be seen whether pressures from Rome and the religious Right in future years, with the dominance of a defensive and pessimistic dualism between 'progress' and the values of the spirit, will render this increasingly difficult.

So, Catholic development agencies today urgently require a renewed catechesis to transform the Church into a mature school for solidarity. If social justice and advocacy is to become part of the Church's lifelong learning and thus an integral part of discipleship, a firm catechetical base is essential. Otherwise the simple demands of justice and the complex task of responding effectively to a globalized economy, with all its inherent injustices, will over the coming years make the Catholic development agencies semi-detached from the Church. And that will be another great and unnecessary loss.

Part III

Sociological Perspectives

9

Young Adult Core Catholics

John Fulton

Post-1945 English Catholics and the Parental Generation

In recent years priests and parishioners have commented on the increasing absence from church of young people, especially young adults, and less willingness to share in the faith of their parents. The observation is almost certainly correct. What is unclear is why. In all likelihood, it suggests a further change in English Roman Catholicism and represents a growing differentiation of the age group from their parents' generation. This chapter looks at the life orientation of those young adults and how they relate to the tradition of their parents. To do this, we first look at the general characteristics of the people's Catholicism in England since 1945 and focus on the generation who parented the present 18–30 group. Then, second, we look at aspects of the contemporary religion and culture of 46 young adult Catholics and former Catholics, paying special attention to those who are most practising. We do this through a study of their life histories, collected as part of an international project examining how contemporary young adult Catholics interpret their faith in the contemporary world. We then conclude with a number of questions and hypotheses about the current religion of young adult Catholics in Britain and their likely religious future.

Post-war Britain still had a culture in which marriage and the family were safeguarded, though it did produce high rates of teenage marriages usually as a result of pre-marital pregnancy. These levels only slightly declined with the legalization of abortion in the 1960s. Despite this privileged place of marriage and the family in the national culture, there was still a transformation taking place in the role of parental authority. Full employment led to relatively high wages among young people. The more they were earning, the more they achieved economic independence and freedom from parental authority. Such a change threatened from within, at least in part, the traditional isolation from the rest of society which Catholics in formerly Protestant countries had previously experienced. In fact, such isolation had been the product not only of the dominant culture enforcing the role of minority status on them but also of a strategy of the Catholic Church leadership. Wherever it formed a minority of the state's population the world over, the life-style of its pre-Vatican II Catholicism was constructed via mechanisms of insularity on the basis of a Tridentine theology. The aim was to isolate as much as possible all Roman Catholics from the surrounding 'sinful' or heretical and Protestant society and to replicate in minority form the monopoly Catholicism of countries like Spain, Portugal and Ireland.

The task of maintaining the separate social and community life of Catholics in and around the Church was done in stages. The first was accomplished by having separate schools for all Catholic children, in so far as material and spiritual resources would permit. The second was done by using the twin pillars of pulpit and confessional to delimit the mind's contact with the surrounding social world. Fulfilling God's will was more or less synonymous with saving one's soul. (For a similar analysis of US Catholics, see Dolan, 1985.) This was the paramount task of the Catholic, and was outlined as such in the Penny Catechism of the day. The world outside was an occasion of sin, and was to be avoided where possible. Allied to this policing of sexual mores was the third stage, the maintenance of stringent laws governing mixed marriage, established by the 1908 *Ne Temere* decree and later written into the Code of Canon Law (1918), and which to all intents and purposes tarred Catholics who married out with the brush of second-class members of the Church, ever in proximate occasion of losing their immortal souls.

This does not mean of course that even the enforcement of this triple-layered discipline was successful. Indeed it was not, as research on the period shows (Hornsby-Smith, 1992). Those migrants who for whatever reason had escaped the net and found the wider society congenial and unthreatening appear to have found little difficulty in leaving behind the taken-for-granted religion which had gone with that package. However, for those laity nearest to the Church and least likely to lapse, the discipline succeeded though they may have kept to themselves any heterodox views they had on Church doctrine and moral teaching. Whether intended or not, the over-formulation of sexual sin in particular was instrumental in keeping devout but 'sinful' Catholics strongly in touch with their leaders, as they were ever running back to confession for necessary absolution from the clergy on whom they were learning by sinful practice ever to depend.

Most of the parents of those aged 18–30 in 1997 were brought up in this pre-Vatican II environment. They were also the first generation of young adults to experience the Vatican II reforms which were put into practice in the period after 1965 while they were still in their teens or their twenties. We must also remember that the Vatican Council reforms had a major setback with the contraceptive pill debate and the papal rebuff of 1968 in the form of *Humanae Vitae* (Paul VI, 1968). This generation of parents was the first to experience a contested Church in the spheres of both worship and sexual life. They were the main ones who would have to take decisions on contraception in a growing climate of personal choice and at a time when the boundaries of their official and confessional religiosity were in flux. However, they arrived at these problems and their solutions in a period of economic stability and often already married, something which we will find not to be the case for today's young adult Catholics.

The introduction of the reforms of Vatican II involved the relaxation of the triple-layered discipline we have outlined, and the redirection of lay spirituality away from over-concentration on personal sin towards concern for one's neighbour and one's role in society as the furtherance of God's kingdom. Such reforms dealt the death blow to the ethnic Church as Catholics became more openly involved in the wider society of which they were members. But the reforms did not appear to provide enough necessary direction and explanation for those for whom the old ways had become an essential feature of personal identity. While many of those who suffered from the loss of the ethnic Church and were too old to change have mostly died, and those who seek to maintain the old model do so with great difficulty and are few in numbers, the parents of today's young adult Catholics have been able to develop their own views, at least those among them who were already oriented towards Church and mission activity. Those already loosely affiliated continued to drift from the Church and were not replaced to the same extent by new waves of Catholic migrants. Also, a number of young adult Catholics both working and middle class, probably left the Church over the contraception debate, just as a number of priests resigned, though with the majority of them staying on as laity.

To an extent, Hornsby-Smith's work documents the change among the laity of the period from this former spirituality to what then emerged. We can use his work, along with that of Kokosalakis, Koopmanschap and Cottrell, to identify some of the new features, especially those which belonged to the young adult generation of the period. Hornsby-Smith focuses particularly on beliefs, practice and morality on the one hand, and on attitudes towards hierarchical authority on the other. From Hornsby-Smith's work as a whole (particularly 1987b; 1989; and 1991; and Hornsby-Smith and Lee, 1979), it is quite clear that around the time of Vatican II and before the publication of its decrees, changes were already taking place, as some clergy and laity were already responding to debates in the Council and modifying ethical perceptions and practices, particularly in the field of sexual ethics.

The above-mentioned research shows English Catholics trying to fit the symbols and rituals of Catholic life (doctrine and worship) to their experiences of life in the contemporary world rather than vice-versa (Kokosalakis, 1971; Koopmanschap, 1978). For one researcher, this involved the marginalization of religion to the boundaries of consciousness itself, with competitive individualism at the centre for most middle-class Catholics (Cottrell, 1985). Core laity from Hornsby-Smith and Penny Mansfield's 1974 sample (Hornsby-Smith, 1991) were clearly already a much-varied bunch in their spiritual orientations as well as in their perceptions of Church authority and of doctrinal and moral teaching. Most had little sense of a fixed Christian calling; rather they were feeling their way in what was already a very complex world. They had little support from the clergy and turned much more to the advice of fellow laity. They were already developing divergent spiritualities often with ecumenical elements. However, most were still oriented towards the importance of Church pronouncements, hence the seriousness of their discomfort on the occasion of *Humanae Vitae*. There was still considerable acceptance of Church teaching, but critique was also apparent and they were upset with the inflexibility of Roman authority. Two-thirds of core members rejected the papal decision on contraception and there was considerable unease at the oversimplification of the issue of abortion.

There were still images of a personal God for core Catholics, though immanent images were preferred. But other Catholics seemed embarrassed at the question of how they saw God. Both personal prayer and set prayer were in evidence but in different sets of people, and many still prayed to saints. There were already calls for a greater share of control for the laity over Church affairs. Only 40 per cent of 18–25-year-olds accepted papal infallibility (though what they meant by it is not at all clear), most respected their clergy, but half were open to having married priests and one quarter to women priests. While they respected the Pope, they were still critical of his teaching. Hornsby-Smith further notes that most no longer feared Church sanctions for breaking its rules on 'frequency of Mass attendance and reception of the sacraments, mixed marriages, intercommunion, and so on' (1991: 139). He further notes how one of his respondents, a 60-year-old, was quite happy to accept the Church's authority himself but his own children (the parental generation of today's young adults) were 'not prepared to take' prohibitions from Church authorities (ibid.: 158).

The above research projects generally looked at adults as a whole, and some were based on purposive or quota sampling of particular groups. But all together they probably give a good picture of the range of Catholic ideologies and forms of adherence at the time, though with little information on the working classes or on regional variations. It can reasonably be assumed that the old ethnic structures binding people into a community separated off in significant ways from its host culture were collapsing, with the Church leadership itself playing a part in 'freeing up' the sense of social isolation, and changing sacramental practice to such an extent that the popular religiosity of sustained continuous guilt withered away.

Theory of Contemporary Culture

The world in which the children of this Vatican II generation have grown up is significantly different from that of their parents. We can suggest key aspects of its culture by looking at the work of Giddens (1990; 1991) and Beck (1992), and some of the work of the postmodernist school of interpretation (Bauman, 1996). The work of Giddens and Beck is often referred to as high or late modernity theory as opposed to postmodern theory. Briefly, the former accept with the postmodernists that there has been in Western society a dramatic shift in culture and consciousness over the last forty or so years. The previous society, while modern and diversified, was still sufficiently organized to provide a sense of belonging and purpose to the majority of their inhabitants and had cultural institutions which were sufficiently powerful to provide 'grand narratives' to explain most of life's purposes.

For the postmodernists, such grand narratives have gone and the power of cultural institutions from religion through to the state has been radically undermined. All that is left is the naked power of technical rationality operating in the market-place and determining what people have to do to survive, but without any internal significance for it being provided. Human beings are totally rudderless and unable to provide significant meaning themselves. The world becomes a superficial place and people live, as it were, on the surface of life, without being able to find or give any deep commitment. Postmodernists, by definition, have no answer to such problems, as there are by definition no answers which can come from human beings living in a postmodernist world.

For high modernists, such meanings are difficult to find, and are almost demanded by the vacuum their lack has created, particularly in a world threatened by weapons of mass destruction, mass global inequalities and suffering, and an ever deteriorating global environment. On the one hand, the main modern institutions of state and business eschew moral responsibility. On the other, a new and enlarged sphere of freedom of personal action and freely embraced relationships – called 'pure relationships' by Giddens – has developed to enrich human life. For Giddens, the key to solving the problems that exist is to re-energize the main modern institutions by restoring their sense of morality and establishing an international order based on humanitarian principles, thus providing corresponding support for personal expression and meaning to those institutions as well as to social life. The focus should be on 'emancipatory' or 'life politics', for example recognizing the way modern living destroys the environment and encouraging life-style changes which enhance rather than threaten the environment, by reforming economic institutions so that they are governed by social and humanistic concerns (Giddens, 1991: 209–31).

If there is truth in the arguments of either postmodern or high modern theorists, then one would expect to uncover in the lives of individuals, including young adult Catholics, some of the fragmentation that these thinkers identify. Indeed, we could perhaps say that high modernists do not go far enough by failing to incorporate sufficiently into their theory the material inequalities which exist within our contemporary Western societies. With reference to young people, we have the collapse of the youth labour market, clearest in the figures for school-leavers in Scotland:

in 1977, 72 per cent of them were already in full-time jobs six months later, but in 1991, only 28 per cent of school-leavers had achieved full-time work over a similar period. Most stay on in school today as a direct result of the collapse of heavy industry. It is also interesting to note that most of today's 26-year-olds who live in the parental home come from relatively disadvantaged backgrounds, have low qualifications and are not continuing with their education (Bynner *et al.*, 1997).

At this point, we might want to say that perhaps the postmodernists have gone too far; the idea that modern people are generally *flâneurs* or strollers, vagabonds, permanent tourists and detached players enjoying the risk of a postmodern dabble (Bauman's description, 1996: 26–32) seems to be a grotesque caricature and totally irrelevant to that significant section of the contemporary population who are condemned to experience their freedom in self-destructive ways, or not to experience it at all.

Today's Young Catholic Adults

With these reflections on the contemporary culture in mind, we now come to look at the young adult Catholics of today and to the research on which the present chapter is based. This research is not of the sample survey type but rather rooted in the study of life histories collected by the author as part of an international study of young Catholics in six Western countries (see Fulton *et al.*, 2000). A quota sample was constructed using (a) religious practice and (b) partner status. Religious practice was used to distinguish core, intermediate, and distant and former Catholics. Partner status was used to distinguish single male, single female and partnered/married (of either sex) categories. A minimum of five people were recruited for each of the $3 \times 3 = 9$ combinations. Financial considerations meant that the research had to be limited to the Home Counties, though graduates have come from as far north as Edinburgh and as far west as Swansea. Sixteen interviewees had spent at least their pre-teen years outside of the South-East. This gives a measure of the geographical spread and experience of the opportunity sample. Three-quarters are graduates or final year under-graduates and the entire age range from 18 to 30 is included. A small number of additional interviews with 35-year-olds and with parents of our target generation are being conducted, and occasional meetings with 18-year-old school-leavers have also been conducted. The research is essentially qualitative and seeks to understand mentalities and ways of life, rather than how many hold views on this or that, or how frequently they go to church.

So far some 46 life histories have been collected, with another eight envisaged to complete some under-recruited quotas. It has proved too difficult to recruit sufficient numbers of working-class Catholics (those still in the working class as opposed to those working-class born who have moved up to middle-class positions by virtue of their education and/or job position and whom we have numbered among the middle class). From this point of view the sample has limitations. However, for the main constituent of the contemporary Church in England, which is increasingly middle class, the sample is likely to have a fair degree of representativeness in terms of the range and types of Catholic experience and outlook. It should be remembered that the Church in this country has lost a significant part of its working-class constituency, and that the middle class is the backbone of its parish organization.

Some initial remarks on the sample are helpful. Our sample of graduate and graduand sons and daughters of middle- and working-class parents were well aware of the labour market advantage most of them have been given over the 70 per cent of their cohort who have not had the same educational opportunities. However, the men were more likely to have moved into business careers and the women into working with people, with some of both sexes going into teaching. This division roughly follows the national employment trend for young adults (Bynner *et al.*, 1997). Those who were lower middle class and upper working class (cooks, mechanics, etc.) were mainly overworked, underpaid and tired at interview, a possible, though partial, explanation of why some working-class people have been difficult to recruit for the research.

One further point on the sample needs to be made. Considerable extra work would have been necessary to match men and women in each of the religious classifications used (core, intermediate, and former and marginal). The 'average' (intermediate) female single Catholic appears to be somewhat more active and committed than their male counterparts. Additionally, it proved far more difficult to find former Catholic women than it was to find former Catholic men. Yet again, 18–30 married or partnered core were very difficult to trace, and very unlikely to be involved deeply in any Church-oriented activities other than regular Mass attendance. However, at this point we have to note that fewer young people in the age group are marrying, mainly because of the instability of the labour market and the shortage of long-term employment (Bynner *et al.*, 1997).

From about halfway through collecting the life histories for England, it became very clear that women, whether partnered, married or single, but particularly if single, had to be further divided between 'ordinary core' and 'super-core'. Super-core is defined as those people who have assumed a significant pastoral role in the Church because of their prime dedication to their calling within the structures of the religious institution itself. The 'super-core' group of single women were relatively easy to find, whereas I could only trace with the same amount of application one young man in the same category, and he was going off as a lay missionary to Africa. Consequently the number of single female core was expanded to eight, containing five super-core, and three ordinary core. One woman in the married/partner group is also a super-core member.

Moral Identity and Autonomy of Conscience

First we deal with the general life orientation and moral identity of the Catholics and former Catholics in the sample. A key element to participation in social life is 'ontological security' (Giddens, 1991; Collins, 1997; 1998). The term refers to a sense of basic trust in life rooted in a certain level of mental, emotional and social stability, sufficient to enable both this trust and the establishment of a basic set of satisfactory human relationships. All members of the group showed this. The most common response to the question 'What is the most important thing in your life?' was 'my family and friends'. Like the majority of respondents, Teresa (super-core) considered self-esteem and freedom important aspects of her life. She also asserted the central importance of her close group of friends. A sense of self-assuredness appeared present among almost all, with only two, both churchgoers, showing signs of severe pressure on their personal sense of worth or purpose. All but these two also considered themselves to be 'in charge' of their life, as opposed to feeling 'dominated' by something.

The second and general characteristic of the group is their basic conviction of moral and personal autonomy in the sphere of personal ethics. This disposition is at its clearest in their pervasive attitude towards authority. Obedience is no longer a virtue, and there is no such thing as disobedience. It has been replaced by personal moral discernment and following one's conscience. This is the characteristic of all the life histories, and differentiates the present generation of young Catholics as a whole from post-war Catholicism, with its sense of obedience as virtuous and right, as opposed to disobedience as sinful and wrong. It also differentiates them from their parents' generation of Catholics, which was quite possibly divided on the subject.

This generally shared disposition does not prevent them from rejoicing in the name of Catholic. For example one of the super-core, whose whole life appears to be permeated by her faith, saw the present Pope as an obstacle to the present life of the Church:

> The Church's teachings are wonderful, but the encyclicals, the catechism are extremely negative, and [the Pope] has dejected the Catholic Church. It's being poorly structured, very poorly run. He believes in the sort of spiritual dimensions of, you know [you hear a lot of] the apostleship down from Peter and it's stilting the Catholic Church. I've got a lot of disappointment, and I hear a lot of that now that I'm at home. [People are] full of anger. (Paula, super-core, political activist and member of a Catholic lay community)

In terms of their relationships with their parents, some respondents even found their conservative mothers accepting of their own morality:

> *Interviewer:* Your mother is concerned about you?
> *Beth*: She's very concerned about my happiness ... She won't mind whatever I do, she won't mind that I am not the norm. She knows I am my own person and she will allow me to be like that. (Former Catholic)

While not a few commentators might see this view as one of individualism, we must point out that there were very few genuine individualists among them. There are one or two 'loners' in the life history group, people who seem to have few friends, but all the others feel they have and need support groups, family and close friends. As Beth, who was one of the few suspicious of the intimacy of marriage, says:

> You see I can't imagine just being with one person in a house. Really, my ideal would be to live on a farm. I would love to live on a farm and have lots of children. But I can't see a husband there. (Beth, former Catholic)

This sense of moral semi-autonomy applies at its most clear on sexuality.

The life histories reveal near unanimity that moral judgement on one's sexual conduct is something for the individual to decide and that there are no easy rules or prohibitions in the area. For example Linda ('Christ is the centre of my life'), who lives a celibate life herself, has 'an open mind' on relationships before marriage, and felt the Church was 'too narrow and eccentric' on such issues. Teresa (a counsellor), who sees herself as once 'narrow-minded' in this area, has come to share similar views. All but two of the life histories collected (both male and both marginal Catholics) show that sexual orientation and corresponding sexual practice are viewed in the main as a given, which people should accept and tolerate. A number explicitly stated that they did not accept the official Church position on the issue.

We now look at the religious faith and commitment of sections of the sample. We do it by looking at the differences and similarities between the three main classes of respondent, namely those of core, intermediate, and distant/former Catholics. First and mainly, we will deal with the core group.

Core Catholics

All of the super-core group, including Eddie (the missionary) and Dec (partnered, but who has been a salaried lay Church minister and now teaches religious education) want what we might term a professional life as a religiously active person, that is they want to earn their daily bread in this way, and are not particularly bothered either with how much bread they might be able to earn doing so. All but one of them have theology degrees. Also, they are all looking forward to pursuing these careers in their married life, though some wish to take time out bringing up a family. So these are not proto-religious order people (though they could be proto-married clergy). They are active in a variety of ways: some are deeply committed to the liturgy and to spending long hours in its preparation, be it in terms of music and song or in developing faith themes for celebration. One wishes to become a professional Catholic school counsellor. Another is deeply involved in human life politics and might end up a lay leader of a corresponding organization in the future. One person has a job in the caring professions, yet still finds time – virtually all her spare time – for public worship preparation and activity. Some are either involved as teachers of religious education in Catholic schools or are training for such.

All six women in the super-core category are also critical of the Church to which they are so committed in terms of the burning issues of current Church organization, namely married clergy and women priests. While they appreciate the outstanding witness of many clergy, they are also critical of what they consider the limitations of a large number of priests, feeling that some are simply not suited to their vocation or position in the Church for lack of appropriate talents, narrowness of outlook, or lack of suitability to the celibate life. Their treatment of women with equal talents to their own is a case in point. The experience of a school chaplain, Teresa, reflects their concerns:

> I know some priests who I think are wonderful and who have fulfilled their role ... seem to manage it very well. But there are others who, I think, are very lonely, and they are impossible to deal with. They surround themselves with admin. There's the example of a meeting that took place a couple of months ago, [involving] ... the priest who oversees ... my job. This other guy said I don't have to go to the meeting. [The priest] said I did, and finished up with, 'But look, I wanted you to make the coffee.' At this point I turned and walked out. This is at half six, having already done a ten hour day. In the evening you know! At this point I blew up. I can follow that with a comment about the following week ... We were in a liturgy committee meeting and he [the same priest] said [when] the husband of this lady made the coffee, 'Wouldn't it be good if priests had wives!' i.e. to make coffee during the meetings. This attitude, whether said in jest or not [pauses] ... – he wasn't joking.

The views of these core Catholic women reinforces the findings of Sharp, who found that her sample of parish women in the South-West were looking for more democracy in the Church, with those actively involved expressing dissatisfaction at not being allowed more authority and decision-making powers, especially the professional women among them (Sharp, 1998: 173).

These six young women have varying spiritualities, two centred on Christ as their closest friend and companion, two others more oriented to the Spirit, one simply experiencing the presence of God in her life and activities, especially having religious experiences through music and liturgy, and one primarily focused on meditation on the word of God. The other ten core members so far recruited (three single and two married women, and four single and one married man) are active as Catholic school teachers, participate in Lourdes pilgrimages and frequent retreats. They are mainly progressive in outlook also, though they vary in their views on celibacy and women priests. They are, in the main, set on a Catholic life course and are likely to be involved in ministries in the future. While some are clearly in periods of experimentation with life values, it seems that, so far, no serious rift or alienation is on the horizon which would take them away entirely from Church belonging. They seem well equipped to weather the storms of controversial Church teaching. It is their Church and they cannot imagine ever being pushed out. In fact there is virtually no way in a society like ours that they could be – only priests and religious can be controlled for faith by the Church hierarchy. At the same time, these core members share with the super-core a critical stance towards Church statements on public mores or policies, and are also critical of the dearth of meaningful liturgy in English Catholic churches.

The Spiritualities of both Core and Intermediate Catholics

Aspects of the spiritualities of our young adult churchgoers include silent worship and devotion to Mary. Sacred spaces are the Lourdes grotto, the community in celebration, a quiet chapel. But priests and bishops are no longer shrouded in sacrality, and pomp is viewed ambiguously. So while there may be fewer ecclesial sacred spaces and people, and the devotionalism to saints other than Mary has virtually disappeared, the sacred is still there, but has shifted to other locations. There is no yearning for the old ways also because those ways have never really been known. Our only representative of the old spiritualities was one of two 35-year-olds, whose life histories were documented to see to what extent they bore similarities to the 18–30 group.

While there is an acceptance by many that good liturgies do exist – one or two admit they have never experienced a 'decent' one at all (but these are confined to people whose liturgical experience is of one or two places only) – they all want greater preparation and enthusiasm in the Sunday liturgy. The Eucharist they appreciate is a community affair, where God is experienced as present within the assembly. At the same time, only a few of them have any sense of an encounter with Christ on reception of Communion. I probed continually on the matter, and found little sense of real eucharistic presence or of communion with Christ. One super-core member admits to having a significant problem with the Church's teaching on this; however, on probing, it appeared that she was confusing scholastic theology of transubstantiation with belief in the real presence, but then, many priests do too.

The most prevalent spirituality of worship was in terms of a sense of simple divine presence. Almost all had felt uncomfortable with being asked how or with what image they thought of God. For this generation, God is what God is not, a kind of *via negativa* of understanding the divine. In this way, the research tends to confirm work in Europe such as that of Dobbelaere in Belgium (1998) on the abstractness of contemporary religious perception. Perhaps the abandonment of devotionalism in the 1960s was so wholesale that encounters for succeeding generations with the humanity of Christ often disappeared along with it and might need great efforts to rebuild. Whether or not this is a sign of postmodernity is for the reader to judge.

The main spiritual renewal experiences these young people have encountered – and two-thirds of them have done so – are those of the retreat and the pilgrimage. Some retreats and 'overnights', on the occasion of Confirmation or a sixth-form special event, have had significant impact on a number of young adults, sufficient to re-orient or strengthen their religious faith. Nine have also experienced Lourdes pilgrimages with the handicapped. For three of these, a complete religious change has been the result. For four of the others, it has meant a deepening of their Christian faith. For one of these, it has meant a break-out from a life concerned with herself and her needs to one where she wishes to have a career working for other people. It is noteworthy that a substantial minority of interviewees had been confirmed before their teenage years, and have never had the opportunity which other 14–16-year-olds have of benefiting from the occasion to renew their religious faith through retreats and overnights. It is surprising that some dioceses still continue with this practice. From the impact of such occasions, it is clearly a golden opportunity lost at one of the crucial ages in the construction of personal identity and morality.

The caring professions and teaching were *preferred careers* for the majority of this sample. Only 20 out of 46 are or want to be involved in the world of business and administration. Having a meaningful job is greatly prized, and they generally do not wish to pursue a career to which they are not drawn. Significantly, only three so far put getting rich as a key goal, and these are in the distant and former Catholic category. Even the only confirmed woman atheist (Beth) in the sample – also wary of marriage – wishes to spend her life working with children and is drawn to the idea of a working community living off the land and to craft activities.

Some of the young adults are still mainly concerned with their own close circle of life. In fact a significant minority are not spontaneously aware of nation-wide issues they want to be dealt with. Of those who are, some are concerned with social breakdown:

> *I*: What's wrong with the country?
> *Ursula*: I think it's a total mess ... Where do you start. The laws for a start, they are a joke ... our society, I hate the way values – money is more important than human life.
> *I*: You think people should come first?
> *U*: Yes ... A lot needs to be done with children, they can go wild, they need play schemes for them.
> *I*: More needs to be done for young people, centres where they can play, clubs?
> *U*: But ... properly organized and properly supervised, not just have a place that will let them go riot still. Everyone needs to get a grip of their values, no-one seems to care any more and it's just a mess, it really is. (Intermediate, with experience of working-class housing estates)

Vera recognizes the extent to which her politics are linked to her own interests, and requires a government to be careful in spending her hard-earned money:

> [My opinions are] not unusually strong but I do think the questions of taxation and who's getting taxed and where the money is going and basically the state of the country and what has happened to it and why you see more and more people on the streets and why you can't get hospital treatment; so I think it's more a social awareness of if I am a taxpayer and I am paying all this money, why isn't the state of the country being brought up to [standard]. (Former Catholic)

Among churchgoers in particular, there is a strong sentiment of justice, particularly with regard to the way our society tolerates poverty and homelessness, and towards the plight of the developing world:

Neil: I think there is a lot more that could be done for homeless people in London because obviously I see that quite a lot and I think it would be very easy to do something about it. (Businessman; intermediate)

On the Third World, Luke, who finds it very difficult to express his opinions, has been very active in fund-raising for CAFOD projects by putting on charity meals and cooking them himself. All but one of the super-core were passionate about social justice across the board, whether at home or abroad. The sentiment is equally strong towards the maintenance of a welfare state, more than one might have expected from the average English undergraduate or graduate.

I: What's wrong with the country?
Terry: Our public services. It's frustrating. The education system. It drives me mad. It's the fact that – and the health system – this choice thing, they say you've got the choice to send your children to whatever school you think is fine. But of course you can send your children to whatever school would like them. And then what happens is ghetto-like schools. Some schools get good results which put them at the top, bound to be full, and the result is the other school is under-achieving. You know, we must do something about it ... (Non-graduate; in business; intermediate)

There is equally a strong environmental consciousness and much sense of the inadequacy of what they personally could do. In fact, despite the awareness, there is little consciousness of the role politics might play in tackling these issues, perhaps a sign of the gap which has opened in our society between moral consciousness and political action with the fragmentation of social class allegiances.

Life issues

The moral problems of abortion, euthanasia and capital punishment are keenly felt by core and intermediate Catholics, with distant and former Catholics having the least sensitivity, and some of the latter also approving generally of these practices. This does not mean that they have a total root and branch approach. Only capital punishment is viewed in absolute terms of rejection or acceptance. Views on abortion and euthanasia are less so, with substantial aversion to abortion in particular balanced by views on what might sometimes be seen as a necessity and by the warning that only the woman facing up to the choice can really make the moral choice. None of the interviewees, including a pro-Life activist, actually voiced the opinion that abortion should be criminalized or totally banned.

When they do comment, most take the stance of Evelyn (intermediate Catholic) who is quite aware she disagrees with the official Church position on the subject: 'Everyone is entitled to their own choice ... It's a hard choice for any woman. [But] I do have reverence for life.' A significant number of women go on to say, like Brenda (intermediate), 'But I would never have one.' In general, Gill (intermediate) summarizes the general opinion of the overwhelming majority: 'I never just say yes it's right just because the Church says. I do very much have my own opinion.' Then, echoing the views of both intermediate and core Catholic women, she goes on to say, 'I am very much interested in what the Church teaches, but my own view is that it's just not practical ... it's just out-dated. But I am influenced by the Church.' Some of the pro-Life feelings of the women were based on experience. Ursula (intermediate) resisted the efforts of her practising Catholic parents to get her to have an abortion. She was being taken into the operating theatre when she finally decided she had had enough pressure, got off the trolley, voided her consent and walked out of the hospital.

Influence of Other Religions

Despite the popular view that young people are experimenting with all kinds of Eastern religion, modern sects and movements like paganism, New Age and other cults, there is very little in our sample to suggest much in the way of leanings to these. While surveys tend to highlight extensively popular beliefs in such things as superstition, reincarnation, astrology and spiritualism, in teenagers (Francis and Kay, 1995; 1996) and adults (27 per cent of the British population according to Harding *et al.*, 1986: 46), our young adults have little if any interest in them. If people are ticking boxes in surveys to indicate they believe in reincarnation, one wonders if they have either confused the topic with the incarnation or have simply ticked an interesting idea which they think might be true, rather than having anything like a significant belief (though clearly a small minority of Western adults definitely do).

Distant and Former Catholics

It has been relatively easy to find young men in the distant or former Catholic category but somewhat more difficult to find single women in the same. This suggests the possibility that either there may be less loss to Catholicism among women compared with men, or that women leavers rather than men put more distance between themselves and the Church. We have called people 'distant' in the life-history sample if they call themselves 'Catholic' despite their convictions that the Church itself is quite irrelevant to their lives and the actual absence of what might be termed Catholic sensitivities, such as abortion and concern for the Church. Eight of the life histories have been identified as of this kind so far, seven from the children of practising Catholics and one the child of a non-practising one.

Rather than believing or belonging, theirs is a form of association, an identity badge worn by a distant supporter of the people who call themselves Catholic, with or without actual association with the institution or its beliefs. In fact there is generally little time for the Church as an institution among this group. The main positive feeling is one of acknowledgement of the 'good basic moral education' they have had from their family and Catholic school. Malcolm, son of traditional Irish Catholic parents, and Kevin, son of a practising Catholic father, see the Church as a meaningless and boring place and the costs of going outweigh any benefit. As an institution it has provided either the wrong solutions or none at all to the problems of today's world. For some of this group's members a modicum of affection for the Church remains, but the majority have largely left it behind, along with their childhood.

The data here suggest a research question long neglected by social scientists, namely whether Church decline is much affected by steady family dissociation from the Church over three or four generations. If this were to be the case, then the study of individually conscious Church 'leavers' (the subject of Richter and Francis's study, 1998) would represent only one path of Church decline. It would become important to complement such studies with the three-generational research of families, to trace whether and how such familial Church dissociation takes place.

Finally, there are six self-designated former Catholics so far in the sample. They include Beth, an atheist, who was a children's liturgy leader in her parish although she had, even then, little inclination to religious belief. She had to attend church because of her (Irish) mother. Because she liked children, she found it easier to tell stories about Jesus and supervise activities than sit in church and undergo the pain of boredom. George, while at university, has become convinced that there is no God, or insufficient evidence to believe, despite having a sound Catholic education and an exemplary Catholic mother. Harry has joined an evangelical sect along with his mother, partly in distaste at continuing Catholic over-concern with the saints and Mary, as opposed to Jesus and because of the 'bad' example of a priest. Sam, the son of committed and active Catholics, no longer identifies a personal God, but has found reverence in the aesthetic aspects of human existence, his own artistic creativity, and the environment.

A Changing Catholic Identity

The sample of young Catholic believers reveals a number of lively and deeply committed young adult Catholics, for whom their Christian faith is a driving force in their lives. The super-core among them is made up mainly of single women who wish to devote themselves full-time to institutional Church ministries. But they are highly critical of the clerical Church and in the main promote a married clergy and, at least in the long run, the ordination of women. Perhaps Church leaders will be most worried about the lack of perception and conviction on the Eucharist, despite the gain of a communal sense of the sacred which has developed over the past 35 years.

A second group of Catholics share with the first a commitment to careers particularly in working for other people, but are less fired up with their Christian Catholic faith and they keep it ticking over rather than feeling it as central. They remain practising Catholics but have less than weekly attendance. Like core Catholics, they have left the ghetto Church behind, along with its focus on the cycle of sin. They are in the main oriented to a positive evaluation of their life and to what they can do rather than what they can avoid.

A third group, very anomalous in their cultural and moral orientations but all having largely given up their Church attendance, show a willingness and desire to be identified as Catholics, but exhibit varying degrees of marginality. Their children are unlikely to continue with the same minimum degree of identification, unless something like a career as a Catholic school pupil intervenes – and some distant Catholics say they will choose this for their own children. A fourth, also anomalous group, no longer present themselves as being Catholic and only one of them remains a Christian by faith.

One overall conclusion is that, at the personal level, a subtle but significant change in Catholic identity has occurred over the past thirty years, one which is incremental to that experienced in the post-conciliar period, and which manifests itself in the lives of our young adults. Precepts will not stick with this generation. As clergy very well know, exhortations on 'no sex before marriage' will not be heeded unless their personal experience tallies with the message. Liturgy is important to them but only when it is meaningful and participatory. They continue to stay in the Church even if they disagree with its leadership.

However, core Catholics do get upset about such disagreements. This might mean they could begin a lengthy process of disconnection if the balance of satisfaction were tipped the wrong way and disenchantment or anomie set in. But rather than they themselves disaffiliating, it might be their children, influenced by their parents' negative experiences and never having had the powerful commitment that Mum or Dad had, who experience increased marginality, with a subsequent generation no longer identifying with the faith at all. Perhaps the very precarious nature of success or failure in contemporary society will increase their personal distance, and the suspicion which some of them have about the bonds of matrimony will be mirrored in their ambiguity over their Catholic belonging. In this sense their participation in the high modern culture of self-reflexivity and uncertainty (Furlong and Cartmel, 1997) will be extended to their religious consciousness, which may even lapse altogether.

At the institutional level, the Church today is certainly leaner so far as young adults are concerned. But there are also signs of fitness in that it is developing a significant and strong core of committed, mainly progressive activists. But more women than men are experiencing a 'vocation' in this way, yet do not find the appropriate institutional structures in which to express and expand this vocation. If on the one hand the materialist institutions of consumerism make inroads on the conscience and consciousness of the new generation of young adults, on the other hand the spiritual institutions of the Church bar the spiritual aspirations of its young women from what they feel are their appropriate places in the ranks of Christian authority and ministry.

From this angle, the research would support the viewpoint that the celibate and male priesthood as exclusive power-holder, authority and gate-keeper to the sacramental life of the Church is an obstacle to the wealth of religious energy possessed by women in contemporary Western and, in this case, English society. Perhaps one of the ways forward for Church reform is the inculturation of Church order and diversification according to country and people's spiritual culture.

10

The Religio-Ethnic Identities of Teenagers of Irish Descent

Mary J. Hickman

Catholicism and Irish Identity

The aim of this chapter is to explore certain aspects of the relationship between Catholicism and Irish identity amongst people of Irish descent in England. Irish identity or being of Irish descent is usually viewed as of declining significance in any account of contemporary Catholicism in England. My contention is that it remained relevant long after its dated demise, and that if the relationship between Catholicism and Irish identity is changing now it is doing so for different reasons to those usually cited as explaining its diminishing importance.

An identifiable Irish Catholicism is generally recognized to have existed in England until the 1950s. For example, the Church of England's report *Faith in the City* (1985), which is an indictment of the failure of the Anglican Church in the inner cities, offers the following analysis of the factors which caused the Catholic Church and the Catholic working class to stick together long after that relationship had disintegrated for other Churches:

> Its English history after the Industrial Revolution is quite different because of the influence from the mid-nineteenth century onwards of the large migrations from Ireland to many English cities. For many of the migrants from Ireland (where the ruling class was mainly English and Protestant) Roman Catholicism seemed to be in tune

with Irish nationalism and to be marked by a pastoral presence among the poor ... For the Irish immigrant to England therefore, the Roman Catholic Church with its quota of Irish priests was a natural focal point for communities in poor housing and with poor job security in an urban environment, and facing in addition the threat of the loss of cultural identity. As Roman Catholics felt themselves becoming accepted in the wider community, secularization took its toll and religious practice declined. Irish migration, however, was a process continuing at various levels over more than a century. The lapsation from practice was therefore marked by a periodical reinforcement of the Irish community – a reinforcement which is now largely in decline. (Quoted in Darwen, 1986: 268)

Faith in the City implies that the assimilation/fading away of the specifically Irish Catholic experience has led to secularization.

In contrast, Hornsby-Smith (1987b; 1991), who has written extensively on the subject, argues that the assimilation of Irish Catholics has resulted in normative convergence with English Catholicism and the disappearance of a persistent and distinctive subculture of Irish Catholicism in England. Hornsby-Smith argues that normative convergence occurs in the first generation. In particular, he cites convergence of non-creedal beliefs, e.g. on moral issues such as abortion, contraception and divorce. The implication is that on migration the Irish move more quickly to a rejection of the Church's teaching in these areas than if they had stayed in Ireland.

His argument is, therefore, that meaningful belonging for English Catholics has been transformed from a religio-ethnic identity to a voluntary religious commitment. He also argues that the large decline in Mass attendance figures since the 1950s does not necessarily indicate that Catholicism in England is losing its social significance; rather that Catholic identity has shifted from the involuntary 'collective-expressive' form to the voluntary 'individual-expressive' form, with the growth of a rational-pragmatic world-view amongst Catholics.

As argued elsewhere (Hickman, 1995), one aim of the Catholic Church during the past 150 years has been to render invisible the Irishness of its predominantly Irish congregation and to achieve a situation where Catholicism became the significant identity of the Irish working class in England. The Catholic Church, in the decades after Catholic emancipation, had as its central objectives the prevention of leakage of Irish migrants and the enhancement of the respectability and legitimacy of the

Church. The Irish in Britain threatened the desired respectability and as a result the Catholic Church constructed its mission to the Irish as a mission of retention and incorporation. The Catholic Church developed a strategy to win its Irish congregation to a version of Catholicism which entailed denationalization, attempting to substitute a religious identity for the Irish national identity which constituted the hallmark of Irish working-class communities in England.

The long-term aim of the Catholic Church, therefore, was to strengthen the Catholic identity of Irish migrants at the expense of weakening their national identity. Education became a central element of this strategy of the Church, especially with respect to the second and subsequent generations. The 1836 Report, *The State of the Irish Poor in Great Britain*, outlined the advisability of regulating the Irish: '... their mode of life is very slowly and very slightly improved unless some civilising influence descends upon them from above, some external moving force independent of their own volition, as of masters, employers, super-intendents, education ...' (quoted in Jones, 1977: 61). In particular, the moral regulation of the second-generation Irish was thought to be possible. Various Catholic priests gave testimony to this effect; for example, an English Roman Catholic priest stated in evidence: 'The children of Irish, born in Liverpool, generally go on well; they learn the habits of the English, are more careful and provident than those born in Ireland. They are willing and active. There is a decided amelioration in the English-born Irish; the longer they stay the more they improve' (ibid.: 50).

A Roman Catholic bishop argued the case, at the 1836 Inquiry, for state aid to Catholic schools: 'To improve the feelings, the conduct, the morals, and the loyalty of the Irish Roman Catholic poor in this country, it would be necessary that the Government should, at least, extend the same assistance for education as is granted to them in Ireland' (ibid.: 62). In this statement, not only is education posited as the means by which a transformation of the Irish could be achieved, it is also argued that education would be the best means of securing the loyalty of the Irish. The problem of loyalty did not arise in the same form with the other constituent parts of the working class. The loyalty of the Irish could only be won by a process of denationalization. This was to be implicit in any educational response to the 'Roman Catholic problem' in education.

The aims of Catholic schools, as articulated by the Catholic Poor School Committee, were to transform the Irish into useful citizens, loyal subjects, respectable members of the working class and good Catholics.

The interests of the government and the Church were consistently presented as mutually reinforcing. The expansion of Catholic education was carried out in a manner which ensured the control by the clergy of the schools. Catholic schooling was increasingly subject to central direction of the Catholic Poor School Committee and, therefore, some uniformity in the experience of Catholic education could be assumed.

The incorporating and denationalizing aims of Catholic education were implemented by interrelated strategies. The school involved the local Irish community, practising and non-practising alike, in raising funds for and building the schools and in sending their children to the schools. This involvement of Irish communities in constructing and supporting Catholic education became the very means of incorporating the Irish working class. The involvement of the Irish community in creating the Catholic education system became a crucial means of strengthening their Catholic identity.

From the beginning of the Catholic elementary system the content of the secular education of Irish working-class children in Britain contained little reference to Ireland. What mention was made of Ireland in the new Catholic readers, which replaced the Irish lesson-books later in the nineteenth century, primarily praised the Catholicity of the Irish as their outstanding feature and otherwise contained lessons on the political economy of Ireland. These characteristics of the Catholic schools' curriculum were little changed over a century later. The identity of Irish working-class children as Catholics was implanted and constantly reinforced in the schools by the priority placed on religious instruction, in the effort which went into religious instruction, and in the manner in which the religious pervaded all the rituals of school life. This was a strategy of incorporation. There was a corresponding silence in the curriculum content of Catholic schools about Ireland. This was a strategy of denationalization.

The long-term success of the Church lay not in the eradication of all Irish identities (although denationalization was successful in specific conjunctures) but in gaining acquiescence to the necessity of a low public profile for Irish Catholic communities and individuals. Thus the low public profile, or invisibility, of the Irish in Britain is the main achievement of the state and institutional response to the Irish presence in nineteenth-century Britain. The success of the incorporatist strategy of the Church lay in its being the agency of a low public profile for the Irish in Britain. The production of this low public profile is frequently misrecognized as a process of assimilation. A low profile is not evidence of assimilation but of a specific response by Irish people to the various anti-Irish and anti-Catholic discourses and practices which have been encountered and negotiated within the context of specific communal institutions. In contrast, issues which were sanctified by the Church, for example education, did not have a low profile, because these issues had not only the backing, but the exhortation, of a powerful institution.

In Catholic histories of education there is a clear acknowledgement that an extensive Catholic state education system would not have developed in the nineteenth century but for the migration of the Irish to Britain. Selby (1974), writing about the Catholic reaction to the 1870 Education Act, comments that: 'it is always important to remember that without the Irish there would have been no Catholic elementary-school problem in the second half of the century' (Selby, 1974: 119). The 'problem' Selby is referring to is that of the need to provide sufficient Catholic school accommodation at the time of the introduction of board schools in 1870. Apart from a few areas in northern England – for example, Preston – and certain parts of Scotland, the pressing need to build more Catholic elementary schools was a response to the presence of Irish Catholics and their offspring in Britain.

The small number of histories of Catholic education available chart the struggle to both establish and control Catholic schools. Relatively little attention, however, is given to the pupils the schools were teaching or to what it was they were being taught. The emphasis is on the obstacles the Church faced in the course of the construction of its school system. The main obstacles described are the poverty of the Catholic population and the need to defend denominational schooling, which increasingly became the policy of the Church from the 1850s onwards. The fact that Catholic elementary schools were full of Irish Catholics is not explored in great detail in these histories. For example, Beales in 1946, in one of his many essays on Catholic education, mentions in passing that the Irish famines of the 1840s added to the ranks of the 'uneducated Catholic poor'. This obscures the reality that most of the 'Catholic poor' already in the country were Irish or of Irish descent.

Evennett (1944), in the course of reviewing over a century of progress in Catholic education, pointed out that: 'Organised Catholic school policy has inevitably been dictated by the social composition of the Catholic community. A large Catholic working class, much of it Irish in origin, has grown up in the big industrial and commercial centres and forms the largest element in the total Catholic population' (Evennett, 1944: 9). Evennett recognizes that the social composition of the Catholic population has been a prime influence on Catholic schooling. However, his reference to the Irish is as brief as any other amongst the published histories of Catholic education. Catholic elementary schools, which served 'the largest element in the total Catholic population', are covered hurriedly in Evennett's study, which devotes most of its text to Catholic grammar and public schools. This reflects a general tendency to view the public and grammar schools, which served the English Catholic aristocracy and growing Catholic middle class, as the pinnacle of Catholic educational achievement. Consequently there are more studies of these schools than of Catholic elementary schools.

This tendency is replicated in recent texts. For example, Arthur (1995) discusses the critical developments of the 1830s–1840s entirely in terms of divisions within English Catholicism about elementary schools. He does not refer at any point to the wider debate of the place of Irish Catholic working-class children in national education arrangements. Arthur sees the principle obstacle to securing government grants for Catholic education as the refusal to sanction the reading of the Authorized Version of the Bible in Catholic schools. He therefore does not take account of the contradictions which existed: on the one hand, the orchestrated opposition to any funding of Catholic education and, on the other hand, the strong local campaigns to ensure that Irish working-class children were not educated with other working-class children. Nor is there any allusion to the complex relationship between Churches and the state and between religion and national identity which informed all debate about schooling for the working class in that era.

So accepted has the account of the assimilation of Irish Catholics become that recent books about Catholic education do not in any way explore the contemporary relationship between Catholicism and Irish identity; the assumption appears to be that these matters are of historical interest only. For example, McLaughlin *et al.* (1996) is a good example of a text which historicizes the Irish Catholic contribution to the English Catholic Church. Although recognizing that Irish immigrants form one of the distinct strands in the post-Reformation English Catholic community, this is discussed largely as a nineteenth-century phenomenon. No mention is made of the mid-twentieth-century migration from Ireland to England when over a half a million Irish migrants, predominantly Catholics, augmented the body of English Catholics.

Given the history of strategies which the English Catholic Church has had towards what in the state schooling system has been a majority of its constituency, it behoves anyone arguing for or assuming assimilation to demonstrate that issues of Irish heritage and/or identity are no longer relevant. It is not sufficient to assume the process has taken place because certain sets of questions do not reveal these allegiances.

The analysis presented here will attempt to explore the basis of the relationship between their Catholicism and Irishness for teenagers of Irish descent. My general proposition is that for teenagers of Irish descent different definitions of the Church/Catholicism will be related to variations in their national/regional identity. This means that differences in how the relationship to Catholicism is expressed by different groups of people of Irish descent are to be expected and these differences may be more sharply apparent whenever the questions make reference to Ireland or Irishness.

Teenagers of Irish Descent in London and Liverpool

This exploration of the meaning of Catholicism for teenagers of Irish descent in London and Liverpool took place in a wider research project, designed to examine the relationship between the British state, the Catholic Church and Irish immigrants in Britain (Hickman, 1990). The focus of the empirical research was on the role of Catholic education and identity in shaping the experience of those of Irish descent in England. Over a hundred in-depth structured interviews were conducted with teachers and pupils in four schools in London and Liverpool. Amongst many other questions they were asked some which specifically explored their national identity, the significance of Catholicism in their lives and their views about Catholic schools. In this chapter I am going to concentrate on the responses of the pupils.

National/Regional Identities

The small number of surveys which have been carried out about the identity of those of Irish descent in this country all confirm that, amongst the second generation, Irish identities are strong. It is significant that these studies have primarily been undertaken by interviewing teenagers who attend Catholic schools. This is obviously because the schools are an institutional location in which the second-generation Irish will be easily found. In the author's survey of the identity of pupils in Catholic schools in London and Liverpool, the pupils interviewed were all born in England; in London they were all second generation, in Liverpool they ranged from third to fifth generation. Amongst the London pupils 81 per cent named either 'Irish' or 'of Irish descent' as their primary identity, thus privileging their parents' national origins over the national identity of the country in which they were born. In Liverpool, in contrast, only 13 per cent chose an Irish identity as primary. On the other hand 65 per cent of the Liverpool sample perceived themselves to be Liverpudlians (Scousers) before all else, thus privileging a regional identity over the national identity of the country in which they were born. Only 18 per cent of the pupils of Irish descent selected 'British/English' as their primary identity (Hickman, 1990).

This is consistent with the other surveys of the identity of children of Irish descent in Catholic schools (*Irish Post*, 23 December 1970: 5; Ullah, 1985). In these surveys a maximum of a quarter of the second generation identify solely as British/English. This is striking given all the assumptions made about the assimilation of the Irish. Ullah (1985), a social psychologist, investigated the extent to which the second-generation Irish feel that they belong to a group which is defined as a low-status group, and the psychological strategies they utilize to avoid the negative feelings which can result from this. He concluded that there was ample evidence that the second generation Irish considered that they belonged to a group who were viewed as of low status.

The London pupils I interviewed lived in a strong, self-expressive Irish community, with their own sense of identity tied closely to the importance of the family in their lives. The large majority of the pupils and their families visited Ireland regularly and participated in Irish social and cultural activities. All the London pupils were second generation with both their parents born in Ireland. Social-class background had no impact on ties of allegiance to Irishness of the London sub-sample. The London pupils represented the raw material which for several generations Catholic schools have received and which has been subject to strategies of incorporation and denationalization. In contrast, the Liverpool sample included pupils whose parents, grandparents or even great-grandparents were second-generation Irish entering Catholic schools; they had been the raw material entering the schools in the past. The Liverpool pupils, as expected, provided an opportunity to examine a sample of pupils whose families and community had been subject to incorporation and denationalization for a number of generations.

Significantly, very few of the Liverpool pupils have visited Ireland or participate in Irish social and cultural activities. The Irish roots of the Catholic population in Liverpool are masked by an identity, Liverpudlianism, based on the perception of the city as unique. One feature which makes Liverpool different from the rest of the country is the high proportion of Catholics in the population. Liverpudlianism is essentially a working-class identity emerging out of the history of the city which is made up of the experience of a number of migrant groups, the largest of which is Irish Catholics. My research suggested that the weakening of identification with Irish origins over the generations in Liverpool can only be understood as the outcome of a complex set of factors. In particular, this has involved the strengthening of the Catholic identity of the city's Irish population, the development of a strong mediating identity and processes of social mobility. The analysis of the responses of the Liverpool pupils suggested that Liverpudlianism is a mediating identity which can encompass identification with Irishness or Britishness.

The findings reveal that, although Irish identity does weaken with generation, this is not the consequence of an inevitable process of adjustment to British society, rather that the weakening of Irish identity is the consequence of the pressures of incorporation. Social class, region and participation in Irish cultural practices are significant factors both in the denationalization of the Irish and in the resistance to incorporation. The survival of Irish identity is more likely if the individual of Irish descent is of working-class origins, lives in an Irish area, visits Ireland regularly and participates in Irish social and cultural activities. In these circumstances someone of Irish descent who is third- or fourth-generation Irish would select an Irish identity to describe himself or herself.

Meaning of Being a Catholic

When asked: 'What does being a Catholic mean to you?', the responses of the interviewees fell into three categories: Catholic communality; family; and religious practices. 'Catholic communality' entails a 'sense of belonging' to a specific community which is embracing. The responses grouped under the heading of 'family' are those where the meaning of Catholicism is directly linked to being brought up a Catholic within the family. A final group of respondents detailed the practices and beliefs of Catholicism as representing its essential meaning.

Eighty-eight per cent of the pupils interviewed in London and 82 per cent in Liverpool stated that their religion was meaningful to them. What divergence there was between the samples lay in the reasons given for the relevance religion had in their lives. Seventy-three per cent of the London pupils stated that their religion was important to them in terms of a communal or family identity. In Liverpool the equivalent responses were given by 56 per cent of the pupils. However, in Liverpool, 28 per cent indicated that it was the religious beliefs and practices encompassed by Catholicism which were most meaningful to them. In London the equivalent response was given by 15 per cent of the pupils.

When the samples were examined separately the main variation was discovered in the London sample. Fifty-two per cent of the pupils in London who selected an Irish identity as primary said that it was a communal identity which rendered their religion meaningful to them. In contrast none of the pupils in London who selected either a regional or British/English identity gave this reason. Despite the small numbers involved this difference is statistically significant. In London, therefore, the tendency to perceive Catholicism in terms of community meanings rather than as a religious entity can be accounted for by the responses of those who chose an Irish identity as most significant for them.

Taken overall 62 per cent of the pupils said that the strength of Catholicism lay in the fact that it is intertwined in their family and/or community identification. The quotations below are examples of what pupils who emphasized Catholic communality stated:

Catholicism is my identity; I have a fellow-feeling to all Catholics.

It's quite important, I'd have quite a lot in common with a Catholic, background and that.

I go to church, it's quite important for most Irish isn't it?

I'm not a very strict Catholic, but it sticks with you. I'd always argue back if anyone put the Catholic faith down and I'd look twice at anyone Orange.

I go to church every week. Round here, old-fashioned Liverpool, it's very Catholic. I like being a Catholic, belonging to it.

The strong sense of connectedness either to their immediate community or to Catholics as a body is clear in these statements. Catholicism had to embrace both aspects if it was to become rooted in the Irish working-class areas which have formed the majority of Catholic parishes in England. Interestingly, when asked about the connection between Irishness and Catholicism in this country 62 per cent of the London pupils thought that Irishness and Catholicism were synonymous in England. In Liverpool, in comparison, 28 per cent of the pupils thought that the two were synonymous. However, despite this difference the vast majority of the pupils, 86 per cent, thought that Irishness and Catholicism were associated to one degree or another.

Thus my research in an Irish area associated with nineteenth-century migration, Liverpool, and one typical of the 1950s emigration, London, shows that Catholic communality remains the prime reason given for the meaning of Catholicism. This has a number of implications for the argument about the continuing salience of religio-ethnic identity and a collective-expressive form for Catholic identity being developed here.

Responsibility of Catholic Schools

The vast majority of the pupils in both London and Liverpool, 91 per cent, were of the view that there should be more teaching about Ireland in schools. They were more divided about how this should be facilitated and about whether Catholic schools had any special responsibility in this respect. The reasons the pupils in both London and Liverpool gave for thinking that curriculum content on Ireland should be expanded fell into three main categories. For some, particularly in Liverpool, the chief rationale was that many people had their 'roots' in Ireland and ought to have the opportunity of learning about Ireland in that context:

Yes, a lot come from Ireland but don't understand much about it.

Yes, a lot of people in Liverpool are Irish descendants and hardly know anything about it.

Yes, most people in this school have an Irish background and we don't think about it enough, what I know comes from relatives or being over there.

Yes, it's near to us and if anything happens there it will affect us and people want to know about their background.

Yes, it's only across the water and there's a lot of Irish descent, only have to look at this school, and it would be interesting to know about our ancestors.

These responses reveal an interest in and wish to know more about their background on the part of the Liverpool pupils, and are a further indication of the extent to which this interest is not catered for at the present time. Ireland is consequently an unknown country even though geographically close. This is summed up in the following quotation: 'Yes, not many know about the Irish, they're a bit unknown.'

A number of other pupils, again especially in Liverpool, thought that the main reason for extending curriculum content on Ireland was because of the existence of prejudiced views about the Irish:

Yes, we're blaming them for everything and don't know what they are like, people themselves, culture and that.

Yes, everyone thinks Ireland is a trouble country but it's not all like that and we could learn about it.

Yes, everyone hates them for being stupid and they're not, then they'd understand all their problems instead of just thinking they kill each other.

Yes, because there is a lot of prejudice against them.

A number of other pupils wanted more teaching on Ireland in the hope that it would enable people to understand the situation in Northern Ireland better:

Yes, there's a lot of political statements about Northern Ireland; people don't understand why troops are there and why people don't want them. They just show shooting and bombing on telly, not the people.

Yes, because we'd get to know what they're fighting about, can't tell on telly.

Yes, should let more people know what's going on over there, not just rely on the media, about the difficulties of ordinary people.

Yes, about the IRA, why they're there and why soldiers are there, because sometimes you don't know about it and why they are shooting might be a good reason.

The emphasis in Liverpool is on wanting to know more about Northern Ireland, as they clearly felt that there was no real source of information on the subject. In London the import was more that there should be teaching about Northern Ireland so that other people would find out the true situation, the implication being that these pupils were already aware. Whether to learn about their background, to combat prejudice or to clarify what is happening in Northern Ireland, most of the pupils think there should be more teaching about Ireland than is currently the case.

The pupils were also asked whether Catholic schools had any special responsibility to teach about Ireland. Although 91 per cent had stated that they thought there should be more teaching on Ireland generally in England, when it came to the question of Catholic schools only 43 per cent considered that these schools had a particular responsibility to increase the curriculum content on Ireland, while 50 per cent of the pupils said that Catholic schools definitely did not have such a responsibility 8 per cent were uncertain. In both cities they were divided on this issue.

Those who did not think teaching about Ireland should be expected at Catholic schools any more than at other schools were divided into two groups. On the one hand, it can represent caution about the impact on other minorities in the school or, on the other hand, caution about prescribing on such matters for the school. Both types of reply appear defensive of the context of Catholic education. It is also possible that a negative response to this question could represent a further affirmation of the pupils' view that all schools should learn more about Ireland and that such learning should not be confined to those of Irish descent.

There was a preponderance of wary replies in London amongst the pupils who answered 'yes' to this question. The pupils in Liverpool emphasized that Catholic schools do have a special responsibility. The reason for this special responsibility is either because so many attending the schools are of an Irish background or because of the need to explain the situation in Northern Ireland.

The divergence in views between the London and Liverpool pupils on this question reflects the different situations in which they were responding. In London not only was a great deal of attention paid in the 1980s to the issue of multicultural or anti-racist education, but most of the discussion was in terms of the need to address the needs of black children. In the London schools, where the cautionary statements were made about the impact of the introduction of an Irish dimension, the pupils who were not second-generation Irish were mostly black, reflecting the mainly black and Irish area of London in which the schools were situated.

In Liverpool, because of the area of the city in which the schools were located, the pupils were predominantly white and inevitably, given the history of Liverpool's Catholic population, were of Irish descent. The patterns of residential segregation established in Liverpool in the nineteenth century between the black and white and the Catholic and Protestant populations still persist where people have not been rehoused beyond the city boundary. When these interviews took place there had been less attention given to multicultural or anti-racist education in Liverpool. This was especially true at the level of local education authority advice to schools. In London a large number of educational authorities offer such advice and especially in the area where the sample schools are located. Thus the replies of the pupils in Liverpool were more clearly focused on the responsibilities of Catholic schools to the people of Irish descent attending them. In comparison, in London the question was inevitably more complex for the pupils to answer and this possibly accounts for the wary tenor of many of their replies.

There can be no doubt that there has been a silence in most Catholic schools about Northern Ireland during the past thirty years. The issue has been so sensitive that even the dominant consensus in the 1980s in England (that the crisis in Northern Ireland is of Irish making and the British presence is primarily that of peace-keeper) was not transmitted. Catholic schools were one of the few institutional sites where this consensus might have been challenged, because the pupils potentially had access to alternative accounts of British–Irish relations. However, the strong identification of pupils of Irish descent with Catholicism means that many are reluctant to assign specific responsibility to Catholic schools for introducing teaching about Ireland. This is the case even though an overwhelming majority would like more teaching about Ireland included in their schooling.

Catholic schools' practice of ignoring Ireland, especially Northern Ireland, despite the concern of the pupils who attend the schools, has formed a continuing strategy of denationalization. This strategy has varying degrees of success, as has always been the case. In London, second-generation pupils are frequently the recipients of accounts of Irish history at home, and their views on Northern Ireland can be correspondingly divergent from the dominant consensus. A majority of the London pupils I questioned viewed the relationship between Britain and Ireland as the root cause of the conflict and supported a United Ireland or negotiations which included Sinn Fein (Hickman, 1990). Their acquiescence that Northern Ireland is a taboo subject at school (most reported they did not discuss the subject at school) is therefore all the more striking. This acquiescence may signify their investment in education which requires that they maintain a low profile in order to do well, even if this requires an apparent acceptance of dominant British values.

The evidence presented in this chapter indicates that the relationship between Catholicism and Irish identity is complex for teenagers of Irish descent. For a majority of the respondents Catholicism represents their family/community. For the London pupils Catholic communality is bound closely to the Irish Catholic communities in which they live. The Liverpool pupils who refer to Catholic communality also mean that it gives them 'a sense of belonging', but to a body of Catholics rather than an identifiable national grouping. This suggests that herein lies part of the basis of the incorporation of the Irish in England, whereas in London a 'communality' exists which is perceived as fusing Irishness and Catholicism.

These findings also suggest that it has been a struggle for the Church to ensure that a religious identity is ascendant amongst its Irish congregation. The Church has won the struggle in the public sphere. However, the responses of the pupils in general about more teaching about Ireland indicate the extent of the interest that exists about Ireland and the effects of the lack of such teaching. In the private sphere, at home or in the community, Ireland is talked about and Irishness remains relevant. This is demonstrated in the replies of the London pupils.

For the Liverpool pupils the situation is different. They have been reared in a city in which Catholicism is acknowledged as a major religion although the Irish context of its history is masked in the public sphere. This is revealed both by the descriptions of the curriculum of the schools and by the pupils' overwhelming response in favour of more teaching about Ireland. The suggestion is that their interest in knowing more about Ireland stems from having been reared in a Liverpudlian culture which, in the private sphere, includes awareness of the Irish antecedents of much of the city's population.

National, Regional and Catholic Identities

The responses of the pupils in both London and Liverpool, when asked which identity they would select to describe themselves, are important data. A majority in each city did not select the nationality of the country they were born in as their primary identity. In London the vast majority of the pupils chose either 'Irish' or 'of Irish descent' to describe themselves. In Liverpool two-thirds of the pupils selected Liverpudlian as their primary identity. Only 18 per cent of the pupils interviewed selected British or English as their primary identity. This finding is important because it suggests that incorporatist strategies are not as effective in denationalizing the Irish as in strengthening the Catholic identity of the Irish in Britain.

It could be argued that the selection of the areas for research and of the pupils' sample increased the likelihood of producing this finding. This is true but does not undermine the importance of the finding, for three reasons. First, the widespread acceptance of the assimilation thesis about the Irish in Britain made it imperative for this investigation to establish that alternative identities are held by people of Irish descent. It is valid, in the circumstances, to commence research in areas where the hypotheses of incorporation and denationalization might most clearly be examined. Later, larger studies can explore the complexities of Irish identity in a wider range of locations. Second, the samples of pupils were small and selected in circumstances which may have produced different but homogeneous samples in each city. However, expected similarities did emerge between the London and Liverpool pupils about Catholicism and about the curriculum. Further, sufficient differences are produced within each sample to point to the role of social class, region and generation in Irish identity (see Hickman, 1990). Third, London has been the chief destination for Irish migrants since the Second World War and findings about the second generation in that city can plausibly claim to be representative of the descendants of the 1950s exodus from Ireland.

My own research, therefore, would question Hornsby-Smith's conclusions for the following reasons. The communal sense of belonging recorded as the predominant meaning attached to Catholicism by those of Irish descent suggests that a religio-ethnic identity remains strong. This is especially the case in London, where the majority of respondents were second-generation. In Liverpool the attachment to community also remains strong, though less explicitly linked to a sense of an Irish community, although that is a significant part of the oral history of the local culture which many commented on. This is not surprising given that for over a century the Catholic Church has been pursuing a strategy of denationalization and that in Liverpool the strategy has been pursued for a number of generations.

What, however, my findings do suggest is that a 'collective-expressive' form remains a linchpin of Catholicism in Irish areas, both new and old. The interviews with teachers in the same schools reinforced this conclusion (see Hickman, 1990). The experience of the 1940-1960s Irish immigrants is not documented in anything like the detail of those of the nineteenth century. However, evidence available (e.g. O'Grady, 1988) suggests that the Church and Catholic organizations were a central feature of the chief areas of Irish settlement. Significantly, the vast majority of Irish people in the 1950s-1970s continued to send their children to Catholic schools. It is the children of that phase of Irish immigration that are the second generation today.

These findings concern those who are actively involved in Catholicism. What of those who are not? Unlike Hornsby-Smith, I think the evidence does point to a degree of secularization. The crucial variables are probably social class and identity. For those of Irish descent who are socially mobile and become middle class, the likely routes are secularization, convergence with English Catholicism or retaining a collective-expressive basis to the meaning of their Catholicism. The stronger the Irish identity, the more likely that the first or the third path will be chosen. For those who are secularized their critique of the Church is not necessarily based on the Church's teaching on moral issues (this form of critique is encompassed within English Catholicism), but is possibly also based on a critique of the role of the Church in relation to the Irish community: for example, criticisms of the lack of teaching about Ireland and/or the Church's silence about Northern Ireland. For working-class Catholics of Irish descent the likely paths are either secularization or retaining a strong 'collective-expressive' meaning to Catholicism, still linked strongly to their Irishness for the first generation.

11

English Catholics and Divorce

Timothy J. Buckley CSSR

A New Social Context

In preparing a mission for a large Catholic secondary school in the Midlands, I and my fellow Redemptorists sought to engage a group of sixth-formers in the planning and presentation of the event. No longer did we consider it sufficient simply to turn up with our package and hope that it would work. The enthusiasm and interest of the group surprised us, but there were some telling moments in those preliminary discussions which reminded us of some of the radically different perspectives with which the younger generation is growing up. For example, when the sacrament of reconciliation was broached, one of the group immediately commented: 'But going to Confession is not something even people who go to Church do any more.' It is true that one young man immediately protested that he did, but it was clear that he was the exception.

One small sample does not provide us with a definitive indicator of the national situation. However, in my experience the reactions of those sixth-formers reflected a widespread attitude towards many aspects of Church teaching, which are born not of a theoretical understanding of the subject in question but simply from their experience of how things work. The fact is that fewer and fewer Catholics of any generation still regularly confess their sins. While older Catholics might be inclined to feel guilty about not going to Confession regularly because it has been instilled into them that this is necessary, the younger generation seem to experience no such tension.

I will not presume at this juncture to offer a value judgement; suffice it to say that for the most part people seem to be voting with their feet. No longer do they feel constrained to adhere to beliefs or practices because they are authoritatively taught; rather they seem to be determining their practice according to what they find helpful and life-giving. Much research remains to be done among the younger generation of Catholics to determine what influences are shaping their understanding of the faith, but my own research among the separated and divorced supports the above conclusion. What became clear was that once people are confronted with a critical situation in their own lives they are more inclined to reassess the principles that have previously governed their understanding. If these principles fail to provide convincing arguments in the face of the new situation, they are likely to adjust their behaviour accordingly.

In his review of my book *What Binds Marriage?* (1997), Kevin Kelly wrote:

> Buckley's book is timely and important. ... his is above all a 'listening' book. In fact, a very interesting feature of the book is the way he makes use of the findings of his listening exercise. He does not attempt to present tables of statistics or complex analyses of responses to set questionnaires. Instead he weaves quotations from various participants into his excellent reporting on the different support groups he listened to. (*Priests and People* (1998): 158–9)

It was encouraging to read this affirmation of my work, the result of an extensive piece of social and theological research between 1990 and 1995. Originally commissioned by the Conference of Bishops for England and Wales through their Marriage and Family Life Committee, I reported a summary analysis of my findings to the bishops in 1994 and completed the doctoral thesis for London University in 1995. Hundreds of people were involved in the social research as I sought to present an account of their experiences in the Catholic community and identify the causes of any dissatisfaction or distress.

The theological history of this question is long and complicated. The book isolates the Catholic definition of the bond as the key factor in limiting the Church's pastoral effectiveness for so many people. In my theological analysis I offer a way forward out of the impasse and challenge the magisterium to address the question in view of the considerable injustices that arise out of the present dispensation. In this chapter I will concentrate on a further analysis of the findings of my social research as it reflects the Catholic community's struggle with authority at the end of the second millennium. It is always difficult to make accurate diagnoses of how the prevailing social conditions help to shape people's opinions and behaviour, but there is ample evidence that Catholic opinion on a wide range of ethical issues has significantly shifted during the second half of the twentieth century (see Hornsby-Smith, 1991: 117–209).

Certainly my research would support the conclusion that in general even many committed Catholics are no longer willing to accept the opinion or judgement of the Church as sacrosanct simply because it is backed by the authority of the magisterium. I propose that there are two major contributory factors that have led to this change of attitude. The first is the reform undertaken within the Church itself and given expression above all in the documents of the Second Vatican Council. The second is the influence of the wider society, where for many people a liberal and *laissez-faire* attitude tends to hold sway. There is a certain irony in the fact that the Catholic Church has partially invited this challenge to its authority by its own reforming process, and to that extent the two influences go hand in hand.

While the Church remained in its fortress mode, defending the faith by means of apologetics and viewing the outside world as a threat – something from which the faithful had to be protected – the majority of Catholics tended to be subservient. There was an implicit trust that those in authority knew what was right and had a duty to proclaim it. But with the advent of Vatican II something radically new was called for: a dialogue with the world. The Pastoral Constitution on the Church in the Modern World, *Gaudium et Spes,* not only claims to have a message for 'the whole of humanity' (§2; in Abbott, 1966: 200), but also explicitly seeks 'the proper fostering of mutual exchange and help in matters which are in some way common to the Church and the world' (§40; ibid.: 239).

The struggle has been played out in no more acutely sensitive an arena than that of sexual ethics. Vatican II coincided with the sexual revolution of the Sixties. Attitudes inside and outside the Catholic Church changed radically as people broke free from the old social and religious strictures and experimented with new forms of relationship and lifestyle. Again it was *Gaudium et Spes* that provided the basis for a changing mentality among Catholics. Chapter 1 of Part II, *The Dignity of Marriage and the Family,* reversed centuries of negative and taboo attitudes towards sex, presenting it rather as something 'noble and honourable', stating that 'the truly human performance of these acts fosters the self-giving they signify and enriches the spouses in joy and gratitude' (§49; ibid.: 253).

It would be difficult to exaggerate what a remarkable development this was, escaping from the age-old oppression of Gnostic and Stoical influences which have bedevilled the theology of marriage throughout the Church's history. Now the love of the spouses is taught to be at the very heart of the mystery of Christian marriage (see Lawler, 1993: 70–2; Dominian, 1991: 3-7). Thirty years later this may not sound very revolutionary, but once the subject of sex could be viewed as a gift to be rejoiced in, not a problem to be tolerated, Catholic attitudes were bound to change. Some of this change may have been unconscious and almost imperceptible, but allied to the external influences of changing social attitudes in Britain the result was that in some areas Catholic opinion and practice seems to have differed little from the rest of society. Divorce is one such subject. As early as 1978 Hornsby-Smith was able to state that 'overall, Catholics are not any less prone to divorce than members of the population at large' (Hornsby-Smith, 1991: 183).

My perception is that this remains an accurate reflection of the current situation. I base this judgement both on my research among the divorced as well as on a considerable amount of anecdotal evidence, especially from Catholic schools and colleges, which report high percentages of children and young people from broken homes and/or living with step-parents. A recent survey on the Catholic Church in Ireland would suggest that similar changes in attitude and practice are now taking root in the Irish Republic (*Irish Independent*, 4 February 1998: 1).

Of course the usefulness of such random polls, using generic questions, is limited. They should be interpreted with caution because in such surveys there are few checks and balances with regard to such important variables as the person's understanding of the Church's teaching on the said matter or the respondent's level of association with the Church. Having said that, these findings are in keeping with the perceived trends outlined above and serve to reinforce the point I am making: namely that people are no longer willing to accept directives simply because they are proclaimed from on high. More and more they will seek rational explanations and if these are not convincing they will adjust their thinking and behaviour accordingly.

My own qualitative research in the field of divorce and remarriage produced some interesting and at times unexpected findings. In this chapter I will review some of these, particularly insofar as they challenge the Church at its teaching and institutional levels.

Divorced Catholics Shaping Opinion in the Church

One of the first major insights of the research was the realization that for many Catholics the trauma of divorce had been compounded by the fact that they belong to the Catholic Church. This problem was not just the result of how they anticipated or experienced others in the community viewing or treating them, but in the first place their own feeling of self-deprecation. It was remarkable how many people confessed to having been harshly judgemental of others before they had faced the breakdown of their own marriages. Of course some considered themselves to be the innocent parties and therefore suffered a double sense of grievance at what they perceived to be the uncaring attitude of the Church and its representatives. Those who have stayed within the Church family – and it is clear that many have not – have learnt much about the fundamental gospel call to compassion, and as a consequence have had a major influence in reshaping the thinking and the attitude of the Church authorities and the wider Church community.

The comment of a member of the Association of Separated and Divorced Catholics (ASDC) at a group meeting epitomizes this whole process: 'I think sometimes the Catholic Church doesn't realize we are human as well as Catholic' (Buckley, 1997: 93–4). Such insights, born of experience, serve to highlight the great tension that exists in the Church when it comes to interpreting the Scriptures and equating the teaching on divorce with the fundamental gospel imperative of compassion and forgiveness. I should add that my research suggests that this tension has been well understood by most of the English and Welsh hierarchy and many of their clergy for some considerable time. An examination of how the bishops have sought to bring pastoral relief in this area should provide comforting reading for those who feel neglected or abandoned. Clearly a lot of work remains to be done and the teaching Church is still constrained by the paradox of the situation and the limitations imposed by its canonical position. However, the fact that the bishops are willing to acknowledge that the situation is unsatisfactory is itself a heartening reminder that a better way of proceeding must be found.

Once the Conference of Bishops of England and Wales had identified divorce as a growing and intractable problem in the 1970s they set up a fairly high-powered commission, comprising a range of theological opinion. This commission, chaired by Bishop Moverley, reported in 1979. Unfortunately the members were unable to agree a common position and so presented two reports, leaving the bishops asking for further guidance. Nevertheless, armed with the results of their consultation at the National Pastoral Congress in Liverpool the following year (Anon., 1981), their concern was such that both Cardinal Hume and Archbishop Worlock made notable interventions at the Roman Synod on the family in 1980. Archbishop Worlock said:

> Yet despite our best efforts, some marriages fail and family unity is destroyed. To these victims of misfortune, not necessarily of personal sin, or of sin which has not been forgiven, the Church, both universal and local, must have a healing ministry of consolation.
>
> Moreover, many pastors nowadays are faced with Catholics whose first marriages have perished and who have now a second and more stable (if legally only civil) union in which they seek to bring up a new family. Often such persons, especially in their desire to help their children, long for the restoration of full eucharistic communion with the Church and its Lord. Is this spirit of repentance and desire for sacramental strength to be for ever frustrated? Can they be told only that they must reject their new responsibilities as a necessary condition of forgiveness and restoration to sacramental life?
>
> Some pastors argue that the Church's teaching on marital fidelity and contractual indissolubility are here at risk. They fear lest other Catholics would be scandalised and the bond of marriage weakened. Our pre-synodal consultation would question this assertion. Those who vigorously uphold the Church's teaching on indissolubility, also ask for mercy and compassion for the repentant who have suffered irrevocable marital breakdown. There is no easy answer. But our Synod must listen seriously to this voice of experienced priests and laity pleading for consideration of this problem of their less happy brethren. They ask that the Church should provide for the spiritually destitute to the same degree as it strives today to meet the material needs of those physically starving. (Kelly, 1996: 71–2)

In 1981 Pope John Paul II published his Apostolic Exhortation on the Family, *Familiaris Consortio*. In §84 his tone was indeed conciliatory, calling 'upon pastors and the whole community of the faithful to help the divorced, and with solicitous care to make sure that they do not consider themselves as separated from the Church'. However, he reaffirmed that those who remarry are banned from eucharistic communion. This is not the place to enter into a detailed theological argument; I have rehearsed those in my book. Nevertheless it must be remembered that much anguish and distress arise from this particular directive. The anomalies and injustices that lead from it have continued to exercise the minds of the bishops to this present day.

In 1986 the standing committee of the Bishops' Conference proposed a further study into the question. Among the nine reasons advanced in a memo were the following:

1   Exclusion from the Eucharist is becoming a countersign; from saying that we are serious about marriage being for life, it is now saying there is no forgiveness whatsoever on earth for you.
2   We can no longer treat everyone as if they are in the same situation. *Familiaris Consortio* makes some differentiations.
3   To ignore the quality of Christian life maintained over a long period could be verging towards a refusal to acknowledge signs indicating the presence of grace.
4   Traditional practice works on the assumption that law can adequately deal with all situations. Pastorally, this has never been the case.

It was this new initiative that led to the research that I undertook. I agreed to the following aims and objectives:

1   To get in touch with the experience of Catholics in the breakdown of marriage and family, and discover how the Church in England and Wales responds in such situations.
2   To discover to what degree those in canonically irregular marriages consider themselves to be members of the Church, and what steps the Church takes to integrate such people into itself, with particular reference to sacramental practice.
3   To suggest a coherent pastoral policy based on a sound theology of sacrament and Church.

After I had reported to the Conference in the Low Week of 1994, the bishops issued a joint statement. They spelt out the need to address the inadequacies of the Church's present discipline, but their emphasis was on the need to reach out to people in their pain and sadness:

> We also note with concern that among those Catholics whose marriages have failed, many have not experienced the 'solicitous care' which Pope John Paul II insisted they must receive when he wrote his Exhortation on 'The Role of the Christian Family in the Modern World' (*Familiaris Consortio*, §84). We acknowledge that many in the midst of the pain and trauma of marital breakdown have felt alienated and ostracised. As pastors we feel a special sense of responsibility towards them and therefore we wish to reach out to the separated and divorced who have experienced hurt within the Church. We regret our failings and those of our communities in this regard, and encourage those in this situation always to seek help and support in their local parish community.

The issue remains high on the bishops' agenda and when they made their official visit to Rome, Cardinal Hume included this passage in his address to the Pope on 23 October 1997:

> In this work of reconciliation we are continually confronted, as pastors, with the situation of those in an 'irregular union' for whom there is no perceived possibility of canonical regularization. We must maintain the clear and consistent teaching of the Church concerning marriage. We must also act pastorally toward those in this situation whether Catholics already or seeking full communion in the Church. In this century especially, the relationship between membership of the Church and reception of Holy Communion has been affirmed and appreciated. It is not surprising that, despite reassurances, those who are not permitted to receive Holy Communion find themselves estranged from the family of the Church gathered for the Mass. We are conscious of your deep concern for these couples and their families and your invitation 'to help them experience the charity of Christ ... to trust in God's mercy ... and to find concrete ways of conversion and participation in the life of the community of the Church' (24 January 1997). We are anxious to receive encouragement from you to explore every possible avenue by which we may address this important and sensitive aspect of our pastoral ministry. (*Briefing* 27/11 (20 November 1997): 8)

It takes time for this growing understanding and compassion to filter through to those who are in distress. But gradually the climate is changing, thanks largely to the untiring efforts of support groups like the Association of Separated and Divorced Catholics (ASDC), the Beginning Experience (BE) and the Rainbow Groups in Liverpool. It is to the work of these organizations that we will now turn our attention.

Divorced Catholics Learning to Minister to One Another

It became clear in the very early days of my research that it was possible to trace a remarkable development in ministry among the separated and divorced. It was born of their own determination to find a way forward when the Church at an institutional and administrative level was struggling to find a compassionate way to respond to them. Thus in 1981 a simple letter in the Catholic press led to a mass meeting in Manchester, from which was born the ASDC. The following year the Archdiocese of Liverpool took its own initiative by setting up a group support system called Rainbow. Although the Liverpool initiative was an ecclesiastical one, effectively their groups, like those of ASDC, function according to the principle that people suffering in similar circumstances are often the most effective ministers to one another. In fact these groups provide a genuine example of lay ministry in action. In 1983 the first Beginning Experience (BE) group met in Britain. Again it was in response to the personal initiative of someone in deep distress who discovered that this movement was operating in the USA. BE is somewhat different to both ASDC and Rainbow in that it is built on an intensive bereavement therapy programme. However, the work of the BE teams often complements that of the ongoing support groups and many of their members take part in BE programmes.

An examination of the contrasting work of these support groups and programmes will provide us with some important clues as to how people who are caught up in the trauma of marital breakdown in the Catholic Church have learned not only to support one another but to cope with the anomalies and injustices of the Church's pastoral practice.

The BE programme was devised in Texas in 1974 by a professional family counsellor, Sr Josephine Stewart, and a divorced Catholic, Mrs Jo Lamia. Their aim was to bring relief to those bereaved by death, separation or divorce, by enabling them to come to terms with what had happened and move on. While it had its roots in Catholic tradition and sacramental practice, from its inception the movement was ecumenical. In my experience of BE this was a particularly significant factor. It means that the emphasis is on ensuring that as a result of good psychological practice supported by sound theological principles, people who are hurting can be enabled to pass through the stages of grief to the point where they have so recovered that they are able to reach out to care for others. Such a process is seen to be rooted in the passion, death and resurrection of Jesus. The national chaplain of BE, Fr Luke Magee CP, explained:

> We cannot 'pray away' our distress, ask God to perform some kind of magic; that would be to miss the life-giving effect of resurrection. ... Sometimes a person may express the feeling of being trapped in a marriage; the resurrection experience may be the opportunity offered to bring to wholeness those parts of their lives buried or diminished by the marriage. (Buckley, 1997: 112)

Once people are liberated at that level they gain a new perspective on their lives and the problems that beset them. They are dealing with that more basic issue of the human person in distress. Remember the plea: 'we are human as well as Catholic'. I did not find those engaged with the BE process preoccupied with the Church's teaching on divorce and remarriage or annulments or the regularization of canonically irregular marriages, or even on who is or who is not entitled to receive the Eucharist. That is not to say that these questions do not arise for them, but they do not dictate the agenda when even more fundamental questions are at stake. For some that will include their very sanity and the ability to cope with life itself. Undoubtedly the most compelling testimony I received throughout all the years of my research was from a man who had recovered from the trauma of the breakdown of his marriage through BE (see Buckley, 1997: 102–3). In doing so he had learnt to live with the anomaly of his situation *vis-à-vis* Catholic teaching and jurisprudence. He concluded:

> I have come to terms with my relationship with God. I am accepting responsibility for my life as it is now, and if I thought I could grow in a loving relationship, then I would have no qualms about entering into one. In fact I have made it almost a criterion for judging whether I trust God enough. (ibid.: 103)

I should add that the man in question had been a monk for several years in his early life and was clearly able to reflect at some depth on the spiritual and theological complexity of his situation. The BE programme coupled with his own personal history enabled him to achieve a perspective that freed him to live at peace with himself, with God and with the Church. Such mature judgement does not come easily and many older-generation Catholics remain haunted by the knowledge that they are not in good standing with the official Church.

My impression is that BE pays little attention to the Church's official policy, not because it is dismissive of it, but simply because its purpose initially is to attend to those more urgent and fundamental issues affecting hurting individuals mentioned above. Its ecumenical dimension also prevents it from becoming too preoccupied with the specifically Roman Catholic way of doing things. By contrast ASDC from the outset has been deeply concerned to ensure that it builds and maintains good relations with the hierarchical Church. From the beginning it secured the patronage of the Bishop of Salford and it has always taken heart from the encouragement it has received from the hierarchy since it was founded in 1981. Indeed any suggestion from its members that it should be more forceful in lobbying for change has always been roundly resisted at executive level. I think there will always be a tension in this area and it is probably a healthy one. I would judge that the motivating force behind the desire to remain in good standing at an official level is born of the heartfelt desire of so many Catholics to know that they are acceptable and accepted, that they still have a place in the community.

Interestingly it is possible to contrast this particular aspect of the tradition of ASDC with that of Rainbow. Rainbow, being an ecclesiastical initiative, does not need to try and establish good relations with the bishops and their clergy. The danger here is that official oversight might restrict their freedom and I sensed a certain frustration among those responsible for the groups in Liverpool that they have not always enjoyed the scope they might have wanted. Suffice it to say that these contrasts, while interesting, are not critical. What is more significant is that both these organizations have contributed much by way of educating their members on a range of issues. Among these and of particular importance is the annulment process.

Interest in annulments is considerable because Catholics realize it is the one way in which they may be able to resolve otherwise intractable problems. I was informed that when someone (generally a priest from the diocesan tribunal) is invited to address a local group on the subject, the attendance for that meeting will be considerably larger than usual. One Rainbow member explained: 'There must be a great need. We have had as many as fifteen in the group. That night we had forty or fifty people' (Buckley, 1997: 155). Furthermore the groups make books on the subject available, and members exchange information from their own personal experiences. While all this can be enormously beneficial and lead people to happy resolutions of their situations, it can also lead to bitter disappointment and disillusion. My research revealed that the more some people learned about the theory and practice of Catholic jurisprudence the more likely they were to be disillusioned and even scandalized. And here we are not talking about the common complaint that only the rich and influential can work the system, but rather the very substance of the process and the anomalies and injustices that arise from it.

In my work for the bishops and in my book I have been careful to give a balanced account, presenting the full range of experiences and acknowledging that 'for some people the annulment process was an important part of their growth and healing'. I concluded that 'for too many others it has been a harrowing experience, characterised by insensitive handling at every level, including intrusions into the most private and personal aspects of their lives, forcing them to revive painful memories from which they were desperately trying to recover' (Buckley, 1997: 157).

I am of the opinion that the development of the annulment process as a means of dealing with the problem of broken marriages among British Catholics is probably levelling out. In the wake of Vatican II the dioceses of England and Wales followed the lead given by the Church in North America, and during the 1970s there was a rapid increase in the number of petitions being processed. However, from the mid-1980s the numbers settled down and nowadays between 1,000 and 1,250 are decided each year. If it is true that Catholics are remarrying in comparable numbers to the rest of society, and this seems to be the case, then at a conservative estimate less than 10 per cent are able to do so validly in the eyes of the Church as a result of annulments.

This poses the question: how do the remainder adjust their thinking and practice? Undoubtedly a large percentage give up the practice of the faith. This will include those who have lost faith in God and the Church, sometimes as a result of their experiences, as well as those who feel they cannot live a life of duplicity. Among those who remain within the family of the Church are some who feel aggrieved that there is apparently no solution to their problem, but whose attachment to the Church is such that they cannot envisage abandoning it; others who accept that they have broken the rules and are willing to live in a sort of limbo; others still who find a sympathetic priest/counsellor with whom they resolve their problems in the conscience forum and return to the Eucharist, albeit unofficially.

There is one other group, which I estimate to be growing. This comprises the people who have petitioned successfully, but for whom the annulment is no longer significant. In other words should they meet someone whom still they could not marry validly in the Catholic Church, they would be prepared to marry elsewhere. I have wondered about this group of people and can only conclude that while initially they were willing to submit their cases to the diocesan tribunal, in the end they failed to be impressed with the integrity of the process. It is almost as if the more they learnt about how the system works the less convinced they were that this was a satisfactory way of dealing with their problems. Interestingly, I found many others, including some of the priests and people who work for the tribunals, coming to similar conclusions. The remainder of this chapter will concern itself with examining the issues surrounding this question, because it not only influences the individual cases of those who petition to have their marriages annulled, but also affects the wider mission of the Church.

Annulments: A Hindrance to Mission

For a long time the annulment process was surrounded by a certain mystique. It was as if no one should really expect to understand the proceedings except those who had been specially trained for the purpose. When the numbers were small and the Church's authority was rarely questioned such an approach worked successfully. Today, as people become better educated and want to know what is happening and why, it is less easy to maintain such a position. Understandably they ask why this seems to be the only solution the Catholic Church can offer to most of those who turn to it for help in the face of a broken marriage.

I have examined the theology and the practical implications of the annulment process in my book (1997). The Church has locked itself into a position from which it is finding it difficult to extricate itself. Ironically this is the product of a long and complicated history of trying to bring pastoral relief to those in difficult marital situations while at the same time upholding its belief in the sanctity and permanence of marriage. As a result the Church is left with the one option of trying to establish that in the first instance a true marriage never actually took place.

It should be noted that I am not quarrelling with the notion that certain marriages may well be invalid, that sometimes it can be proved that there was something defective in the consent of the couple, which would render a marriage null and void. In those circumstances it is perfectly reasonable either for the state or the Church to issue a declaration of nullity. The difficulties arise when one's theology so restricts one's options that this provides virtually the only avenue of escape for those whose marriages fail. In those circumstances the whole process is almost certain to become contrived.

In recent times the Church has extended the grounds for nullity to include the generic psychological ones: 'lack of discretionary judgement' and the inability 'to assume the essential obligations of marriage' (Canon Law Society, 1983: Canon 1095). As a result there are a few canon lawyers who will argue that whenever a marriage irretrievably breaks down, it should be possible to establish the root causes of its destruction within those categories. Clearly that is not the position being advanced by Rome. Nevertheless Cardinal Ratzinger and Archbishop Bovone, in a letter from the Congregation for the Doctrine of the Faith (CDF) to the bishops of the world (a letter occasioned largely in response to a pastoral initiative of three leading German bishops), state that the grounds for nullity have now been extended so that every reasonable case should be resolvable in the tribunal forum.

> The discipline of the Church, while it confirms the exclusive competence of ecclesiastical tribunals with respect to the examination of the validity of the marriage of Catholics, also offers new ways to demonstrate the nullity of a previous marriage in order to exclude as far as possible every divergence between the truth verifiable in the judicial process and the objective truth known by a correct conscience. (Kelly, 1996: 124–5)

It is not just the laity whose cases come before the tribunals who often find this all hard to understand or accept. Many of the clergy are likewise bewildered and frustrated. Here are the comments of a priest who had worked for eighteen years for his diocesan tribunal:

I would say there are many more grounds . . . but nevertheless it is all hedged around with rules and regulations. If you don't fit into the pattern it is no use to you really. . . . The only thing that makes it worthwhile as a task for me in life is to be able to say I have helped some people officially. But I don't think it is anything more than a loophole to be honest. The crucifixion of the whole thing comes when you have got a weeping person in front of you wanting something that you can't give on that level. (Buckley, 1997: 122–3)

The problem is highlighted even more dramatically by the problem of those seeking reception into full communion in the Catholic Church, but coming with irregular marriage situations *vis-à-vis* Catholic canon law. In my research I addressed this problem separately, visiting a number of RCIA (Rite of Christian Initiation of Adults) teams across the country and noting their different responses (ibid.: 143–9). I recall a number of situations in different parishes, recently brought to my attention, where people were not going to be admitted to eucharistic communion, although they were due to be received into the Church at the Easter Vigil.

Such an extraordinary state of affairs cannot be left unresolved for too long or grave scandal will result. There are so many anomalies and *non sequiturs* to be addressed in relation to this question that it is impossible to explore them here. Suffice it to say that for many people the problems were in their early life, long before they had any association with the Catholic Church or were seen to receive the gift of faith. Common sense dictates that something is seriously wrong with legislation which so cramps the apostolic opportunities and limits the missionary activity of the Church.

I have used the word scandal above, advisedly. It is one of the two reasons that Pope John Paul II uses in *Familiaris Consortio* (1981: §84) in reaffirming his decision not to readmit to eucharistic communion those in irregular marriages. My research findings would suggest that if that were the case in 1981 it no longer holds today. The overwhelming weight of evidence points to the fact that now the scandal is rather that the teaching Church has not found a way of reassessing this situation. Other Christian traditions, most notably the Orthodox, have an equally strict and uncompromising belief in the sanctity, sacramentality and permanence of marriage, but their theological tradition has not so hampered them that they are unable to bring pastoral relief to broken human beings seeking forgiveness and a fresh start.

The problem for the Catholic Church is often vividly illustrated when its canon law and jurisprudence come into conflict with the discipline of other Christian traditions. We have seen the problem as it affects those wishing to be received into the Catholic Church. It can also become an issue when it affects the non-Catholic partner of a Catholic who is seeking an annulment.

Annulments: An Ecumenical Problem

A recent example is the much-publicized case of Sheila Rauch Kennedy in the United States. Being associated with America's most famous family, this case is receiving a considerable amount of publicity even on this side of the Atlantic. In her book *Shattered Faith* (1997) Sheila Kennedy details the disturbing story of her battle with the tribunal of the Catholic Archdiocese of Boston. Of course the book offers her side of the story, but it is fair to say that the issues she raises are not uncommon and I have no reason to suppose that she is exaggerating. In summary her story is that she was able to cope with the divorce after her twelve-year marriage to Joseph Kennedy, the eldest son of Senator Robert and Ethel Kennedy, but she could not countenance the idea of an annulment granted by the Catholic Church.

The difficulty for Sheila, and for many others confronted with the Church's official investigation of a broken marriage in the annulment court, is that the process is designed to establish that a true marriage never actually took place. For her this was totally unacceptable and she has been determined to fight the Church every inch of the way. Indeed, although the Boston tribunal eventually granted the annulment at the first instance on the grounds of Joseph's 'lack of due discretion', she has forced an appeal to Rome and awaits its decision. Sheila Kennedy catalogues many grievances including the fact that her own mental stability was for a long time called into question, but the issue which really seems to have distressed her most was the implication that her children were not born in a sacred union. During my own research I met many people who were deeply concerned about the legitimacy and status of their children if the Church had declared or was to declare that their marriages had never existed in the first place. Despite all the reassurances that an annulment in no way affects the legitimacy of the children, many remained unconvinced and spoke of their children's distress at what they perceived to be the implications of the annulment process for them.

This position is understandable. Few people will be well versed in the niceties of the law, and distinctions between the effects of civil and canon law. Thus while the Church authorities can satisfy themselves that legitimacy is purely a civil matter, it is not easy for people to make such fine distinctions when faced with the news that at another level their union never really existed. Sheila Kennedy on the other hand was taking this a spiritual step further. Hers was not a problem with legitimacy, but with the spiritual status of her twin boys and the union into which they were born. She writes:

My concern about an annulment and its effect on my children was spiritual, not legal. To me, the spiritual domain was clearly a Church responsibility and one which its priests had stressed repeatedly before I married. The same Church that had so eloquently discussed with Joe and me the importance of sanctity for our soon-to-be-conceived children now wanted to declare that the union that had produced them was flawed from the beginning and had never been sanctified at all. I now saw this Church as not only abandoning my children but, by hiding behind civil law and an irrelevant legitimacy issue, as failing to address the spiritual issues that had been its rightful domain and responsibility for almost two thousand years. (Kennedy, 1997: 14)

Kennedy presents a powerfully argued case and refuses to be deflected from her purpose. Brought up in the Episcopal Church she was not willing to sacrifice her own convictions about the sacredness of her marriage, albeit that subsequently it had failed. Interestingly when she confronted her former husband about whether he took his marriage to her seriously he responded in a way which now he may well regret:

Of course I took our marriage and the children seriously. And of course I think we had a true marriage. But that doesn't matter now. I don't believe this stuff. Nobody actually believes it. It's just Catholic gobbledygook, Sheila. But you just have to say it this way because, well, because that's the way the Church is. (ibid.: 11)

The phrase 'Catholic gobbledygook' may be extreme but it does reflect a confusion and lack of understanding even within the ranks of Catholics themselves. While I did not encounter such cynical responses among my interviewees I did meet many people who understood little not only of what the annulment process was about but why it is employed. Thus I was forced to conclude:

> The research revealed that the majority of people, including those who are grateful for having received annulments from the Church, see the process as little other than the Church's way of resolving the problem of broken marriages. The state grants divorces, the Church annulments. Thus while people may learn something of *how* the annulment process works, few gave any indication that they understood *why* the Church operates the system. (Buckley, 1997: 157)

Certainly the Catholic Church's dependence on the annulment process is unique within Christianity and many commentators point to the more liberal approach of the Orthodox Churches as a reminder that other ways of pastorally responding to the problem have developed even from the Patristic period. It would be naive to suggest that somehow the Catholic Church could simply adopt the Orthodox principle of *oikonomia* (the economy of God which enables the Church through its bishop – the *oikonomos* or householder – to ensure the good running of the community so that God's saving presence may reach into every situation). Nevertheless this should surely have its place in an ongoing ecumenical dialogue as we seek a way towards the organic unity that Pope John Paul II has set as a Millennial project. I am convinced that such a dialogue would furnish the Catholic Church with new and enriching insights into its own tradition and may help to break through the impasse with which we are confronted.

Seeking that dialogue for myself I arranged what turned out to be a fascinating meeting with Archbishop Gregorios of Thyateira and Great Britain (see Buckley, 1997: 174–5). It took some time for me to realize that we were talking totally different theological languages. I was searching for an explanation of how the Orthodox notion of *oikonomia* works in practice; he was trying to explain to me that it was not a system which operates, but a way of living and experiencing God's saving presence in Christ. For him that saving presence can reach into every situation. Therefore he could not understand how the Catholic Church has trapped itself into a position in which this one group of people – namely the divorced and remarried – is excluded.

The Challenge to Dialogue over Pastoral Policy

As the incidence of marital breakdown has increased amid a complex mass of social pressures at the end of the twentieth century, the majority of Roman Catholics in the Church in England and Wales – bishops, priests and people – are struggling with the limited available pastoral options. It is not surprising that there is a tension between official Church teaching, seeking to uphold the ideals of marriage and family life, and the pastoral experiences of priests and people in the field. However, the question at present is whether that tension is healthy or not. I fear that it is becoming so strained that the teaching Church is in danger of losing credibility even among those of more moderate views.

I have already drawn attention to the discussion of scandal in *Familiaris Consortio*. The other reason advanced in the same document for not admitting those in irregular marriages to Holy Communion is a philosophical one: namely that the disunity in these people's lives is in conflict with the unity expressed in the Eucharist. It is in this context that Cardinal Ratzinger and Archbishop Bovone included the following in their letter to the bishops of the world:

> The faithful who persist in such a situation may receive Holy Communion only after obtaining sacramental absolution, which may be given only 'to those who, repenting of having broken the sign of the covenant and of fidelity to Christ, are sincerely ready to undertake a way of life that is no longer in contradiction to the indissolubility of marriage. This means, in practice, that when for serious reasons, for example, for the children's upbringing, a man and a woman cannot satisfy the obligation to separate, they "take on themselves the duty to live in complete continence, that is, by abstinence from the acts proper to married couples".' In such a case they may receive Holy Communion as long as they respect the obligation to avoid giving scandal. (Kelly, 1996: 122–3)

Some theologians have expressed surprise that this teaching was taken up by John Paul II in *Familiaris Consortio* and reiterated there. For many there is a real difficulty about whether this teaching is sound psychologically. I suspect it would be hard to find many reputable psychiatrists/psychologists, Catholic or otherwise, who would advocate this practice as a norm. Undoubtedly there are some Catholics who have heroically accepted this solution and have lived out their lives accordingly, but I would suggest that as we enter the new millennium there will be very few who can or will accept this teaching as God's will for them or for others.

The question here is one of how theology can be in dialogue with other disciplines which have a direct bearing on its understanding of God and human relations. We have seen that Vatican II opened the way to this dialogue with the modern world amidst all its scientific and technological advances. The challenge for the Church is to find a language in which that dialogue can be fruitful, and that is not easy if medieval philosophical categories still dictate the terms of reference. People today are better educated and understandably they will ask how a teaching which appears not to be based on good psychology can be based on good theology.

The fact is that even if many have not articulated the question in those terms, a growing number in the Catholic community, reflecting on their experience, have a gut feeling that the Church's present pastoral policy regarding the separated, divorced and remarried is hopelessly inadequate. On the evidence of my research this appears to be the vast majority. The fact that the bishops themselves continue to search for solutions and are willing to make their voice heard in Rome reflects the tension that still obtains. It is to be hoped that as we enter the new millennium fruitful dialogue will right the balance and lead to a healthier state of affairs.

12

What Became of the Children of Mary?

Mary Eaton

Catholic Women's Organizations

In 1937 my mother, then a young woman, came to England from Ireland. She found a job, enrolled at the local technical college and quickly became involved in parish life. She joined the Children of Mary and the Legion of Mary, and it was at a parish social that she met her future husband (my father). After the war they married and throughout their lives lived within walking distance of a Catholic church. Both were active in the parish. My mother was a member and an officer in the Union of Catholic Mothers – this involved providing the refreshments at parish social functions, making the produce for bazaars, and organizing and running frequent jumble sales. Fund-raising through cooking and sewing, through organizing and administering, was a major project for my mother and her friends. Most of her friends were fellow parishioners. Such activities ran parallel to religious practice and devotion – discussion groups and daily rosary. This was a pattern of activity to be found throughout Britain in the years following the Second World War – a pattern documented by sociologists (Hornsby-Smith, 1989) and described in fiction (Lodge, 1993).

Growing up, I too was part of the parish activity – a member of the Guild of St Agnes and later the Children of Mary – helping with the fund-raising ventures and attending the parish church. But I did not go on to join the Union of Catholic Mothers (UCM) or the Catholic Women's League (CWL). Parish-based women's organizations have not been part of my adult Church membership. In this my behaviour is consistent with the national picture of recruitment to these organizations (See Tables 12.1 and 12.2).

The Catholic Women's League was established in 1907 in order to promote communications between Catholic women and to promote Catholic influence within the country. The founder, Margaret Fletcher, wanted lay women to play a part in bringing the Christian message to the social and educational questions of the day. Local lectures, debates and social gatherings were organized and members were available to give help to the clergy where it was needed. The Union of Catholic Mothers began as a committee of the Catholic Women's League in 1913 and became autonomous in 1938. The original aim of the UCM was to instruct

Table 12.1 Post-War Membership of the Union of Catholic Mothers

1956	23,718
1957	24,142
1964	26,305
1966	28,000
1970	24,199
1971	21,070
1972	19,839
1978	16,907
1987	13,723
1990	11,200
1992	10,954
1994	9,723

(*Source:* Union of Catholic Mothers)

Table 12.2 Post-War Membership of the Catholic Women's League

1945	13,800
1946	16,567
1955	21,852
1958	20,092
1959	22,309
1964	23,800
1966	22,800
1968	22,000
1970	21,292
1971	19,000
1976	15,938
1980	14,600
1981–4	fluctuates between 12,000 and 13,000
1986–7	both 11,000
1989	10,026
1990	9,668
1991	8,912
1996	6,441
1997	6,227

(*Source:* Catholic Women's League)

mothers in the teaching and the practice of the faith. The UCM was usually found in inner-city parishes (Noble, 1991).

For both the Catholic Women's League and the Union of Catholic Mothers the decline in membership began in the mid-1960s. Both organizations attribute this decline to a failure to recruit rather than to the resignation of existing members. The years that saw this decline were also the years that saw the post-war babies becoming adults, leaving full-time education, entering the job market, marrying and having their own children. These are women who might have been Children of Mary, children in Catholic parishes in the Fifties and Sixties, but who did not go on to become organized adult Catholic women. This is the situation explored by Valerie Noble (1991) in her study of the history of women's organizations in the Catholic Church.

Noble set her study in the context of *Do Not Be Afraid* (NBCW, 1991) – the report published as the result of work on the concerns and perceptions of women in matters affecting them in the life of the Church and in the world. This work was undertaken by the National Board of Catholic Women at the request, in 1988, of the Bishops' Conference of England and Wales. Based on responses from 2,884 individuals and 78 groups, *Do Not Be Afraid* revealed a wide range of opinion existing amongst women who consider themselves to be committed members of the Catholic Church. The opinions ranged from a total satisfaction with the *status quo*, and a resistance to any change, right though to anger and resentment at the marginalization and oppression of women by the Church. From either end of this spectrum two new women's groups have emerged in recent years. Neither is parish-based.

The Catholic Women's Network (CWN) was established in 1984 following a weekend meeting at Roehampton addressed by the feminist theologian Rosemary Reuther. The aim of the CWN is to provide a network of support that will empower women to grow and mature in their spiritual life; work towards the participation of women in every aspect of church life; encourage and enable women to engage in theology; and create new ways of worshipping together. Members pay an annual subscription and receive the quarterly journal *Network*. Local groups organize liturgies, shared meals, discussions, speakers and other events which take forward the aims of the organization. *Network* provides members with details of such events locally, nationally and internationally, as well as articles, book reviews and reports on recent conferences. The CWN may be seen as the organization of women who wish to challenge the established traditions of the Church through a call for a return to gospel values of freedom and justice for all. Currently the CWN has a membership of approximately 350. Since its foundation in 1984 there has been a membership of between 300 and 400 – apparently women join for a few years and then move on, to be replaced by new recruits so that there is an average turnover of between 30 and 40 members each year.

The Association of Catholic Women (ACW) began in 1989 and describes itself as 'women from all parts of the country who find happiness and fulfilment in giving glad assent to the Church's teaching as proclaimed by the magisterium'. There is no fixed subscription but donations are requested. The ACW produces a quarterly *Review* and organizes study days and meetings. Men are welcome as supporters. The ACW has disassociated itself from *Do Not Be Afraid* and the president has challenged its accuracy in the mass media (Noble, 1991: 45). In terms of perspectives, the ACW could be located with those Catholic women who staunchly resist change. Their current membership is estimated to be between 1,300 and 1,500. Neither the CWN nor the ACW claims a membership to match that of the CWL or the UCM today, let alone the numbers these more established organizations commanded at their peak.

The National Board of Catholic Women (NBCW) is the main forum for the official representation of Catholic women in England and Wales. Established in 1938, the NBCW is composed of representatives of all the women's organizations in the Church and those organizations with women members, a total of 32. Recently membership has broadened to include representatives from the dioceses. The NBCW is a consultative body of the Bishops' Conference and is thus an opportunity for women to be represented in the decision-making of the Church. It was a request from the Bishops' Conference that led to the production of *Do Not Be Afraid* by the NBCW, and it was in response to this document that the Joint Dialogue Group (JDG) was established to encourage and facilitate dialogue between women, bishops and clergy.

The JDG conducted a wider survey, *Working Together,* on the involvement and inclusion of women in the work of the Church. This second survey confirmed the findings of *Do Not Be Afraid* and identified eight concerns: the need to improve communications; the need to make proper use of the gifts and skills of women; the need to examine the power of the parish priest to enable or restrict the involvement of women; the need to clarify the role of the ordained priesthood; the need to involve women in decision-making processes; the need for inclusive language; the need for adult spiritual formation; and the need to relate the gospel to people's everyday lives (NBCW *et al.*, 1998: para. 2.3). Following the publication of *Working Together* two national meetings have been organized. These meetings confirmed the relevance of, and began to address the concerns of, *Working Together* (ibid., para.: 2.5).

However, despite these initiatives at a structural level, there is recognition that many women are unrepresented and uninvolved:

> awareness of the NBCW among women active in parish or diocesan life remains relatively low and awareness of the opportunity to provide input to the Bishops' Conference is even lower. In practice the level of women's involvement in diocesan and national Church structures depends on the initiative of individual bishops and groups of women. The encouragement offered by parish priests is also important. Thus the levels of women's involvement are patchy, varying between dioceses and between parishes within dioceses. (ibid.: para 2.5)

What, then, of those women who are not represented at any forum, who belong to no formal organization, who have not had their opinions canvassed in any survey, and yet who are members of the Catholic Church? In the following sections I aim to give a voice to a group of these women, to understand something of the lived realities behind the pattern of non-joining, to learn what became of those who were, or might have been, Children of Mary.

A Pilot Study

The data are derived from individual and loosely structured interviews with nine women. All had been students, with me, at a Catholic College of Education in Central London in the late 1960s. I contacted the women through the past students' association and the recommendation of friends. No woman was still in contact with more than one other of the women interviewed. In most cases I was aware of the Catholicity of the respondent, either through personal knowledge or through others, but I always asked if the woman considered herself to be a Catholic and in answering this question each woman defined this as necessarily involving attending Mass on Sunday. One woman did not attend Mass, instead she and her husband and two teenage children were involved in the parish life of the local United Reformed Church. Because of the husband's job the family had moved several times during the last 25 years. As a family they had taken a decision to select their worshipping community on criteria other than adjacent Catholicism. The woman's childhood and early life had been characterized by close involvement with Church and parish life. It was not until she left college and took a job in a non-Catholic comprehensive school that she experienced any alternative. Although her situation is not one which she or any of the others in this group would categorize as 'practising Catholic', I decided to include her since she voices criticisms and comments which are echoed in other interviews. The difference is in the way in which she responded to these criticisms.

Each interview lasted approximately an hour, but some were set in the context of a much longer meeting which gave me the opportunity of a fuller discussion of the subjects raised. The interviews covered four main areas: (1) religious practice of the woman's childhood; the Catholicism of her parents and their involvement in parish life; schooling and her childhood involvement in parish organizations; (2) Catholic college: the reasons for its selection and expectations of it; first and lasting impressions of it; and its felt impact on her adult religious practice; (3) post-college life: work, parish life, marriage and children; and (4) issues facing the Church today: including women and their role, and her views on the ordination of women.

With only one exception, each woman attended weekly Mass, most did much more, none was a member of an established Catholic women's organization. In many respects there was considerable variation between the women in terms of lifestyle, disposable income and personal history. There were also common characteristics relating to family, marriage and Church involvement. All but one had married; one had been widowed in her early forties; the rest were still apparently happily married. It is interesting to note that while for their parents' generation it had been customary for a non-Catholic partner to convert on marriage, for these women marriage to a non-Catholic had posed no problem, either at the time of the wedding or subsequently. Only two of the nine had married Catholic men.

In this the interviewees reflect the national trend on the proportion of Catholics marrying non-Catholics. During the late Fifties and early Sixties mixed marriages accounted for approximately half the marriages among Catholics. Through the Seventies this figure rose to two-thirds and remained at this level until the mid-Nineties. All the married women had children, usually between two and four; one had six. Whilst none of the women had elderly relatives living with her, two had parents living nearby for whom they accepted some responsibility. Both of these women were also in full-time employment in challenging educational environments. Four others were in full-time employment, three teaching children with special needs, one as a headteacher. Two were teaching part-time. One had recently moved and was not in paid employment at the time of the interview.

Good Catholic Girls

Of the nine women interviewed, seven had two Catholic parents and four of these parents had converted to Catholicism in order to marry. For most of the women the parish had been an important focus of family life:

> My mother belonged to the UCM and still does although it's not so active in the parish now because it is an old parish and so most of the members are older ladies. They still meet together as a social group. My father was in the St Vincent de Paul. The Church has always been a big part of their lives and most of their socialising was through the Church.

From the accounts of childhood emerges a picture of the 1950s parish – men as members of the Catenians, Knights of St Columba (KSC), St Vincent de Paul Society (SVP); women as members of the UCM and CWL involved in cleaning the church, flower arranging, jumble sales. Most of the children went as a matter of course to a Catholic school.

> I went to a local Catholic primary school and then there wasn't a local Catholic secondary school so through some hardship and a lot of struggle I went to the local Catholic convent school. That was seen as the only right option.
>
> From what I can ascertain, the parish priest more or less stated that unless children were sent to Catholic schools in the area it would be deemed a mortal sin, which my mother took seriously.

Two of the women had not attended a Catholic secondary school, one because of the poor academic reputation of the local convent school, one because of the lack of a school in the area; both had attended religious instruction provided by the parish. Schools did not feature prominently as recognized influences on these women. One woman spoke favourably of her convent school education citing her teachers as role models and mentors; one woman was critical of the over-sentimental and rule-bound religious education that she had received. The others voiced indirect criticism of their schoolteachers when they spoke of the contrasting impact of their college education. While at school a number of the women were involved in parish-based organizations:

> The Legion of Mary was a way of doing things for other people. When you were very young it was things like cleaning the wax off the candlesticks, cleaning the altar, it was very much part of the parish.

Sometimes the altruism and sense of duty overrode strong personal aversion.

> My job was to visit a certain couple of ladies. One lived in an old persons' home. I hated it because it smelled of cabbage and wee. But I had to do it, it was my job. I had to go and visit her on a Sunday. And I also had to visit another lady who lived near me, who actually had cancer of the breast. I was rather frightened because there used to be a plastic bucket on the floor with soiled dressings in. And I remember as a child being quite frightened – but I thought 'No, I've got to do this.'

The Catholic College

One characteristic that all these women share is that from the mid-Sixties to late Sixties they attended a Catholic College of Education in Central London where they trained to be teachers. The college of 300 students was run by women religious. The principal, and several members of staff, were members of that order and lived in the convent adjacent to the college. The college was residential and single-sex.

None of the women was aware of having consciously chosen to go to a Catholic college; for each it was an automatic decision based on the assumptions of family and teachers. The decision to go to that particular college was usually made because of the central London location. Once there as young women they were delighted at what they found – from the presence of the sisters to the content of the syllabus.

I thought it was wonderful because the convent thing gave you a whole degree of security. There was a great presence – you always felt there was somebody there. I think the whole ambience of the place crossed over into the secular staff – I felt too that it permeated the students. If you've got enough of that around you, in the end it's contagious.

Despite the ever present reality, the sisters were not seen to be intrusive:

The nuns there were very ahead of themselves for the time, I think. Obviously there was the aspect of gate hours but you expected that. My children now can't believe I had to be in by 10.30 pm when I was at college. I thought they might have made sure that we went to church on Sundays, but they didn't. There was none of that. Your religion was your business and they didn't check up on whether you were practising, so they were forward thinking really.

For some women the opportunity to encounter post-Vatican II catechetics had a significant impact on their spiritual lives. One woman described how she had been rescued from empty formulae and had been given new focus.

A thing I do remember about the first year at college is going to Mass on a Sunday. I dropped off quite a bit through a combination of reasons – laziness, general non-motivation. And I remember the thing that jarred me into action again was Mr M's lectures about your faith being Christ-centred. Because I had all these hang-ups about novenas and nine first Fridays running round in my head – praying to saints – and that was a bit of a problem to me. So I made a conscious decision to centre my life on Christ and the Mass. The saints and Mary became much more peripheral. That suited me fine because I wanted to be like that. I wanted to remove all the trappings of a convent-orientated adolescence. You prayed for specific intentions – nine novenas – nine separate prayers – and I was too frightened to stop in case I didn't get what I wanted. I just went on and on. I knew it wasn't right and it was only when I removed all the trappings of that that I felt far more secure in my faith, that my faith is Christ-centred, and that was Mr M who made things quite clear in my second year.

Others too spoke of significant influences encountered at that time:

> It was fabulous – fabulous years. I think we were very lucky in lots of ways. We had the best of liturgies and when you think of the people who influenced us in our religious development, we were very very fortunate – Peter de Rosa, Michel Quoist's prayers.

The religious influence of the college was also seen in the vocational training for teaching in the wish to provide the best possible education for pupils.

> Every time I go into a classroom I'm looking around. Are the children comfortable? Is the window open? Are the walls suitably embellished with the children's work? Are the books marked? It wasn't just teaching it was a mission to do all these things and do them properly. Mrs S gave teaching a mission – not just a task to be undertaken but a way of life. You didn't just go in and present facts. She made you feel that your whole life had to be involved in it or you weren't doing it properly.

Of the six former students currently teaching full-time, one is a headteacher and the other five are all involved in provision of education for children with widely differing, but recognizably special, needs. None had originally trained to teach children with special needs although some subsequently went on to take such training.

> The fact that I've ended up working with deeply disturbed children perhaps is something that came from [the college]. It's something that I don't find difficult and I'm always surprised that people say 'I don't know how you can do it' because I don't have a problem doing it. I really do believe that a place like [the college] engenders in you a sense of caring for other human beings as individuals. You do your job and you should do it well. If something doesn't constitute a viable educational experience you shouldn't be doing it.

Parish Life

On leaving college most of the women found jobs in Catholic schools and started attending Mass in a local parish. As single women with no visible ties to the community they did not find it easy to make contacts. The experience of many is summed up in one woman's words:

I didn't feel any community feel of the Church. I did not get involved and to me it was quite difficult and I thought it was actually contravening the whole point of going to church and being part of the community. I thought 'This is funny.' We are supposed to be Christians and supposed to be so caring about the community and you go along and nobody says anything to you. I was willing, I had been brought up to be part of it. There seemed to be no way. It didn't matter whether you went to the same time Mass, none of them ever seemed to open up their community to single women without children.

One way for the childless to find a place in the parish community was to worship in the parish in which they taught. Speaking of her early years of marriage one woman describes the involvement that follows when there is a recognizable connection to the community.

I was teaching in a Catholic school and we lived in the parish too. I did folk Masses and things at church. I think if you teach in the primary school that's attached to the local Catholic church you haven't got much choice.

For most of the women involvement in parish life began when they had young children, but not necessarily. One woman described her experiences in three different parishes in the same area:

We moved down to Reading and I had to find myself another church again so I went to the local Catholic church – St John's – and it was very old-fashioned, very dark. Again, I felt I didn't belong. I went to Mass on a Sunday, it was quite hard really. Nobody ever spoke to me, I went because that's what you do.

Later they moved within the area and she found herself in a parish with a better atmosphere. However, she was not drawn into parish life until a new parish priest was appointed:

He was an ex-army chaplain and I loved him. He was very brusque but absolutely fantastic and the parish expanded greatly under Fr R. And he used to come and visit us. He found it difficult, particularly to relate to women, with being an army chaplain, but he tried his best and I really, really liked him. The parish was really booming. There were lots of activities going on. I belonged to the baby-sitting group, I took part in the First Communion preparation, I sang in the choir. It was good to be involved.

Another move took the family to another parish and to one which this woman describes as the best parish experience of her life:

I remember that first Sunday we went to Mass, myself and the two children, Oliver was nine and Lucy was seven. And I remember a lady coming to sit next to us, with red hair, and straight away she said 'Hello, you're new here. I'm Mary Docherty and welcome to the parish.' And it was the best welcome I've had in any parish. We were there three years only and I was desolate to leave that parish, absolutely desolate. Because it was so small we knew everybody. Again, I sang in the choir there, I was on the church cleaning rota, I helped with the crèche for the children, I went to this wonderful area centre where we had these family days organized by the diocese ... I was a catechist for the Confirmation group this time, the older ones, through the parish priest Fr B, who was wonderful. We had girls on the altar, total involvement of the congregation in the liturgy. We had a rota for bidding prayers and each road would do a bidding prayer every couple of months or so. We had a super group of people in our road who all sang in the choir and we all went together. That was the happiest, happiest church in my whole life ...
It was the combination of the priest and the people that made that such a wonderful place. I was desolate, desolate to have to leave that.

That experience in so many ways illustrates the common features of success and failure in parish involvement for the women that I interviewed. All but one tenaciously continued to attend their parish church despite rejection and marginalization. All were willing to be drawn into parish life and most were drawn in once they had young children. Children's liturgies and preparation for the sacraments were the dominant roles played by these women, perhaps because they were trained teachers.

The role of the parish priest was vital in this. It was he who created and sustained the conditions in which lay participation was possible. One woman told how her parish priest had the express intention of drawing all his parishioners into the life of the parish.

> There may be about a thousand in the parish and he has 260 doing little jobs – my son reads – he'll have other people doing the collecting, other people doing ministry of welcome and he asked me to be a minister of the Eucharist.

Up to that point she had had little involvement beyond attendance at Mass. Becoming a eucharistic minister has not only brought her into the parish community, it has also deepened her spiritual life:

> I feel it's very important – I'm always nervous about doing it but I feel I'm doing something special when I'm doing it. And because I'm a minister of the Eucharist I also feel obliged very much to pray for the sick and my family because of the healing power of the Eucharist. I suppose without realizing it you do grow closer to the spirituality of the Church, it just develops gradually without you even realizing it – the closeness with the work of the Church.

These women are not dependent on the close involvement of a priest in carrying out their work but he is necessary as a catalyst and facilitator. Even the most enthusiastic and motivated find it hard to develop their parish projects if the priest will not promote those projects. One woman has recently started a mothers' prayer group in her parish. Those who attended had found it a beneficial experience but the parish covers a large area and there is the potential for other groups to start in different locations. The priest is not hostile to the idea and notices have appeared in the newsletter but he is reluctant to give any support from the pulpit:

> Unfortunately for us, although he's a dear, he's very lazy. He's fine if you go to him with ideas, he's all keen for it but he won't give any input – he wants you to do it. And he has this odd belief that nothing should be mentioned from the pulpit unless it's to do with the liturgy of the Word and the Gospel for that particular Sunday. So he makes no announcements from the pulpit.

Such seeming indifference, or reluctance to be involved, is frustrating to the active parishioner. Several women expressed disappointment at what they saw as a further distancing from the congregation by priests who did not visit parishioners in their homes. However, despite the widespread experiences of unwelcoming parishes and indifferent or hostile priests, only one of the women interviewed decided to seek an alternative worshipping community. Others might have articulated similar needs and been duly thankful when they found themselves in a parish which met these needs, but they did not look beyond the Catholic Church and, in most cases, the local Catholic Church. The one exception does not repudiate her Catholic upbringing but sees her current practice as an appropriate development. Her husband is not a Catholic and although the children were baptized in the Catholic Church the parents have both prioritized religious experience over denominational conformity:

> We wanted to give our kids the chance to see that being a Christian isn't automatically a Catholic and that there are different views and as this existed in our family already we wanted there to be an element of choice.

Unhappy with their experiences in the local Catholic Church they began to look around and select a community on the degree to which all the family – parents and children – benefit from it. Frequent moves have made this an accepted pattern within the family.

> I have to say that when you do these surveys of going round the different churches it is mind-boggling. For one thing, when you go in you have this feeling of whether the people actually want to be there or not ... You also notice the number of people and the age-range, whether they're all old or young and with a family, especially at the impressionable age of teenagers ... Then how are they when you go there as a visitor? You don't want people to be grabbing you but is there a warm feeling? Some of the places ... usually said, after a couple of times of going there, 'Oh, I've seen you several times, how nice to see you. Where have you come from?'

The characteristics of the good parish were consistent for all the women interviewed: a place to belong, a place to enjoy, a place to contribute.

What of these women's membership of the traditional parish-based women's organizations? I asked each woman about her contact with and possible membership of the CWL and the UCM. The overwhelming response was 'It wasn't for me.' As others have noted (Noble, 1991) women today have many demands on their time. The group I interviewed were no exception; child-rearing was being combined with teaching and in two cases care of elderly parents. Nevertheless many were involved in parish life, and had been throughout their adult lives, as catechists, liturgists, eucharistic ministers, readers, members of prayer groups and discussion groups. The perceived relevance seems to have been a more important factor than time, and much of this relevance is based on a perceived 'fit' with an existing group. Explaining why she had not joined the CWL or the UCM, one woman echoes the sentiments of others:

I didn't feel as a young mother I should belong, I felt it was a middle-aged or elderly woman's domain. I felt it wasn't for me. I belonged to the baby-sitting circle and I had children to my house. I was a catechist.

One had joined the UCM when as a young married woman she was approached after Mass one Sunday but she observed: 'I only went a few times. It didn't feel very relevant. It was full of older women who seemed to run everything in the parish.' Age was frequently mentioned as a factor by these women who were in their twenties in the 1970s when recruitment to the UCM and CWL was beginning to fall. Failing to recruit at an earlier stage may have begun a downward spiral as potential members looked at organizations which had none of their own generation. Furthermore their generation was finding other ways of contributing and many of these ways drew on the training received as students at a Catholic college. One woman saw the decline of the women's parish-based organizations as sad but inevitable:

The mothers used to be very active in my parish, but the mothers turned to grandmothers and the mothers were mostly working. There wasn't a new membership and the parish activities now tend to be run on more social committee lines and this is organized by the parish council who are elected by the parish members.

None of my sample mentioned the CWN, the ACW or the NBCW. In fact, the status of women, their problems or issues, their possible representation, was not mentioned, unprompted, by any of the women interviewed. Even when asked about the issues facing the Church the position of women was not mentioned. Only when asked directly about their views on the position of women in the Catholic Church did the respondents voice their opinions.

Issues Facing the Church Today

While a number of issues were mentioned by individuals: birth control, marriage, technological and medical change, maintaining high standards, a lack of social mix in the pews, speaking out on social issues, vocations, the one subject which dominated when the women were asked what they considered to be the main issues facing the Church today was youth.

Keeping the Youth Involved

Most of the women were parents, all of the women were teachers. It is not surprising that this was such a major concern. In discussing this issue the women moved from their experience of their own children to their experience of the teaching of religious education in schools. Concern was not confined to those whose children no longer practised their religion. Some compared the Catholic Church to other apparently more successful Churches:

> I think one of the big issues at the moment is how to get the youngsters to stay, how to keep the youth in the Church. Opposite where we live is a Chapel of Unity and that is bursting at the seams every Sunday and there is a large young population who go to it. Any denominations can go there – it is very thriving. Ours have lost it or are losing it, certainly where we live the youngsters don't come. Perhaps modern day society is so 'I want it and I want it now.' Maybe they're bored because it's the same old service ...

Others linked church attendance to an involvement sponsored through religious education and an understanding of the meanings behind liturgical practice; meanings which should go beyond the daily or weekly ritual to inform everyday life. Without this education youth seemed to be the group most in danger from corruption by a materialistic age:

What frightens me is that we've had a political environment and materialistic society for so long that a lot of our children find it very difficult to stand up and say: 'This is something I really believe in.' We get all wrapped up in morality and sex and abortion and other things that they get a bit lost. We've got this great programme [for RE] *Here I Am* – great, lovely, but at some stage they've got to know if not what's right and wrong then what hurts people and what doesn't hurt people.

Another woman, responsible for religious education in a school, was far more forthright about a programme which she sees as failing to give a firm foundation in either Scripture or doctrine:

I've sat in on RE meetings where you are told not to be involved in catechetics, it's religious education. At one stage someone put up their hand to ask a question – this is a hall full of primary teachers – and said 'Are we not to mention anything from the Gospel other than is mentioned in *Here I Am*?' The answer is 'No, you are categorically forbidden to drag in little bits that you see fit to put in.' And I think, 'Well if a child goes to Mass on a Sunday they are going to hear the story of whatever Gospel reading.' It was just ludicrous. Not only are children not being taught the practice of their faith, they are not being given scriptural background knowledge. It's all very well to say that it is the job of the parents, but the parents need support and guidance and they're not getting it either.

Concern at the requirement placed on parents was voiced by another woman who feared she was failing as both teacher and parent. Unlike the previous speaker her criticism is levelled at herself rather than the scheme. As her own children attended the school she had two roles:

I was very keen that my children were brought up as Catholics but I couldn't understand the way that Catholic education was going and I found it very difficult that they were not taught doctrine. [*Veritas*] was meant to be very much tied up with involving parents – sending their little books home and asking parents to comment on various statements that had been made. This is where I really can't come to terms with myself. Although I declare that I wanted these children to have a religious background, I was dreadful at teaching this particular scheme. I don't think it really hit the point that I wanted it to.

The fact that their own children were no longer practising Catholics was a source of considerable sadness for many of the women. Of the eight mothers interviewed, two had all their children still practising, three had some of their children (those still at school) practising, three had none of their children practising although one daughter had joined another Church and was very involved in a local evangelical fellowship. That their children, and others, were leaving the Catholic Church was, for these women, a major concern.

Changes to the Priesthood

It was only when each woman was asked directly about her views on women priests that she began to discuss this as an issue – and to broaden the subject to include married men as priests. Neither the status of women within the Church, nor the ordination of women, was a subject mentioned spontaneously by any of the women interviewed. This is not a subject on which they hold strong views, either pro or anti, and all wanted to see this in the wider context of vocations to the priesthood. Those who were in favour of the ordination of women were also in favour of the ordination of married men and thought this less drastic step might pave the way for future change. There was a recognition of the weight of tradition impeding any change and a reluctance to challenge such tradition since such a challenge would cause distress and disturbance.

> I wouldn't beat the drum for women priests in that we must have them, but I don't see why not with women becoming so involved during the last twenty years. I can remember not being allowed to go on to the altar to change the flowers unless I had permission. It all just seems to be very very slow. The fact that Christ didn't ordain women priests at the time was surely a cultural thing. I don't know that I would be that comfortable but I wouldn't be totally uncomfortable. But me being me, I would like it to be accepted first rather than rebel.

Women commented favourably on their experience of women ministers both in life and fiction. While for some this augured well for the future of women priests in the Catholic Church, for others it was irrelevant. What was important was that 'committed people are what we need'.

> I have had some experience of Anglican women priests and deacons. They were fine, very caring, great ... but somehow – I'm probably just too traditional.
>
> As a feminist I should say 'yes' to women priests, but there are other issues involved. I haven't really got an informed decision on this subject yet. I just find that a tricky one, I really do. Whereas celibacy of priests I don't have problems, I'd have no problems with priests being married. I haven't any experience of women ministers of other faiths. I listen to *The Archers* and I hear Janet being the vicar there – I just think in the Catholic Church, I can't see it but I have no real reason why not.

One woman told of a local Anglican priest, a married man with children, who had become a Catholic and was now recognised as a Catholic priest. His conversion was not based on an opposition to the ordination of women:

> Even so, there were people demonstrating against this man being a Catholic priest and yet it was so lovely to see him with his family around him. It was a lovely contrast because the week before in the press we'd had another priest who's been had up for child abuse, which was just horrible.

Another woman contrasted the reception of married Anglican clergy into the Catholic Church with the rejection of ordained Catholic priests who break their vows of celibacy.

Of the nine women who talked to me, five were in favour of women priests and four were opposed – at present. Those who were opposed said that they might change their minds in time and with changing circumstances. Those who were in favour did not want any innovations forced on an unready congregation. None was explicitly opposed to a married male clergy but even this change was recognized as posing problems.

Church membership was an important part of the lives of these women; many described it as central to their very being. If they had given much they felt they had gained more. The Church was a community to which they belonged; they did not expect perfection:

There is the peace of mind – does that sound trite? It's not a smugness, I'm only too aware of the responsibilities, but there is a feeling of belonging. It's quite a warm feeling, for all the errant priests and scandalous behaviour.

Belonging brought a sense of duty. Several spoke of the responsibility of being a Catholic, to meet a higher standard of behaviour:

It's a bit like a permanent safety net, I suppose. My faith is very important to me but it's not a soft option. I do things because I think I ought to, which, I think, is the Catholic influence.

Some discussed the darker times in their lives when bereavement and loss, depression and pain had made it hard for them to carry on. One woman spoke of a time of great distress when her faith was her support:

I would go to church, either in Mass or just go to church, and plead that I could have strength. So there must have been some deep underlying feeling that something was there for me that was worth going for. I had been so negative in so many other ways that that was the only positive thing I did and I can say that it really, really held us together.

Others spoke of comfort provided at times of bereavement:

We've had various things in our lives – my sister had a cot death and the priest who married us and baptized the babies was there within hours from the other end of the country. It's a terrible thing to say but you do frequently find that the Church is there when you need it. It's the extra thing that helps you through.

The thoughts of the others can be summarized in one woman's words:

It's part of my life in the same way as training to be a teacher was or being a mum. I wouldn't be without it because I think it expands my life. It makes my life easier to cope with because I have that at the basis of everything I do. I've got that fundamental belief that God is there, he's with me, he's watching over me. It helps me to see the good, despite all the bad. I always quote Padre Pio; he said 'Pray, hope and don't worry.'

Post-War Women in the Church

This then is what became of nine of the Children of Mary, nine members of that generation who were brought up in traditional Catholic families in traditional Catholic parishes after the Second World War. They did not join the organizations to which their mothers had belonged (CWL or UCM) nor did they join the new organizations which have formed more recently (CWN or ACW). They were unaware of experiencing any problems as women and were not aware of the representative body which acts on their behalf (NBCW). For them there was very little consciousness of the place and role of women within the Church.

However, these are women who have lived through a time of recognized change in the Catholic Church (Hornsby-Smith, 1987b; 1989; and Hornsby-Smith *et al.*, 1995). During the 1950s they witnessed the introduction of the dialogue Mass, during which the congregation speaks in response to the celebrant priest. During the 1960s they saw the translation of that Mass from Latin to the vernacular. Post-Vatican II they have also seen the reorganization of the sanctuary so that the priest can face the people across the altar, and the introduction of men and women as lay readers and ministers of the Eucharist. Each of these changes was intended to increase the involvement of the laity in the work and worship of the Church. Yet during this period there has been a gradual decline in the numbers of Catholics attending Mass on a regular basis. The mid-1960s saw approximately half the Catholic population as regular attenders; by the mid-1990s the number was fewer, not much above one-quarter.

The accounts of parish life given by these women may throw light on these statistics. For the nine women interviewed, childhood and education had taken place within a tradition of Catholicism that prioritized parish involvement and commitment to religious beliefs and practices clearly defined by parents, priests and teachers. As student teachers these women were introduced to the ideas of the Second Vatican Council, but this introduction was supported by scriptural and theological authority which endorsed, and was endorsed by, the teaching of the Church. On leaving college these women were willing to serve both the parish and the wider community. Their commitment to the wider community may be measured by their continuing involvement in the more demanding aspects of teaching in roles involving leadership or the teaching of children with special needs. Their wish to serve the parish in ways informed by post-

Vatican II ideals may be measured by their response when the possibility of service was offered. Good parishes were defined by the opportunity to participate.

From the accounts given by these women comes a picture of a laity willing and eager to collaborate in parish ministry. Sadly that opportunity was not always present. Too often these women encountered parishes which offered no welcome and priests who gave no recognition to new, or even long-standing members. Such experiences not only denied the women an opportunity of contributing to parish life but also denied their children the experience of belonging to a parish in which they and their parents were valued members. The women could draw on earlier experiences to sustain them in these situations. The children were being denied access to similar experiences, in many cases by both parish church and school. Several of the women were critical of the failure of religious education to engage with the new ways of thinking that they had encountered as students. All were critical of parish priests who seemed unable or unwilling to facilitate the spiritual and social development of the parish; unwillingness was most frequently cited as the problem. One woman spoke of the valiant and successful attempts made by a priest whose army background had made him unused to working with women. Another spoke of her priest's reluctance to publicize parish activities from the pulpit.

As *Working Together* and *Do Not Be Afraid* noted, the parish priest plays a powerful part in the building or frustrating of the parish community. Without the experience of a community of faith the coming generation of parishioners is severely disadvantaged. The national decline in Mass attendance was mirrored in the concerns of the women interviewed. Most of these women had children who no longer attended Mass once they had left school. The future of their children, indeed of all children within the Church, was their major concern. No other issue claimed the same degree of support. What they wanted for their children was what they wanted for themselves – a place, a parish – to which all belonged and in which all were actively involved, women and men, old and young.

The CWL and the UCM were both established in the early part of the twentieth century to foster the contribution of women to the life of the Church. They flourished throughout a time of greater consensus on the roles of women within the Church and within the wider society. Like other Church organizations their recruitment fell dramatically in the last two decades of the century. Although all the women I interviewed were willing to participate in parish life none was attracted to either the CWL or the UCM. The NBCW exists to publicize and promote the interests of women within the Church; not one of the women I interviewed was aware of this. As the NBCW recognizes, the degree of involvement of women at all levels is 'patchy' and much depends on the initiatives of significant groups and individuals, particularly parish priests. Clearly the women with whom I spoke had much to offer, but this was not always recognized by their parish priests, or even by the women themselves. These Children of Mary had not become members of the CWL or the UCM, or even of the CWN or the ACW. However, where a parish priest had prompted or promoted them, theirs was a contribution as vital as that of their mothers' generation – a truly collaborative ministry to their fellow parishioners.

13

Reordering Perspectives in Catholic Schools

Bernadette O'Keeffe

The Catholic School System

Reflecting on the efforts of the pioneers of Catholic education in the nineteenth century Bishop Beck noted that 'The struggle of the Catholic body to make provision for the education of its children has been long and arduous.' It was a time of 'financial scraping and scratching, of piecemeal and inadequate building, and of heroic sacrifice on the part of priests, teachers and people' (Beck, 1950: 595). The struggle was sustained by unswerving loyalty to the Church and a commitment to provide an education for the poor and those on the margins of society. Schools were built primarily to educate the children of the poor who constituted the greater part of the Catholic community at that time.

When the Catholic Poor School Committee was instituted by the bishops at the close of 1847 its role was one of 'promoting the cause of education, and especially religious education among the Catholic poor' (Catholic Poor School Committee, 1848: 5). Energies were directed towards major school-building programmes. Large numbers of poor working-class children, mainly Irish children, received their education in a Catholic atmosphere. The committee's financial objective was pursued in two ways, first, by raising funds from within the Catholic community and involving it in both the building and support of schools, and second, in pursuing for Catholic schools a share in the national grants for education.

For a century or more the goal of Catholic decision-makers was a Catholic school for every Catholic child to be taught by Catholic teachers. This goal was never fully realized (Beck, 1950: 599).

In 1847 the Committee received a small grant from the state to help maintain existing schools. Thus the seeds of partnership between Church and state were sown from as early as 1847, eventually maturing into the full complex relationships of the Dual System which is in place today. State funding for new school buildings was raised from 50 per cent in 1936 to 75 per cent in 1959, 80 per cent in 1967 and 85 per cent in 1975. The running costs of maintained Catholic schools are entirely state-funded. Capital costs are funded at 85 per cent for voluntary aided schools and 100 per cent for grant-maintained schools. By the year 2001, all primary schools must ensure that no class of five-, six- and seven-year-olds will have more than 30 pupils per class. Acknowledging the popularity of many denominational schools, the government has announced that a 100 per cent government grant will be made available for necessary building work where the expansion of such schools is deemed necessary.

A purposeful system of Catholic-maintained schools developed in England and Wales, underpinned by the combination of personal sacrifice within the Catholic community, the dedication and commitment of Catholic teachers, both religious and lay, and the loyalty and support of priests and parishioners. The intensity of religious bonds between parish, school and home was a mainstay for the Catholic Church in its mission of 'preserving the faithful' in an environment shielded from secular influences and hostilities. Working together, the home, the school and the parish displayed characteristics of common bonding, solidarity and a sense of mutual obligation.

One measure of the success of this educational endeavour was the growth in pupil numbers. Whereas in 1850 there were 41,382 school places in 'all age' Catholic schools, just twenty years later this figure had more than doubled to 101,556 places (Beales, 1950: 371). Elementary schools multiplied and statistics for 1950 put the number of Catholic schools at 1,833 and the number of pupils attending these schools at 395,000 (Beck, 1955: 78). It is against this background of endeavour, enterprise, commitment and sacrifice that I now address contemporary developments in Catholic education provision.

I shall confine my explorations to those strands of influence that have significantly defined today's context for Catholic state-maintained schools in England and Wales. First, the demographic changes that have given rise to a multicultural, multi-racial and religiously diverse society. Second, there are those developments springing from the Second Vatican Council that have generated changes in the self-understanding of the Church, in particular, the Catholic Church's teaching with regard to other faiths. The third area focuses on the ways in which educational policies and priorities of successive governments have exerted powerful influences on the Catholic school system.

The 1944 Education Act firmly established a national system of education. As Fletcher notes:

> It was a point of arrival and a point of departure in the fullest sense – accomplishing a consolidation of all that had been achieved in the making of the education system so far, but also reconstructing this in the light of the new *addition* of a comprehensive system of education. (Fletcher, 1984: 188)

The restructuring of education culminating in the 1944 Education Act was a landmark in the development of the Catholic school system in England and Wales. For the Catholic Church, in its educative role, it signified a shift from the margins of educational endeavour towards a more pivotal role in an enhanced partnership with the state in a publicly funded education system. The unswerving determination of the Catholic bishops to seek justice in terms of the natural rights and duties of Catholic parents to have their children educated in their faith by teachers of their own faith, and not to be financially discriminated against, had paid dividends. It is significant that the expansion of school development at that time was undertaken with a minimum of encroachment on the Church's autonomy.

Following the 1944 Education Act and the introduction of 'secondary education for all' the Catholic school network in England and Wales experienced continuous growth until the mid-1970s. The task of expanding the Catholic school system in line with population mobility and patterns of variation was an overriding concern of the administrators of Catholic schools.

The year 1974 was in some respects a high-water mark for the Catholic education project in England and Wales. Commentators ascribe contrasting characteristics to the direction of Catholic education before and after that year. For Hornsby-Smith the preoccupation of Catholic education before 1974 was crucially 'quantitative' – illustrating a major concern over school buildings and pupil populations. After 1974, reflecting a decline in pupil numbers and a depressed economic environment, the emphasis was redirected to what he describes as 'qualitative' outcomes with 'an increasing concern to explore facts about the quality of Catholic schools' (Hornsby-Smith, 1978: 37).

Within the wider education scene, Catholic schools from the 1950s underwent reorganization along comprehensive lines and the subsequent dismantling of the tripartite system of grammar, technical and secondary modern schools. The progressive ideals of both liberal Conservatives and radical Labour Party politicians tended to converge in their search for the maximization of talent, equality of opportunity and parity of prestige, for all schools. It was also a time of major reports (Ministry of Education, 1959 (Crowther); Newson, 1963; Robbins, 1963; and Department of Education and Science, 1967 (Plowden)).

Furthermore, in the early 1950s the arrival of large numbers of immigrants from New Commonwealth countries had far-reaching implications for schools. Secular reforms stemmed from pragmatic concerns with a focus on education, ease of pupil transfers, equality of opportunity and academic selection. Catholic reorientations, emanating ultimately from Vatican II, reflect the transfiguring nature of Catholic tradition and the refusal of that tradition to be confined 'in a museum of nostalgias' or to 'retreat into a world of privacy' (Kiberd, 1995: 292). Since Vatican II there has been an increasing emphasis on service to the community, involvement in the secular world and contributing to a more just society (*Gravissimum Educationis*; in Abbott, 1966: 637–51).

Statistical profiles of the Catholic school system in England and Wales showing clergy and religious teaching in schools, non-Catholic teachers, contraction in school numbers, pupil populations, numbers in receipt of free school meals, pupils from ethnic minority backgrounds and numbers of non-Catholic pupils are given in the tables below. Statistics concerning the social composition in Catholic schools are not available.

Catholic schools have changed significantly in respect of the staffing profile. In terms of numbers, religious staff in schools declined from 5,857 in 1964 to 3,813 in 1974, a drop of 65 per cent. Table 13.1 shows that the decline in the number of clergy and religious involved in teaching in Catholic schools has continued, while Table 13.2 reveals a marked increase in the proportion of non-Catholic teachers employed in Catholic schools.

Table 13.1 Clergy and Members of Religious Orders Teaching in Catholic Schools

	1980		1990		1996	
Primary	1,238	(7.0%)	471	(2.7%)	221	(1.2%)
Secondary	975	(4.4%)	331	(1.7%)	155	(0.8%)
Independent	1,101	(22.9%)	497	(10.0%)	206	(5.1%)

(*Source:* Catholic Education Service (CES))

Table 13.2 Non-Catholic Teachers in Catholic Schools

	1980		1990		1996	
Primary	1,365	(7.6%)	1,893	(11.2%)	2,248	(13.1%)
Secondary	7,522	(33.6%)	7,239	(39.3%)	7,773	(42.5%)
Independent	1,665	(34.6%)	2,071	(41.7%)	1,815	(45.1%)

(*Source:* CES)

A survey carried out by the Diocese of Arundel and Brighton (1991) highlighted the increasing difficulties faced by Catholic schools in recruiting Catholic teachers. One of the main conclusions in *The Supply of Catholic Teachers to Catholic Schools*, compiled by the Catholic Education Service (CES, 1994), in respect of teacher recruitment and the nature of teacher shortages in Catholic schools, stresses that the difficulty in recruiting Catholic teachers is more apparent in the key posts for which the appointment of a Catholic is essential. Statistics for the number of Catholic teachers teaching in secular schools are not available.

In the early 1950s there were 400,000 pupils in Catholic maintained schools; by the early 1970s this figure exceeded three quarters of a million (Hornsby-Smith, 1978: 16). Since then the sharp drop in the birth rate and subsequent falling pupil numbers have affected all schools in England and Wales, including Catholic schools. Over the same period Catholic baptisms declined. Table 13.3 highlights the contraction in the number of Catholic primary and secondary schools since 1980.

Post-war affluence and upward social mobility, resulting in large numbers of Catholics moving out of traditional inner-city parishes and into new suburbs, housing estates and new towns, necessitated the building of new schools in areas where large numbers of Catholics had

Table 13.3 Contraction of Catholic School Provision 1980–96

	1980	1990	1996
Primary schools	2,117	1,930	1,854
Secondary schools	525	418	392
Independent schools	291	224	178
Direct grant schools	12	–	–
Special schools	22	17	14
Total	2,984	2,589	2,438

Note: 17 sixth-form colleges are included under the category of secondary schools. There are 120 grant-maintained schools. Included in the above figures are 2 primary and 8 secondary jointly managed schools, shared between the Catholic and Anglican Churches.
(*Source:* CES)

settled. Today, Catholic schools, reflecting this movement of people, are to be found not only in traditional working-class areas and in some of the most deprived areas in the country but also in the leafy suburbs with predominantly middle-class pupil intakes and in rural areas.

Since 1980 there has been an 18.3 per cent decline in the number of schools. Radical restructuring of education and the accompanying amalgamations played a significant part in the contraction of Catholic schools. The decline has been most marked in the independent sector with a 39 per cent fall. The number of maintained secondary schools fell by 25 per cent for the same period. The contraction of maintained primary schools has been less marked, with a decline of 12 per cent in the number of schools.

The 1988 Education Act provided a legal framework for schools to 'opt out' of the control, funding and administration of Local Education Authorities and choose whether to become grant-maintained schools. There were 120 Catholic grant-maintained schools which were funded and administered directly by central government. All capital works were 100 per cent funded from public money, eliminating the 15 per cent contribution which had to be found by Catholic voluntary aided schools. The introduction of grant-maintained schools brought to an end a unified policy of voluntary aided Catholic schools. The Catholic bishops expressed grave reservations about the 'opting out' of Catholic schools in respect of episcopal control and the planning of Catholic school

Table 13.4 Pupils attending Catholic Schools 1980–96

	1980	1990	1996
Primary schools	417,593	409,357	440,957
Secondary schools	363,412	283,904	314,950
Independent schools	79,138	65,614	51,693
Direct grant schools	7,622	–	–
Special schools	1,579	1,276	1,174
Total	870,430	760,151	808,774

Note: In addition in 1980, 1,086 pupils were receiving their education in Community Homes, formerly known as Approved Schools.
(*Source:* CES)

provision as a whole. Under the present government, opted-out status will be abolished. Although the bishops have urged schools that have opted out to take up their voluntary aided status again, it would appear that only one school has, at the time of writing, provisionally opted out. If this happens the Church would lose control over the employment of the head, staff and religious education.

In 1974 the number of pupils attending Catholic schools reached a peak of 942,545 pupils (Hornsby-Smith, 1978: 170). Table 13.4 gives the statistics for pupil numbers for the period from 1980 to 1996. Between 1980 and 1996 the pupil population dropped by 7 per cent. The independent sector experienced the sharpest fall in pupil numbers (34.7 per cent). In maintained secondary schools there was a 13 per cent fall in pupil numbers for the same period. However, there was an increase of 5.6 per cent for pupils entering primary schools.

An important indicator of the social and economic backgrounds of pupils is their entitlement to free school meals. The national average for pupils eligible for free school meals is 18 per cent of pupils per school. Tables 13.5 and 13.6 provide statistics for pupils who are receiving free school meals in Catholic primary schools and secondary schools.

Further analysis of these data reveal that over one third (38 per cent) of Catholic primary schools have above national average intakes of pupils from disadvantaged backgrounds. Fewer secondary schools than primary schools, 36 in every 100, have above the national average intake of pupils from disadvantaged backgrounds. The lower numbers may be partly explained by a more rigorous secondary school admissions policy.

Table 13.5 Percentage of Pupils in Catholic Primary Schools Receiving Free School Meals

% Free schools meals	Number of schools
0 < 10%	563
10 < 20%	527
20 < 30%	269
30 < 40%	185
40 < 50%	125
50 < 60%	68
60% or more	35
Total	1,772

(*Source:* The statistics for the Tables 13.5, 13.6, 13.7 and 13.8 were compiled by the Catholic Committee for Community Relations and are based on data supplied by the Office for Standards in Education (Ofsted) (January 1997). The Ofsted statistics do not include infant schools. This explains variations in statistics provided by the CES in previous tables.)

Table 13.6 Percentage of Pupils in Catholic Secondary Schools Receiving Free School Meals

% Free school meals	Number of schools
0 < 10%	89
10 < 20%	137
20 < 30%	61
30 < 40%	24
40 < 50%	21
50 < 60%	14
60% or more	9
Total	355

Note: Sixth-form colleges and special category schools are not included in the above statistics.

Table 13.7 The Percentage of Ethnic Minority Pupils in Catholic Primary Schools

% of ethnic minority pupils	Number of schools
5 < 10%	167
10 < 20%	119
20 < 30%	68
30 < 40%	51
40 < 50%	26
50% or more	26
Total	457

Table 13.8 The Percentage of Ethnic Minority Pupils in Catholic Secondary Schools

% of Ethnic Minority Pupils	Number of Schools
5 < 10%	47
10 < 20%	42
20 < 30%	13
30 < 40%	17
40 < 50%	12
50% or more	12
Total	143

Today, ethnic minorities account for approximately 6 per cent of the population of Britain. In schools they account for a larger percentage of the school population, possibly as high as 10 per cent. This ethnic diversity is reflected in many Catholic schools. It is important to mention that in many areas the diversity of the pupil population extends beyond ethnicity and includes significant numbers of pupils of faiths other than Christian. Tables 13.7 and 13.8 provide statistics for schools with 5 per cent or more ethnic minority pupils.

Just over a quarter (26 per cent) of all Catholic primary schools have 5 per cent or more ethnic minority pupils. 63 per cent of these primary schools have 10 per cent or more ethnic minority pupils. Over half (58 per cent) of schools with sizeable numbers of ethnic minorities are to be found in major cities, with the greatest concentration (35 per cent) in London. Thirty per cent of all Catholic secondary schools have 5 per cent or more ethnic minority pupils. Thirty-eight per cent of these schools have 20 per cent or more ethnic minority pupils.

The distribution of the ethnic minority population is largely centred within the major conurbations. Accordingly, there is a significant variation in pupil populations from area to area with a preponderance of diverse pupil rolls located within deprived working-class areas. Bishop Konstant draws attention to the 'problems which many of these schools face' and which are virtually unknown in more affluent areas. He cautions that 'it is imperative that we do not leave them alone in their struggle' (CES, 1997).

The link between disadvantage and diverse school populations is underlined in a Report published by the Bishops' Conference of England and Wales *A Struggle for Excellence* (1997). To take an example – a secondary school in a deprived London borough provides the following statistics for the ethnic mix of pupils: British (37.8 per cent); other European (including Irish) (34.5 per cent); Jamaica/Trinidad (6.8 per cent); other Commonwealth (6.7 per cent); other non-British (6.5 per cent); East African (2 per cent); Ghana/Sierra Leone (4.2 per cent); China/Hong Kong (0.8 per cent); India/Sri Lanka (0.5 per cent); Malaysia (0.1 per cent) (p. 15).

The above Report, which is based on research undertaken in Catholic secondary schools in urban poverty areas, found that of the Catholic schools with high concentrations of ethnic minority pupils many are located in some of the most deprived areas in the country. The ethnic diversity of pupil intake is accompanied by increased numbers of pupils from other faith backgrounds. It is clear that the remit of 'mission' to the poor, once mainly Irish Catholics, is not quite so obvious today. The poor are heavily represented among ethnic minority groups of diverse religious and cultural backgrounds.

Table 13.9 shows that throughout the 1980s there was a significant increase in the number of pupils in Catholic schools who were not Catholic. While admission policies for schools continue to give priority to Roman Catholics, it is clear that many schools have flexible admissions policies in place. The marked change in the school population has given rise to an increasingly diverse Catholic school system. While some schools cater only for Catholic pupils, other schools with spare places admit pupils from other Christian traditions and other faith backgrounds.

Table 13.9 The Percentage of Non-Catholic Pupils in Catholic Schools

	1980		1990		1996	
Primary	19,384	(5%)	39,263	(9.5%)	49,098	(11%)
Secondary	12,882	(3.5%)	38,195	(13.4%)	56,004	(17.7%)
Independent	33,782	(42.6%)	32,185	(49%)	26,092	(50.4%)

(*Source:* CES)

To sum up at this point, since 1980 Catholic schools have engaged more lay teachers and an increasing number of teachers who are not Catholics. Schools are more diverse in respect of race, ethnicity and indeed, of faith backgrounds. These factors now constitute significant features on the landscape of Catholic education. Approaches to the admission of pupils are now varied and far removed from a once ordered, unitary and coherent scheme of thought and action. An important departure is noted by Hypher in the following way:

> Catholic schools founded with one set of objectives are now being required to adapt to new objectives relating to openness, dialogue, mission, other faiths, option for the poor, racism and religious freedom, while at the same time remaining true to their original purpose (Hypher, 1996: 230).

Needs of Ethnic Minority Children

Ethnic Diversity in Catholic Schools

A number of working parties have explored key aspects of ethnic diversity in Catholic schools with their implications for all pupils being taught in Catholic schools. Central to the work of these groups was the recognition that there is a 'long way to travel' on the question of how best to fulfil the Church's mission of education and service in Catholic schools in response to the changes in society. In 1975, the then Catholic Commission for Racial Justice (CCRJ) carried out research in 25 Catholic schools and published its findings under the title *Where Creed and Colour Matter: A Survey of Black Children and Catholic Schools*. It found little evidence to suggest that these Catholic schools had adapted sufficiently in response to their experience of a more ethnically, racially and religiously diverse pupil population, or developed appropriate practices that took into account their wider variety of needs. In essence, Catholic schools were 'making a very small contribution to the education of immigrants' (p. 8). In 1982 the CCRJ stressed that 'Though the obligation to prepare our children for life in a multi-racial society falls on all of us, and on all our institutions, the Church and Church schools specifically, have an important role to play' (1982: 2).

A second working party was set up at a time when Church schools were at the centre of a wide-ranging debate. Their place in the dual system was being increasingly challenged by educationalists, pressure groups and politicians. The Socialist Education Association questioned the continuing role of Church schools in its pursuit of the 'principle of harmonization of all schools'. Admissions policies were a major source of tension. They were seen as divisive and a means of preserving a 'privileged selective intake; and a skewed social or racial intake as well' (O'Keeffe, 1986).

A group of Christians committed to racial justice voiced their concern over admissions policies in the following way: 'Some Church schools emphasize their Christian basis and thereby ... exclude, in practice, children of other faiths, thus becoming unrepresentative of their neighbourhood. Thus in some areas Church schools have become white enclaves using religion as a means of discrimination' (Christians Against Racism and Fascism, 1985).

The starting point for the working party of the Department for Christian Doctrine and Formation of the Bishops' Conference had, as a central concern, the need for Catholic education to provide for 'the education of all Catholics for life in a multi-racial, multi-cultural society, and the specific educational needs of Catholics who are members of racial or cultural minorities' (1984: 8). In its published report *Learning from Diversity*, the working party found many encouraging instances of good practice. Yet much remained to be achieved, especially in attitudes of schools towards tackling the prevailing racism in the wider society. It argued for an education that 'prepares children to live in, and help to create a multi-cultural society, based on unity in diversity', characterized by justice and equality, in which racism is a thing of the past (ibid.: 18–19). The working party also noted that an 'all white' Catholic school in a racially mixed neighbourhood 'can, unless great care is taken to foster links with the local community, stand out as a symbol of racial segregation contradicting the good work which may be attempted within the school itself' (ibid.: 29).

Cardinal Hume's Advisory Group on the Catholic Church's commitment to the black community in its report *With you in Spirit?* (1986) put the defeat of racism as a top priority for Catholic schools: 'There is an urgent need for those responsible in Catholic schools to put their house in order and to demonstrate to the black community that the system of education they are offering is fair and just for all God's people' (Cardinal Hume's Advisory Group, 1986: 28). The group reported the widespread misgivings among black parents over what they saw as 'the raw deal they get from the Church in education' (ibid.: 21). Black parents spoke of the practices which adversely affected their children's education and hampered their hopes, aspirations and achievement levels (ibid.: 24). They emphasized that 'Catholic schools should be in the forefront – showing the way to others by eliminating racist attitudes and practices within their institutions. To date there is little evidence that they consider this a priority' (ibid.: 27).

It is noteworthy that these working parties in the 1970s and 1980s accepted the need for Catholic schools to play their part in creating a more just and fair society. What emerged from the above reports was the need for all schools to implement programmes for action to develop mutuality of respect between different cultural and ethnic groups and to promote racial justice and equality of educational opportunity for all pupils.

The concern for social justice moved further centre stage when the Committee for Community Relations was established in 1984 as an advisory body to the Catholic Bishops Conference of England and Wales. Its remit covers the areas of racial justice, urban poverty and community development (Annual Report, 1997). The following were some of the Committee's key areas of concern during 1997: urban poverty issues in Catholic schools and in the wider society; achievement of ethnic minorities in schools; Catholic schools in urban poverty areas; other faith issues and 'Islamaphobia'; racism and the criminal justice system.

Encountering Other Faiths

Catholic schools located alongside multi-faith communities often face requests for admission from families of other faiths. In a number of inner-city parishes, where many parishioners have moved to the suburbs, the Church school may find its very survival at stake. The presence of a large pupil market, albeit of other faith backgrounds, can be a spur to a re-examination of admissions policies. In some such areas, where schools have experienced a fall in the applications from Catholic parents, they have widened their admission criteria.

Other schools do not adapt. Their admissions criteria continue to be based solely on the school's trust deeds and places are offered only to Catholic pupils. Where there are insufficient Catholic pupils, schools have closed and the Church has effectively withdrawn from sensitive areas of human and social affairs in areas often characterized by marked deprivation.

The hazards, facing those schools whose response is purely pragmatic and who fail to reorder their objectives and practices to match their new intake, are soon evident. They may, for instance, without adapting existing policies and practices, admit pupils of other faiths on condition that they participate fully in all aspects of school life. Inevitably, in the absence of special provision the religious needs of these pupils are placed in jeopardy. The faith dimension by which the Church places such great store, and which for the Catholic child is fully integrated and expressed within the school, is for a child of another faith tradition invisible and absent from the school environment unless specifically and fully catered for.

A comparatively small but significant number of Catholic schools have made a principled decision to accept pupils of other faiths and have sought to develop policies in response to a more diverse pupil population. The stress is on the school as a community that meets the human and religious needs of pupils and looks beyond its frontiers to challenge and serve a religiously, culturally and racially diverse society. The emphasis shifts beyond the concept of providing 'an education for the Catholic community' to incorporating the Post-Vatican II understanding of mission by providing 'a Catholic school for the community' (Murray, 1996: 250).

In 1991, the bishops established a consultation to review and re-evaluate the work of schools in the light of the development of a more diverse Catholic school population. The report of the consultation, *Catholic Schools and Other Faiths* (Bishops' Conference, 1997b), was the culmination of a five-year joint project involving the Committee for Community Relations, the Committee for Other Faiths and the Department for Catholic Education and Formation.

The report outlines policies for Catholic schools that incorporate the vision of Vatican II towards people of other faiths while 'having care to preserve the essential Catholic nature of our schools within the dual system' (Bishops' Conference, 1997c: 2). The report addresses all schools whether or not they open their doors to pupils who are members of other faiths, or are situated in multi-faith areas. All Catholic schools will 'need to find ways in which its pupils can learn to engage in dialogue' (1997b: 22) and to develop an attitude of respect for religious diversity.

The report highlights a number of tensions for Catholic schools in their response to the challenges of our multi-faith society. These include tensions: 'between faithfulness and openness, between being a teacher and being a learner, between being mandated to proclaim a message and mandated to engage in dialogue, between forming faith and respecting religious freedom and personal conscience' (1997b: 19). These tensions arise not just from practical circumstances 'but from the fullness of the Church's teaching'. In addition, they concern not only religious realities and experiences and a valuing of diversity, but also the search for cultural harmony. Furthermore, the Bishops' Working Party remind us that fidelity and openness are:

> two sides of one response to Christ; they do not contradict each other, but complement each other. Fidelity, without the openness the Church asks of us, is no longer true fidelity but merely choosing which parts of the Church's teaching we like. Equally openness, without fidelity, is no longer an openness based on faith and truth, but merely a bland broad-mindedness. (1997c: 4–5)

Confronting these tensions we can seek to translate them into factors of creative possibility, aided by a sense of the past that has not 'lost its future, its power to challenge and disrupt' (Kiberd, 1995: 294).

The report reminds schools of the necessity for a clear rationale for admitting pupils of other faiths and which will find expression in policies and practices of the school (1997b: 23). It puts forward three approaches as a way forward for schools which admit or are thinking of admitting pupils of other faiths. These three approaches or rationales, while distinct, are not necessarily mutually exclusive. While in practice they may often overlap, they nevertheless point to a difference in emphasis in the way schools see their role.

First, schools may decide to offer a form of *hospitality* to Muslim, Hindu or Sikh pupils whose parents are looking for a faith environment in which their children can be educated. It is anticipated that these pupils would constitute a small minority. There would be a greater emphasis on similarities rather than on their differences in these schools. All pupils would be encouraged to live harmoniously together. However, the school environment would be one in which children from other faith communities would find 'an atmosphere of sincere respect and friendship' (1997b: 24).

A second approach speaks to those who see their schools as *servants* to the local community and at the service of other communities of faith. These schools would display an active concern for social justice. In socially deprived inner-city areas this 'servant' model is particularly relevant. Their actions would enable schools to: 'provide a Catholic and Christian presence, as an effective sign of faith in Jesus, placed at the service of the local community in order to meet both social and religious needs of the poorest' (1997b: 24). Reflecting on the 'servant' model, Vince Murray makes an important observation: 'While it is possible to make a logical distinction between education for justice and education for interfaith understanding, the reality is that commitment to the former will often incorporate the latter as a necessary form of "acting justly" in Britain's bigger cities' (Murray, 1996: 250).

A third approach is for those responsible to see their school as fundamentally a place of *encounter, dialogue* and *partnership* between the Catholic community and other faith communities. The report suggests that the joint Christian school already in existence might provide a paradigm of ways in which a Catholic school could be developed as a joint Roman Catholic/Other Faith school. However, for legal and practical reasons, establishing a basis for such a partnership is unlikely to happen in the near future (1997b: 24). The report draws attention to the fact that:

> When a school admits children from Other Faith communities it takes on a commitment to and enters into a relationship with pupils, their families and their communities which demand both openness and dialogue ... A Catholic school taking on such a commitment is allowing itself to be both challenged and enriched by opening its doors (as well as its mind and heart) to people of Other Faiths. (1997b: 21)

In a second publication of the Bishops' Conference, *Guidelines for the Study and Implementation of 'Catholic Schools and Other Faiths'* (1997c), the focus is on practical issues for Catholic schools, for example, mission statements, worship, in-service training, pupil admissions, curriculum and staffing. There has been considerable debate concerning the proportion of non-Catholic pupils who can be admitted without diluting the Catholic identity of a school. In the case of St Philip's Catholic Sixth Form College in Birmingham, the Oratory Fathers as foundation governors decided to close the college because they considered that only 32 per cent of Catholics was insufficient to maintain its Catholic character. In the *Guidelines*, the bishops are 'not ... proposing a new concept of open enrolment' for Catholic schools. Instead they envisage 'Catholic schools who see themselves as serving both the Catholic community, with a concern for all people, especially the poor and marginalized, and for the spiritual and moral development of each individual' (1997c: 9). Here we see a dual role for the Catholic schools: first, the traditional domestic role – the religious socialization of Catholic pupils, in partnership with Catholic parents; and second, a general role – service to the wider community reflected in the changing nature of the pupil populations of many Catholic schools.

When the presence of pupils from different faith backgrounds is viewed as a positive enrichment and the curriculum reflects explicitly the rich diversity within the school and within society as a whole, pupils are assisted to play their part in the construction of a society that respects religious and cultural diversity. In this way Catholic schools will make their own contribution to building up harmonious relations, tolerance, understanding and combating racism, particularly in multi-ethnic and multi-faith areas.

A Focus for Religious Education

The task for religious education in the contemporary Catholic school is a demanding one. It must 'respond to different levels of faith response' among Catholic pupils (Sacred Congregation for Catholic Education, 1982: no. 28). At the same time it must provide for pupils who believe, those who are searching, and those who do not believe. In addition, the recently published *General Directory for Catechesis* (1997) makes the point that the teaching of religion is 'an academic discipline with the same demands and methods as other disciplines' (p. 26). It highlights the complexity:

The teaching of religion helps those students who believe to better understand the Christian message in relation to the great existential problems common to all religions and the problems facing humanity. Those students who are searching, or who find themselves confronted with doubts can begin to discover in the teaching of religion what is meant by faith in Jesus Christ. They can discern the replies which the Church gives to their questions, so giving them the opportunity of reexamining the decisions they have made ... When students are non-believers the teaching of religion becomes a missionary proclamation of the gospel. It helps to lead towards a decision of faith which catechesis, in a communitarian context, will help to mature. (ibid.: para. 75)

The distinction between catechesis, religious education and evangelization helps us to identify an important shift that has occurred from thinking of religious education as solely concerned with its traditional role of catechesis. This is not to say that catechesis will not have its place in relation to the faith needs and development of Catholic pupils, but it will be within a broader framework of classroom RE. The introduction of *Weaving the Web* as part of 'a flexible framework for curriculum planning' designed for use in secondary schools (ages 11–14) highlights a broadening of the subject matter and a role for RE which 'aims to help young people to be aware of and to appreciate the religious dimensions of life and the way this has been expressed in religious traditions' (*Teachers' Handbook*: 14).

The introduction of *Weaving the Web* into schools provoked much controversy (Arthur and Gaine, 1996: 333–57). A fundamental objection of the critics of this programme was that it was not inherently catechetical. Critics who opposed its introduction into secondary schools seemed unwilling to accept the consequences of a classroom as outlined in the *General Directory for Catechesis* and the need to distinguish between catechesis and religious education.

Secular Standards for Schools

Secular influences from distinct and varied sources impact inevitably on Catholic schools. Schools are required to deliver a National Curriculum which is accompanied by methods of assessment, attainment targets and testing. There is an obligation on schools to publish data performance on, for example, National Curriculum tests and examinations and school attendance. The government maintains control over the National Curriculum and the setting of national attainment targets while delegating its implementation to individual schools. The introduction of a new national system of inspection has forced all schools to review their progress towards providing high quality teaching, high standards of achievement for their pupils and value for money in the use of their resources.

The recently published bill, *The School Standards and Framework Bill,* has for the most part taken on board the education policies of the previous government by focusing on targets, levels of attainment, value for money and efficiency. Success will continue to be narrowly focused on literacy and numeracy targets and on GCSE and A-Level results. It is clear from the Bill that success is the dominant value in education.

Today, schools are among the most competitive institutions in our society. The competitive climate in which Catholic schools carry out their educational task places self-interest, competition, personal choice, power and, above all, success high on the agenda. A major influence today is the 1992 White Paper, *Choice and Diversity,* which sets out five major themes – quality, diversity, increasing parental choice, greater autonomy for schools and greater accountability – as the guiding principles for successive policy changes (p. 2). They 'provide the framework for the Government's aims and together define our goal for Britain's education system' (p. 5). The five themes promoted by the White Paper are set out in summary as follows:

1 *Quality* The search for higher quality in schools lies at the core of government reforms since 1979. A National Curriculum was established to this end.
2 *Diversity* As children have different needs, the provision of education should be geared more to local circumstances and individual needs. Decision-taking is relocated within Local Management of Schools (LMS) schemes.
3 *Parental choice* The claim that 'parents know best' is accepted more and more. Parental choice directly influences individual schools; the more pupils the school attracts the larger its budget.
4 *Greater school autonomy* Power has moved from the LEA, and a school governing body on which parents and teachers would be represented was set up under the Education (No. 2) Act, 1986.
5 *Greater accountability* Seen as the corollary to increased auton-

omy for schools. The publication of data about performance, school attendance and inspection reports makes possible scrutiny by parents, employers and the local community at large.

As I have remarked elsewhere, the task of setting the 'five great themes' in the White Paper, *Choice and Diversity* within an overarching theme of fairness remains to be accomplished (O'Keeffe, 1995).

As a member of the working party on Catholic secondary schools in urban poverty areas, I had the opportunity to listen to and learn from headteachers concerning the ways in which educational reforms have affected their schools. They spoke of the ways in which the introduction of a market culture, a prevailing spirit of competition and the criteria for measuring success have, in some instances, set school against school in the competition for pupils. They found that the taken-for-granted 'commonality of interest' among Catholic schools that had existed for so long is now in decline. As one teacher observed: 'we are not working together'.

In one area a headteacher of a Catholic school in a very deprived area, struggling to maintain pupil numbers, found he was losing his pupils to another Catholic school in a more stable working-class area. This headteacher, in turn, complained of losing the brightest children to a suburban Catholic school. In some areas it would appear that those who are gaining most from a competitive ethos have not only lost sight of those who are gaining least; they have also lost sight of any sense of interdependence and interconnectedness. In other areas, Catholic schools have developed a partnership based on collaboration and co-operation in order to minimize competition between schools.

Where there is an absence of partnership based on collaboration and co-operation, schools become increasingly detached from the 'natural' social community. As Ball points out: 'They may be *in* but are no longer *of* their community. Indeed by virtue of the changes in school governance schools are no longer accountable to or have responsibilities towards their local community, but rather to their immediate clients. Institutional survival rather than social responsibility is the primary concern' (Ball, 1997: 75).

Clearly, the ability of some schools to select pupils comes at a price: 'the creation of an underclass of disfavoured and under funded schools' (ibid). Several studies point to the adverse effects of choice and competition. They point to the ways in which over-subscribed schools screen out or exclude pupils who are difficult or expensive to teach, thus making teaching less demanding and high levels of performance in public examinations more easily obtainable.

In its wide-ranging response to the White Paper, *Choice and Diversity,* the Commission for Racial Equality (CRE) highlights areas of priority for action. First, the need to ensure that the remit of the Race Relations Act 1976 applies to the entire educational arena; that schools' admissions criteria and procedures operate within the Act; that inspection summaries are made available in relevant community languages; that the children of refugees, travellers and the homeless are provided for under the terms of the Education Bill. It requests that special educational needs assessment is undertaken where appropriate in the child's first language, with the availability to parents of necessary translation services. It argues that a broad knowledge of non-Christian faiths be a goal of religious education and that schools foster among their pupils and embody in their practice respect for people of ethnic groups and religions other than their own (CRE, 1992: 14).

The Catholic bishops in their publication *The Common Good in Education* (1997a), while not denying that market forces have brought benefits to some educational institutions, stress that long-term effects are threatening the integrity of educational values and practice. They speak out about the desire to 'succeed at all costs' and the dehumanizing tendency of recent education policies, and call on schools to examine their existing practices 'in the light of fundamental and humane principles' (Bishops' Conference, 1997a: 14).

A Basis for Catholic Schools

The bishops, drawing on the Church's social teaching, provide an alternative vision (1996) to *Choice and Diversity.* They set out the key areas of the distinctive nature of Catholic education based on five principles. The Catholic Education Service (CES) in a document *Learning from OFSTED and Diocesan Inspections,* based on reports of the strengths and weaknesses of 85 Catholic primary and secondary schools, takes up the five principles and suggests the means by which these can be put into practice. It is aimed at all those responsible for Catholic schools to help improve the quality of education and to evaluate the distinctive quality of the education they provide, particularly as it impacts on classroom practice (CES, 1996: 4). The CES has sought to promote the bishops' principles as an integral and informing aspect of the policies and practice in Catholic schools. The five principles are set out below with illustrations of some of the implications for school practice identified by the CES.

The Search for Excellence

The search for excellence is seen as an integral part of the spiritual quest. Christians are called to seek perfection in all aspects of their lives. In Catholic education, pupils and students are therefore, given every opportunity to develop their talents to the full.

The CES emphasizes the need for schools to ensure equality of opportunity for every child. Schools are asked to review and, where necessary, tackle shortcomings so that effective learning opportunities for all children of all abilities are made available (CES, 1996: 15).

The Uniqueness of the Individual

Within Catholic schools and colleges, each individual is seen as made in God's image and loved by him. All students are, therefore, valued and respected as individuals so that they may be helped to fulfil their unique role in creation.

The CES draws attention to the importance of 'consistency in assessment and monitoring of pupils' progress' and the setting of targets which are matched to pupils' abilities. On the issue of exclusions, schools are encouraged to review and, where necessary, improve 'strategies for reconciliation and the reintegration of pupils temporarily excluded from the school community' and to find ways of supporting permanently excluded pupils. It is noteworthy that inspectors found evidence of inadequate support for the spiritual dimension of pupils of other faiths. The responsibility of teachers to meet this need is emphasized (ibid.: 17).

The Education of the Whole Person

Catholic education is based on the belief that the human and the divine are inseparable. In Catholic schools and colleges, management, organization, academic and pastoral work, prayer and worship, all aim to prepare young people for their life as Christians in the community.

In addressing this principle, schools are challenged to offer more opportunities for pupils' spiritual and moral development and provide greater opportunities to promote individual responsibility. Schools are asked to ensure 'the integration of spiritual and moral development into the curriculum as a whole' (ibid.: 19).

The Education of All

Their belief in the value of each individual leads Catholic schools and colleges to have the duty to care for the poor and to educate those who are socially, academically, physically or emotionally disadvantaged.

The CES asks schools to review, and improve where necessary, criteria surrounding the admission of disadvantaged pupils; setting of targets; provision of resources; its place in the local community, especially in response to the most deprived; and the preparation of all pupils for life in a multicultural society (ibid.: 21).

Moral Principles

Catholic education aims to offer young people the experience of life in a community founded on Gospel values. In religious education in particular, the Church aims to transmit to them the Catholic faith. Both through religious education and in the general life of the school, young people are prepared to serve as witnesses to moral and spiritual values in the wider world.

The CES points to the need for schools to ensure that methods, teaching and learning promote individual responsibility; that sufficient opportunities are provided for moral development across the curriculum; that religious education is allocated sufficient time; and that in-service development of teachers of religious education is high on the agenda (ibid.: 23).

McLaughlin cautions against 'platitudinous rhetoric' which offers 'a spurious clarity in the form of slogans'. He suggests that unless principles drawn from Church documents act 'as spurs to deeper discussion' they remain no more than a 'Catholic variant of "edu-babble"' (McLaughlin, 1996: 138–9). His prudence suggests a concern with outcomes. Grace

(1998) points to the need to differentiate between 'a surface level analysis' and deep structural analysis as effective tools for measuring educational outcomes. He notes that Catholic schools 'have most of the surface and visible indicators of success'. However, analysis at the deep structural level 'encourages instead thoughtful reflection about the visible success and more systematic research into the changing culture of Catholic schooling' (Ibid.). Grace's concern for deep structural analysis in Catholic education points to the need for outcome-monitoring procedures capable of assessing the realization of the bishops' five principles.

14

Religious Life After Vatican II

James Sweeney CP

Historical Context

The religious orders are a distinctive feature of the Catholic Church. Other Christian Churches, indeed other world religions, have comparable institutions (Orthodox monasticism, Anglican religious communities, the Church of Scotland's Iona Community, Buddhist monasticism), but Catholicism is unique for the size and variety of its religious life (or consecrated life). This tradition has been built up from the earliest centuries to the present day, a dynamic tradition constantly evolving, creating new types of community, new expressions of religious living, new kinds of apostolic response.

Orders and the diocesan priesthood, existing side by side, have often been in tension with each other. The focus of ministry for the diocesan priest is the parish, while the orders (although sometimes caring for parishes) have concentrated on activities such as preaching, education, health-care and overseas missions; and, of course, the orders are both female and male whereas priesthood has always been reserved for men. The diocesan/order contrast, of course, should not be drawn purely in terms of ministry, as between 'general practitioners' and 'specialists'. Orders, in addition to their chosen form of apostolate (in the case of the apostolic orders), are committed to a distinctive lifestyle built around values of community, contemplation and the profession of the evangelical counsels.

Church authority across the centuries has regulated the practice of ministry of both diocesans and religious, as well as laying down the approved form of religious life. For the orders this has often been a difficult and delicate business. Their inspiration derives not from the perceptions of ecclesiastical authority but from the creative charismatic insight of their founders in response to emerging needs of time and place. Any new order or new form of consecrated life has usually had to go through a protracted period of questioning, and even suspicion, before finding a settled place within the Church.

The established ecclesial practice of today, encompassing both orders and the diocesan priesthood, can be traced to the reforms of the Council of Trent which reshaped and revitalized the Church's pastoral life (O'Malley, 1997). Subsequently, in the nineteenth century, Church authority was vigorous in re-establishing Church institutions, although making no change of direction from that set at Trent, and at this time a great number of new apostolic orders came into existence. Then, with Vatican II, a major innovative phase in the development of pastoral practice began.

Historically, then, the Church's pastoral life has been serviced by two interrelated institutions, two traditions: the diocesan priesthood and the religious life. These are not just complementary corps of pastoral agents, mobilized for different purposes, but are specific approaches to mission, different ways of exercising ministry, particular forms of Christian witness. Both have been profoundly affected by Vatican II's project of renewal.

Models of Church

For the diocesan priesthood the parish, despite criticisms of it as outmoded in today's more mobile society, remains and indeed has been reinforced as the focus of ministry, but the emergence of the proper and active role of the laity has required a certain transformation of the model of parish and of the role definition of the priest. This is set in the context of a fundamental shift in ecclesiology, from a stress on the Church as institution to Church as communion.

What of the religious orders? They, too, have had to redefine themselves in the light of changes in ecclesiology and ministry. Their problem, however, is more intractable. The new emphases on the theology of communion and lay ministry dovetail naturally with the parish as the institutional context which, when suitably reshaped, can accommodate these values in practice. The 'local Church', the diocese, made up of its parish communities, came centre stage at Vatican II and the role and scope of authority of the bishop was enhanced. Orders, however, have traditionally engaged in other sectors than the parish, are exempt from episcopal control and, most fundamentally, have a distinctive approach to mission, not preoccupied with the regular servicing of the life of the Church community (the field of the diocesans) but on the frontiers of emerging needs. Today, however, many of the institutions in which orders have pursued their mission – schools, hospitals, overseas missions – either are not available to them or may no longer be the places where the most urgent needs of the contemporary world can best be served.

Set adrift by these dislocations of their traditional contexts of mission, and attracted by the new model of communion (while also weakened by their own falling numbers, and under pressure to supplement the falling numbers of diocesans), many orders have drifted towards parish ministry. Clerical orders have committed more of their members as parish priests while lay orders (male and female) have taken on roles as parish assistants.

Social Change

Theological and institutional change within the Church since Vatican II has run alongside the sweeping social changes of the late twentieth century, and this has been a primary factor in transforming the make-up of the English Catholic community – and Catholicism in neighbouring Scotland (Boyle and Lynch, 1998). The distinctive sense of community of the previous era, emerging slowly from a memory of persecution and marginalization and maintained in a semi-ghetto environment, has given way as fuller opportunities for participation in the life of society have become available. As a consequence, distinctive Catholic institutions – from the parish to the school to the various services of the religious orders – have weakened as the focus of personal and communal belonging.

Previously, the religious orders appealed strongly to the idealism of the young, who entered them with the enthusiastic backing of their parents, and they were highly valued for their service of the Catholic community through works of religion and ministries of teaching, nursing and spirituality. Today, however, the orders face questioning as to why such good works should be linked to distinctive – and personally costly – institutional life. It is no longer perceived as necessary, or even helpful, to enter religious life in order to dedicate oneself to teaching or nursing or, indeed, to engage in pastoral ministry. Lay people can do all these things. The professionalization of care and the requirement of certified qualifications for the job have further loosened orders' control over their institutions and at the same time opened new career pathways for the laity.

Thus, the social and cultural underpinnings of religious life are dissolved and vocations are no longer forthcoming to anything like the extent previously known. The restricting effect on vocations of smaller families, in contrast to previous socio-cultural norms, also needs to be taken into account – the 'good Catholic family' no longer produces the children 'to give to the Church'.

The consequent move away by orders from their traditional institutions and works is often questioned on the basis that, while their role may have changed, there are new kinds of educational, healthcare and spiritual needs which urgently require their unique form of service. While this is evidently the case – and many religious do continue to work in their traditional contexts – the fact remains that, as a result of change in the social make-up of the Catholic community and at the level of ecclesiology and ministry, orders as institutions can no longer hold on to the role they once had. Orders today, within the Church as a whole and in the specific socio-cultural context pertaining in England and neighbouring countries, are ineluctably forced to a fundamental reappraisal of their identity and purpose.

The Impact of Vatican II

The immediate effect of Vatican II on religious life was not simply the setting in train of renewal, but an unanticipated shaking of the foundations. The late 1960s and early 1970s was a liminal period, a time of deconstruction of a pattern of life within orders which, since the nineteenth-century restoration project and the 1917 Code of Canon Law, had become more and more rigidly institutionalized. While organizationally superb, the restoration had disastrously underplayed the charismatic and personal–spiritual characteristics of the religious lifestyle. Orders took on features of Goffman-style 'total institutions', bulwarks of the 'Fortress Church' (Sweeney, 1994: 61–75).

The reason why a sudden change of direction took hold, with a wholesale rejection of standard practices, is still a matter of dispute –

sometimes bitter in tone (Carey, 1997); but clearly the mandate given by the Council for religious to return to their origins, to excavate the guiding inspiration of their founders, and to adapt their way of life and mission to the needs of the modern world, was seized upon as a liberation from burdens imposed by ecclesiastical ordinance. Religious felt, above all, free: free to respond again in tune with their deepest spiritual and pastoral intuitions (no doubt with some admixture of a less worthy shedding of inescapable burdens and obligations).

Religious life, drawing now upon its own inherent dynamic of response to need, long overlaid by institutionalized routine, vibrated to the fundamental shift of perspective articulated by the Council – the reorientation of the Church in relation to the world (cf. *Gaudium et Spes*, in Abbott, 1966: 199–308). This, together with the interrelated transition already noted from Church as institution to Church as mystery-communion, was the giant step accomplished at Vatican II, transforming the Church's basic pastoral stance from self-sufficient fortress in opposition, to the community of God's People open in service to the world.

The image of religious as monks and nuns shutting themselves away from the world (apart from carefully controlled pastoral duties) was ditched in favour of a lifestyle, tasks and commitments conceived in this-worldly terms and contributing to the advancement of God's kingdom in this life not just the next. As already said, this dramatic shift in outlook and practice was spontaneous – although not without its opponents – and overtook religious orders after the Council (1960s-style) rather than in a planned process. By the time the mandated process of renewal got under way in the late 1960s it had to deal with an already transformed situation. A theory had to be found for the practice!

Preferential Option for the Poor

After the Council, responsibility for initiating renewal (the management of change) was entrusted to the chapters and major superiors of orders, and a period of experimentation lasting twelve to fifteen years was envisaged (*Ecclesiae Sanctae*, 1966). The work carried out at this time – drafting new constitutions, formulating pastoral plans, adapting structures of government, modifying practices of communal life, reshaping ministries – was influenced by, and in some measure influenced, contemporaneous events and trends in the Church at large: papal teaching, particularly the social encyclicals of Paul VI and John Paul II; the deliberations of the Synod of Bishops; the CELAM conferences of Medellín (1968) and Puebla (1979); theological movements, particularly relating to liberation, feminism, ecology, inculturation. This was the crucible in which the preferential option for the poor, so influential in Latin America, came to prominence among the orders, following the lead of the 1975 Jesuit General Congregation which defined the Jesuit vocation as the service of both faith and justice.

The option for the poor is a multi-faceted notion, not so easily explained and all too easily distorted by simplistic reductionism. Its components are biblical-theological (God's choice of the poor), spiritual ('blessed are the poor/poor in spirit'), pastoral (service of the disadvantaged), lifestyle (solidarity with those in need), socio-structural and political (commitment to justice), praxis (conscientizing the poor to equip them as agents of social change). Holding all these elements in balance can be difficult. On the one hand, it may be asserted that this is nothing new – religious orders have always had a bias to the poor – but this underestimates the crucial shift to justice rather than mere 'charity'. On the other hand, it might be taken that the option for the poor is all about social work or political activism – ignoring the foundational belief in God as present among the poor. (For a fuller, ideal-typical description of the religious orders in the light of the option for the poor, see Sweeney, 1994: 35–6; also Azevedo, 1995: 49–62.)

It is hardly surprising that this perspective, so prominent in the post-conciliar Church, received such strong emphasis in the redefinition of religious life and its mission, since it both gives practical application to the Council's new openness to the world and expresses religious life's instinctive orientation to the needs of the times. Moreover, as orders began disengaging from traditional institutions and works, a process threatening to corporate identity, the rhetoric of the option for the poor laid down a marker about basic values.

The ideological and pastoral shift, however, was viewed with disquiet by some Church authorities, especially – and ironically – in the very regions, such as Latin America, where questions of poverty and justice were most critical. Religious renewal was, clearly, political – both in terms of internal relationships in the Church (control, exercise of power, determination of pastoral strategy), and in its possible external consequences (social commitments, political stances). In the wake of the Council, the perennial tension between religious and Church authority erupted in new form. The Vatican took action in 1991 against the Conference of Latin American Religious (CLAR), fearing that the option for the poor was being interpreted 'according to a Marxist code'; CLAR's elections were overturned and Vatican appointees installed. The United States was another major battleground, with the Vatican locked in controversy with religious, particularly the female orders and over feminist issues, leading in 1983 to a formal inquiry into the state of religious life (headed by Archbishop Quinn of San Francisco). Its restrained findings, however, did not substantiate – or satisfy – the views of conservative critics.

In England and Wales such bitter disputes have been largely avoided and orders, individually and collectively, have developed a range of initiatives promoting the option for the poor: small communities located in ordinary housing in areas of multiple deprivation; ministries to deprived groups (migrant workers, the homeless); advocacy of Third World issues, particularly by missionary orders with members serving abroad; public stances taken by the Conference of Religious and its social justice desk, aligning religious in the late 1980s with the declaration of Church Action on Poverty; and a renewed commitment to work with the poor entered into at Mass in Westminster Cathedral with Cardinal Hume in September 1998 (*The Tablet*, 5 September 1998, p. 1164).

New Theory – but Declining Institution

Orders' option for the poor, however, as well as attracting external criticism, is far from being universally embraced internally. Its articulation may have been theory catching up with the spontaneous post-conciliar shift in practice, but now it is practice which lags behind theory.

Renewal was always going to be problematic. What disrupted it was the precipitous drop in vocations which took hold in virtually all orders, as well as the diocesan priesthood, in the mid-1960s, becoming ever more critical in subsequent years. Many older religious on viewing the demands of Vatican II had felt that it would take a new generation to make the required change; when that generation failed to materialize, energy for renewal faltered.

Concern about (the lack of) vocations has always been a Church phobia, even at the height of the vocations boom, but it has become clear, in the Western world at least, that priests and religious are going to be in short supply in forthcoming decades. The sudden and dramatic reversal of the vocations trend – from the 1920s it had been steadily upwards, resulting typically in orders doubling or trebling their membership by the 1960s – raises fundamental questions. In the 1990s, orders are back to pre-boom levels, but now with very few young religious and many elderly. In part, the decline can be attributed to the 1920s and 1930s bulge passing on, but obviously a deeper change is taking place. Is it simply cyclical, something that should right itself with the passage of time? Or are there implications for the present form of priesthood and religious life? And what has been the part of post-conciliar renewal in the crisis? Did it cause it? Deepen it? Or would it have happened anyway?

One unfortunate effect of the Council, although perhaps inevitable, was to leave a certain ambiguity around the status of religious life, thus creating a confusion which was to plague renewal and blunt its effectiveness. The giant step of the opening to the world, and all else involved in it, was a new mandate for the whole Church and its total membership. An integral element was a revaluation of the laity, and not just in terms of role (as active participants, involved in ministry) but as regards their ultimate calling, expressed in *Lumen Gentium* (in Abbott, 1966: 14–101) as the 'universal call to holiness'. The Council abandoned any idea of a two-tier Christian calling: perfect following of Christ undertaken by religious, with the laity (and diocesan clergy?) merely satisfying minimum requirements. This change in ecclesiastical cosmology dethroned religious life from its position as a higher calling. By tampering with a fundamental feature of identity this was destabilizing in that it knocked away a key motive for embracing the religious life. Such knock-on effects of Vatican II, however, were not addressed at the Council (for example, by *Perfectae Caritatis,* the decree on religious life renewal (in Abbott, 1966: 466–82)), and had to be worked out, or muddled through, in the course of implementation (Wittberg, 1994: 232–3).

Inevitably, early in the twenty-first century some orders or provinces of orders will cease to exist. This is nothing new; two-thirds of all orders in the history of the Church have gone out of existence (O'Murchu, 1989: 109). The likelihood is that smaller orders, under severe vocations pressure, and orders with a poorly etched identity will succumb. The nineteenth-century foundations, many without a distinct spiritual tradition or charism of their own, and founded for very specific apostolic purposes, may fare badly. Larger, older orders with long traditions of life, spirituality, scholarship and diversity of historical experience may weather the storm better. New orders may emerge in response to the changed situation; some already have, as well as a new form of consecrated life, the secular institute, which first appeared on the scene in mid-century.

Religious Life at the Crossroads

What connections there may be between post-conciliar renewal and indicators of decline is a question to Catholicism as a whole, not just religious orders. Vatican II's critics make much of the drop in Mass attendance since the Latin liturgy was abandoned, often in a simplistic cause–effect analysis. While contemporary problems, which the Catholic Church shares with other Churches, are closely intertwined with the changes introduced at Vatican II, we obviously need to take account of the wide variety of other factors operative since the 1960s in analysing the key challenges now facing religious life.

A Way of Life

The main characteristics of religious orders have always been the capacity to respond to emerging needs and adherence to a rule or carefully constructed lifestyle. These together give form to the specific charisms of individual orders, and establish religious not so much in some unique set of ministerial activities which they alone perform as in their own tradition and approach to ministry, their own specific mission in the Church. This historic ecclesial tradition is today under pressure, internally from orders' organizational decline and externally from the concentration on the local Church. A further environmental factor is that since Vatican II there are not two but three *loci* of mission: diocesan priesthood, religious life and the laity.

Religious are not a simple corps of workers, but followers of the gospel path, 'virtuosi'. Who and what they are – in terms of witness, lifestyle and community – looms larger in their self-understanding and in how the Church understands them than any functional value. Their capacity to respond to emerging need, therefore, is not just a matter of availability, nor is it simply a keen eye for a challenge. Rather, it arises from the ability, characteristic of founders, to interpret the 'signs of the times', that is to say, to read the realities of the day in the light of the gospel, and to formulate an all-encompassing project of life and action by way of response. Charisma is the defining characteristic. But charisma is unstable; consequently, identity questions feature prominently in the theory and practice of religious life, although fading into the background once institutional concerns induce routinization.

Identity Crisis

Contemporary studies are all agreed on the centrality of the issues of identity, role and purpose of religious life. It is clear that this is an era of transition, and that on the ground there is a widespread crisis of identity. The major study on the future of religious orders in the United States (FORUS) (Nygren and Ukeritis, 1992; 1993; 1994) revealed that 'a significant proportion of religious, particularly women and those in younger age groups, do not have a clear understanding of their purpose or function in the Church today' (Nygren and Ukeritis, 1994: 30; see also, Sweeney, 1994: 209). This complex topic, ranging from the deepest level of communal- and self-expression to the instrumental level of contribution to society, is all-embracing.

As has been pointed out elsewhere, at mid-point in the century when celebrating the centenary of the hierarchy of England and Wales, the concern was for maintenance and consolidation. Since then, the story of religious life has primarily been of moving on from an era of massive institutional involvement – in schools, colleges, hospitals, orphanages, retreat houses, etc. Those projects had entailed great personal and communal sacrifice, had catered in a sustained way for the needs of a poor, marginalized community (a real option for the poor), and had been underpinned by the conviction that religious life was uniquely worthy in the sight of God. Orders were organized around corporate purposes and ministries, with clear goals in view (some taught, some thought, some preached, some nursed, some prayed, etc.).

The inexorable dissolution of it all in the post-war era forced orders to rethink their goals, but new corporate commitments – if such were established, some virtually abandoned them – have almost inevitably been more vague and less tangible (e.g. in place of schools, 'education in its widest sense'). Moreover, since Vatican II the conviction of following a higher calling, setting one apart from others, has had to give way to the less immediately compelling image of religious life as the following of an exemplary path, the purpose of which is not to seek some exclusive heavenly reward but to give special witness to common values and to exemplify in a striking way the universal call to holiness.

Searching for New Identity

Re-expressing identity is accomplished more through praxis than theory. At the ministerial level, it is a matter of creating new roles where they have been lost, reworking roles in need of change, and redefining corporate purposes. Even though the present paucity of personnel inhibits initiative here, many religious orders have taken the risk of assuming striking new individual and corporate commitments, while making provision to hand them over to others in the longer term on the probability of the order not being able to sustain the work. Examples can be cited: the move to live close to the poor and disadvantaged, or major new organizational commitments such as St Gemma's Hospice in Leeds opened by the Sisters of the Cross and Passion in the 1970s in response to an emerging area of need.

In 1985 and 1987, the Conference of Major Religious Superiors of England and Wales (CMRS) conducted in-depth surveys which showed that in the previous decade 340 religious houses were closed by two-thirds of institutes, but over the same period 60 per cent of institutes opened a total of 290 houses. The most common reasons for closure were large houses and finance; for openings, to provide for new forms of ministry and to cater for the elderly (CMRS, 1987: 46–7). Among trends identified were 'smaller communities and changes in life style' and 'movement towards the poor' (ibid.: 31–7).

The key issue of religious life's exemplary role or witness function is developed by grounding it in tangible value commitments: to community living, contemplation, the service of the poor. The theological shift has been from pre-Vatican II portrayal of 'the state of perfection' to today's view of religious life as prophetic: a way of life lived as a parable, proclaiming the values and present reality of God's kingdom, challenging behaviour, forces and structures which inhibit its spread. This model – less the 'city on the hill', more the 'leaven in the lump' – places religious life not apart from 'the world' but precisely at the meeting point of faith and social reality. At this interface, the preferential option for the poor – following Jesus's example of befriending those marginalized by religio-social power structures – grounds the commitment (Cussianovich, 1979; Neal, 1990).

New Directions

It is not difficult to see that redefining role and identity in these terms, while theoretically coherent, is a formidable existential task. The option for the poor is here embedded in a wholesale re-expression of the religious calling as a prophetic imperative with consequences for the totality of life and ministry. The ideological–theological challenge is matched by a practical and moral challenge. Nygren and Ukeritis found that only about 40 per cent of religious felt adequately prepared to work with the poor; 30 per cent felt little commitment to such work. They concluded: 'the ideal outpaces the action and the intention' (Nygren and Ukeritis, 1994: 36).

The practical expression of the option for the poor is more than simply 'working with the poor'. More fundamentally, it is a theological vision and a matter of spirituality, leading to a life-stance of solidarity with those who are marginalized, disadvantaged, excluded, stigmatized. Solidarity takes myriad forms: befriending in the first instance, and entering into the world of the socially excluded; but also by way of activities such as preaching, writing, advocacy, education, socio-political action. The existential challenge before religious orders is: to take on this kind of commitment; to develop a spirituality based on solidarity, allowing it to reforge their communal-personal identity; to mark out their gospel path in terms of the God of the poor; to rework corporate goals and pastoral strategies in relation to the social exclusion, cultural impoverishment and economic poverty of today. The existential challenge of the option for the poor is certainly about action (what must we do?) but it is also about identity (who are we as religious in today's Church?).

New Models

While the option for the poor has application in all forms and styles of religious life (as well as Christian life in general), the flagship projects are those involving 'insertion': that is, those religious living as small groups among local communities in areas of deprivation, in ordinary housing rather than ecclesiastical buildings, taking part formally (through specific projects) and/or informally (as neighbours) in the concerns of the local people. This alters the religious–secular mix: such a community is less readily identifiable as religious, having shed the usual signs including, often, the habit; and the immediate aims and goals are typically not evangelism or religious conversion but witness and service of human-spiritual need.

This ideal of life inspired some orders founded earlier in the twentieth century. The Little Sisters of Jesus (of Charles de Foucauld), for example, live as contemplatives in the midst of urban life and take up secular employment in poorer jobs. The Missionaries of Charity (of Mother Teresa), living in similar circumstances, follow a traditional form of religious life, seeking out and serving 'the poorest of the poor'. Today, many older orders have also set up communities on this model. Among the best known of such communities in England are the Hope Community in Wolverhampton (Goulding, 1994) and the Passionist Inner City Mission in Liverpool (and also London) (Smith, 1983). Most female orders have taken this step, as have the Jesuits, and the Franciscans in Newcastle. It would appear to have gained ground more fully among sisters, probably as a follow-on from the closure of larger institutions, than among orders of priests, who are more likely to be associated with a parish.

Among the older orders, however, such projects often remain on the institutional margins and are viewed as exotic specializations rather than within the mainstream of life and ministry. While superiors are usually keen to advance their importance, practical support is often disappointingly lukewarm, and relationships at times degenerate into opposition and outright hostility. Religious communities remain overwhelmingly wedded to the old traditions of their orders and are ambiguous and ambivalent about any radical departure in terms of the option for the poor. Arbuckle, who has argued the need not simply to renew but to refound religious communities, states that 'the new belongs elsewhere' and that those who set out on this path court marginalization (1988: 41, 125).

The Politics of Renewal

How might this ambivalence verging on hostility be explained? In part, the struggle is the same as that noted earlier between orders and Church authority; renewal is political, parties compete and interests collide. How the future of religious life is to be defined, what direction it is to take, are questions which divide. It may also be seen as a consequence of the vocations crisis. Religious today, fearing for the future of their way of life, take fright at any radical departure from their traditions lest it compound the problem. Reactive responses are also fired by unease at the disputations provoked by renewal, and the deluge of problems afflicting the Church after the Council. Blame is laid on those who have not adhered to the strict letter of the law and allegedly misinterpreted and usurped Vatican II by appeal to the 'spirit of the Council' (Carey, 1997).

Political diversifications of this kind take hold between orders as well as within them. A wave of new orders and movements – begun over the last thirty years in Italy, France, French-speaking Canada, Spain – adhere to traditional, even pre-conciliar, styles of religious life (Lenoir, 1988). Some older established orders have done the same, notably in the United States where, with backing from a section of the hierarchy, they broke away from the Leadership Conference of Women Religious (LCWR), which represents the great majority of orders, and formed their own coordinating body, the Conference of Major Religious Superiors, achieving Vatican accreditation in the early 1990s. Their trump card is that these orders attract vocations!

Vocations

Given that vocations crashed immediately on the close of the Council it is plausible, but simplistic, to blame renewal for the collapse. It is also simplistic to think that because traditional-style orders attract recruits other orders would attract them if they reverted to traditional ways. Today's traditionally minded recruits are a narrower band who, as a social group, do not reflect the breadth and diversity of previous generations of vocations.

Two primary factors need to be explained. Why the established route – the 'good Catholic family', by which such a wide band of young people once entered religious life – no longer functions for this purpose; and why religious orders no longer exercise a power of attraction over the young. For one thing, as already noted, families are smaller, even 'good Catholic' ones. But the vocations collapse has to be seen as part of a wider drift away from religious practice in the context of late-twentieth-century cultural transformations. The steady secularization and value diversification of society makes the passing-on of values and practices across the generations problematic. The cultural bias now works against tradition, in favour of the new and of change. Permanency in location, occupation, relationship, lifestyle, is no longer the norm, and may even be challenged as timid and inflexible. Institutions and ways of life redolent with tradition, making a claim over the totality of personal life and involving a lifetime of sacrificial commitment, are at a cultural disadvantage.

At the same time, the very insecurity and uncertainty of modern life can be an opportunity. This is precisely how fundamentalism works. Traditionalist groups profit by moving against the culture, opposing the spirit of the times. But in contrast, *Gaudium et Spes*, while resolute in opposing the dark side of the modern world, strikes a different note, celebrating human values and experience: 'The joy and hope, the grief and anguish of the people of our time, especially of those who are poor or afflicted in any way, are the joy and hope, the grief and anguish of the followers of Christ as well' (in Abbott, 1966: 199–200). Similarly for religious orders, their option for the poor, while prophetically denouncing injustice, is fundamentally optimistic. In place of the ancient *fuga mundi*, it embraces humanity, society and history as the locus of God's saving work. Why then do orders espousing such a generous, attractive vision apparently find it more difficult to attract vocations?

There are, of course, wider opportunities available for ecclesial service in today's Church, and in view of the value given to the lay role at Vatican II it was always likely that the number offering themselves for service as priests and religious would adjust downwards. But more fundamentally, contemporary cultural transformations do not favour attachment to organizations. As Beckford observes: 'virtually all voluntary associations have been finding it difficult in the last few decades to attract and retain members. In other words, "belonging" has been simultaneously losing its popularity in religion *and* in other fields as well' (quoted in Davie, 1994: 19). The lack of recruits has as much, if not more, to do with societal factors as to the features exhibited by religious orders. In this light, what needs explanation is not so much established orders' failure with vocations, but traditionalist orders' success. How have they managed to buck the social trend?

In fact, it is not only the new, traditionalist orders which attract vocations. Orders go through phases of lean and plenty which are not easily explained. In Britain, for example: Dominican recruitment is notably buoyant at the moment, the Passionists are enduring a long famine; some contemplative monasteries flourish (Pluscarden), others languish (Nunraw); the earlier success of some more traditional orders, hailed as proof that renewal was corrosive, has faded.

Nygren and Ukeritis claim that 'the orders that seem to be stabilizing in membership and direction are those that attend to two fundamental dynamics ... they are faithful to their founding purpose ... and in some ways more importantly in this time, they are responsive to new and emerging needs'. Listing new forms of poverty, new populations of immigrants, unmet human needs, the utter desperation of those who are homeless or with AIDS, and asking about the Church's response, they observe that: 'orders that are indeed attentive to these and similar concerns in the external environment and willing to assess and alter current commitments with the intention of serving the most pressing needs are, indeed, increasing in internal cohesion around an intensified mission. Collaterally, they are often the groups that attract newer members' (Nygren and Ukeritis, 1994: 41).

Renewal, then, is not the cause of the problem, but faint-hearted renewal. Orders which allow themselves to become torn between clinging to their traditions and taking risks with new tasks risk losing all. The secret of success – of both new traditionalist and established orders – seems to be that clearly focused identity manifest in praxis attracts, while existential identity-confusion is a major stumbling-block. Resolving the identity crisis may not bring about revitalization on its own, but clearly it is a necessary condition.

Into the New Millennium: Death or Rebirth?

What is troubling religious life as the century draws to a close is a rather fundamental and all-embracing existential question of identity. Over the last half century the way of life of religious has been radically disrupted at both practical-ministerial and theological levels and their special contribution to English society has, in large part, been overtaken by social and ecclesial change, even as they have laboured to carve out new roles. The approaching millennium now invites futurological speculation, and indeed there are good empirical reasons for asking whether something radically new – for religious life, for the Church as a whole – will be required in the near future. More critically, are such 'futures' likely to fly?

The theory has been proposed that with Vatican II religious life began a major transformation, on the scale of the twelfth-century transition to the mendicant way of life or the emergence of the apostolic model in the sixteenth century (Hostie, 1972; Cada *et al.*, 1979). More recently Wittberg (1994) has examined the patterns of rise and fall of orders applying social movement theory to the data – both contemporary instances and the historical record – analysing the operation of three factors: frame alignment, resource mobilization and communal commitment mechanisms.

Frame alignment issues (changing ideologies) are in play at both the micro level of individual orders (charism, mission, ministry) and the macro level of the institution of religious life as such (its perceived fundamental purpose and the dominant form in succeeding epochs). At the micro level religious life has clearly undergone an ideological transformation, refocusing it on prophetic witness (Wittberg, 1994: 233). What, however, are the macro level implications? How plausible is the hypothesis that the cumulative effect will be the emergence of a new prophetic model of religious life as the dominant form of religious life for the future? This would mean the prophetic model eventually exercising a hegemony over older orders as well as new foundations, in the way the mendicant model not only followed on from the earlier stable monastic form but influenced its further development and, in similar fashion, the apostolic superseded the mendicant (Cada *et al.*, 1979: 11–50; O'Murchu, 1989). Wittberg is doubtful, pointing out contradictions between the prophetic definition of purpose and the trends she uncovered in religious communities in the United States:

> The rising individualism of the communities' members and their competing identities as professionals prevented the concrete enact-ment of the new ideology within a given community. Lack of corporate visibility (whether through common dress or community-run institutions) made it all the more difficult for the order as a whole to be seen to be fulfilling its prophetic role. Instead, many religious communities evolved into voluntary associations of individuals held together largely by affiliative ties.

She quotes a leading commentator, Joan Chittister: 'Religious commu-nities have done a great deal to foster the prophetic individuals in their midst. At the same time, they have done very little to function as prophetic groups' (Wittberg, 1994: 239–40). Wittberg dismisses the chances of a full-blown prophetic model getting going because the rhetoric of its champions is not matched by reality: theoretical identity-clarity is overcome by existential identity-confusion. This came about largely because communities succumbed to the culture of individualism – an observation which finds support in the FORUS study (Nygren and Ukeritis, 1994: 22). It is this corrosive force which also brought about the atrophy of the communal commitment mechanisms which sustain the distinctiveness of religious life (common life and prayer, the habit, shared sacrifices, penitential practices, formation procedures). Finally, this parlous state of affairs was compounded by deep problems of resource mobilization – the vocations famine, loss of secure role ('environmental niche') and, critically, ecclesiastical hostility to the new direction taken by religious (Wittberg, 1994: 257–66).

At the 1994 Synod of Bishops on Consecrated Life some hostility was indeed expressed by a number of bishops, principally from the United States and Latin America and the Roman Curia, but the Synod as a whole, gently led by Cardinal Hume as *Relator*, declined to go down that road, preferring instead to encourage and support. Moreover, the bishops' understanding of religious life improved noticeably as the synodal process unfolded. The early consultation document (the *Lineamenta*) omitted any reference to the prophetic role, and on this and many other points was widely criticized; it appeared to confirm the fears that the Synod would be a disciplinary exercise dominated by a Vatican view. However, subsequent synodal texts and the post-synodal exhortation (*Vita Consecrata*) were a major advance, and all of them fully acknowledged the prophetic dimension (Sweeney, 1995; 1996). Wittberg's dismissal of the prophetic model as lacking the support of Church authority (1994: 223 – written just before the Synod) turned out to be quite wrong, no doubt because her judgement was shaped by the more narrowed, and conflictual, experience of the United States. (Individual addresses given to the Synod by participants from Britain and Ireland were published in *Religious Life Review*, in 1994 and 1995.)

At the same time, Wittberg is driven to the necessity of some form of 'new Catholic virtuoso spirituality'. She suggests tentatively that its seedbed will be the new traditionalist orders and, alongside them, the new lay movements. These, 'responding to the "sharpest anguish" of current Western culture ... focus on spirituality and community rather than on ministerial service ... devoting over half of their days to common prayer or meditation ... (with as a) subsidiary focus ... a strong spirit of poverty, which is interpreted as personal material renunciation ... as well as working exclusively with the poor'. For Wittberg, development is likely to take place under pressure from, and competing with, Protestant evangelicalism on the one hand, and esoteric New Age practices on the other, with an added dash of feminist sensitivity, Native American or Eastern prayer styles and Jungian archetypes (1994: 268–71).

Charisma and Transforming the Religious Life Tradition

Wittberg, like many others (e.g. Carey, 1997), is staggered by the dramatic downturn in the fortunes of religious, particularly in the United States and especially women's orders. Some comfort is taken from history: religious life went into free-fall before, at the Reformation and the French Revolution, but bounced back. This time, of course, it was not external events but an apparent own goal which triggered the crisis. However, events external or internal do not of themselves cause the crisis of an institution whose identity is rooted in the charismatic; the challenge of events is grist to the charismatic mill. If there has been a failure of creative response, we should look for its roots in the routinization of charisma.

The founding charisma of any order or movement inevitably fades as attention turns to consolidation; but for groups whose paradoxical purpose is to institutionalize the charismatic dimension of the Church, it is critical that charisma remains vital. Traditionally this was done by feats of virtuosity – going to a far land on mission, enduring a rigorous penitential lifestyle, excelling as a preacher or teacher, a profound life of prayer – all nurtured by the mystique of an exotic way of life shielded from view behind monastery walls. Most of this has been ironed out of contemporary religious life. Out in the open, orders look and feel pedestrian, and many are left with the feeling that this way of life has had its day. This virtuoso charisma was expressed above all by the individual and at the level of personal spirituality. What new form might it take in present circumstances in the Church?

I take it – in the conviction that with Vatican II the Spirit is leading the Church and disclosing its future – that the truly urgent need today, right across the Church, is to give concrete embodiment to the vision espoused at the Council. To hover uncertainly between the old and the new (faint-hearted renewal), between the past and the future, is to court decline. Desmond Ryan, writing about parish life in England, 'identifies as the core problem the inability of the senior levels of the institution to re-absorb inherited structures, evolved in earlier ages for other tasks, into a continuing process of Vatican II-ization, whereby the opposition between the Church and the world formerly prevalent is transmuted into a dialogue between them' (Ryan, 1996: 2). What the institutional Church appears hesitant about is religious life equipped to pioneer.

Orders are ancient inherited structures – malleable for new purposes if only they can throw off their present sclerosis. In the end they are simply what their members make them to be, and as exempt institutes they have relatively unfettered scope for action. Therefore, they enjoy and can assert the freedom to be innovative about life and ministry; they need not be constrained about a truly open dialogue with the world, a generous ecumenism, a keen engagement with the many spiritual traditions of humanity, a vigorous pursuit of justice. A new era for religious life – its renewed charisma – may be found in the task of fashioning at the heart of the Church contemporary models for life and ministry, prophetic models functioning as parables and speaking with power by virtue only of their inherent evangelical quality. This role is 'on offer', as it were, to today's religious. It waits to be taken up. The wellsprings of charisma, in both theological and sociological senses, wait to be tapped. In the meantime the struggle between the drive to future-oriented transformation and a restorationist tendency is likely to continue (Sweeney, 1994: 145–66).

Ultimately, charismatic forces and energies must find their place within underlying ideological and environmental realities. In the first place, orders, like the diocesan priesthood, will have to adapt to the emergence of the laity. This will be a massive change, as the pastoral life of the Church comes to be routinely served not only by specialist personnel, but by the wider community of the baptized. The FORUS study, in its most unambiguous finding (less than 2 per cent against), demonstrated that religious accept the necessity to work with the laity (Nygren and Ukeritis, 1994: 33).

Although the parish is the obvious and favoured context of lay involvement, it has limitations. The jealous guarding of clerical roles evident in a recent Vatican instruction put out a 'thus far and no further' message to the laity. Moreover, the parish can induce parochialization, with the unfortunate consequence of a narrowing-down of lay involvement to internal Church concerns, whereas lay mission is above all within and to society. A creative and fruitful partnership can be envisaged, therefore, between lay people and religious who seek to make a prophetic response to the signs of the times. Sectors of the laity have always been closely associated with religious: with religious-run churches in preference to their own parishes; as associates in schools and institutions; in third orders. Orders following the prophetic model would be well placed to provide opportunities for new forms of lay involvement. This could develop, to their mutual benefit, in collaboration with lay-ecumenical-professional organizations such as Church Action on Poverty and the Catholic Institute for International Relations which, in a way parallel to exempt orders, stand at a certain distance from the institutional Church.

The Future of the Religious Life Tradition

We began by acknowledging religious life as a distinct tradition of life and ministry in the Church, historically set alongside the diocesan priesthood. Today it has to accommodate the emergent role of the laity; at the same time, it runs the risk of being swallowed up in a generalized pastoral ministry of the parish. Its distinctive characteristic, determinative also for its future, is the charismatic; were religious life to lose contact with its charismatic roots, it would be unable to fulfil its prophetic potential. Religious charismatic forces tend to coalesce around social needs, human hungers, spiritual voids; all of which are as dramatic as ever in today's world. What distinguishes a religious foundation as truly significant, however, is the reading of that need in the light of the gospel.

Vatican II called for a new in-depth reading of human, social, economic and cultural realities. Thus, read in depth, economic poverty is revealed at the human level as social exclusion, at spiritual level as disregard of personal value, and at faith level as disruption of the covenantal love of God's kingdom. It is imperative to be consistent in following the Council's decisive shift away from theological-spiritual dualism (and the over-personalized devotional spirituality of fortress Catholicism) which kept religion separate from secular life – i.e. historically disengaged spiritualism. By contrast, the Council linked spirituality with human experience, community and justice and peace – i.e. communitarian or integral spirituality.

Crafting a way of life on this basis is the work of spiritual masters. Nygren and Ukeritis point out key factors crucial to an order's regeneration – fidelity to purpose, responsiveness to absolute human need understood in the contemporary context, energies collectively focused toward mission – and then conclude: 'outstanding leadership must emerge to carry the process of transformation to completion' (Nygren and Ukeritis, 1994: 41). This is a call for charisma. The danger, though, is that new procedures of decision-making and seeking consensus may have an inhibiting effect and rob leaders of effective authority (Wittberg, 1994: 273). An order fainthearted about renewal is likely to elect as leaders just those who reflect their own existential identity-confusion.

The story of religious life in England over the last half-century may read like one of decline, and on many fronts it is; it is a melancholy tale. Yet, decline in numbers, institutions, works and influence does not touch the heart of what the religious life tradition has been in and to the Church. At its best, this tradition has been a creative gospel response to new times and new challenges. What matters is not that yesterday's response to old challenges is fading fast; it is whether and when the tradition will rise to tomorrow's challenges.

Part IV

Conclusions

15

English Catholics at the New Millennium

Michael P. Hornsby-Smith

In Retrospect

Adrian Hastings has written or edited several collections which helpfully review many of the changes which have characterized the period under review. In the immediate post-war years, from 1945 to 1960, in spite of much expansion generated by large infusions of Catholic immigrants, 'politically, Catholics maintained almost as low a profile as in previous decades'. There was an 'intellectual emptiness' about contemporary Catholicism though there were elements of enthusiasm in the 'great cross-carrying pilgrimage to Walsingham in the summer of 1948', the celebration of the centenary of the restoration of the hierarchy at Wembley in 1950, the first stirrings of liturgical reform and 'the great post-war expansion of Catholic Action' and particularly the Young Christian Workers, inspired by 'the deepest loyalty to the contemporary papacy' and the recognition that they were 'all now in the front line in the struggle with Communism'. Yet this was the time when 'Roman Catholics could not rightly even say the Lord's Prayer with other Christians' (Hastings, 1986: 473–90).

By the 1960s, however, 'Catholicism had moved into the moderate centre of national power' with a Catholic Minister of Education and also Shadow Minister, General Secretary of the TUC, Director General of the BBC and Editor of *The Times*. Pat Keegan, President of the World Movement of Christian Workers, addressed the third session of the

Second Vatican Council. The Mass in English was introduced and 'with the passing of Latin, both the special mystery and the unquestioned clericalism of Catholicism faded fast'. After the Council there was a perceptible thaw in ecumenical relations. The Sword of the Spirit became the Catholic Institute for International Relations. But it was also the decade of *Humanae Vitae* (Paul VI, 1968) and a time of confrontation and decline. Charles Davis left the Church and Herbert McCabe was dismissed as editor of *New Blackfriars*. Letters were sent to *The Times* and there was a 'sharp decline in respect for papal authority' (Hastings, 1986: 561–79).

Bernard Sharratt (1977) provides a detailed review of the 1960s, 'the decade of Vatican II, as predominantly characterized by a process of complex re-education, including the articulation and assimilation of [the conciliar texts]'. The 'deliberately self-perpetuating process of social enclosure', promoted by the separate system of Catholic education and the emphasis on marital endogamy, came under increasing challenge and the strains were exemplified by the clash over and eventual closure of Corpus Christ College. Following the publication of *Humanae Vitae*, a dissenting letter was signed by 55 priests and appeared in *The Times* on 2 October 1968. A dissenting statement signed by 75 lay people, 55 of them in senior positions in Catholic organizations, was published in *The Tablet* on 5 October 1968. Archbishop Cowderoy complained that 'some of our poor, simple people have been misled by disobedient priests'. Sharratt sees the 1960s as promoting the 'rediscovery of Newman'. He concluded that 'the impact of Vatican II in England could be experienced by many of the faithful as an extraordinarily compressed period of "development of doctrine", at the heart of which was the rediscovery of the role of the laity, the laos or whole people of God'. Even so, the policy of 'consulting the faithful' was only implemented 'hesitantly and minimally'.

The next fifteen years, up to the mid-1980s, saw a decline of the clergy and an increasing process of 'laicization', notably in education. Reactionary movements such as the Catholic Priests Association and Pro Fide emerged, as did radical movements such as the Catholic Renewal Movement and the Catholic Charismatic Movement. Archbishop Worlock developed a close working relationship with the Anglican Bishop Sheppard (Sheppard and Worlock, 1989) in Liverpool where the National Pastoral Congress was held in 1980. Pope John Paul II became the first reigning pope to visit the country in 1982. Cardinal Hume was

'quietly protecting the moderate reformism that had come to develop ...
from being snuffed out too brutally' (Hastings, 1986: 630–48).

In Hastings's volume on *Modern Catholicism* (1991) many of the
matters classified as 'unfinished business', including intercommunion,
birth control and celibacy, or various 'aspects of Church life since the
Council', such as the state of the priesthood, the place of women in the
Church, marriage and sexuality, abortion and homosexuality, remain
unsatisfactory as we enter the new millennium. In a chapter on the effect
of Vatican II in Great Britain and Ireland, McClelland offers an account
of the closure of Corpus Christi College, the foundation of Heythrop as a
school of London University, and the ecumenical work of the Anglican–
Roman Catholic International Commission (ARCIC), the National
Pastoral Congress and the Pope's visit.

In sum, the post-war period, and especially the period since Vatican II,
has seen dramatic transformations in English Catholicism. Many of the
old 'certainties' have been challenged by the greater differentiation
between the 'essential' and the 'contextual'. The old assumptions about
clerical dominance and lay deference have been shattered for ever. The
verdict of history will surely be that the publication of *Humanae Vitae* in
1968 was a disaster and a major turning point in terms of the acceptance
of the legitimacy of clerical authority. From now on, Catholics would
make up their own minds on matters where they felt their experience or
conscience was appropriate. Contraception became the norm and Mass
attendance optional and occasional. As David Lodge pointed out: there
was a 'loss of the sense of hell' (1980). From being an ascribed collective
cultural identity, Catholicism became much more an achieved and
voluntary individual identity and it had to compete with all the other
leisure time pursuits on offer in the booming consumer-oriented culture at
the end of the century.

At the beginning of this study we asked four questions: how distinctive
are English Catholics? How have they changed over the past half-century?
What special contribution do they make to English society? Where are
they heading as we enter the new millennium? The contributors to this
volume have offered a rich collage of researches, testimonies and insights
at the end of the twentieth century. It is time to review the evidence they
have provided and the impressions which are suggested, attempt to
answer our original questions, and offer a judgement as to what can
reasonably be inferred about the prospects for English Catholicism in the
twenty-first century.

Reviewing the Evidence

The Distinctiveness of English Catholics

There seems little doubt that with the post-war social, cultural and economic changes, and the post-Vatican II religious changes and the easing of ecumenical relationships, the strong boundary walls which once defended the fortress model of the Church have steadily dissolved away. As Mary Douglas once regretted a quarter of a century ago, 'Now the English Catholics are like everyone else' (1973: 67). The national survey of *Roman Catholic Opinion* in 1978 provided strong evidence to support the thesis that there had been a dissolution of the distinctive Catholic subculture (Hornsby-Smith, 1987b: 208–14). Catholics no longer have to forgo eating and drinking on Christmas Eve if they wish to receive Holy Communion at Midnight Mass. They no longer have to decline meat courses at office parties on Fridays. Holy days of obligation are not as disruptive of work routines. Catholics are no longer forbidden to worship with others, even if the regulations about intercommunion remain strict (Catholic Bishops' Conferences of England and Wales, Ireland, and Scotland, 1998). For all intents and purposes English Catholics are indistinguishable from other English people.

The various researches reported in this book have substantially confirmed this thesis. John Marshall and Timothy Buckley have indicated that for Catholics as for everyone else, family life has been vulnerable to the pressures and tensions of modern life. This has led to a large measure of convergence to the norms of the wider society in such matters as contraception and divorce, though to a much lesser extent, abortion. Catholics are now much more likely to make friendships with and to marry people who are not themselves Catholics. Mildred Nevile and Ian Linden have traced the general decline of a 'confessional' approach to organized social concern. Michael Fogarty has drawn on his wide experience in public affairs to reflect that, unlike 50 years ago, the appearance of a Catholic in a position of public responsibility is no longer an occasion for surprise or alarm. John Fulton and Mary Eaton have drawn attention to the very considerable generational differences which can be identified among Catholics and which reflect the large-scale adoption of the societal norms of autonomy and individual choice. Like other people, Catholics now make up their own minds on matters of both private and social morality in a way which was much less the case fifty years ago. The retention by some teenagers of the Irish identity of their ancestors, which Mary Hickman had noted, runs against the general drift of the evidence for a loss of distinctiveness on the part of English Catholics over the past half-century.

Social and Religious Transformations

What, then, has happened to English Catholics over the past half-century? First, there was the period of 'expansionism' lasting up to the 1960s. Estimates from the Newman Demographic Survey suggested that, largely as a result of high levels of Irish immigration in the late 1950s, the Catholic population increased from 4.7 million or 10.7 per cent of the total population in 1951 to 5.6 million or 12.2 per cent in 1961 (Spencer, 1966: 62). In the early 1960s one in eight marriages was solemnized in a Catholic church and the proportion of Catholic infant baptisms as a proportion of total live births had risen to 16.1 per cent (ibid.: 72). In the two decades after the end of the war the number of parishes increased by one fifth from 1,910 to 2,320 and the number of priests by one quarter from 6,257 to 7,808. In the early 1960s a whole string of indicators peaked: Mass attendances around 2 million; child baptisms around 134,000; receptions (conversions) around 15,000; confirmations around 81,000; and marriages over 46,000 with 50 per cent between two Catholics. The corresponding figures thirty years later are 1.1 million; 75,000; 6,000; 46,000 (for 1985); and 17,000 (with the proportion of marriages between two Catholics around one third).

What does seem to be apparent is that somewhere around the late 1950s and early 1960s there was a distinct shift in the Church. Some (e.g. Dulles, 1977: 1; Hornsby-Smith, 1989: 17) saw the Second Vatican Council as the defining moment of change since it legitimated a new and distinctly different way of looking at the nature of the Church, which had significant consequences in every sphere of its activities from worship and liturgy to its relationship to the world. Others (e.g. McSweeney, 1980: 86; McHugh, 1982: 12 and also 1987) argued that an older ideological homogeneity of an authoritarian Catholicism began to break up with the death of Pope Pius XII.

There was certainly evidence that all was not well in the Church. Nearly two years before Pope Paul VI's encyclical *Humanae Vitae* (1968), Charles Davis, England's foremost theologian and editor of the *Clergy Review*, suddenly left the Church saying that he did not find either a concern for truth or a concern for people in the official Church. Rather 'there is a concern for authority at the expense of truth' and he was 'constantly saddened by instances of the damage done to persons by workings of an impersonal and unfree system' (Davis, 1967: 16; see also Hastings, 1986: 573–4). That similar judgements appear to find resonance at the end of the twentieth century is apparent in the resignation of Fr John Wijngaards from the active ministry in protest at the 'silencing [of] all theological reflection and discussion' about official Vatican teachings against the ordination of women (*Tablet*, 19 September 1998: 1231). Similar criticisms were also evident in the extraordinary letter sent by the National Conference of Priests to the Symposium of European Priests expressing 'growing alarm ... about the increasingly restrictive and sanction-based directives which come from the Holy See and the Roman Curia' and regarding 'recent attempts to foreclose on some theological discussions' as 'even a cause of scandal' (ibid.: 1232).

A senior priest has observed that the 1944 Education Act had been 'the greatest gift to the Catholic community'. There is no doubt that one consequence of this Act was that English Catholics were able to grow a 'new middle class', upwardly mobile as a result of educational achievement and occupational advancement. An indication of this can be gleaned from the pages of the first *Who's Who in Catholic Life* (Cullen, 1997) for 45 years. Here is evidence that Catholics are to be found in the whole range of professional, managerial and administrative occupations. Nearly 60 university professors are recorded. There are Catholic company chairmen and directors, managers and consultants, circuit judges and recorders, solicitors and company secretaries, lawyers, accountants, medical practitioners and consultants, librarians and publishers, journalists and broadcasters, senior officers in the armed services, public officials in local government and the civil service, chief constables and members of a wide variety of public bodies such as health authorities, and large numbers of writers and artists. This process of *embourgeoisement*, the diffusion into all areas of public and professional life, has been a steady and practically unrecognized feature of English Catholicism in the postwar period.

The 1978 survey of *Roman Catholic Opinion* (Hornsby-Smith and Lee, 1979), and research in four parishes in London and Preston, provided the strongest evidence yet of the extent to which Catholics had converged with the rest of the population (see, for example, Hornsby-Smith, 1987b: 109, 165). What these researches demonstrated was that at least by the

1970s Catholics were heterogeneous in terms of belief, practice and morality (ibid.: 47–66). It seems likely that whereas

> [u]p to the 1950s Catholics differentiated relatively little between creedal beliefs, non-creedal beliefs such as papal infallibility, teachings on moral issues ... and disciplinary rules ... in a strongly rule-bound and guilt-ridden Church, where notions of mortal sin and eternal damnation were strongly emphasised ... it also seems likely that with the 'loss of the fear of hell' from the 1960s, this is much less true today. (Hornsby-Smith, 1991: 215)

The evidence suggests that 'there is a distinct "hierarchy of truths" in the minds of most Catholics' (ibid.) and an 'emergent plurality of ways in which religious authority is legitimated' (ibid.: 221–2). While there is no evidence of a generalized anti-clericalism, clerical authority was increasingly likely to be contested where it lacked credibility. Catholics were generally opposed to absolutist moral rules which failed to take account of the situational context. The 'loss of the fear of hell' (Lodge, 1980: 113–27) was particularly strong among young Catholics, with the result that

> more and more Catholics are making up their own minds on more and more things and are getting on with the everyday tasks of living their lives, bringing up their families, and coping with the everyday problems of child-rearing, earning a living and making ends meet, unemployment or redundancy, being good citizens, and so on, as best they can, with whatever support they can get, from whatever source. It would seem that the days of substantial thought-control over all aspects of social life, powerful especially in the defensive ghettos of the fortress Church, are now well and truly over. With the removal of the threat of eternal damnation, going to church has to take its chance along with all the other claims on the discretionary time, energy and interest of Catholics. (ibid.: 226–7)

The sort of Catholic doctrine which taught that 'however slight it may be ... every direct sin ... contrary to holy purity, whether of thought, look, word, or action, is mortal if it receives full consent' (Hart, 1918: 219–20), which was still being taught in the early post-war years, was simply regarded as nonsensical, or 'over the top', or undiscriminating and hence inadequate, by young Catholics a generation later.

It is clear that in the past three or four decades there has been a radical transformation in the way that religious authority has been interpreted (Hornsby-Smith, 1991). On personal matters, such as those concerned with marriage and family life, there was a growing sense in which clerical leaders were not credible so that their pronouncements, therefore, were not accorded legitimacy. There was also a growing desire for dialogue and accountability in the Church. The bishops in their *ad limina* visit to Rome in 1997 raised such concerns diplomatically, but Pope John Paul II replied firmly that different forms of lay participation should be fostered but 'without adopting notions borrowed from democracy and sociology which do not reflect the Catholic vision of the Church and the authentic spirit of Vatican II' (*The Tablet*, 1 November 1997: 1419–21). In *The Sign We Give*, the report of a working party on collaborative ministry (Bishops' Conference, 1995), the bishops attempted to respond to the changing climate but significantly there was no dialogue with some of the bishops' own consultative bodies in the preparation of their statement *The Common Good* (1996).

Special Contribution?

It is difficult to identify any significant and distinctive contribution which English Catholics have made in the last half-century. In the first few years after the war it was possible to mobilize thousands of Catholics for demonstrations in the major cities in favour of what they saw as a fairer degree of state support for Catholic schools. From the passing of the Abortion Act in 1967 Catholics have been prominent in successive campaigns to repeal or amend the Act, but they have failed to mobilize a sufficiently large coalition of like-minded citizens to succeed. Apart from these two areas, the evidence is that Catholics have not been particularly distinctive in any area of public concern.

Fifty years ago Bishop Beck, in his centenary volume, observed that:

It seems to be generally admitted that the influence of the Catholic community in England on public life is by no means commensurate with its size, and there seems to be a good case for arguing that, at least until very recent years, this influence has been throughout the greater part of this century declining ... Politically, since the withdrawal of the Irish Members, the Catholic influence has, on the whole, been negligible. (1950: 602–3).

In the late 1950s a Catholic Labour MP was quoted as saying: 'There is not much to say about the influence of English Catholics on public life: they exert very little' (Scott, 1967: 78). This lack of political clout has been attributed, first, to a historical legacy of defensiveness 'forged especially among the Catholic gentry in the penal years following the Reformation and the continuing expressions of anti-Catholic prejudice well into the twentieth century' (Hornsby-Smith, 1987b: 158), and second, to a general other-worldliness (Lawlor, 1965) as a result of which 'Catholics seem to have been happy to have allowed pluralist politics to take their course and [have] concentrated on the struggle for personal salvation in the "life hereafter" ' (Hornsby-Smith, 1987b: 159).

While in recent decades, as a consequence of both social and religious change, there would seem to have been a decline in the 'other-worldly' orientation of Catholics, there is still little evidence that Catholics are politically influential. It may be that as a consequence of the dissolution of the boundary walls between Catholics and the rest of the population, Catholics have indeed diffused throughout the polity where they make a proportionate contribution to English society. *The Catholic Directory 1998* (Bishops' Conference, 1998: 96–9) has published information about Members of both Houses of Parliament following the General Election of 1997. It is instructive to compare the figures with those a quarter of a century earlier (1973: 24–5). There are now 24 Catholic members of the Privy Council (compared to 16); 85 Catholic members of the House of Lords (compared to 61), of whom 32 were Life Peers (compared to 4). In the House of Commons there were 60 Catholic MPs (compared to 38). There were also nine Catholic Members of the European Parliament. These modest increases are consistent with a steady diffusion thesis. Catholics are still not as influential as their proportions in the population would suggest. It seems, however, that a Catholic affiliation is less likely than it might once have been to disqualify a candidate for political office. Of course, these data are also consistent with the view that religious affiliation no longer has relevance in an increasingly secular and multicultural society.

It may be not so much that Catholics do not make a difference as that there is a trend to serve no longer in a confessional context or overtly as Catholics. A close analysis of the origins of numerous initiatives in the area of social welfare and social concern suggests that individual Catholics have been prominent in such voluntary activities as concern for the homeless where members of the Catholic Housing Aid Society

(CHAS), which had already existed for ten years, were instrumental in the founding of SHELTER. Catholics have also been prominent in such ecumenical campaigning groups as Church Action on Poverty (CAP) and the Churches' National Housing Coalition (CNHC). Members of religious orders are quietly working away in some of the most deprived areas of our run-down inner cities (see, for example, the work of Margaret Walsh in the Hope Community in Wolverhampton, in Sedgwick, 1995: 27–71; and Austin Smith in Liverpool, in Smith, 1983). Catholics have also been prominent in the hospice movement, the Samaritans, and a whole range of care groups and organizations. The Sword of the Spirit was founded by Catholics and evolved as the highly regarded Catholic Institute of International Relations (CIIR). The Catholic Fund for Overseas Development (CAFOD) remains a highly respected aid agency which increasingly works in collaboration with other agencies in matters of great urgency such as famine in Africa or hurricane damage in Central America. It is increasingly common for all such forms of social concern to be undertaken ecumenically, as Mildred Nevile and Ian Linden pointed out.

Main Concerns

The fourth question we set ourselves at the beginning of this study was 'What are the main concerns of English Catholics and in what direction are they heading as they enter the new millennium?' In the first place, there are clear signs of the institutional decline that is apparent throughout Europe. There are fewer priests and the likelihood of an increasing number of priestless parishes within a very short time. Mass attendances have virtually halved in the past four decades, though it seems possible that a much higher proportion of attendances is regular though less frequent than weekly. The serious losses among the younger generations, with the strong possibility that they may not return to communal forms of membership, bodes ill for the future, though it is possible that newer forms of parish-based sacramental catechesis for children will provide a route back for their parents.

There is a sense in which all is not well in the parishes, where the situation is somewhat patchy. Even in the more lively parishes it seems that strategic planning remains insular and ecumenical developments have stalled. It seems that the cultural and stylistic variations of worship between different Christian groupings continue to have a more powerful emotional and aesthetic pull than had been thought, and they remain strong and legitimate at the same time as there have been developing friendships between Christians of different local churches. Individual Catholics are increasingly just getting on with the job of collaborating with Christians from other traditions in responding to local needs for care or for the homeless. In spite of some heroic examples, the general picture one has of English Catholicism at the end of the century is that it is fairly complacent and lukewarm. The end-of-century report might well say: 'could do better'!

We have previously noted the upward social mobility of Catholics in the post-war period. Relatively high proportions of Catholics in the armed forces probably still reflect the long-recognized desire on the part of a defensive minority to express its loyalty to the British state. It would also be nice to think that a high representation, for example in the diplomatic service, might also indicate a respect for standards of honesty and integrity. Catholics seem to be well-represented in the media, in journalism and broadcasting, and in the wider cultural industries which have mushroomed in recent decades. On the other hand they also seem to be well-represented among the prison population as well as their guardians!

The shift of attitudes to clerical authority, manifestly evident among the younger generations, reflects probably one of the most significant developments since the 1960s. The Church has not been immune to the global democratic imperative or the demands for official accountability. Forms of lay deference which persisted until the early post-war years have gone, probably for ever. The tragedy of *Humanae Vitae* was that it utterly destroyed the confidence of lay people that their everyday concerns would be fully and properly taken into account by the ecclesiastical authorities. This is not to say that the encyclical was solely to blame; after all, Charles Davis made his protest two years before its publication. But it is to suggest that after the encyclical all clerical claims for legitimacy and credibility were increasingly treated with great, though polite and silent, scepticism. Whereas there might have been latent or subterranean revolts on the part of a minority of English Catholics, for example over entering a 'mixed' marriage, or over preaching about political policies or industrial disputes, from the 1960s on it seems clear that Catholics generally were increasingly making up their own minds on an ever widening range of issues. The shift was immediately expressed by the young who, unlike their parents, did not regard missing Mass on Sundays or practising contraception or cohabitation before marriage or remarriage after divorce as mortal sins excluding them from Holy Communion.

Although there are no signs of a generalized anti-clericalism among English Catholics there still remain major and distinct power differentials between the parochial clergy and their parishioners which are under-pinned in canon law (Canon Law Society, 1983) and which are observable on major religious occasions such as the concelebration of the Mass by a large number of clergy. In so far as such power is exercised arbitrarily and unilaterally, and in the absence of any consultation and dialogue, it can be perceived as illegitimate and divisive within the local Church. The report on collaborative ministry, *The Sign We Give* (1995), is an indication that more thought is being given to creating a 'people of God' model of the Church in the spirit of Vatican II.

There is some awareness of the fact that increasing participation by the laity and consultation with them, both at diocesan and parish levels, has inevitably bureaucratized much of Church life, increased the workload of priests and reduced the time they can devote to the pastoral work of care and visiting. While there is a small but increasing number of married deacons in the parishes, lay people are increasingly collaborating as special ministers taking Communion to the sick and organizing care for the elderly and housebound. In spite of some dismay at current official positions on married priests and discussion of the possibility of women priests, many Catholics who wish to realize the spirit of Vatican II see these slow developments, unthinkable fifty years ago, as 'signs of hope'.

As we reach the end of the twentieth century, there is some disappointment that the promise of Vatican II seems to have been filtered away, especially under the present papacy. Most of the contributors to this volume have expressed their concerns that there has been a process of centralization and retrenchment in the Church which has stifled the search for pastoral responses to contemporary needs which are appropriate to our own context. Many see the Church as still too rule-bound and inadequately sensitive to human needs and pain. They would point to such areas as the pastoral care of the divorced and remarried, and intercommunion where married partners belong to other Christian Churches, as suggesting that issues of order and authority have been given precedence over human responses to human needs. The contribu-tions of John Marshall and Tim Buckley in this volume have particular relevance to these issues. These may well be areas where pastoral practice responds to latent dissent and quietly becomes the norm which will subsequently be officially legitimated.

Perhaps the greatest concern of ordinary Catholics is the faith and commitment of their children. We have seen in John Fulton's and Mary Eaton's chapters how very different is the nature of the Catholicism of young adults compared to older generations who grew up in the days before Vatican II in the 'fortress' Church. There are two quite separate issues. First, there is the possibility of a failed, or at least inadequate and unconvincing religious socialization of the younger generations (Hornsby-Smith, 1997). There may be something in this and in a lost generation as a result of uncertainties created by Vatican II where previously the unchanging, all-knowing Church had 'absolute truth' (Stourton, 1998).

For those brought up in the 1970s and 1980s there may well have been a lack of theological grounding in the Catholic belief-system. Only subsequently have religious education teachers recovered some confidence, though the requirements of the national curriculum and of knowledge of comparative religions in a multicultural society may well have resulted in some confusion and ambiguity. What seems to have emerged in tune with shifts in the wider culture is a somewhat inchoate belief in God but not in the institutional Church. What also seem to have become more common, and may indeed have lasting consequences, are sacramental preparation programmes at the parish level which are intended to involve the parents of children. There is the suggestion that non-Catholic partners also discover aspects of 'community' through such schemes.

The second and quite distinct issue is that of the nature of Catholic identity which has been transformed as a result of the social and religious changes of the past half-century. In somewhat ideal-typical terms it could be argued that in the years immediately after the war, the English Catholic identity was communal and largely that of a religio-ethnic subculture. 'Once a Catholic, always a Catholic', so it was said. It was an ascribed identity and one could no more rid oneself of one's Catholicism than one could one's gender or ethnicity. But that has been fundamentally transformed. A Catholic identity today is to a much smaller extent a communal and ascribed mark, but is achieved and to some extent chosen, a result of individual, voluntary choice. There is, in the differences between the generations, something of both a transformed socialization and a transformed identity.

Finally, Catholics sometimes ask: 'Is the Church more loving than fifty years ago?' In spite of the concern we have expressed about the limited influence of Catholics in the public life of the nation, the question might be answered with a cautious affirmative. It might be suggested that whereas in the early post-war years there was much concern for the amelioration of suffering and need, this was often tinged with a certain judgementalism and was seen in terms of 'charity' and duty. Catholicism was about loving God and achieving personal salvation. It has been suggested that love of neighbour was not on the agenda fifty years ago but has become increasingly so. Furthermore, there has been a distinct shift of concern from amelioration to seeking the causes of suffering and injustice and working to address their root causes. In such a shift, we believe we see signs of hope for English Catholicism in the next millennium.

Prospects for the New Millennium

What, then, are the prospects for English Catholicism as it enters the third millennium? First, it can be said to have been substantially assimilated into English society over the past fifty years or so. The strong boundary walls which defended the fortress and closed Church against a hostile world up to the 1950s were substantially dissolved away in the solvent of both post-war social and post-conciliar religious changes. A few legislative forms of discrimination remain but they are no more than those experienced by the new English with an Islamic faith. English Catholics have become respectable, particularly under the leadership of the much-liked Cardinal Hume. Perhaps they have also become complacent as well as congenitally defensive and they have not offered instances of prophecy to match those given by the Church of England in its several challenges to the state in recent decades. Sadly, it seems they have become a rather cosy and unchallengingly domesticated denomination. In this process it seems likely that the new, younger generations of cradle Catholics have substantially lost an awareness, and hence a pride in, their historical roots. There is a weakened sense of a distinctive community evoking a sense of identity and commitment.

The ecumenical climate has been totally transformed in the past four decades. At the beginning of the period bishops were still explaining why it was not proper to join with non-Catholics in saying the Lord's Prayer. Since then there have been the remarkable convergences reported by the Anglican–Roman Catholic International Commission (ARCIC), reciprocal visits and loving exchanges between popes and archbishops of Canterbury, the growth of ecumenical worship, study and friendships at the local level, and the steady emergence of social action organized on an ecumenical basis. Rather than interpret ecumenism as the survival strategy of Churches in decline (Wilson, 1966: 126), it can perhaps be interpreted more positively as evidence of a growing awareness that the historical divisions are a scandal and that there are good reasons why Christians of different traditions should work together in order to bring the 'Good News to the Poor' in an otherwise secular society. Such awareness is apparent in the ongoing and developing collaboration between CAFOD and the other aid agencies and in the memberships of such organizations as the CIIR, CAP and CNHC.

So while it is undoubtedly true that over the past half-century there have been numerous changes and some instances of decline, some of which have been indicated in the earlier sections of this chapter, it is also the case that there is evidence of a more highly educated Catholic community, more self-confident, and more fully involved in the everyday workings of the Church in this country. As *The Common Good* (Bishops' Conference, 1996) indicated, quite apart from the very large system of Catholic schools, the contribution of Catholics to informal and voluntary forms of social welfare is very considerable. With the setting up of the Catholic Agency for Social Concern (CASC), the possibilities of this work being developed in a more systematic and self-conscious way have been much enhanced.

It would be a wild exaggeration to suggest that all vestiges of the static, hierarchically organized and clerically dominated Church for the 'simple faithful' have disappeared. But it would also be fair to interpret the broad drift of the transformations in English Catholicism as to some extent a shift towards a more open, less arrogant and complacent, more humble pilgrim people of God, not in a static, unchanging Church, but in one which anticipates changes in the sort of world we are currently living in. Inevitably these changes will be mediated by the nature and strength of relationships with the centralized bureaucracy of the universal Church in Rome and by the character and charisma of the local leadership of bishops and priests. But as we enter the new millennium it is clear that lay people will have to play a more central part as the number of priestless parishes increases. My judgement would be that lay people are not, on the whole, fearful of this prospect but are increasingly confident about their lay ministries and, to a much lesser extent than previously, are much less dependent on clerical leadership to initiate pastoral responses and action. It also seems likely that there will be a major reappraisal of the place of women in the Church quite early in the new millennium.

English Catholics have a number of major weaknesses which they carry with them into the new millennium. As we have noted previously, they carry a legacy of defensiveness which reflects the survival strategies learned over several hundreds of years since Reformation times, and this legacy has not been seriously eroded as a result of the transformations of the past fifty years. The easing of hostility has resulted in a certain sloppiness and laziness. Catholics are notoriously bad at evangelization, at offering a challenging witness to their neighbours and fellow country-men and women. While there has undoubtedly been a slow diffusion of Catholics into positions of power and influence in the country, it is not so obvious that they have had a significant impact in Christianizing their work and domestic environments. The contribution of Catholics to the political life of the country remains weak.

A second weakness is educational. In spite of the enormous efforts put into the provision of Catholic schools, one suspects that younger generations of Catholics have a weaker grounding in their Catholic faith and the rich tradition of Catholic social teaching than was the case a generation ago. There seems to have been no development of the notion of the lay apostolate for a changed world and a more sympathetic ecumenical climate. Young Catholics leaving school or university seem to have little awareness of their 'calling' or vocation in their domestic, marital and occupational lives. Without the appropriate 'formation' as lay people with a God-given vocation it seems hard to see where a significant Catholic witness in marriage and family life, in politics, trade unions, professional associations, boardrooms and offices will come from.

English Catholics are a significant segment in this country today. Whether they will make a distinctive contribution to the life of the nation in the next millennium must remain an open question. Perhaps one hopeful sign is that the accommodation which the Church has made to English society since Catholic emancipation and to the reforms deriving from the Second Vatican Council has been 'contested' (Seidler, 1986). There are numerous Catholics who have been inspired by the vision of Vatican II who are not satisfied with both the preparations for the pilgrimage which have been made and the direction in which the pilgrims are facing. The future depends largely on the energy, commitment and vision of those who are prepared to struggle against the powerful forces of inertia and fear in order to realize the conciliar vision and to bring the 'Good News to the Poor'.

Bibliography

Abbott, W. M. (ed.) (1966) *The Documents of Vatican II*, London: Geoffrey Chapman.

Alderman, G. (1989) *London Jewry and London Politics 1889–1986*, London and New York: Routledge.

Altermatt, U. (1972) *Der Weg des Schweizer Katholiken ins Ghetto*, Zürich: Benziger.

Anon. (1980) *Congress Report: Documents of the National Pastoral Congress*, London: CTS.

Anon. (1981) *Liverpool 1980: Official Report of the National Pastoral Congress*, Slough: St Paul Publications.

Arbuckle, G. (1988) *Out of Chaos: Refounding Religious Congregations*, London: Geoffrey Chapman; Mahwah, N.J.: Paulist Press.

Archer, A. (1986) *The Two Catholic Churches: A Study in Oppression*, London: SCM.

Arthur, J. (1995) *The Ebbing Tide: Policy and Principles of Catholic Education*, Leominster: Gracewing.

Arthur, J. and Gaine, S. (1996) '"Catechesis" and "Religious Education" in Catholic Theory and Practice', in L. Francis, W. Kay and W. Campbell (eds), *Research in Religious Education*, Leominster: Gracewing.

Ashford, S. and Timms, N. (1992) *What Europe Thinks: A Study of Western European Values*, Aldershot: Dartmouth.

Atterbury, P. and Wainwright, C. (1994) *Pugin: A Gothic Passion*, New Haven and London: Yale University Press.

Azevedo, M. (1995) *The Consecrated Life: Crossroads and Directions*, New York: Orbis.

Baily, P. (1995) *A History of Catholic People's Weeks: 1945–1995*, Wilprint Group.

Ball, S. (1997) 'Markets, Equity and Values in Education', in R. Pring and G. Walford (eds), *Affirming the Comprehensive Ideal*, London: Falmer.

Barker, E., Beckford, J. and Dobbelaere, K. (eds) (1993) *Secularization, Rationalism and Sectarianism*, Oxford: Clarendon.

Barnes, E. (ed.) (1976) *Together in the Church: Report of the Laity Commission 1972–6*, London: Catholic Information Office.

Bartlett, Alan (1988) *The Churches in Bermondsey 1880–1939*, unpublished PhD thesis, University of Birmingham.

Bauman, Z. (1996) 'From Pilgrim to Tourist: Or a Short History of Identity', in S. Hall and P. du Gay (eds), *Questions of Cultural Identity*, London: Sage, pp. 18–36.

Beales, A. C. F. (1950) 'The Struggle for the Schools', in Beck, *English Catholics*, pp. 365–409.

Beards, A. (1992) 'The Relevance of a Liturgical Language', *The Downside Review* 110, pp. 30–44.

Beck, G. A. (ed.) (1950) *The English Catholics: 1850–1950*, London: Burns Oates.

Beck, G. A. (1955) *The Case for Catholic Schools*, London: Catholic Truth Society.

Beck, U. (1992) *Risk Society: Towards a New Modernity*, London: Sage.

Berger, P. L. (1973) *The Social Reality of Religion*, Harmondsworth: Penguin.

Bishops' Conference of England and Wales (1971) *Commissions: Aid to a Pastoral Strategy*, London.

Bishops' Conference of England and Wales (1980) *The Easter People: A Message in the Light of the National Pastoral Congress, Liverpool 1980*, Slough: St Paul Publications.

Bishops' Conference of England and Wales (1982) *In the House of the Living God: Report following 'The Easter People' with a Briefing Note*, London.

Bishops' Conference of England and Wales (1990) *Homelessness: A Fact and a Scandal. A Report Published by the Department for Christian Social Responsibility and Citizenship*, London: CHAS.

Bishops' Conference of England and Wales (1995) *The Sign We Give: Report From the Working Party on Collaborative Ministry*, Chelmsford: Matthew James.

Bishops' Conference of England and Wales (1996a) *The Common Good and the Catholic Church's Social Teaching*, Manchester: Gabriel Communications.

Bishops' Conference of England and Wales (1996b) *Education in Catholic Schools and Colleges: Principles, Practices and Concerns*, London: CES.

Bishops' Conference of England and Wales (1997a) *The Common Good in Education*, London: CES.

Bishops' Conference of England and Wales (1997b) *Catholic Schools and Other Faiths*, London: CES.

Bishops' Conference of England and Wales (1997c) *Guidelines for the Study and Implementation of 'Catholic Schools and Other Faiths'*, London: CES.

Bishops' Conference of England and Wales (1998) *Catholic Directory 1998*, Manchester: Gabriel Communications.

Bishops' Conference of England and Wales and the National Conference of Priests (1973) *The Church 2000: An Interim Report Offered by the Joint*

Working Party on Pastoral Strategy, Abbots Langley: Catholic Information Services.

Black, P. (ed.) (1971) *Report to the Laity: The Work and Experience of the Provisional Laity Commission 1967–71*, London: Living Parish Pamphlets.

Bossy, J. (1975) *The English Catholic Community, 1570–1850*, London: Darton, Longman & Todd.

Boswell, J. (1994) *Community and the Economy: The Theory of Public Co-Operation*, London: Routledge.

Boswell, J. and Peters, J. (1997) *Capitalism in Contention*, Cambridge: Cambridge University Press.

Bourne, J. (1994) 'Stories of Exclusion', in J. Bourne, L. Bridges and C. Searle (eds), *Outcast England*, London: Institute of Race Relations.

Boyle, R. and Lynch, P. (eds) (1998) *Out of the Ghetto? The Catholic Community in Modern Scotland*, Edinburgh: John Donald.

Brannen, J. and Collard, J. (1982) *Marriages in Trouble: The Process of Seeking Help*, London: Tavistock.

Brech, R. (1972) *The Church: Joint Venture of Priests and Laity*, London: Living Parish Pamphlets.

Brierley, P. (ed.) (1991) *Prospects For the Nineties: Trends and Tables From the 1989 English Church Census*, London: MARC Europe.

British Council of Churches (1981) *Understanding Christian Nurture*, London: BCC.

Brogan, M. (1992) 'The Newman and Women's Role in the Church', in Cheverton *et al.*, *A Use of Gifts*, pp. 60–3.

Brothers, J. (1964) *Church and School: A Study of the Impact of Education on Religion*, Liverpool: Liverpool University Press.

Brown, S. (1940) *Novels and Tales by Catholic Writers: A Catalogue*, Dublin: Catholic Central Library.

Bryden, J. (1998) *Behold the Wood: A History of the Student Cross Pilgrimage 1948–1998*, London: The Student Cross Association.

Buchanan, T. (1996) 'Great Britain', in T. Buchanan and M. Conway (eds), *Political Catholicism in Europe, 1918–1965*, Oxford: Clarendon, pp. 248–74.

Buckley, T. J. (1997) *What Binds Marriage? Roman Catholic Theology in Practice*, London: Geoffrey Chapman.

Bull, G. (1993) 'Reasons for Disbelief', *The Tablet*, 20 February, pp. 240–1.

Bunting, M. (1998) 'For Hume the Bells Toll', *The Guardian*, 24 February.

Butler, C. (1981) *The Theology of Vatican II*, rev. edn, London: Darton, Longman & Todd.

Butler, Sara (1996) 'The Ordination of Women: A New Obstacle to the Recognition of Anglican Orders', in R. W. Franklin (ed.), *Anglican Orders: Essays on the Centenary of 'Apostolicae Curae' 1896–1996*, London: Mowbray, pp. 96–113.

Bynner, J., Ferri, E. and Shepherd, P. (eds) (1997) *Twenty-Something in the 1990s*, Aldershot: Ashgate Press.

Cada, F. and Fitz, R. (1979) *Shaping the Coming Age of Religious Life*, New York: Seabury.

Caldecott, S. and Morrill, J. (1997) *Eternity in Time: Christopher Dawson and the Catholic Idea of History*, Edinburgh: T & T Clark.

Canon Law Society of Great Britain and Ireland (1983) *The Code of Canon Law*, London: Collins.

Cardinal Hume's Advisory Group (1986) *With You in Spirit? Report on the Catholic Church's Commitment to the Black Community*, London: The Print Business.

Carey, A. (1997) *Sisters in Crisis: The Tragic Unfolding of Women's Religious Communities*, Indiana: Our Sunday Visitor Publishing Division.

Catholic Agency for Social Concern (1998) *Second Annual Review 1997*, London: CASC.

Catholic Agency for Social Concern (forthcoming) *Contributing to the Common Good: Yesterday, Today and Tomorrow*, London: CASC.

Catholic Bishops' Conferences of England and Wales, Ireland, and Scotland (1998) 'One Bread One Body: A Teaching Document on the Eucharist in the Life of the Church and the Establishment of General Norms on Sacramental Sharing', *Briefing* 28/10 (15 October) pp. 3–10.

Catholic Commission for Racial Justice (1982) *Catholic Education in a Multiracial Society*, No. 11 (April), London: Rye Express.

Catholic Education Council (1955) *The Case for Catholic Schools*, 2nd edn, London: CEC.

Catholic Education Service (1996) *Learning from OFSTED and Diocesan Inspections: The Distinctive Nature of Education in Catholic Primary and Secondary Schools*, London: CES.

Catholic Education Service (1997) *Differentiation: A Catholic Perspective*, London: CES.

Catholic Institute for International Relations (1985) *Challenge to the Church: A Theological Comment on the Political Crisis in South Africa: The Kairos Document*, London: CIIR/BCC.

Catholic Institute for International Relations (1989) *The Road to Damascus: Kairos and Conversion: A Document Signed by Third World Christians*, London: CIIR/Center of Concern/Christian Aid.

Catholic Poor School Committee (1984) *Minutes*.

Charles, B. (1986) 'Liverpool: A City in Crisis', *The Month* (February), pp. 47–52.

Châtellier, L. (1989) *The Europe of the Devout: The Catholic Reformation and the Formation of a New Society*, Cambridge: Cambridge University Press.

Cheverton, E. *et al.* (eds) (1992) *A Use of Gifts: The Newman Association, 1942–1992*, London: Newman Association.

Christians Against Racism and Fascism (1985) *Issues in the 80s*, London: CARAF.

Cleary, J. M. (1961) *Catholic Social Action in Britain 1909–1959*, Oxford: Catholic Social Guild.

Clifton, M. (1993) *The Alliance of Dissent: Turning the Church Upside Down*, (privately published).

Collins, S. (1997) *Young People's Faith in Late Modernity*, unpublished PhD thesis, Guildford: University of Surrey.

Collins, S. (1998) 'Immanent Faith: Young People in Late Modernity', in L. J. Francis (ed.), *Sociology and the Curriculum: A Theological Perspective*, London: Cassell.

Coman, P. (1977) *Catholics and the Welfare State*, Longman.

Commission for Racial Equality (1992) *Response to Choice and Diversity: A New Framework for Schools*, London: CRE.

Conference of Major Religious Superiors (1987) *Religious Institutes in England and Wales: Surveys 1985 and 1987: A Report*, London: CMRS.

Congar, Y. (1965) *Lay People in the Church*, London: Geoffrey Chapman.

Congregation for the Clergy (1997) *General Catechetical Directory*, London: CTS.

Connolly, G. (1985) 'Irish and Catholic: Myth or Reality? Another Sort of Irish and the Renewal of the Clerical Profession among Catholics in England, 1791–1918', in Swift and Gilley, *The Irish in the Victorian City*, pp. 225–54.

Cottrell, M. (1985) *Secular Beliefs in Contemporary Society*, unpublished DPhil thesis, University of Oxford.

Council of Churches for Britain and Ireland (CCBI) (1997) *Unemployment and the Future of Work*, London: CCBI.

Cullen, M. J. (ed.) (1997) *Who's Who in Catholic Life 1997*, Manchester: Gabriel Communications.

Cumming, J. and Burns, P. (eds) (1980) *The Church Now: An Inquiry Into the Present State of the Catholic Church in Britain and Ireland*, Dublin: Gill & Macmillan.

Cussianovich, A. (1979) *Religious Life and the Poor: Liberation Theology Perspectives*, Dublin: Gill & Macmillan.

Dalrymple, J. (1995) *Jack Dominian: Lay Prophet?*, London: Geoffrey Chapman.

Daniel, P. (1997a) 'The Catholic Union and Its Priorities for Action', *The Newman*, 40 (January), pp. 14–17.

Daniel, P. (1997b) *For the Common Good: An Account of the Work of the Catholic Union of Great Britain 1975–1997* (mimeo).

Daniel, P. (1998) *For the Common Good*, London: Newburgh Books/Catholic Union.

Darwen, R. (1986) 'Why the Church Fails the City', *The Month* 19/7–8 (July–August), pp. 267–70.

Davie, G. (1994) *Religion in Britain Since 1945*, Oxford: Blackwell.

Davis, C. (1967) *A Question of Conscience*, London: Hodder & Stoughton.

D'Costa, G. (1998) 'On Cultivating the Disciplined Habits of a Love Affair *Or* On How to do Theology on Your Knees', *New Blackfriars* 79, pp. 116–36.

De Broucker, J. (1971) *The Case for Collegiality (The Suenens Dossier)*, Dublin: Gill & Macmillan.

Department for Christian Doctrine and Formation (1984) *Learning from Diversity*, London: Catholic Media Office.

Department for Catholic Education and Formation (1997) *A Struggle for Excellence*, London: CES.

Department for Education (1992) *Choice and Diversity: A New Framework for Schools*, Cmnd 2021, London: HMSO.

Department of Education and Science (1967) *Children and Their Primary School. Report of the Central Advisory Council for Education (England) (The Plowden Report)*, London: HMSO.

Department of Education and Science (1981) *West Indian Children in Our Schools, (The Rampton Report)*, Cmnd 6869, London: HMSO.

Department of Education and Science (1985) *Education for All: The Report of the Committee of Enquiry into Education of Children from Ethnic Minority Groups (The Swann Report)*, Cmnd 9453, London: HMSO.

Diocese of Arundel and Brighton (1991) *Report of the Special Committee on Catholic School Provision in the Diocese.*

Dobbelaere, K. (1988) 'Secularization, Pillarization, Religious Involvement, and Religious Change in the Low Countries', in T. M. Gannon (ed.), *World Catholicism in Transition*, London: Collier Macmillan, pp. 80–115.

Dobbelaere, K. (1993) 'Church Involvement and Secularization: Making Sense of the European Case, in E. Barker *et al.* (eds), *Secularization, Rationalism and Sectarianism*, Oxford: Clarendon.

Dobbelaere, K. (1998) 'Relations Ambigues des Religions à la Société Globale', *Social Compass* 45/1, pp. 81–98.

Dolan, J. P. (1985) *The American Catholic Experience: A History From Colonial Times to the Present*, New York: Doubleday.

Dominian, J. (1975) *Cycles of Affirmation: Psychological Essays in Christian Living*, London: Darton, Longman & Todd.

Dominian, J. (1977) *Proposals for a New Sexual Ethic*, London: Darton, Longman & Todd.

Dominian, J. (1981) *Marriage, Faith and Love*, London: Darton, Longman & Todd.

Dominian, J. (1991) *Passionate and Compassionate Love: A Vision for Christian Marriage*, London: Darton, Longman & Todd.

Dorr, D. (1992) *Option for the Poor: A Hundred Years of Vatican Social Teaching*, Dublin: Gill & Macmillan.

Douglas, M. (1973) *Natural Symbols: Explorations in Cosmology*, Harmondsworth: Penguin.

Duffy, E. (1992) *The Stripping of the Altars*, New Haven and London: Yale University Press.

Dulles, A. (1977) *The Resilient Church: The Necessity and Limits of Adaptation*, Garden City, N.Y.: Doubleday.

Ester, P., Halman, L. and de Moor, R. (eds) (1993) *The Individualizing Society: Value Change in Europe and North America*, Tilberg: Tilberg University Press.

Evennett, H. O. (1944) *The Catholic Schools of England and Wales*, Cambridge: Cambridge University Press.

Fagerberg, D. W. (1998) *The Size of Chesterton's Catholicism*, Indiana: University of Notre Dame Press.

Felknor, L. (ed.) (1989) *The Crisis in Religious Vocations: An Inside View*, Mahwah, N.J.: Paulist Press.

Fielding, S. (1993) *Class and Ethnicity: Irish Catholics in England, 1880–1939*, Buckingham and Philadelphia: Open University Press.

Finnis, J. M. (1983) *Fundamentals of Ethics*, Oxford: Clarendon.

Finnis, J. M. (1991) *Moral Absolutes: Tradition, Revision and Truth: The Michael J. McGivney Lectures of the John Paul II Institute for Studies on Marriage and Family*, Washington D.C.: Catholic University of America.

Finnis, J. M. (1993a) *Natural Law and Natural Rights*, Oxford: Clarendon.

Finnis, J. M. (1993b) 'Bland: Crossing the Rubicon', *Law Quarterly Review* 109, pp. 329–37.

Flanagan, K. (1991) *Sociology and Liturgy: Re-Presentation of the Holy*, Basingstoke: Macmillan.

Flannery, A. (ed.) (1996) *Documents of Vatican II*, Dublin: Costello/Dominican Publications.

Flessati, V. (1991) *The History of a Catholic Peace Society in Britain 1936–1971*, unpublished PhD thesis, University of Bradford.

Fletcher, R. (1984) *Education in Society: The Promethean Fire: A New Essay in the Sociology of Education*, Harmondsworth: Penguin.

Florovsky, G. (1972) 'The Function of Tradition in the Ancient Church', in *Bible, Church, Tradition: An Eastern Orthodox View*, Massachusetts: Norland.

Fogarty, M. P. (1963) *The Rules of Work*, London: Geoffrey Chapman.

Fogarty, M. P. (1995) *Phoenix or Cheshire Cat?*, Christian Democrat Press.

Ford, C. (1996) 'Female Martyrdom and the Politics of Sainthood in Nineteenth-Century France: The Cult of Sainte Philomene', in F. Tallett and N. Atkin (eds), *Catholicism in Britain and France since 1789*, London and Rio Grande: The Hambledon Press, pp. 115–34.

Foster, C. (1989) 'The American Catholic Bishops' Economic Pastoral', paper given at Conference at St George's House, Windsor.

Francis, L. J. and Kay, W. K. (1995) *Teenage Religion and Values*, Leominster: Fowler Wright.

Francis, L. J. and Kay, W. K. (1996) *Drift From the Churches: Attitudes Towards*

Christianity During Childhood and Adolescence, Cardiff: University of Wales Press.

Fulton, J., Abela, A., Borowik, I., Dowling, T., Marler, P. and Tomasi, L. (forthcoming) *Young Catholics and the New Millennium: Private and Social Consciousness in Six Western Countries*, Dublin: University College Dublin Press.

Furlong, A. and Cartmel, F. (1997) *Young People and Social Change: Individualization and Risk in Late Modernity*, Buckingham: Open University Press.

Furlong, P. and Curtis, D. (eds) (1994) *The Church Faces the Modern World: 'Rerum Novarum' and its Impact*, Hull: Earlsgate Press.

Gallagher, T. (1987) *Glasgow: The Uneasy Peace: Religious Tension in Modern Scotland 1819–1914*, Manchester: Manchester University Press.

Gamber, K. (1993) *The Reform of the Roman Liturgy: Its Problems and Background*, San Juan Capistrano, Calif., and Harrison, N.Y.: Una Voce Press and The Foundation for Catholic Reform.

Gannon, T. (ed.) (1987) *The Catholic Challenge to the American Economy*, Macmillan.

General Synod of the Church of England (1985) *Faith in the City: A Call for Action by Church and Nation: The Report of the Archbishop of Canterbury's Commission on Urban Priority Areas*, London: Church House.

Gerard, D. (1985) 'Religious Attitudes and Values', in M. Abrams, D. Gerard, and N. Timms (eds), *Values and Social Change in Britain*, Basingstoke: Macmillan/EVSSG, pp. 50–92.

Giddens, A. (1990) *The Consequences of Modernity*, Cambridge: Polity.

Giddens, A. (1991) *Modernity and Self-Identity*, Cambridge: Polity.

Gilley, S. (1984) 'The Roman Catholic Church and the Nineteenth-Century Irish Diaspora', *The Journal of Ecclesiastical History* 35, pp. 188–207.

Gilley, S. (1987) 'Labour and the Catholic Church: A Tale of Three Cardinals', in T. Murphy and C. J. Byrne (eds), *Religion and Identity: The Experience of Irish and Scottish Catholics in Atlantic Canada*, St John's, Newfoundland: Jesperson.

Gilley, S. (1989) 'Catholics and Socialists in Scotland, 1900–30', in Swift and Gilley, *The Irish in Britain 1815–1939*, pp. 212–38.

Gilley, S. (1997) 'Newman and the Convert Mind', in Ian Ker (ed.), *Newman and Conversion*, Edinburgh: T & T Clark, pp. 5–20.

Goulding, G. (1994) *On the Edge of Mystery: Towards a Spiritual Hermeneutic of the Urban Margins*, unpublished PhD thesis, University of Edinburgh.

Grace, G. (1998) 'The Future of the Catholic School: An English Perspective', in J. M. Feheney (ed.), *From Ideal to Action: The Inner Nature of a Catholic School Today*, Dublin: Veritas.

Grisez, G. (1983) *The Way of the Lord Jesus*, I: *Christian Moral Principles*, Chicago: Franciscan Herald Press.

Grisez, G., Finnis, J. and May, W. E. (1994) 'Indissolubility, Divorce and Holy Communion', *New Blackfriars* 75, pp. 321–30.

Haigh, C. (ed.) (1987) *The English Reformation Revised*, Cambridge: Cambridge University Press.

Hammond, P. E. (1988) 'Religion and the Persistence of Identity', *Journal for the Scientific Study of Religion* 27/1 (March), pp. 1–11.

Hamnett, I. and Mills, J. O. (eds) (1987) 'Class and Church: After Ghetto Catholicism: Facing the Issues Raised by Anthony Archer's *The Two Catholic Churches*', *New Blackfriars* 68 (February).

Hanley, D. (ed.) (1996) *Christian Democracy in Europe: A Comparative Perspective*, London: Pinter.

Harding, S. and Phillips, D., with Fogarty, M. (1986) *Contrasting Values in Western Europe: Unity, Diversity and Change*, London: Macmillan/EVSSG.

Hart, C. (1918) *The Student's Catholic Doctrine*, London: Burns Oates & Washbourne.

Hart, J. F. (1971) *Some Statistics of Social Contrast*, Liverpool: Liverpool Council for Voluntary Services.

Hastings, A. (ed.) (1977) *Bishops and Writers: Aspects of the Evolution of Modern English Catholicism*, Wheathampstead: Anthony Clarke.

Hastings, A. (1986) *A History of English Christianity, 1920–1985*, London: Collins.

Hastings, A. (1991) *A History of English Christianity 1920–1990*, London: SCM.

Hastings, A. (ed.) (1991) *Modern Catholicism: Vatican II and After*, London: SPCK.

Heenan, J. C. (1971) *Not the Whole Truth*, London: Hodder & Stoughton.

Heenan, J. C. (1974) *A Crown of Thorns*, London: Hodder & Stoughton.

Heimann, M. (1995) *Catholic Devotion in Victorian England*, Oxford: Clarendon.

Hennessy, P. (ed.) (1997) *A Concert of Charisms: Ordained Ministry in Religious Life*, Mahwah, N.J.: Paulist Press.

Hickey, J. (1967) *Urban Catholics: Urban Catholicism in England and Wales from 1829 to the Present Day*, London: Geoffrey Chapman.

Hickman, M. J. (1990) *A Study of the Incorporation of the Irish in Britain With Special Reference to Catholic State Education: Involving a Comparison of the Attitudes of Pupils and Teachers in Selected Catholic Schools in London and Liverpool*, unpublished PhD thesis, Institute of Education, University of London.

Hickman, M. (1995) *Religion, Class and Identity: The State, the Catholic Church and the Education of the Irish in Britain*, Aldershot: Avebury.

Hobsbawm, E. (1994) *Age of Extremes: The Short Twentieth Century 1914–1991*, London: Michael Joseph.

Hornsby-Smith, M. P. (1978) *Catholic Education: The Unobtrusive Partner*, London: Sheed & Ward.

Hornsby-Smith, M. P. (1982a) 'What Sort of Catholic?', *The Tablet*, 8 May.

Hornsby-Smith, M. P. (1982b) 'What Sort of Catholic? (2)', *The Tablet*, 15 May.

Hornsby-Smith, M. P. (1982c) 'Two Years After: Reflections on "Liverpool 1980"', *New Blackfriars* 63 (June) pp. 252–60.

Hornsby-Smith, M. P. (1987a) 'The Church's New Face', *The Tablet*, 11 July.

Hornsby-Smith, M. P. (1987b) *Roman Catholics in England: Studies in Social Structure Since the Second World War*, Cambridge: Cambridge University Press.

Hornsby-Smith, M. P. (1989) *The Changing Parish: A Study of Parishes, Priests, and Parishioners After Vatican II*, London: Routledge.

Hornsby-Smith, M. P. (1991) *Roman Catholic Beliefs in England: Customary Catholicism and Transformations of Religious Authority*, Cambridge: Cambridge University Press.

Hornsby-Smith, M. P. (1992) 'Recent Transformations in English Catholicism: Evidence of Secularization?', in S. Bruce (ed.), *Religion and Modernization: Sociologists and Historians Debate the Secularization Thesis*, Oxford: Clarendon, pp. 118–44.

Hornsby-Smith, M. P. (1996) 'The Catholic Church and Education in Britain: From the "Intransigence" of "Closed" Catholicism to the Accommodation Strategy of "Open" Catholicism', in F. Tallett and N. Atkin (eds), *Catholicism in Britain and France Since 1789*, London: Hambledon.

Hornsby-Smith, M. P. (1997) 'Echec de l'impregnation religieuse ou transformation du religieux? Catholiques anglais et circonstances historiques', *Recherches Sociologiques* 28/3, pp. 51–64.

Hornsby-Smith, M. P. (1999, forthcoming) 'The Changing Social and Religious Context of Catholic Schooling in England and Wales', in M. Eaton (ed.), *Commitment to Diversity: Catholics and Education 1850–2000*.

Hornsby-Smith, M. P. and Mansfield, M. C. (1975) 'Overview of the Church Commissions', *The Month* 8/3 (March), pp. 84–9.

Hornsby-Smith, M. P. and Lee, R. M. (1979) *Roman Catholic Opinion: A Study of Roman Catholics in England and Wales in the 1970s*, Guildford: University of Surrey.

Hornsby-Smith, M. P., Brown, J. and O'Byrne, J. (1983) 'Second Thoughts on the Pope's Visit', *The Month* 16/4 (April), pp. 131–3.

Hornsby-Smith, M. P. and Foley, M. (1993) 'British Catholics in the Labour Movement: A Study of Religious and Political Marginalization?', *Social Compass* 40/1, pp. 45–54.

Hornsby-Smith, M. P., Fulton, J. and Norris, M. (1995) *The Politics of Spirituality: A Study of a Renewal Process in an English Diocese*, Oxford: Clarendon.

Hostie, R. (1972) *Vie et Mort des Ordres Religieux: Approches Psychosociologiques*, Paris: Desclée de Brouwer (translation and limited English edition, 1983), Washington: CARA.

Houck, J. W. and Williams, O. F. (eds) (1984) *Catholic Social Teaching and the*

US Economy: Working Papers for a Bishops' Pastoral, Washington D.C.: University Press of America.

Howes, J. (1996) *History of the Catholic Housing Aid Society*, unpublished manuscript, London: CHAS.

Hughes, P. (1950) 'The English Catholics in 1850', in Beck, *English Catholics*, pp. 42–85.

Hypher, P. (1996) 'Catholic Schools and Other Faiths', in T. McLaughlin *et al.*, *Contemporary Catholic School*, pp. 216–31.

Jacobs, M. (1996) *The Politics of the Real World: Meeting the New Century*, London: Earthscan Publications.

Jansen, T. (1989) *Efforts to Define a Christian Democratic Doctrine*, European People's Party.

John XXIII, Pope (1959) *The Catholic Missions (Princeps Pastorum)*, London: CTS (Do 315).

John XXIII, Pope (1961) *New Light on Social Problems (Mater et Magistra)*, London: CTS (S 259); in Walsh and Davies (1984), *Proclaiming Justice and Peace*, pp. 1–44.

John XXIII, Pope (1963) *Peace on Earth (Pacem in Terris)*, London: CTS (S 264); in Walsh and Davies (1984), *Proclaiming Justice and Peace*, pp. 45–76.

John Paul II, Pope (1981) *Familiaris Consortio: Apostolic Exhortation on the Role of the Christian Family in the Modern World*, London: CTS (S 357).

John Paul II, Pope (1988) *Christifideles Laici: Post-Synodal Apostolic Exhortation on The Vocation and the Mission of the Lay Faithful in the Church and in the World*, London: CTS (Do 589).

Jones, C. (1977) *Immigration and Social Policy in Britain*, London: Tavistock.

Kaiser, R. B. (1987) *The Encyclical That Never Was: The Story of the Pontifical Commission and Population, Family and Birth, 1964–66*, London: Sheed & Ward.

Kalilombe, Lubin, Muart, Igwara, Menezes (1991) *Black Catholics Speak: Reflections on Experience, Faith and Theology*, London: Catholic Association for Racial Justice.

Kandiah, M. D. and Seldon, S. (1996) *Ideas and Think Tanks in Contemporary Britain*, 2 vols., Ilford: Frank Cass.

Katholisch-Soziales Institut (1996) Konsultationprozess, Archdiocese of Köln.

Keating, J. (1996) 'The British Experience: Christian Democrats Without a Party', in D. Hanley (ed.), *Christian Democracy in Europe: A Comparative Perspective*, London: Pinter, pp. 168–81.

Kelly, K. T. (1996) *Divorce and Second Marriage: Facing the Challenge*, London: Geoffrey Chapman.

Kelly, K. T. (1998) 'What Binds Marriage?', *Priests and People* 12/4, pp. 157–9.

Kennedy, S. R. (1997) *Shattered Faith*, Dublin: Poolbeg.

Kenny, A. (1986) *A Path From Rome: An Autobiography*, Oxford: Oxford University Press.

Keynes, J. M. (1936) *The General Theory of Employment, Interest, and Money*, London: Macmillan.

Kiberd, D. (1995) *Inventing Ireland*, London: Jonathan Cape.

Kitson Clark, G. (1965) *The Making of Victorian England*, London: Methuen.

Kokosalakis, N. (1971) 'Aspects of Conflict Between the Structure of Authority and the Beliefs of the Laity in the Roman Catholic Church', in M. Hill (ed.), *A Sociological Yearbook of Religion in Britain 4*, London: SCM, pp. 21–35.

Konstant, D. (Chairman) (1981) *Signposts and Homecomings: The Educative Task of the Catholic Community: A Report to the Bishops of England and Wales*, Slough: St Paul Publications.

Koopmanschap, T. (1978) *Transformations in Contemporary Roman Catholicism: A Case Study*, unpublished PhD thesis, University of Liverpool.

Lash, N. (1977) 'Modernism, Aggiornamento and the Night Battle', in Hastings, *Bishops and Writers*, pp. 51–80.

Lash, N. (1986) *Theology on the Way to Emmaus*, London, SCM.

Lawlor, M. G. (1993) *Marriage and Sacrament: A Theology of Christian Marriage*, Collegeville, Minn.: Liturgical Press.

Lees, L. H. (1979) *Irish Migrants in Victorian London*, Manchester: Manchester University Press.

Lenoir, F. (1988) *Les Communautés Nouvelles*, Paris: Fayard.

Leo XIII, Pope (1949 f.p. 1891) *The Workers' Charter* (*Rerum Novarum*), Oxford: Catholic Social Guild.

Leslie, J. H. (1986) *Resistance to Change in a North Midlands Parish*, unpublished PhD thesis, Guildford: University of Surrey.

Leys, M. D. R. (1961) *Catholics in England 1559–1829*, London: Longman.

Linden, I. (1994) *Back to Basics: Revisiting Catholic Social Teaching*, London: CIIR.

Litvack, L. B. (1996) 'The Psychology of Song; the Theology of Hymn: Songs and Hymns of the Irish Migration', in Patrick O'Sullivan (ed.), *The Irish World Wide*; *History, Heritage, Identity*, V: *Religion and Identity*, London and New York: Leicester University Press, pp. 70–89.

Lodge, D. (1980) *How Far Can You Go?*, London: Secker & Warburg.

Lodge, D. (1993) *The Picturegoers*, Harmondsworth: Penguin (first published 1960).

Louden, S. (1998) *The Greying of the Clergy: An Assessment of Role, Stress, Burnout, and Personality Among Roman Catholic Parish Clergy in England and Wales*, unpublished PhD thesis, University of Wales.

Loughlin, G. (1998) 'Rains for a Famished Land', *The Times Literary Supplement* 4958, p. 12.

Louth, A. (1983) *Discerning the Mystery: An Essay on the Nature of Theology*, Oxford: Clarendon.

Maccagno, D. (1971) *The Origins of the YCW Movement*, unpublished thesis (YCW Archives).

McClelland, V. A. (1962) *Cardinal Manning: His Public Life and Influence, 1865–1892*, London: Oxford University Press.

McClelland, V. A. (1973) *English Roman Catholics and Higher Education 1830–1903*, Oxford: Clarendon.

McClelland, V. A. (1991) 'Great Britain and Ireland', in Hastings, *History of English Christianity 1920–1990*, pp. 365–76.

McGuinness, J. J. (1986) *Joseph Cardijn's YCW Movement and the Re-Discovered Role of the Laity in the Church*, dissertation submitted in partial fulfilment for the Postgraduate Diploma in Pastoral Theology, Heythrop College, London University.

McHugh, F. P. (1982) *The Changing Social Role of the Roman Catholic Church in England, 1958–1982*, unpublished PhD thesis, University of Cambridge.

McHugh, F. P. (1987) 'Two Churches: The Significance of the Political', *New Blackfriars* 68 (February), pp. 89–98.

McLaughlin, T. (1996) 'The Distinctiveness of Catholic Education', in T. McLaughlin *et al.*, *The Contemporary Catholic School*, pp. 136–54.

McLaughlin, T., O'Keefe, J. and O'Keeffe, B. (eds) (1996) *The Contemporary Catholic School: Context, Identity and Diversity*, London: Falmer.

McLeod, H. (1974) *Class and Religion in the Late Victorian City*, London: Croom Helm.

McLeod, H. (1981) *Religion and the People of Western Europe 1789–1970*, Oxford: Oxford University Press.

McLeod, H. (1984) *Religion and the Working Class in Nineteenth-Century Britain*, Studies in Economic and Social History, London: Macmillan.

McLeod, H. (1989) 'Popular Catholicism in Irish New York, c 1900', pp. 353–74 in W. J. Sheils and D. Wood (eds), *The Churches, Ireland and the Irish*, Studies in Church History, 25, Oxford: Blackwell.

McLeod, H. (1996) *Piety and Poverty: Working-Class Religion in Berlin, London and New York 1870–1914*, New York and London: Holmes & Meier.

McSweeney, B. (1980) *Roman Catholicism: The Search for Relevance*, Oxford: Blackwell.

Mansfield, P. and Hornsby-Smith, M. P. (1975) 'Consultation, Consensus and Conflict: Some Observations on the Structures and Working of the International Justice and Peace Commission', *The Month* 8/5 (May), pp. 138–45.

Mansfield, P. and Collard, J. (1988) *The Beginning of the Rest of Your Life? A Portrait of Newly-Wed Marriage*, Basingstoke: Macmillan.

Marshall, J. (1963) *The Infertile Period: Principles and Practice*, London: Darton, Longman & Todd.

Marshall, J. (1968) 'A Field Trial of the Basal-Body-Temperature Method of Regulating Births', *The Lancet* 2, pp. 8–10.

Marshall, J. (1995) *Love One Another: Psychological Aspects of Natural Family Planning*, London: Sheed & Ward.

Marshall, J. (1996) *Fifty Years of Marriage Care*, London: Catholic Marriage Care.

Marshall, J. and Rowe, B. (1970) 'Psychological Aspects of the Basal Body Temperature Method of Regulating Births', *Fertility and Sterility* 8, pp. 14–19.

Mays, J. B. (1962) *Education and the Urban Child*, Liverpool: Liverpool University Press.

Miles Board, D. (1980) *Responses: An Account of the Correspondence which Followed 'The Church 2000' and 'A Time for Building' – the Two Reports of the Joint Working Party on Pastoral Strategy*, Abbots Langley: Catholic Information Services.

Miller, A. (1995a) 'Where Have All the Catholics Gone? 1: Rebels With a Cause', *The Tablet*, 12 August, pp. 1022–3.

Miller, A. (1995b) 'Where Have All the Catholics Gone? 2: God's Human Touch', *The Tablet*, 19 August, pp. 1050–1.

Ministry of Education (1959) 15–18 vol. I (*The Crowther Report*), London: HMSO.

Mordaunt Crook, J. (1981) *William Burges and the High Victorian Dream*, London: John Murray.

Murray, V. (1996) 'Other Faiths in Catholic Schools: General Implications of a Case Study', in McLaughlin *et al.*, *Contemporary Catholic School*, pp. 239–53.

National Board of Catholic Women (NBCW) (1991) *Do Not Be Afraid: A Report on the Responses of Catholic Women to the Discussion Paper, 'Women – Status' and Role, Life and Mission'*, ed. R. Gallagher, London: Redemptorist Publications.

National Board of Catholic Women, the Bishops' Conference of England and Wales, and the Joint Dialogue Group (1998) *Response by the Catholic Church in England and Wales to the CCBI Report on the Ecumenical Decade of Churches in Solidarity with Women*, London.

Neal, F. (1988) *Sectarian Violence: The Liverpool Experience, 1819–1914: An Aspect of Anglo-Irish History*, Manchester: Manchester University Press.

Neal, M. A. (1990) *From Nuns to Sisters: An Expanding Vocation*, Mystic, Conn.: Twenty-Third Publications.

Nevile, M. (1984) *Living the Gospel*, III: *Doing Justice*, London: CAFOD.

Nevile, M. (1995) 'Not Just Housing', *Christian Action Journal* (Spring).

Newman, J. H. (1848) *Loss and Gain: The Story of a Convert*, 1891 edn, London: Longmans, Green & Co.

Newman, J. H., Cardinal (1961) *On Consulting the Faithful in Matters of Doctrine*, ed. J. Coulson, London: Geoffrey Chapman (first published 1859).

Newsome, D. (1993) *The Convert Cardinals: John Henry Newman and Henry Edward Manning*, London: John Murray.

Newson, J. H. (Chairman) (1963) *Half Our Future*, Report of the Central Advisory Council for Education, London: HMSO.

Nichols, A. (1996) *Looking at the Liturgy: A Critical View of its Contemporary Form*, San Francisco: Ignatius Press.

Nichols, A. (1997) *Dominican Gallery: Portrait of a Culture*, Leominster: Gracewing.

Nichols, V. (1995) 'The Church's Mission in Education in a Multi-Faith Society', *Briefing*, Education Special Edition (June).

Noble, V. (1991) *A Mission for Women: A Reflection on the History of Women's Organizations in the Catholic Church and Their Relevance Within the Contemporary Church*, a dissertation submitted for the Postgraduate Diploma in Pastoral Theology, Heythrop College, University of London.

Norman, E. (1984) *The English Catholic Church in the Nineteenth Century*, Oxford: Clarendon.

Novak, M. (1965) *The Experience of Marriage: 13 Married Couples Report*, London: Darton, Longman & Todd.

Nygren, D. J. and Ukeritis, M. D. (1992) 'Research Executive Summary: Future of Religious Orders in the United States', *Origins* 22/15, pp. 257–72, Washington.

Nygren, D. J. and Ukeritis, M. D. (1993) *The Future of Religious Orders in the United States: Transformation and Commitment*, Westport, Conn.: Praeger.

Nygren, D. J. and Ukeritis, M. D. (1994) 'Transforming Tradition: Shaping the Mission and Identity of Religious Life in the United States', in Union of Superiors General, *Consecrated Life Today*, pp. 17–45.

O'Brien, S. (1988) '*Terra Incognita*: The Nun in Nineteenth-Century England', *Past & Present* 121, pp. 110–40.

O'Brien, S. (1992) 'Making Catholic Spaces: Women, Decor, and Devotion in the English Catholic Church', in D. Wood (ed.), *The Church and the Arts*, Studies in Church History, 28, Oxford: Blackwell, pp. 449–64.

O'Donnell, R. (1983) *Roman Catholic Church Building in Great Britain and Ireland*, unpublished PhD thesis, University of Cambridge.

O'Donnell, R. (1994a) 'The Re-Ordering Debate: A Better Way Forward', *The Tablet*, 26 March, p. 389.

O'Donnell, R. (1994b) 'Pugin: A Passion for Gothic'; 'The Church Must Act On the Heritage', *The Universe*, 'Our Heritage' Supplement, 9 July.

O'Donnell, R. (1997) 'How to Use a Church', *The Tablet*, 19 July.

Office for Standards in Education (1996) *Recent Research on the Achievements of Ethnic Minority Children*, London: HMSO.

O'Grady, A. (1988) *Irish Migration to London*, Irish Studies Centre Occasional Publications Series, London: Polytechnic of North London.

O'Keeffe, B. (1986) *Faith Culture and the Dual System: A Comparative Study of Church and County Schools*, Lewes: Falmer.

O'Keeffe, B. (1995) 'Fairness: A Missing Theme in Education', in The Edmund Plowden Trust, *Law and Justice, The Christian Review* (Autumn).

O'Malley, J. (1997) 'One Priesthood: Two Traditions', in Hennessy, *A Concert of Charisms*, pp. 9–24.

O'Murchu, D. (1989) *The Prophetic Horizon of Religious Life*, London: Excalibur.

O'Sullivan, B. (1979) *Parish Alive*, London: Sheed & Ward.

O'Sullivan, P. (1992–7) *The Irish World Wide: History, Heritage, Identity*, 6 vols, London and New York: Leicester University Press; esp. V: *Religion and Identity* (1996).

Papini, R. (1997) *The Christian Democrat International*, London: Rowman & Littlefield.

Parkinson, M. (1985) *Liverpool on the Brink*, Liverpool: Hermitage UK Policy Journals.

Paul VI, Pope (1964) *The Church and the Modern World (Ecclesiam Suam)*, London: CTS (Do 354).

Paul VI, Pope (1967) *The Development of Peoples (Populorum Progressio)*, London: CTS (S 273); in Walsh and Davies (1984), *Proclaiming Justice and Peace*, pp. 141–64.

Paul VI, Pope (1968) *The Regulation of Birth (Humanae Vitae)*, London: CTS (Do 411).

Paul VI, Pope (1975) *Evangelization in the Modern World* (*Evangelii Nuntiandi*) London: CTS (S 312); in Walsh and Davies (1984), *Proclaiming Justice and Peace*, pp. 204–42.

Paz, D. G. (1992) *Popular Anti-Catholicism in Mid-Victorian England*, Stanford, Calif.: Stanford University Press.

Pereiro, J. (1998) *Cardinal Manning: An Intellectual Biography*, Oxford: Clarendon.

Pickstock, C. (1998) *After Writing: On the Liturgical Consummation of Philosophy*, Oxford: Blackwell.

Pius XI, Pope (1951) *Christian Marriage* (*Casti Connubii*), London: CTS (Do 113) (first published 1930).

Pooley, C. G. (1989) 'Segregation or Integration? The Residential Experience of the Irish in Mid-Victorian Britain', in Swift and Gilley, *Irish in Britain 1815–1939*, pp. 60–83.

Pütz, H. (1985) *Die CDU*, 4th edn, Droste-Verlag.

Quinn, D. (1993a) *Patronage and Piety: The Politics of English Roman Catholicism, 1850–1900*, Stanford Calif.: Stanford University Press.

Quinn, D. (1993b) 'Distributism as Movement and Ideal', *The Chesterton Review* 19, pp. 157–73.

Reid, C. J. (ed.) (1986) *Peace in a Nuclear Age: The Bishops' Pastoral Letter in Perspective*, Washington D. C.: The Catholic University of America Press.

Rerum Novarum (1997) *Rerum Novarum: Ecriture, Contenu et Reception d'une Encyclique*, Collection de L'Ecole Francaise de Rome, 232, Palais Farnese.

Rex, R. (1993) *Henry VIII and the English Reformation*, Cambridge: Cambridge University Press.

Richter, P. and Francis, L. J. (1998) *Gone But Not Forgotten: Church Leaving and Returning*, London: Darton, Longman & Todd.

Robbins, Lord (Chairman) (1963) *Higher Education* (Robbins Report), Cmnd 2154, London: HMSO.

Ryan, D. (1996) *The Catholic Parish: Institutional Discipline, Tribal Identity and Religious Development in the English Church*, London: Sheed & Ward.

Ryan, M. (1981) *Yesterday Recalled: A Jubilee History of the Catholic Women's League 1906–1981*, London: CWL.

Rynne, X. (1965) *The Fourth Session*, London: Faber & Faber.

Sacred Congregation for Catholic Education (1977) *Lay Catholics in Schools: Witness to Faith*, London: CTS.

Samuel, R. (1985) 'The Roman Catholic Church and the Irish Poor', in Swift and Gilley, *Irish in the Victorian City*, pp. 267–300.

Sanders, J. (1997) 'Pugin & Pugin and the Diocese of Glasgow', *Caledonia Gothica: Pugin and the Gothic Revival in Scotland Architectural Heritage*, VIII, Edinburgh: Edinburgh University Press, pp. 89–107.

Saward, J. (1997) *The Beauty of Holiness and the Holiness of Beauty: Art, Sanctity, and the Truth of Catholicism*, New York: Ignatius.

Scarisbrick, J. J. (1984) *The Reformation and the English People*, Oxford: Blackwell.

Schiefen, R. J. (1984) *Nicholas Wiseman and the Transformation of English Catholicism*, Shepherdstown: Patmos.

Scott, G. (1967) *The R.C.s: Report on Roman Catholics in Britain Today*, London: Hutchinson.

Scurfield, A. (1982) 'A Question of Orthodoxy', *The Tablet*, 25 September.

Sedgwick, P. (ed.) (1995) *God in the City: Essays and Reflections From the Archbishop's Urban Theology Group*, London: Mowbray.

Seidler, J. (1986) 'Contested Accommodation: The Catholic Church as a Special Case of Social Change', *Social Forces* 64/4 (June), pp. 847–74.

Selby, D. (1974) 'Manning, Lord Howard of Glossop and the Catholic Education Crisis Fund 1870–1871', *Paedagogica Historica* 14.

Sharp, G. (1998) *Patriarchy and Discordant Discourses in the Contemporary Roman Catholic Church: The Voices of Priests and Women in Parish Settings*, unpublished PhD thesis, University of Plymouth.

Sharratt, B. (1977) 'English Catholicism in the 1960s', in Hastings, *Bishops and Writers*, pp. 127–58.

Sheppard, D. and Worlock, D. (1989) *Better Together: Christian Partnership in a Hurt City*, Harmondsworth: Penguin.

Sheppard, D. and Worlock, D. (1994) *With Hope in Our Hearts*, London: Hodder & Stoughton.

Sire, H. J. A. (1997) *Father Martin D'Arcy: Philosopher of Christian Love*, Leominster: Gracewing.

Smith, A. (1983) *Passion for the Inner City*, London: Sheed & Ward.

Socialist Education Association (1983) *The Dual System of Voluntary and County Schools*, London: SEA.

Spencer, A. E. C. W. (1966) 'The Demography and Sociography of the Roman Catholic Community of England and Wales', in L. Bright and S. Clements (eds), *The Committed Church*, London: Darton, Longman & Todd, pp. 60–85.

Spencer, A. E. C. W. (1973) 'The Catholic Community as a British Melting Pot', *New Community* 2/2 (Spring), pp. 125–31.

Stourton, E. (1998) *Absolute Truth: The Catholic Church in the World Today*, London: Viking.

Stourton, E. and Gumley, F. (eds) (1996) *Christian Values*, London: Hodder & Stoughton.

Suenens, L.-J., Cardinal (1968) *Co-Responsibility in the Church*, London: Burns & Oates.

Sweeney, J. (1994) *The New Religious Order: The Passionists and the Option for the Poor*, London: Bellew.

Sweeney, J. (1995) 'The Synod: Was it Worth It?', *Religious Life Review* (January–February), pp. 3–16, Dublin: Dominican Publications.

Sweeney, J. (1996) 'Vita Consecrata: Commentary on the Document', *Religious Life Review* (July–August), pp. 218–28, Dublin: Dominican Publications.

Swift, R. and Gilley, S. (eds) (1985) *The Irish in the Victorian City*, London: Croom Helm.

Swift, R. and Gilley, S. (eds) (1989) *The Irish in Britain 1815–1939*, London: Pinter.

Swift, R. and Gilley, S. (forthcoming) *The Irish in Britain: The Local Dimension*, Dublin: Four Courts.

Taaffe, P. and Mulhearn, T. (1988) *Liverpool: A City That Dared to Fight*, London: Fortress.

Taylor, A. J. P. (1965) *English History 1914–1945*, Oxford: Clarendon.

Thorn, J. M. (1997) 'Towards a History and Interpretation of the Distributist League', *The Chesterton Review* 23, pp. 305–28.

Thornes, B. and Collard, J. (1979) *Who Divorces?*, London: Routledge & Kegan Paul.

Ullah, P. (1985) 'Second-Generation Irish Youth: Identity and Ethnicity', *New Community* 12/12 (Summer).

Union of Superiors General (1994) *Consecrated Life Today: Charisms in the Church for the World*, Slough: St Paul Publications.

Vaillancourt, J.-G. (1980) *Papal Power: A Study of Vatican Control Over Lay Elites*, London: University of California Press.

Van Kersbergen, K. (1995) *Social Capitalism: A Study of Christian Democracy*, London: Routledge.

Vereker, C. and Mays, J. B. (1961) *Urban Redevelopment and Social Change*, Liverpool: Liverpool University Press.

Walker, C. (1994) *Worker Apostles: The Young Christian Workers Movement in Britain*, London: CTS.

Waller, P. J. (1981) *Democracy and Sectarianism: Liverpool 1868–1939*, Liverpool: Liverpool University Press.

Walsh, M. (1980) *From Sword to Ploughshare: Sword of the Spirit to Catholic Institute for International Relations, 1940–1980*, London: CIIR.

Walsh, M. (1990) *The Tablet, 1840–1990: A Commemorative History*, London: The Tablet Publishing Company.

Walsh, M. (1992) 'What Newman Members Could Be Reading', in Cheverton *et al., Use of Gifts*, pp. 70–2.

Walsh, M. and Davies, B. (eds) (1984) *Proclaiming Justice and Peace: Documents From John XXIII to John Paul II*, London: Collins/CAFOD.

Ward, C. K. (1965) *Priests and People: A Study in the Sociology of Religion*, Liverpool: Liverpool University Press.

Ward, G. (1996) 'Between Postmodernism and Postmodernity: The Theology of Jean-Luc Marion', in K. Flanagan and P. C. Jupp (eds), *Postmodernity, Sociology and Religion*, Basingstoke: Macmillan, pp. 190–205.

Weber, M. (1968) *Economy and Society: An Outline of Interpretive Sociology*, 3 vols, ed. G. Roth and C. Wittich, New York: Bedminster Press

Whyte, J. H. (1981) *Catholics in Western Democracies: A Study in Political Behaviour*, Dublin: Gill & Macmillan.

Wilson, B. R. (1966) *Religion in Secular Society: A Sociological Comment*, London: Watts.

Winter, M. (1985) *Whatever Happened to Vatican II?*, London: Sheed & Ward.

Wittberg, P. (1994) *The Rise and Fall of Catholic Religious Orders: A Social Movement Perspective*, New York: State University of New York Press.

Wolffe, J. (1991) *The Protestant Crusade in Great Britain, 1829–1860*, Oxford: Oxford University Press.

Wood, I. S. (1990) *John Wheatley*, Manchester: Manchester University Press.

Wright, L. (1992) 'The Spread of Ugliness', in Cheverton *et al., Use of Gifts*, pp. 54–7.

Ziesler, K. I. (1989) *The Irish in Birmingham 1830–1970*, unpublished PhD thesis, University of Birmingham.

Zipfel, P. (no date) *Catholic Association for Racial Justice: An Outline History 1973–1988*, unpublished manuscript, London: CARJ.

Index